Laboratory Research in Political Economy

Laboratory Research in Political Economy

Edited by Thomas R. Palfrey

Ann Arbor
The University of Michigan Press

Copyright © by the University of Michigan 1991
All rights reserved
Published in the United States of America by
The University of Michigan Press
Manufactured in the United States of America

1994   1993   1992   1991   4   3   2   1

Library of Congress Cataloging-in-Publication Data

Laboratory research in political economy / edited by Thomas R.
   Palfrey
        p.   cm.
   Includes bibliographical references.
   ISBN 0-472-10203-6 (cloth : alk.)
   1. Political science—Mathematical models.   I. Palfrey, Thomas
R., 1953–
JA74.L22   1991
320'.01'51—dc20   91-8937
                                                       CIP

British Library Cataloguing in Publication Data
Laboratory research in political economy.
   1. Political science. Methods
   I. Palfrey, Thomas
   320.01

   ISBN 0-472-10203-6

Distributed in the United Kingdom and Europe by
Manchester University Press, Oxford Road,
Manchester M13 9PL, UK

Contents

Part 3. Coordination and Cooperation

Introduction

Thomas R. Palfrey

Laboratory experimentation has recently become an influential methodology for conducting empirical work in political science. Traditional political science has restricted its use of data to either public opinion surveys or historical records such as electoral outcomes or roll call votes. The increasing acceptance of formal theoretical models as a legitimate mode of analysis in political science has led to a need for greater reliance on data from carefully controlled laboratory environments. Many of the predictions and theoretical findings that emerge from such analyses are couched in terms of variables and parameters that are extremely difficult to measure using either of the traditional data methodologies (surveys and historical data). Largely because of this, political scientists are increasingly inclined to turn to the laboratory to evaluate these relatively abstract models of political processes.

Moreover, until the recent development of reliable laboratory methods, very little serious testing of these formal theories was undertaken. The result was a situation in which model development far outpaced model testing. This imbalance is undoubtedly one major source (perhaps *the* major source) of the early skepticism and controversy about the usefulness of the formal approach to studying political processes and political behavior.

Fortunately, the situation has changed a great deal in the past ten to fifteen years. Now experimental work designed to test formal theory is being conducted at many major research institutions—Caltech, Arizona, Indiana, Michigan, Michigan State, Carnegie-Mellon, Penn, Haifa, and elsewhere. It has, in fact, become the dominant empirical methodology for evaluating these formal models, and research results are increasingly found in the leading political science journals.

The purpose of this volume is to collect, in one place, some of the best current research being conducted in this area. None of these articles have been published elsewhere (although they certainly could have been) and most have been completed in the last few months. This gives the reader an unusual opportunity to see a representative cross section of current research by leaders in the field.

The contributions are organized in the following way. The types of experiments in formal theory now being conducted by political scientists can be loosely placed into three categories. First, and perhaps best known, are laboratory elections. A second category is committee decision making. A third category (and probably the most extensive in terms of both the total number of experiments that have been run and the breadth of application in political science) explores game theoretic models of how groups might overcome problems of coordination and cooperation.

Political Science Laboratories

Before introducing the ten articles in this volume, it may be helpful to those who have never conducted a laboratory experiment to briefly describe the techniques that are used. In the decade or two since the early pioneering experiments, quite a bit has been learned about experimental techniques, and, perhaps most influential, technology has allowed for both greater control and flexibility.

The first "modern" experiments in political science were the laboratory committees explored by Plott and his collaborators in the early 1970s. Largely motivated by a rather strange theoretical combination of equilibrium predictions and gloomy theorems about the impossibility of equilibrium and the inevitability of chaos, that initial work showed that not only were there strong regularities where the theory predicted we should see strong regularities, but the experimental data also had some systematic features that the theory was unable to usefully predict.

Those experiments were conducted "by hand," meaning that the experimenter and/or research assistants recruited subjects for the experiment, sat them down in a room together, and ran an experiment. Subjects engaged in discussion and made decisions that were written down on pieces of paper and collected and recorded by the person running the experiment. These decisions (occasionally supplemented by tape-recorded conversations) constituted the "data" from the experiment.

Since the theories being tested relied heavily on "economic arguments" of individual maximization of utility, a technique of "induced preferences" borrowed from the work of Vernon Smith in experimental economics was developed. According to this technique, subjects are told they will be paid different amounts for different outcomes that the committee ends up deciding on. This means, in turn, that different decisions they make will give them different earnings at the end of the experiment. The underlying formal model is then applied, treating these payment schedules, or "induced preferences" as the subjects' utility functions. By changing the payment schedules, the experimenter can vary the predictions of the theories, for which the utility functions are environmental parameters. The control achieved in the laboratory, to a large extent, relies on an assumption that this induced preference technique has successfully induced the utility functions that are, in turn, used to make theoretical predictions of the experimental outcomes.

A second important consideration in these experiments is to make sure subjects understand the rules, and understand how their earnings in the experiment are derived. Without this understanding, there is no reason to believe that preferences will have been successfully induced and the resulting data would be nearly worthless. Consequently, there is extensive training, where instructions are read aloud to the subjects, practice examples are worked through, questions are answered, and quizzes to verify comprehension are given. In some cases, practice rounds for which subjects are not paid are conducted.

Besides learning the rules, subjects also learn how other people behave in the course of an experiment. Thus a common treatment variable in these experiments is "experience." To the extent that many committee experiments are testing theories of how "expert" subjects might behave (such as legislators), experience can be a very important treatment variable.

Finally, because much of what goes on in "by hand" experiments involves interactions between experimenter and subject, there is a real possibility of "experimenter effects." That is, different experimenters may inadvertently but systematically bias the outcomes in different ways.

With the advent of reliable and fast computer networks, much of the potential difficulty with experimenter effects has been circumvented. Most experiments are now conducted on a computer network. This also makes it easier for the experimenter to control other environmental parameters, such as face-to-face contact and/or communication. A third virtue of the computer setting is that many of the time-consuming details of an experiment (such as collecting ballots) are streamlined, resulting in a massive time savings. Because of boredom problems, an experimenter cannot expect to have the undivided attention of the subjects for more than a couple of hours. A time savings of as little as fifteen minutes can mean that one more treatment can be run during that experimental session.

There are many more details of the experiments that will become apparent when reading the experimental instructions that are included at the end of most of the articles. In fact, I strongly encourage readers—especially the uninitiated—to carefully read through the instructions. Doing so will answer many questions that you would automatically think of while reading the main body of the articles, and may also help you better understand the outcomes. The instructions are also useful in understanding the theory, since they provide, in many cases, the experimenter's attempt to replicate in a "real" environment the assumptions of an abstract theoretical model.

Laboratory Election

In the three decades since Anthony Downs wrote *An Economic Theory of Democracy,* a variety of formal models have been used to try to understand the theoretical underpinnings of competitive, democratic, mass elections. The first part of the book will include several important recent papers that test three different kinds of formal models of elections.

The part begins with an article by Charles R. Plott that is cast in the familiar "spatial model" and explores the consequences of representative democracy. The behavioral properties of two-candidate elections, three-candidate elections, and large committees are explored, and these properties are compared to ones theorized in recent formal models. The political processes were created under laboratory conditions that hold other variables constant. Plott shows that the core/equilibrium of a spatial model of competition is an accurate predictor of outcomes but the outcome variance is higher under three-candidate processes than it is under the other two processes. The experiments also examine the effects of voting costs on turnout. In particular, the experiments reproduce the widespread empirical phenomenon of "irrational turnout," in the sense that almost everyone votes, even though to do so is irrational because the chance of affecting the outcome is so small.

In the second article, Boylan, Ledyard, Lupia, McKelvey, and Ordeshook explore the interaction of deficit spending and economic performance with retrospective voting and the dynamics of candidate competition. It is an innovative study both theoretically and experimentally. Specifically, they run experiments on a one-sector model of economic growth, in which decisions on capital accumulation and consumption are made through a political process: Prior to each election, candidates adopt positions indicating the level of investment and consumption that they will deliver by the final period of their term of office, and voters then vote. The candidate who obtains a majority becomes the incumbent, and must adopt a policy for each period of the term of office. The process repeats itself, with a random ending rule to induce preferences that discount future earnings. They investigate how closely the path of investment approximates optimal capital accumulation. Evidence of political business cycles are found in the data, but there is also evidence that in this simple stationary environment, two-party competition can lead to efficient consumption-savings paths. The article goes on to explore how the theoretical properties of a dynamic electoral equilibrium depend upon the extent to which candidates or parties may be able to commit to a particular set of policies.

The third article, by Forsythe, Nelson, Neumann, and Wright, summarizes an intriguing set of results from a "political stock market" that operated continuously during the 1988 presidential election, where 190 traders bought and sold "shares" of the presidential candidates. Shares paid off in proportion to the percentage of the vote each candidate won. Formal theories developed from financial economics tell us that the trading prices of the candidates' shares can be transformed into predictors of expected vote percentages according to formulas derived from a system of equations. Therefore, the trading prices provide, at least in theory, a continuous opinion poll. This article provides a comparison between commercial opinion polls and candidate share prices over the course of the last five months of the 1988 campaign.

The article by Williams examines the effects of voter information costs on how well candidates reflect the median preferences of the electorate. In a well known set of papers, McKelvey and Ordeshook theorized that, in order for elections to be informationally efficient and produce representative elected officials, only a very small fraction of the electorate needed to be well informed about the candidates. Economic theory (and common sense) tells us that the fraction of the electorate that becomes informed is inversely related to information costs: as these costs go up, fewer and fewer voters will bother to become informed. Nevertheless, McKelvey and Ordeshook tell us that this really does not matter, as long as at least some voters become informed. Williams explicitly tests this remarkable prediction by manipulating information costs in a laboratory environment and finds evidence that strongly supports it.

Committee Decision Making

Nearly all legislatures and representative bodies make political and policy decisions using a combination of majority-rule voting and bargaining. The articles in part 2 examine the effects of a variety of features of the bargaining process and the voting rules on outcomes. Specific theories that have been recently developed are applied to the laboratory environments and evaluated. Of special interest is the dynamics of decision making by committees. A common feature of committee decision making is that a sequence of decisions is made (an "agenda"); therefore, strategic, dynamic models seem particularly appropriate for studying committee behavior. Only recently have we developed such models, perhaps the best known being the model proposed by Farquharson. A common criticism of that model involves the cognitive ability of the committee members to anticipate outcomes of the later stages of the agenda when making their voting decisions in the early stages of the agenda. An analogous problem arises when the agenda is not fixed but proposals must be made, and, in static settings, when there are multiple candidates or alternatives to be voted on so that an individual's expectations of other members' voting decisions play a critical role.

The first article, by McKelvey, tests a variant of the recent Baron-

Ferejohn model of bargaining under majority rule. That approach analyzes a "divide the pie" game in a committee environment in which members are randomly selected to propose a split, followed by a majority vote to ratify the split. The pie they are splitting is declining in value over time. The bargaining game ends as soon as one of the proposed splits is successfully ratified. A key assumption in the theory is that players adopt stationary strategies. Thus, for example, players may not be excluded from future proposed splits because of their vote on past proposals. McKelvey examines an environment that is slightly different from simply dividing a pie, but retains the same basic feature of delay costs. He finds strong evidence that the player's strategies are history dependent and, therefore, rejects the Baron-Ferejohn solution. This may not seem surprising to many congressional scholars, since folk wisdom has long held that there are strong reputational considerations in committee and legislative decision making, and legislators may gain or suffer in future bargaining situations with their fellow legislators, depending on their past voting behavior.

The article by Herzberg and Wilson examines the effects of bargaining costs on outcomes, when outcomes are determined by majority rule. Incorporating such costs into an otherwise "institution-free" majority-rule game is sufficient to produce stable and predictable collective choices. They experimentally test the theoretical predictions of the agenda cost game using five-person laboratory committees. They explore how the introduction of these costs might systematically affect the strategies of decision makers, and thereby yield those more predictable outcomes. From their theoretical model and laboratory experiments, they are able to offer generalizations about the effects of a particular class of decision-making costs—agenda access costs.

The article by Rapoport, Felsenthal, and Maoz presents an extensive experimental test of four competing models of sophisticated voting in laboratory committees. The models range from strictly noncooperative to tacitly cooperative models of behavior, and the experiments are conducted under both plurality and approval voting systems. In plurality systems, they find pervasive patterns of strategic behavior, and show that a process model that approximates a sequential-decision algorithm fits the data quite well and, in fact, significantly outperforms more standard game-theoretic criteria based on dominance solvability. They also find significant amounts of strategic behavior in approval voting. This finding is especially significant in view of the claims, by its proponents, that one of the great virtues of approval voting is that the incentives to behave strategically are negligible.

Coordination and Cooperation

Strategic issues relating to the trade-off between securing personal gains at the expense of group gains are pervasive in political science. For example, in the study of foreign policy and international relations, problems of stability of alliances, arms races, trade wars, immigration and emigration policy, international sanctions, and other interesting subjects all involve such trade-offs. Other examples abound in legislative and bureaucratic politics, political participation, and elsewhere.

Noncooperative game theory is the primary formal theoretical approach for studying situations of this sort. Experiments in this area attempt to either directly confront the theory with data or to probe the frontiers of the theory by studying environments in which the current theory is agnostic or else thought to be flawed or incomplete. Much of this work is serving to narrow the gap between social psychological models of behavior and more rigorous game-theoretic models.

The first article in part 3, by Palfrey and Rosenthal, studies coordination problems in a simple "social dilemma" game in which at least some minimal subset of a group must make a personal sacrifice in order for all the members to gain. Several variables are experimentally manipulated to test very precise theoretical predictions about both the direction and the magnitude of the effects of these variables on the successful coordination of the group. Treatment variables include the amount of diversity in the group, the relative value of the group benefit compared to the individual costs of sacrifice, group size, and the number of members required to make the sacrifice. The findings are highly supportive of a modification of the standard noncooperative equilibrium model, adapted to allow for systematic biases in the players' prior beliefs about each others' choice behavior.

The article by Isaac and Walker explores the effects of group discussion on the ability of the group to coordinate, and attempts to identify the dynamics of how costly communication and coordination are related. In view of the well-documented fact that communication increases the group's ability to cooperate, the group decision of whether or not to pay a cost to communicate transforms a simple public goods game into a two-stage, public goods problem, where the first stage is a threshold game like the one analyzed by Palfrey and Rosenthal. Isacc and Walker find strong evidence in support of a mixed strategy, Nash equilibrium behavior in the first stage (deciding whether to contribute to the communication costs) of the game.

The final article, by Ostrom and Walker, reports strong evidence for the power of face-to-face communication in a repeated, common-pool resource setting. Such environments are frequently the source of important international political conflicts, for example when the use of water and air resources are at issue. The repeated nature of their experimental design enables them to look at the ability of the group to deal with parties who renege on agreements for their own short-term personal benefit, and study the interaction of these selective punishments with barriers to the group's ability to coordinate strategies. When communication was provided as a "costless" institution, players successfully used the opportunity to develop successful strategies for cooperating.

As the authors point out in part 3, it is very unusual for communication to be costless in field settings. The provision problem players faced in these costly communication experiments was not trivial and did, in fact, create a significant barrier to cooperation. In all three experiments, the problem of providing the institution for communication had a detrimental effect on the success of the group.

In summary, there are at least three strong themes of recent experimental work and formal theoretical models that are reflected in this volume. First is the importance of *strategic behavior*. Nearly all the papers involve compli-cated strategic situations for the individuals involved. For the last two de-cades, rigorous political analysis has turned more and more to game theory and related approaches to study the complex, strategic interactions of political agents. This basic approach is mirrored in the experimental designs presented here.

Second is the importance of *incomplete and asymmetric information*. This complicates the strategic issues for the players in particular ways that are of importance in political situations: in particular, problems of reputation building, coordination, communication, and signaling. That these are crucial features in many political settings is recognized widely by most political scientists, formal theorists and more traditional scholars alike. Whether one reads Key or Schattschneider, Riker, Downs, or, more recently, the fine sur-veys by Banks and Calvert, the theme of decision making in a strategic and information-poor environment is ever present.

Third, there is an emerging trend toward explicitly incorporating *dy-namics* into the theory, a relatively recent development in formal theory, and one for which experimental methods, as witnessed here, can be quite il-luminating. The importance of dynamics is evident in the traditional literature on party ID, realignments, incumbency effects, retrospective voting, and political business cycles, but there has been relatively less success in coming to grips with these issues in rigorous theoretical formulations until the last five years or so. This direction of research is in its infancy. Not surprisingly, the same is true for the experimental work in this area.

Part 1
Laboratory Elections

A Comparative Analysis of Direct Democracy, Two-Candidate Elections, and Three-Candidate Elections in an Experimental Environment

Charles R. Plott

This study explores the behavioral properties of political processes in a very simple environment. The processes are two-candidate elections, three-candidate elections, and large committees. These alternative political processes are implemented under laboratory experimental conditions in which the issues and underlying population preferences over issues are held constant. This allows the behavioral implications of the decision rule to be observed without the compounding complications caused by changing issues and attitudes. Such a setting provides a method for checking the predictive accuracy of spatial models and related game-theoretic models of candidate competition. If the models are sufficiently inaccurate in simple laboratory environments, then they might readily be rejected as applicable to the much more complicated, naturally occurring systems. In addition, the experimental design provides a comparison of selected aspects of behavior of these alternative processes.

Laboratory methodology should be viewed as complementary to field data and not as a complete substitute. The idea is to study the operation of very simple political processes in an attempt to identify poor theories and models, and thereby remove them from further consideration. Indeed, if the models are sufficiently inaccurate in simple laboratory environments, then a special burden is placed on those who would apply the models to more complicated, naturally occurring systems. In addition, the laboratory provides an opportunity to compare the behavior of different political processes independent of our ability to understand or model the reasons for any observed

The financial support of the National Science Foundation and the Caltech Program for Enterprise and Public Policy is gratefully acknowledged. The Guggenheim Foundation and the Center for Advanced Study in the Behavioral Sciences also provided time and the research assistance of Lynn Gale and Ron Rice.

differences. The observation and documentation of the differences in the behavior of different political processes provide an opportunity and a special challenge to theorists to modify and improve their theories to account for the differences.

The experimental techniques used in this paper can be viewed as an extension of those developed in Fiorina and Plott (1978) and Plott and Levine (1978). Those two papers initiated an investigation into the conditions under which majority-rule, equilibrium models accurately predict political choices. Subsequent research has focused primarily on relatively small groups. In this article, the techniques are extended to include much larger groups and different political processes.

This article has a rather awkward position relative to other, closely related, published papers. When it was first widely circulated (Plott 1982), nothing comparable existed in the experimental literature.[1] Several papers, subsequently published, replicated the results and then continued to generalize the theory and extend the experimental investigation into substantially more stringent information conditions than those that are studied here. Those interested in two-candidate elections should consult the recently published works of McKelvey and Ordeshook (1984, 1985a, 1985b, 1986, 1987, 1990a, 1990b). The results reported in this article regarding three-candidate elections and direct democracy are new to the published literature and, of course, the direct comparison of the three types of processes is also new.

The study is divided into four sections plus concluding remarks. Section 1 outlines the research questions. The procedures and parameters are in section 2. Section 3 contains the experimental results. Section 4 discusses the results of an auxiliary experiment designed to examine the decision to vote. There is no extensive discussion about the problems and limitations of experimental methods themselves. Many scholars harbor legitimate reservations about what might be learned from such an exercise. The methodological issues are addressed extensively in Fiorina and Plott 1978 and Plott 1978 and 1981, so the interested reader is referred to those sources. Obviously, political scientists have been interested in processes infinitely more complicated than those studied here and, even within the context of these simple experiments, a variety of complicating factors, alternative procedures, or alternative parameters could have been imposed. Presumably, these alternatives will be explored as experimental technology and experience is acquired.

---

1. The content of this chapter was delivered at the 1977 annual meeting of the Public Choice Society.

Research Questions Studied

The groups studied are characterized by four prominent features.

   a) The options available to the group are well specified and involve no
   uncertainty. This removes from consideration groups that traditionally
   have been called "problem-solving" groups.
   b) Individuals have "strong" incentives. There is no large-scale "indifference" among decision makers.
   c) There are no premeeting meetings or agreements. Thus, the individuals meet to decide the issues without preformed coalitions.
   d) Information about individual preferences is privately held by the individual alone.

   When such groups operate using majority rule and a fixed agenda, the
form of the agenda essentially determines the outcome (Plott and Levine
1978). When the agenda is not fixed but is determined endogenously as the
group uses majority rule and common parliamentary procedures, small-group
decisions can be modeled as a cooperative game without side payments. By
treating the majority preference relation as a dominance relation and comput-
ing the associated core, one obtains a reasonable prediction of the group's
choice. Although exceptions to this empirical generality do exist, the reasons
for their existence are somewhat of a paradox (a review of major results is
contained in McKelvey and Ordeshook [1990b]). The current study was designed to answer three questions that naturally emerge from the results found
in the literature.

   1. Does the majority rule equilibrium predict the outcome when the
   group (committee) is "large"? Several lines of reasoning can lead to a
   negative prediction. In a large group, an individual feels less influential and is thus likely to accept poor terms more readily. Thus, according to this argument, the outcomes would be more erratic as the group
   size increases and individuals readily accept the first options they are
   offered. In addition, the potential for leadership influence and the
   related conformity tendencies of followers would increase the likelihood of coalition formation. A coalition, once formed, would not
   likely choose the core equilibrium.
   2. Does the group choice diverge from the equilibrium/core when the
   decision is made by means of a majority-rule, two-candidate election
   process? Is there a difference between the policy-choice behavior of a
   large committee and procedures when the winner of a competitive
   election chooses the policy? Spatial models of candidate competition

(see Riker and Ordeshook 1973 for a summary) suggest that the model used here to describe the choices of small committees applies equally well to the choice behavior of electorates choosing between two candidates. Data in support of such claims are sparse and alternative modes of thought lead readily to different conclusions. If, for example, candidates put together a coalition, or if individuals vote for personalities rather than preference, or if candidates become loyal to subsets of supporters and thereby fail to move too far from them, then the outcome will not be the core.

3. What are the differences between two-candidate election processes and three-candidate processes? Existing models apply only to the two-candidate case. The intuitive reasoning that underlies the two-candidate models suggests that three-candidate elections will behave substantially differently. Candidates who adopt the core position can be "squeezed out" by the other two candidates. Thus, the core position might not tend to be chosen.

Existing models do not have an exceptionally strong base in the theories of individual choice and behavior. Many aspects of individual behavior stand as near paradoxes against the reasoning that lies behind the models. Existing theories are pushed hard to explain why people vote (Ferejohn and Fiorina 1975). In three-candidate elections, how an individual votes is as perplexing as why he or she votes. Furthermore, the optimum strategy for a candidate is not obvious, so there is sufficient theoretical latitude to support almost any result. The experiments described here provide an opportunity for us to study the behavior of some simple cases of these processes.

Procedures and Parameters

Subjects were recruited from the California Institute of Technology, Pasadena City College, Los Angeles City College, University of California at Los Angeles, Cal State Los Angeles, Cal State Fullerton, and Cal State Northridge. Large classes were used where possible; otherwise subjects were recruited and paid $4 (which was promised them) plus whatever they earned during the experiment, as dictated by the payoff chart explained below. All payments were made in cash immediately after the experiment.

The procedures are essentially those reported in detail in Fiorina and Plott 1978. The "issue space" was the blackboard. A preference for each individual was induced using monetary incentives. That is, where the blackboard was given a coordinate system, each individual i was assigned a function $u^i(x,y)$ indicating the amount of money he or she would receive from the experimenter expressed as a function of the point chosen by the group. Since

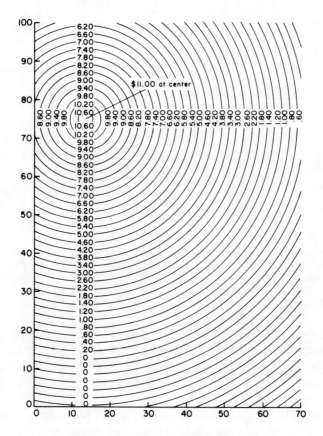

Fig. 1. Example payoff chart

no side payments were allowed, this function induced preferences for points on the blackboard according to $(x,y)R^i(x',y') \Leftrightarrow u^i(x,y) \geq u^i(x',y')$. The gradients of the functions $u^i(x,y)$ were generally between \$1 and \$3 per unit over relevant ranges of the blackboard. A typical payoff chart is included here as figure 1. In the election experiment, the winning candidate was paid \$10 and the losing candidate was paid \$1.

The indifference curves of each individual were circles centered around his or her most preferred point. The distribution of most preferred points for thirty-five subject experiments is shown in figure 2. Because recruitment was difficult, the number of subjects frequently differed across experimental sessions. The formula for adding or subtracting subjects from the standard thirty-five person design shown in figure 2 is outlined in table 1. For sessions with fewer than thirty-five subjects, subjects were removed in pairs starting with

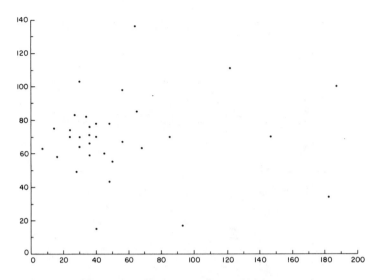

Fig. 2. Distribution of individual optimums

the locations indexed as first, which are the preferences of individuals 32 and 33. The second pair removed was individuals 28 and 29, etc. When more than thirty-five participants were available, subjects were added by giving pairs preferences in the same order. Thus, individuals 36 and 37 had the same preferences as individuals 32 and 33, etc.

The distribution of ideal points (fig. 2) satisfies a condition of radial symmetry around the point (40,70) for all experiments. For each individual, there is another individual whose most preferred point is on the "opposite side" of (40,70). This condition has been shown (Plott 1967) to constitute a sufficient condition for (40,70) to be a core/equilibrium. Notice, however, that (40,70) is not the mean of the distribution of ideal points nor is (40,70) near the middle of the range of the distribution of ideal points. Thus, theories based on such properties of the distribution cannot be used as alternative explanations of outcomes.

After subjects were seated, volunteers were recruited for the position of candidate in the election experiments. The instructions (see the appendix) explained how to read their payoff charts and the procedures. In all experiments, no individual had information about payoffs of others, and individuals were not allowed to indicate the amounts or make side payments even though statements about preferences were admissible.[2]

_____

2. For a discussion of this see Fiorina and Plott 1978.

TABLE 1. Removal Sequence

Subject Number	Maximum Point	Position in Removal Sequence	Subject Number	Maximum Point	Position in Removal Sequence
1	(40,70)		19	(147,70)	
2	(24,70)	8th	20	(30,64)	3d
3	(85,70)	8th	21	(65,85)	3d
4	(24,74)		22	(36,59)	5th
5	(182,34)		23	(64,136)	5th
6	(27,83)	7th	24	(36,76)	9th
7	(93,17)	7th	25	(50,55)	9th
8	(28,49)		26	(36,71)	12th
9	(56,98)		27	(68,63)	12th
10	(48,43)	10th	28	(36,66)	2d
11	(30,103)	10th	29	(48,78)	2d
12	(16,58)		30	(14,75)	6th
13	(122,111)		31	(56,67)	6th
14	(7,63)		32	(34,82)	1st
15	(187,100)		33	(45,60)	1st
16	(40,15)	11th	34	(40,70)	4th[a]
17	(40,78)	11th	35	(40,70)	4th[o]
18	(30,70)				

Note: For experiments with more than thirty-five in the electorate, positions were added in the same order as the removal sequence.

[a] This position is never removed in the three-candidate election.

[b] This position is always removed from all three-candidate elections.

The dynamics of all three types of processes can be identified by a series of periods that are more precisely defined in the election processes. For the large committee experiments the process started with a motion on the floor (200,150). This motion could be amended, with the amended motion becoming the new motion on the floor, until the question was called and a majority accepted the motion as amended. Each successful amendment can be viewed as a stage, since the effect was to change the motion on the floor from one point to another.

The election processes began with all candidates at the same point (200,150). Candidates were free to change their positions at any time. The group choice was the position of the winning candidate at the time of the election. A period could be identified with the opportunity for a candidate to gain information about preferences by asking polling questions: "How many would like for me to move to point _____?" Such opportunities were given to candidates in turn, and the answers obtained were public information. Every several minutes a Gallup poll was taken ("If the election were held now, how many would vote for _____?"). The results of these polls were public.

Experimental Results—Outcomes

For all experimental sessions, the equilibrium/core is the point (40,70). Ten experimental sessions were conducted for each of the three processes. As can be seen in figures 3 and 4 as well as table 2, the equilibrium/core is an excellent predictor for all three processes. The mean outcomes are (38.3,69.8), (38.8,70.9), and (39.2,70.5), respectively, for direct democracy, two-candidate elections, and three-candidate elections. Standard deviations for the committee and two candidates are small and about one-third of the standard deviation of the three-candidate election.

The central results are easy to state. The mean outcome from all three processes is essentially the same. On average, all three processes tend to produce core/equilibrium outcomes.[3] The variances of direct democracy and two-candidate elections are approximately equal, but the variance of the three-candidate process around this mean is higher than the other two.[4]

From an anecdotal or "qualitative" point of view, the large committees do seem to be different from small committees. The small groups we have observed (Fiorina and Plott 1978) are interactive. Large groups are not. Only a small subset of the large group seems to participate, and the meetings seem to go much faster. People simply voted their interest without bothering to argue,

---

3. The null hypothesis that the outcome is the mean of the individual maximums or that the outcomes are uniformly distributed over the range of preferences can easily be rejected in favor of the alternative that the outcome is the core/equilibrium. In fact, the null hypothesis that the outcomes are the core/equilibrium cannot be rejected at a 10 percent level of confidence. The Hotelling T^2-tests are as follows:

	$\bar{\mu} - (40,70)$	T^2	F	ρ	df
Committees	$(-1.7,-0.2)$	5.8295	2.5909	.136	(2, 8)
2-candidate	$(-1.2,0.9)$	3.7303	1.6579	.250	(2, 8)
3-candidate	$(-0.8,0.5)$	0.6640	0.2951	.752	(2, 8)

4. A box test for equality of variance-covariance yields the following results.

	df	χ^2	ρ
Committees vs. 2 candidates	3	5.3705	.15
Committees vs. 3 candidates	3	16.9675	<.001
2 candidates vs. 3 candidates	3	17.737	<.001

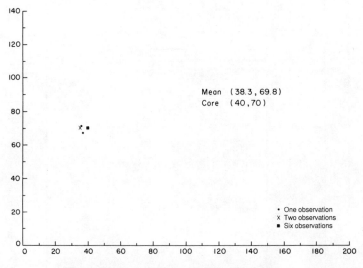

Fig. 3. Large committee outcome distribution

compromise, or persuade others. This supports a conjecture that large groups will be much more susceptible to procedural influences, such as those reported in Plott and Levine 1978, than are small groups.

The experimental outcomes for the two-candidate elections leave little

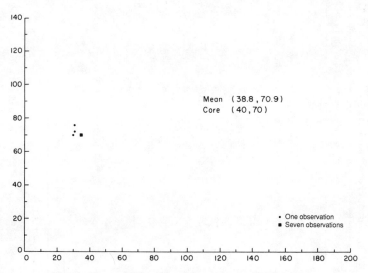

Fig. 4. Two-candidate elections outcome distribution

TABLE 2. Individual Experiment Data

Committees

Exp. No.	N of Subjects	Final Choice
101	35	(40,70)
102	35	(37,67)
103	23	(35,70)
104	27	(35,70)
106	35	(40,70)
107	45	(36,71)
108	23	(40,70)
109	35	(40,70)
110	31	(40,70)
111	33	(40,70)
Outcome mean		(38.3, 69.8)
$\left[\sum \dfrac{\|(x_1^i, x_2^i) - (40,70)\|^2}{10}\right]^{1/2}$		(2.92)

Two-Candidate Elections

Exp. No.	N of Subjects[a]	Candidate Final Points[b] S	Candidate Final Points[b] T	Votes S	Votes T
203	23	(38,72)	(40,70)	12	13
204	41	(45,60)	(40,70)	9	33
205	33	(40,63)	(40,70)	16	19
206	19	(45,75)	(40,70)	8	13
207	23	(35,75)	(36,76)	10	15
208	19	(35,70)	(42,65)	15	6
209	19	(50,60)	(40,70)	9	12
210	27	(37,73)	(36,72)	15	14
211	35	(40,70)	(35,70)	15	14
212	41	(39,70)	(40,70)	18	23
Outcome mean		(38.8, 70.9)			
$\left[\sum \dfrac{\|(x_1^i, x_2^i) - (40,70)\|^2}{10}\right]^{1/2}$		(3.08)			

Three-Candidate Elections

Exp. No.	N of Subjects[a]	Candidate Final Points[b] S	Candidate Final Points[b] T	Candidate Final Points[b] U	Votes S	Votes T	Votes U
301	22	(53,70)	(36,70)	(34,70)	10	7	8
302	22	(21,65)	(75,75)	(60,40)	12	8	5
303	28	(40,69)	(40,70)	(41,69)	8	13	10
304	22	(40,70)	(35,70)	(45,70)	13	5	7
305	30	(38,70)	(40,70)	(45,75)	12	7	13
306	26	(40,70)	(40,71)	(41,68)	8	8	13
307	48	(42,72)	(45,70)	(42,72)	5	18	27
308[b]	28	(35,70)	(55,65)	(45,60)	15	10	5
309	24	(30,75)	(35,70)	(60,65)	2	12	11
310	24	(31,75)	(40,70)	(35,75)	10	13	4
311	33	(60,80)	(40,70)	(35,75)	12	3	18
Outcome mean		(39.2, 70.5)					
$\left[\sum \dfrac{\|(x_1^i, x_2^i) - (40,70)\|^2}{10}\right]^{1/2}$		(8.32)					

[a] Ns exclude candidates.

[b] The winning candidate's final points are underlined.

[c] Due to an administrative error, charts were not distributed in accord with table 1. The core of this game is (40,70), but no subject had a maximum at that point. The observation is eliminated from all calculations below.

room for debate. The candidates tend to converge both together and to the generalized median, core, or equilibrium (depending upon how you derived the point). Clearly, for this class of institutions and situations, the principles that underlie the spatial models of candidate competition stemming from the work of Downs (1957) are correct.

Again, generalization from personal observations leads to some interesting speculations. Candidates' behavior is very sensitive to the information they receive from the electorate. Candidates tend to change their position primarily in response to Gallup polls that show they are behind. They gather information about preferences on issues from every opinion poll available but tend not to act on the information unless they are behind (as revealed in the Gallup poll).

In eight of the experiments in which proper records exist on the details of candidate movement, candidates made a total of fifty-eight moves. Of these, forty moves (69 percent of the total) were made by the candidate who was losing in the previous Gallup poll. (The null hypothesis that movement by winners and losers is equally likely can be rejected at the .01 level of significance.) When forced to move, they then seem to follow a type of gradient procedure whereby they simply go in the direction that would yield the most votes.

The distance candidates move tends to be much greater than the steps taken in large committees. This suggests that the information revealed by the polling techniques in this experiment does not allow the candidates to adjust their positions as finely to individual preferences as might otherwise be the case, and that in situations where decision costs are low, direct democracy might adjust "more closely" to preferences than do competitive election processes. A reasonable conjecture is, for example, that, had the equilibrium not been in multiples of five or ten, say at (36,73), the elections would have still gone to (40,70) while the direct democracy would have gone to (36,73). Of course, if the process is costly in terms of polls or in terms of a personal cost to those who propose amendments, the comparative performance might be very different indeed.

The fact that candidates in these processes have no personal preferences over issues leads to another interesting variable. If, for example, a candidate has his or her own independent preferences over issues, he or she may be willing to risk losing the election for the additional reward he or she would gain if, when elected, he or she is able to implement decisions that are to his or her personal liking. If candidates are allowed to have preferences in addition to winning, then the system may behave differently and be sensitive to the process of candidate selection.

Other institutions, such as polling techniques, appear to be exceptionally important. In these experiments, candidates basically asked "how many would prefer me to move to _____?" although other questions were asked

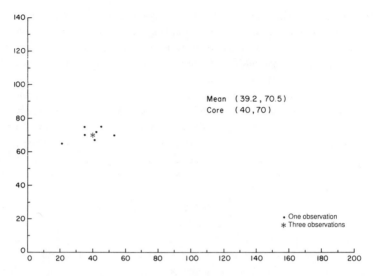

Fig. 5. Three-candidate elections outcome distribution

whenever candidates could find a way to articulate them (e.g., "How many are to the right of fifty on the x?" "How many want me to move up?" "How many would vote for me if I moved to _____?"). Preliminary experiments conducted as pilots for these experiments suggested that the system would not generally converge if candidates were not allowed to take opinion polls. That is, if the candidate knows only whether he or she is ahead or behind and has no other information about where people's preferences lie, then the system may exhibit different behavior. Because theory was completely lacking, this problem of information was not pursued at the time of the research. However, the structure of the conjecture has now been investigated extensively by McKelvey and Ordeshook (1987).

Outcomes of the three-candidate elections are shown in figure 5. Because of the lack of theory, generalizations are difficult to make. The pattern indicates that, on average, the process will result in the median, but the variance is large. An impression about the dynamics of the behavior leads to the following conjecture about the patterns. Candidate competition drives all candidates to the median. Once there, however, the "middleman" is squeezed out by the candidates on both sides. If the election is held when candidates are in this configuration, one of the outliers will win. If candidates still have the opportunity to change positions, the "middleman" will move away from the equilibrium, thereby initiating a new cycle converging toward the equilibrium. The distribution of outcomes seems to depend critically upon the timing of the election, since that will determine the phase of the cycle on which the experiment is terminated.

There are observations, however, that cast doubts on this conjecture. Notice the position of the candidates for experiment 304 in table 2. Candidate S at (40,70) is boxed in on both sides by T on his left at (35,70) and U on his right at (45,70). If individuals had voted sincerely for the candidate whose position would yield the most money, the vote would have been five for S, ten for T, and ten for U. Candidate S won because he got five votes that T would have gotten by sincere voting and three votes that U would have gotten, thereby bringing his vote to thirteen. Comments volunteered by subjects afterward supported the hypothesis that voters were consciously using strategic voting strategies. Some voters who preferred an outlying candidate decided to vote for the person in the center because their favorite candidate had not been doing well at the polls and the voters did not want to "waste" their vote. They therefore shifted support to the median. If such strategic voting is generally characteristic of three-candidate processes, the instability discussed above may not occur. Here we definitely need more theory, and that theory should incorporate the probability of winning as perceived by the voter.

The Decision to Vote

For some of the two-candidate elections, the experimental design had a feature not revealed in the instructions. After individuals had marked their ballots indicating for whom they were planning to vote, they were told there would be a poll tax. If an individual wanted his or her vote counted, a poll tax of $.50 would be deducted from earnings. Subjects were assured that they would be paid according to the position of the winning candidate, independent of the decision to vote. The decision not to vote could only affect an individual's payment by influencing the outcome of the election. Those who wanted their vote counted and were willing to pay the $.50 were asked to place an X on their ballots. Actually, the poll tax was not collected and all individuals' votes were counted in determining the winner.[5]

Figure 6 contains the frequency of decisions to vote as a function of the monetary difference between the two candidates, as seen from the subjects' point of view. While the observations are not as numerous as we would like, a pattern is definitely beginning to emerge. The relative frequency of voting clearly increases as the difference between the candidates increases. This can be seen impressionistically from the figure and from the logit model estimated and plotted in the figure against the data.

---

5. Prior to the vote count, subjects were told that we needed those data resulting from their decision and, in fact, there would be no tax. Subjects then voted and the winner was determined.

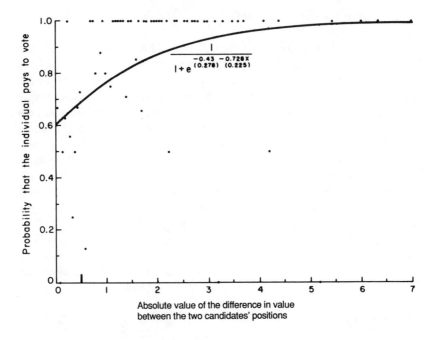

Fig. 6. Decisions to pay cost of voting

Of particular interest is the high frequency of voting that occurs when the difference between the candidates is less than $.50, the cost of voting. Sixty-three percent of the subjects for whom the difference between the candidates was $.50 or less paid $.50 to vote. These people voted even though the cost of voting exceeded or equaled the maximum possible monetary return from voting. Whether or not this behavior is a result of a feeling of "duty" has yet to be determined, but the data are very supportive of a model such as the one found in Riker and Ordeshook 1973.

Concluding Remarks

The conclusions are easy to summarize. For the political situations studied here in which the citizens had well-formed preferences over an issue space characterized by certainty, and where there were no premeeting meetings, there was very little difference between the behavior of large committees and two-candidate electoral behavior. They all resulted at the core or equilibrium. The spatial models in these settings are very accurate predictors of policy outcomes. Three-candidate processes can produce different process behavior. The median of individual preferences will emerge, on average, as the group choice, but the variance is larger than for the other two processes. Thus, in the three-candidate processes, individuals who are "far" from the center are more likely to get favorable policies than is the case with two-candidate elections.

A satisfactory explanation of these results is not available. The exact process of convergence may be sensitive to the nature of the polling institutions and practices that provide candidates with feedback on their strategies. Candidate decisions are clearly influenced by the state of their current information. Research should not focus on the dynamic properties of candidate decisions alone, however, as is the natural tendency in game-theoretic models. Voting patterns in three-candidate elections and in response to voting costs suggest there is much that remains to be explained, even within political settings as simple as these.

APPENDIX

Instructions for Two-Candidate Elections

Change as in Brackets [ ] to Obtain Instructions for
Three-Candidate Elections

General

You are about to participate in an electoral process experiment in which one of two [three] candidates (*S* or *T*) [*U*] will be elected. The purpose of the experiment is to gain insight into certain features of complex political processes. The instructions are simple. If you follow them carefully and make good decisions, you might earn a considerable amount of money. You will be paid in cash.

Instructions to Voters

Your task is to elect either candidate *S* or candidate *T* [or candidate *U*]. The task of the elected individual is to choose one of several competing alternatives, represented by points on the blackboard. After the elections, he or she will choose one and only one point. Your compensation depends on the particular point chosen by the elected individual (see attached payoff chart).

[In the original instructions, a small copy of a figure similar to fig. 1 was inserted here.]

For example, suppose your payoff chart is that given in the Figure 1, and that the elected individual's choice is the point $(x,y) = (170,50)$. Your payment as read from Figure 1 would be $7,000.

For points which lie between curves, the chart should be read in the following manner. Suppose the elected individual chooses the point (140,125). This point, (140,125) is halfway between the curve marked $7,000 and the curve marked $8,000. So your payment is halfway between $7,000 and $8,000, i.e., $7,500. If the point is one-quarter of the distance between two curves, then your payment is determined by the same proportion. As an example (75,50) lies one-fourth of the way between the curve marked $8,000 and the curve marked $9,000, so you get $8,250.

The payments charts may differ among individuals. This means that the patterns of preferences differ and the monetary amounts may not be comparable. The point which would result in the highest payment to you may not result in the highest payment to someone else. You should decide what final decision you want and do whatever you wish within the confines of the rules to get things to go your way. *The experiments, however, are not primarily concerned with whether or how you participate so long as you stay within the confines of the rules.* Under no circumstances may you mention anything *quantitative* about your payment. You are free, if you wish, to indicate which point you like best, the ones you like least, the direction of your preference, etc., but you cannot mention anything about the actual monetary amounts. Under no circumstances may you mention anything about activities which might involve you and other committee members after the experiment (i.e., no deals to split up afterward or no physical threats).

From time to time you will be asked to participate in opinion polls by a show of hands. You are free to answer in any manner you like. Please record the appropriate data on the voter record sheet.

Instructions to Candidates

If you win the election, you will be paid $10.00. If you lose, you will receive $1.00. Do not mention the amount of this payment and do not assume the payment to the other candidates is the same. Please do not talk to anyone aside from what is necessary to conduct polls and indicate your tentative point choices.

Election Organization

The election will be held _____ minutes after the instructions are completed. At the end of this period each candidate will choose a final point on the blackboard. The election will be held. Your payment will be determined by the final point chosen by the candidate who receives a majority vote.

Each candidate must maintain a tentative point choice during the election period. Both candidates will begin at the Point (200,150). A candidate is free to change this tentative choice at any time during the election period and as many times as he/she wishes.

Two types of polls will be conducted—opinion polls and Gallup polls. Candidates will have the opportunity to ask "Would you prefer me to move to the point (_____,_____)?" The opportunity to conduct such opinion polls will occur in turn with the first decided by lot. Every _____ minutes a Gallup poll will be conducted. The experimenter will ask, "If the election were held now, would you vote for S or T [or U]?" The results of all polls will be made public.

At the end of the election period each candidate must submit a final point. He will submit it in writing prior to learning about his opponent's choice. The candidates will then announce their final points and the election will be held.

The candidate who receives the largest number of votes wins the election. Voter's payments are determined by the final point chosen by the winning candidate. Are there any questions?

Prior to beginning, we would like all voters to answer the questions on the attached voter test sheet.

Instructions for Committees

General

You are about to participate in a committee process experiment in which one of numerous competing alternatives will be chosen by majority rule. The purpose of the experiment is to gain insight into certain features of complex political processes. The instructions are simple. If you follow them carefully and make good decisions, you might earn a considerable amount of money. You will be paid in cash.

Instructions to Committee Members

The alternatives are represented by points on the blackboard. The committee will adopt as the committee decision one and only one point. Your compensation depends on the particular point chosen by the committee (see attached payoff chart). For example, suppose your payoff chart is that given in Figure 1, and that the committee's final choice of an alternative is the point $(x,y) = (170,50)$.

[In the original instructions a small copy of a figure similar to fig. 1 was inserted here.]

Your compensation in this event would be $7,000. If the policy of the committee is (140,125) your compensation would be computed as follows:

The point (140,125) is halfway between the curve marked $7,000 and the curve marked $8,000. So, your compensation is halfway between $7,000 and $8,000, i.e., $7,500. If the policy is one-quarter of the distance between two curves, then your payoff is determined by the same proportion (i.e., at (75,50) which is one-quarter of the way between $8,000 and $9,000, you get $8,250).

The compensation charts may differ among individuals. *This means that the patterns of preferences differ and the monetary amounts may not be comparable. The point which would result in the highest payoff to you may not result in the highest payoff to someone else.* You should decide what decision you want the committee to make and do whatever you wish within the confines of the rules to get things to go your way. *The experimenters, however, are not primarily concerned with whether or how you participate so long as you stay within the confines of the rules.* Under no circumstances may you mention anything *quantitative* about your compensation. You are free, if you wish, to indicate which ones you like best, etc., but you cannot mention anything about the actual monetary amounts. Under no circumstances may you mention anything about activities which might involve you and other committee members after the experiment, i.e., no deals to split up afterward or no physical threats.

Parliamentary Rules

The process begins with an existing motion (200,150) on the floor. You are free to propose *amendments* to this motion on the floor. Suppose the motion on the floor is (170,50) and you want the group to consider the point (140,125). Simply raise your hand and when you are recognized by the chair, say "I move to amend the motion to (140,125)." The group will then proceed to vote on the amendment. If the amendment passes by a majority vote, the point (140,125) is the new motion on the floor and is subject, itself, to amendments. If the amendment fails the motion (170,50) remains on the floor and is subject to further amendment. Thus, amendments simply change the motion on the floor. You may pass as many amendments as you wish.

At any time during the consideration of an amendment or the motion on the floor a *motion to end debate* is in order. If there are no objections, an immediate vote will take place. If there are objections, the motion to end debate will itself be put to a majority vote. If the motion to end debate fails, the amendment process continues. If it passes, a vote on the amendment or motion will take place.

To sum up, the existing motion on the floor is (200,150). You are free to amend this motion as you wish. The meeting will not end until a majority consents to end debate and accept some motion. Your compensation will be determined by the motion on the floor finally adopted by the majority.

Voter Test Questions

Voter Number _____

1. If the final platform of the winning candidate is (90,105) my payment would be $_____.

2. The point where I receive the most money is (_____,_____) which yields a payment of $_____.

3. Suppose the final point choice S is (50,55), the final point choice of T is (85,60), and the final choice of U is (120,110); then the election of candidate _____ would yield me the most money. The amount would be $_____.

****

Voter Ballot

Voter Number _____

I wish to vote for candidate _____.

****

Each subject was given additional materials which included (i) a sheet of small grid graph paper with a 200 × 200 coordinate system that could be used to track candidate positions and; (ii) a voter record sheet on which each subject recorded the candidate's tentative point, the candidate's proposed point and the subject's vote on the candidate or poll. The record sheet was maintained for every poll and for the final rate.

Voter Test Questions

Voter Number _____

1. If the final platform of the winning candidate is (90,105) my payment would be $_____.

2. The point where I receive the most money is (___,___) which yields a payment of $_____.

3. Suppose the final point choice S is (50,55), the final point choice of T is (85,60), and the final choice of U is (120,110); then the election of candidate _____ would yield me the most money. The amount would be $_____.

****

Voter Ballot

Voter Number _____

I wish to vote for candidate _____.

REFERENCES

Downs, A. 1957. *An Economic Theory of Democracy.* New York: Harper.
Ferejohn, John, and Fiorina, Morris P. 1975. "Closeness Counts Only in Horseshoes and Dancing." *American Political Science Review* 69:920–25.
Fiorina, Morris P., and Plott, Charles R. 1978. "Committee Decisions under Majority Rule: An Experimental Study." *American Political Science Review* 72:575–98.
McKelvey, Richard D., and Peter C. Ordeshook. 1984. "Rational Expectations in Elections: Some Experimental Results Based on a Multidimensional Model." *Public Choice* 44:61–102.
McKelvey, Richard D., and Peter C. Ordeshook. 1985a. "Elections with Limited Information: A Fulfilled Expectations Model using Contemporaneous Poll and Endorsement Data as Information Sources." *Journal of Economic Theory* 36:55–85.
McKelvey, Richard D., and Peter C. Ordeshook. 1985b. "Sequential Elections with Limited Information." *American Journal of Political Science* 29:480–512.
McKelvey, Richard D., and Peter C. Ordeshook. 1986. "Sequential Elections with Limited Information: A Formal Analysis." *Social Choice and Welfare* 3:199–211.
McKelvey, Richard D., and Peter C. Ordeshook. 1987. "Elections with Limited Information: A Multidimensional Model." *Mathematical Social Science* 14 (1987):77–99.
McKelvey, Richard D., and Peter C. Ordeshook. 1990a. "Information and Elections: Retrospective Voting and Rational Expectations." In *Information and Democratic Processes,* ed. J. Ferejohn and J. Kuklinski. Champaign: University of Illinois Press.
McKelvey, Richard D., and Peter C. Ordeshook. 1990b. "A Decade of Experimental Research on Spatial Models of Elections and Committees." In *Government, Democracy, and Social Choice,* ed. M. J. Hinich and J. Enelow. Cambridge: Cambridge University Press.

McKelvey, Richard D., Peter C. Ordeshook, Kenneth, E. Collier, and Kenneth C. Williams. 1987. "Retrospective Voting: An Experimental Study." *Public Choice* 53:101–30.

Plott, Charles R. 1967. "A Notion of Equilibrium and Its Possibility under Majority Rule." *American Economic Review* 57:787–806.

Plott, Charles R. 1978. "The Application of Laboratory Experimental Methods to Public Choice." In *Collective Decision Making: Applications from Public Choice Theory,* ed. Clifford S. Russell. Dordrecht, Holland: D. Reidel.

Plott, Charles R. 1981. "Experimental Methods in Political Economy: A Tool for Regulatory Research." In *Attacking Regulatory Problems: An Agenda for Research in the 1980s,* ed. Allen R. Ferguson. Cambridge, Mass.: Ballinger.

Plott, Charles R., 1982. "A Comparative Analysis of Direct Democracy, Two-Candidate Elections and Three Candidate Elections in an Experimental Environment." Caltech.

Plott, Charles R., and Michael E. Levine. 1978. "A Model of Agenda Influence on Committee Decisions." *American Economic Review* 68:146–60.

Riker, W., and P. Ordeshook. 1973. *An Introduction to Positive Political Theory.* Englewood Cliffs, N.J.: Prentice-Hall.

Political Competition in a Model of Economic Growth: An Experimental Study

Richard Boylan, John Ledyard, Arthur Lupia, Richard D. McKelvey, and Peter C. Ordeshook

1. Introduction

We report here on a series of experiments on a one-sector model of economic growth in which decisions on consumption and capital accumulation are made by politicians elected in a competitive political process. The basic question we want to study is how political systems, in which candidates have limited tenures, make decisions on issues that involve capital investment planning. There has been much work investigating the one-sector growth model from the point of view of an economic planner. But not much has been done to study the types of consumption-investment paths that would be generated by political processes in this framework. We are concerned with two aspects of the paths that are generated. First, we want to see how the paths generated by a political process compare with so called optimal paths that would be chosen by an economic planner. Second, we want to see if there is any evidence of political business cycles in the data.

When one leaves the setting of growth theory, there is a fair amount of work that has attempted to characterize the type of fiscal and monetary policy that would be generated by political processes. A recurrent theme in this literature is that if politicians are allowed to make economic decisions, it will generate "political business cycles"—business cycles coinciding with the term of office of the politicians. Nordhaus (1975) originally derives such results in a model in which the incumbent office holder must choose among different points along a Phillips curve. He also presents some empirical evidence that supports the existence of political business cycles in some countries. Nordhaus's theoretical argument depends crucially on voter myopia.

Support for this research was provided, in part, by NSF grant #SES-8604348 to the California Institute of Technology.

Subsequent papers by Rogoff (1990) (see also Rogoff and Sibert 1988) and Alesina (1987) have derived political business cycles without having to assume voter myopia. Rogoff and Rogoff and Sibert show that the introduction of asymmetric information over the competency of political candidates can generate a political business cycle. In this model, a business cycle emerges as a signaling equilibrium in which the size of the cycle is used, by the candidate, to signal its competency to the voters. Alesina assumes that different political parties have different preferences over the trade-off between inflation and unemployment levels. He then gets political business cycles emerging even when voters have rational expectations, due to the fact that the election provides a random shock. Both of the above models are partial equilibrium models. Rogoff's economy does not have the capability of real growth, while Alesina's political parties have exogenously given policy positions.

A second theme that emerges in the literature is that political candidates have short time-horizons, since they are only concerned with the performance of the economy while they are in office. Consequently, they make decisions that are not optimal in the long run. In Nordhaus's model, for example, the candidates pick a higher level of inflation and lower level of unemployment than is optimal for the voters. If candidates are really shortsighted, then, in a model that allows for savings and investment, one might expect that politicians would invest less than would be socially optimal.

We began this study with these questions in mind. The simplest possible framework in which to study them seems to us to be the one-sector model of economic growth, where decisions are made by candidates who compete in a two-candidate electoral process. In this article, we study these questions from an experimental point of view.

In a related paper (Boylan et al. 1990), we study the same questions addressed here, but from a theoretical point of view. We summarize some of those results here. First we present the basic model.

2. The Model

We consider the simplest possible framework—a one-sector model with two-candidate competition. The economy is one in which there is one good that can be consumed or invested (for example, corn, which can be planted or eaten). Following the classical economic model, the technology of growth and production is as follows:

Let y_t be the per capita output on date t, let k_t be the per capita capital stock at the beginning of date t, let ι_t be the per capita investment on date t, let c_t be the per capita consumption on date t, and let λ be the rate of depreciation of the capital stock. At time t, output y_t is determined by the capital stock k_t,

$$y_t = f(k_t), \tag{2.1}$$

where f is the production function.[1] The output y_t in any period can be either consumed or saved (invested). Thus,

$$y_t = \iota_t + c_t. \tag{2.2}$$

The capital stock at time $t + 1$, k_{t+1}, equals the capital stock at time t, minus depreciation, plus the output invested at time t. That is,

$$k_{t+1} = \iota_t + (1 - \lambda)k_t. \tag{2.3}$$

We write $F(k_t) = f(k_t) + (1 - \lambda)k_t$. The technology can be summarized in the fundamental equation of growth theory: we are given $\bar{k} > 0$, and for $t = 0, 1, 2, \ldots$,

$$c_t + k_{t+1} = f(k_t) + (1 - \lambda)k_t = F(k_t), \tag{2.4}$$

where

$$k_0 = \bar{k}, \ k_t \geq 0, \ c_t \geq 0. \tag{2.5}$$

Any path $z = \{(c_t, k_t)\}_{0 < t < \infty}$ satisfying equations 2.4 and 2.5 is a *feasible consumption-investment path*. Let Z represent the set of feasible consumption-investment paths. For any $z \in Z$, write $z = (c, k)$, where $c = \{c_t\}_{0 < t < \infty}$ is the corresponding consumption path, and $k = \{k_t\}_{0 < t < \infty}$ is the corresponding capital path. Since k_t is determined from c_{t-1} and k_{t-1} by equation 2.4, a consumption-investment path is determined completely by the corresponding consumption path. Let $\mathscr{C}$ denote the set of feasible consumption paths.

Letting $N = \{1, \ldots, n\}$ denote the set of n voters (consumers), we assume that for each voter $i \in N$, one period preferences over consumption are represented by a concave function $u_i \colon \mathscr{R}_+ \to \mathscr{R}$ satisfying $u_i'(c) > 0$, $u_i'(0) = \infty$ and $u_i''(c) < 0$ for all $c \in \mathscr{R}$. Further, for each voter, there is a positive real number $\delta_i < 1$ representing the voter's discount factor. The voter's utility function $U_i \colon \mathscr{C} \to \mathscr{R}$ over consumption paths is then given by

$$U_i(c) = \Sigma_{0 < t < \infty} \delta_i^t u_i(c_t).[2]$$

---

1. We assume throughout that f is twice continuously differentiable, with $f' > 0$, $f'' < 0$, $f(0) = 0$, $f'(0) = +\infty$, and $f'(\infty) = 0$.

2. One might worry about the distribution of c_t across voters, but for simplicity we will treat this as a public good. That is, the elected candidate will pick c_t, the amount of y_t to be consumed, yielding voter i a utility level of $u_i(c_t)$ for that period.

This economic growth model has been studied extensively in the case where a particular social welfare function is defined. This approach amounts to assuming that there is just one voter, so that we can solve for a feasible consumption-investment path that maximizes the welfare function for that one voter. That is, for any $c \in \mathscr{C}$, $U(c) = \sum_{t=0}^{\infty} \delta^t u(c_t)$, where $u: \mathscr{R}_+ \to \mathscr{R}$ satisfies $u'(c) > 0$, $u'(0) = \infty$, and $u''(c) < 0$ for all $c \in \mathscr{R}_+$.

The solution $[(c_t^*, k_t^*)]_{0 < t < \infty}$ can be characterized by a pair of functions $g(k)$ and $h(k)$ for the optimal consumption and capital, respectively, such that $k_0^* = \bar{k}$, $k_{t+1}^* = h(k_t^*)$, and $c_t^* = g(k_t^*)$. The functions g and h satisfy $g(k) = F(k) - h(k)$, and $\delta u'\{g[h(k)]\} = u'[g(k)]/F'[h(k)]$, where h satisfies $h' > 0$ and $\mathrm{h}(k) < k^*$ for $k < k^*$, and $h(k) > k^*$ for $k > k^*$, and k^* is defined by

$$f'(k^*) = \lambda + r, \tag{2.6}$$

where $r = 1/\delta - 1$.[3] This result means that $k_{t+1}^* = F(k_t^*) - c_t^*$, and $\delta u'(c_{t+1}^*) = u'(c_t^*)/F'(k_{t+1}^*)$. The optimal path of capital begins at k_0 and converges monotonically to k^*. Similarly, the optimal path of consumption converges monotonically to $c^* = f(k^*) - \lambda k^*$.

Boylan et al. (1990) offer a theoretical analysis of political processes within the framework of the one-sector model of economic growth described here. There, decisions about the consumption-investment path are decided by a two-candidate political system in which the candidates compete for office through the consumption paths that they propose to the voters. They consider two different models: In the first, candidates are able to commit to a path of consumption over their entire term of office. In the second model, they are only able to commit themselves for the current period.

In the first model, where candidates can commit to consumption streams, under very mild conditions on the heterogeneity of voter preferences, there is no majority-rule equilibrium.[4] More specifically, if different voters have dif-

---

3. To see this, let $v^*(k) = \underset{c}{max} \{u(c) + \delta v^*[F(k) - c]\} = \underset{h}{max} \{u[F(k) - h] + \delta v^*(h)\}$ be the value of being at state k. Then $v^*(k) = u[F(k) - h(k)] + \delta v^*[h(k)]$, where for all k, $h(k)$ satisfies $\frac{\partial v^*}{\partial h} = 0 \Rightarrow u'[F(k) - h(k)] = \delta v^{*\prime}[h(k)]$. Now, by the Envelope theorem, $v^{*\prime}(k) = \frac{\partial v^*}{\partial k} = u'[F(k) - h(k)]F'(k)$. Hence $u'[F(k) - h(k)] = \delta v^{*\prime}[h(k)]$ $= \delta u'\{F[h(k)] - h[h(k)]\}/F'[h(k)] \Rightarrow u'[g(k)] = \delta u'\{g[h(k)]\}F'[h(k)]$. Note that if $h(k) = k$, then $\delta u'[g(k)] = u'[g(k)]/F'(k) \Rightarrow F'(k) = 1/\delta \Rightarrow f'(k) = \lambda + r$. The value function, v^*, is continuous, differentiable, strictly increasing, and strictly concave. That is, $v^{*\prime}(k) > 0$, and $v^{*\prime\prime}(k) < 0$. For more details, the reader can consult Harris 1987.

4. A feasible path $c \in \mathscr{C}$ is said to be a *majority-rule equilibrium*, or *majority core* if there is no other feasible path, $c' \in \mathscr{C}$ such that a majority of voters prefer c' over c. That is, $\|i \in N: U_i(c') > U_i(c)\| > n/2$.

ferent discount rates, then, even if their one-period utility functions are the same (i.e., $u_i = u$ for all i), there is no majority-rule core equilibrium. One might expect that in the case where voters differ only by their discount rates, there would be an equilibrium at the optimal path for the voter with a median discount factor. However, this path can be defeated by a coalition of voters with higher and lower discount rates as follows. Perturb the path to increase consumption slightly in the current period, reduce consumption considerably in the second period, and raise consumption even more in the third period. The second period reduction in consumption can be used to finance the third period rise in consumption in such a way that one returns to the original path in the fourth period. This perturbation is preferred by voters with lower discount factors since they get more immediate consumption in the long run, and it is preferred by voters with higher discount factors because they get larger total consumption. In the case where there is variation in the utility functions, but no variation in discount factors, the optimal path for every voter converges to the same steady state level of consumption. It follows that a path that starts at this level and stays there forever will be a majority core. However, if one takes into account the initial constraint, then generically there will be no core in this case either.

In the second model, where candidates can commit only to the policy to be adopted for the current period, Boylan et al. find different results. The instability in the first model depends on the ability of candidates to commit to policies. But multiple-period commitment may not be credible in political processes, where candidates have limited terms of office. Since policies must be implemented over time, coalitions such as ones between voters of high and low discount factors may unravel: once policies that help one part of the coalition are implemented, those individuals no longer have incentives to support the remaining portion of the proposed policy. Thus, if one assumes that candidates cannot commit to future policies, but only to the policies that are adopted in the current period, then Boylan et al. find that there is a unique, subgame-perfect, stationary, symmetric (for the candidates) equilibrium. The equilibrium follows the optimal consumption path of the voter with the median discount rate.

In all of our experiments, voters have the same discount factors, but different utility functions. Thus, in our experiments, there is no majority equilibrium if multiperiod commitment is allowed. However, if the path ever reaches the optimal steady state for the voters, then even with multiperiod commitment, that steady state is a majority rule equilibrium. It is not clear what the implications of the nonexistence of a majority core are for our data, since we do not know the nature of the majority cycles, and if for example, the Pareto set or uncovered set are small. Presumably, nonexistence of a core would lead to consumption paths that are different from experiment to experiment, and which do not show any specific patterns. On the other hand, in our experiments, while we allow candidates to specify multiperiod plans, we do not provide any means of commitment. In the case of no commitment, there is an equilibrium at the optimal path of the median voter. So in the analysis of our results, we will compare our outcomes with the optimal path for the median voter.

3. Experimental Design

In this article, we look at the behavior of voters and candidates in an experimental laboratory setting so that we might learn some of the factors that influence policy selection by candidates in the one-sector growth model. We ran two versions of the basic experiment. Version A incorporates features that go beyond the confines of preexisting theoretical models but which make the experiment "realistic." This version includes polls, incomplete information, and ambiguous message spaces. In version B, we eliminate several of these features. The version B experiments try to isolate the source of cyclical economic behavior that we observe in the more realistic version A experiments. We first describe the version B experiments, and then describe the version A experiments by indicating the ways in which they differ from the version B experiments.

Version B

Each experiment consists of a series of elections in which two candidates compete for a four-period term of office. Prior to each election, candidates make a campaign promise indicating the consumption levels they plan to select in each of the four periods of their term of office. After observing the campaign promises of both candidates, the voters vote for one of the two candidates. The candidate who obtains a majority of the votes becomes the incumbent for the next four periods.

During each period of the term of office, the incumbent observes the current total real income, $y_t = f(k_t)$, and must choose how to divide this between investment, ι_t, and consumption, c_t.[5] After the incumbent makes a policy choice, all voters are told the decision, and for each voter, i, the payoff $u_i(c_t)$ is computed and reported to that voter. Given the incumbent's policy choice, we use equations 2.1–2.3 to compute the total real income, y_{t+1}, available for the next period. All participants observe this figure, and the process described above continues for the remaining three periods of the incumbent's term of office. Thus, in each period, the incumbent divides the current real income

---

5. One important fact for the interpretation of the data is that not only was $c_t \geq 0$ required but also $\iota_t \geq 0$. Thus, candidates could not run a deficit and borrow against the future.

into investment and consumption, and the voters observe that policy choice and their own payoffs from this choice. After the fourth period there is a new election. Both candidates make new campaign promises, indicating the consumption levels they plan to achieve during each of the four periods of their term of office, and the voters select the incumbent for the next four periods.

In our experiments, we use the production function

$$f(k_t) = a(1 - e^{-bk_t}),$$

and utility functions of the form

$$U_i(c) = \sum_{t=0}^{\infty} \delta^t d_i c_t^{e_i}.$$

The values of the parameters k_0, λ, a, and b in the production function, as well as the the parameters d_i and e_i in the utility functions, are given in table 1. These parameters are chosen so that all voters are risk averse, and have a payoff of $v_i(100) = 10$. The discount rates are equal across voters, with $\delta_i = \delta = .97$ for all i. The discounting is imposed by having a probabilistic end to the experiment. Thus, after each period, a random number between 0 and 1 is selected, and if it is greater than .97, the experiment is terminated. If it is less than or equal to .97, then the experiment continues to the next period, with all voters accumulating the additional payoff from the decision of that period.

With the preceding specification of the problem, we can solve for the optimal steady state consumption level for the voters using equation 2.6:

$$f'(k^*) = \lambda + r \Rightarrow abe^{-bk^*} = \lambda + r \Rightarrow k^* = \frac{1}{b}\ln\left(\frac{ab}{\lambda + r}\right).^6 \quad (3.1)$$

Thus,

$$y^* = f(k^*) = a\left(1 - e^{\ln\left(\frac{\lambda + r}{ab}\right)}\right) = a\left(1 - \frac{\lambda + r}{ab}\right), \quad (3.2)$$

$$i^* = \lambda k^*, \quad (3.3)$$

and

$$c^* = y^* - i^*. \quad (3.4)$$

---

6. Note that since $\delta_i = \delta$ for all i, the optimal steady state consumption level is the same for all i.

TABLE 1. Experimental Parameters

	Production Function		Voter	Utility Function	
	1	2	i	d_i	e_i
a	300	400	1	1.00	.50
b	.003	.004	2,6,10	0.79	.45
λ	.3	.4	3,7,11	1.26	.55
k_0	100	13	4,8	0.63	.60
y_0	77	20	5,9	1.58	.40

Table 2 reports the values of y^*, i^*, and c^* for our experiments, both for the value of $\delta = .97$ induced in the version B experiments, and for the value $\delta = 1.00$, corresponding to the solution that maximizes the long-run value of consumption.

Notice that we can suppress the role of capital in the model, and simply write real income at time $t + 1$ as a function of real income and investment at time t. From equations 2.1–2.3 it follows that

$$y_{t+1} = f(k_{t+1}) = f[\iota_t + (1 - \lambda)k_t] = f[\iota_t + (1 - \lambda)f^{-1}(y_t)]. \quad (3.5)$$

So, setting $y_t = f(k_t) = a(1 - e^{-bk_t})$, it follows that $f^{-1}(y_t) = -\dfrac{1}{b}\ln(1 - \dfrac{y_t}{a})$. So

$$y_{t+1} = a(1 - e^{-[b\iota_t - (1 - \lambda)\ln(1 - \frac{y_t}{a})]}) \equiv G(\iota_t, y_t). \quad (3.6)$$

Thus, in each experiment, subjects are given a plot of the function $y_{t+1} = G(\iota_t, y_t)$, with representative contours on a two-dimensional grid. Figure 1

TABLE 2. Optimal Steady State Values

	Production Function 1		Production Function 2	
	$\delta = .97$	$\delta = 1.00$	$\delta = .97$	$\delta = 1.00$
k^*	333.50	336.20	327.95	346.57
y^*	189.69	200.00	292.26	300.00
i^*	100.05	109.86	131.18	138.63
c^*	89.64	90.14	161.08	161.37

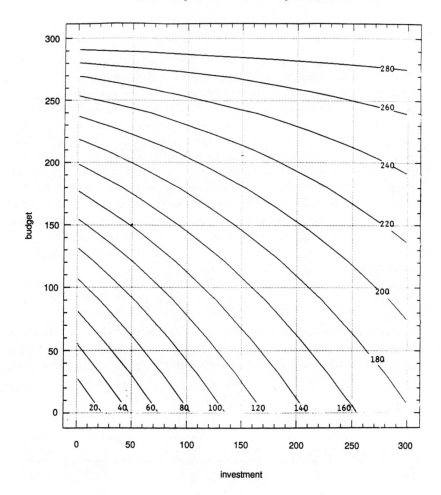

Fig. 1. Plot of production function 1 given to subjects

illustrates the plot of G given to the subjects for experiments 1–7. (A similar plot, using the payoff function generated by the parameters of column 2 of table 1 is used in experiments 8–9.) Thus, in a given period, the incumbent candidate has a budget, y_t, which must be split between investment and consumption. Using function G, a candidate can determine what the next period budget will be, given y_t and the investment choice ι_t, by reading the appropriate contour for the point (y_t, ι_t) off figure 1.

Version A

The version *A* experiments differed from the version *B* experiments in four ways. First, the voters and candidates are not told the functional form of the voter utility functions. They are only told that the utility functions are increasing with consumption, but not that they increase at a decreasing rate. Second, the candidates do not make a promise for a consumption path over the entire four-period term of office. Rather, they make a consumption-investment promise only for the last period of the term of office. Third, the voters are polled between each period of the term of office about their approval or disapproval of the incumbent's performance while in office. Fourth, the discounting is done somewhat differently in the version *A* experiments than in the version *B* experiments. Rather than having a fixed discount rate over the course of the experiment, we have a discount rate that declines in time. Thus, $\delta_{it} = \delta_t = \rho^t\delta$, where $0 < \rho < 1$. This procedure gives us somewhat greater control over the length of the experiment.

4. Data

We ran a total of sixteen experiments using undergraduates at the California Institute of Technology as subjects—ten version *A* experiments, with six groups of subjects, and six version *B* experiments, with four groups of sub-

TABLE 3. **Experimental Design**

Experiment	Group	Version	Production Function	Number of Voters	Number of Periods
1A	1	A	1	7	32
2A	2	A	1	9	31
3A	2	A	1	7	40
4A	3	A	1	7	24
5A	3	A	1	7	14
6A	4	A	1	9	40
7A	4	A	1	9	40
8A	5	A	2	11	40
9A	5	A	2	11	38
10A	6	A	2	11	40
1B	7	B	1	9	40
2B	8	B	1	9	40
3B	8	B	1	7	40
4B	9	B	2	9	29
5B	9	B	1	9	40
6B	10	B	2	9	88

jects. Because of the way in which the discounting was implemented, we had no control over the length of the experiment. Thus, with those groups in which time permitted, we ran two experiments. With this procedure, we obtained two experiments with six of the groups, and one with the other four groups.[7] Table 3 describes the experiments we ran.

5. Candidate Behavior

Figures 4–19 show candidate behavior in each of the experiments. These figures plot the path of consumption and investment chosen by the incumbent candidates. The lower path represents the consumption chosen in each period, while the upper path represents the corresponding total budget. The investment in period t can then be computed as the difference in the consumption and budget in period t. The left axis of each figure shows the number of units of consumption and the total budget that the paths refer to. The upper horizontal line represents the equilibrium value for total budget, which was obtained using equation 2.2 and is displayed in table 1, while the lower horizontal line represents the corresponding equilibrium value for consumption, from equation 2.4. Figures 2 and 3 summarize the data for all of the experiments, giving average values across experiments of the consumption and total budget. Figure 2 gives summaries for the experiments run with production function 1, and figure 3 gives a summary of the data for experiments with production function 2.

Version A

The results of the Version A experiments are given in figures 4–13. As is clear from these figures, candidates tend to converge toward values that are near the long-run equilibrium values of consumption and budget. However, there is a tendency in many of the experiments to overinvest, even when the path is compared to the optimal values generated by $\delta = 1.00$. In some of the experiments, the overinvestment disappears with time, as in experiment 6A (fig. 9), but in others it seems to persist. The tendency to overinvest is curious, especially in light of the fact that the effects of discounting and risk would be to lead to lower levels of investment than that which sustains optimal consumption.

---

7. We chose λ to give an expected length of around ten elections. In addition, for all but the last experiment, we imposed a maximum length of forty periods, or ten elections. This explains the large number of experiments that ended at forty periods. Neither subjects nor experimenters were aware of the maximum length. With those groups in which time permitted, we ran two experiments.

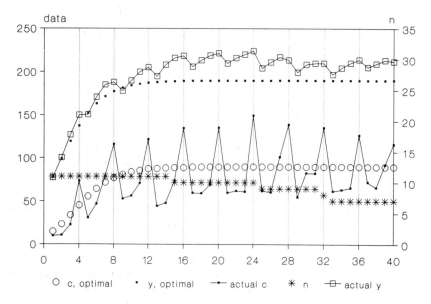

Fig. 2. Optimal and actual (average) behavior for production function 1

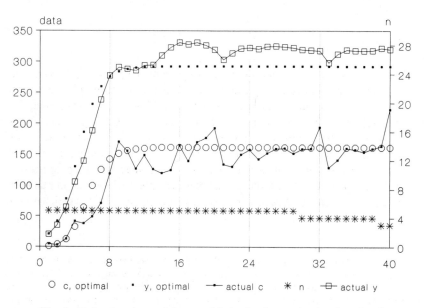

Fig. 3. Optimal and actual (average) behavior for production function 2

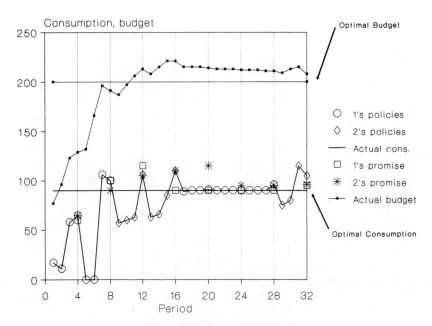

Fig. 4. Growth experiment 1A

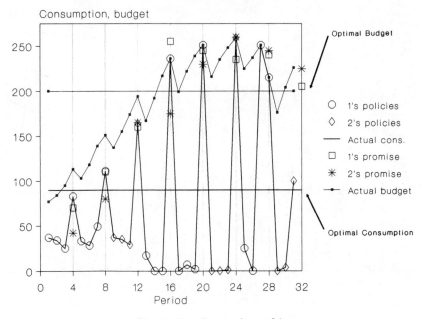

Fig. 5. Growth experiment 2A

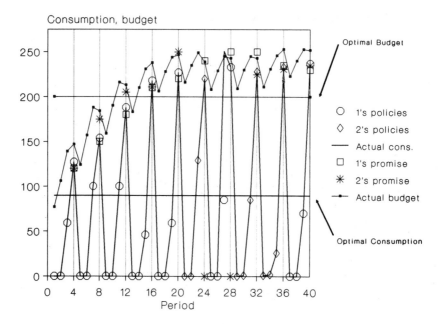

Fig. 6. Growth experiment 3A

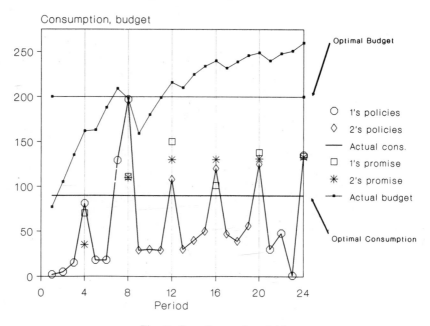

Fig. 7. Growth experiment 4A

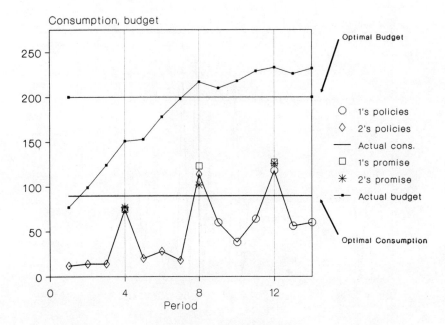

Fig. 8. Growth experiment 5A

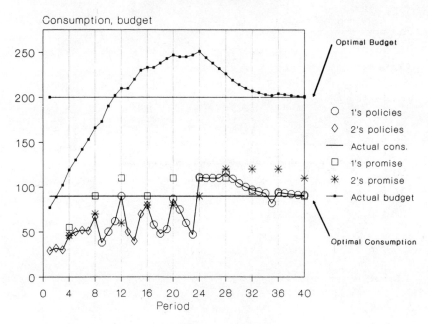

Fig. 9. Growth experiment 6A

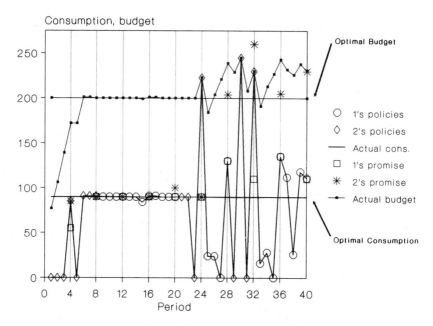

Fig. 10. Growth experiment 7A

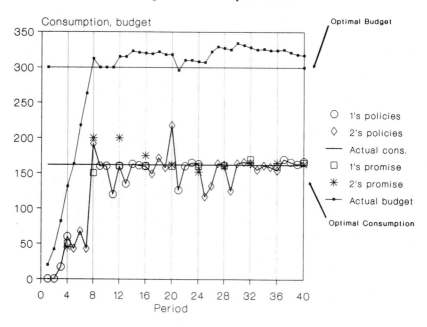

Fig. 11. Growth experiment 8A

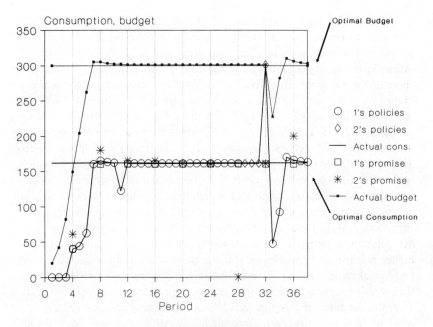

Fig. 12. Growth experiment 9A

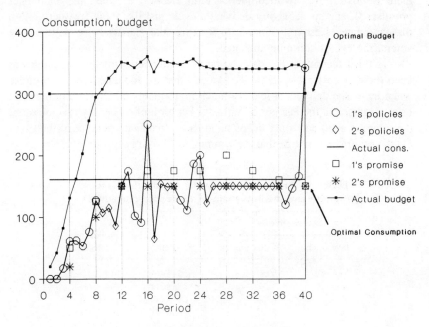

Fig. 13. Growth experiment 10A

A second feature of the data is that many of the experiments exhibit a political business cycle, in which the candidate overinvests in the first few periods of his or her term in office, and overconsumes in the last few periods. We attribute this cycle, in part, to the role of the candidates' promises. In some of the experiments, voters tend to vote for candidates who promise the higher value of consumption. This behavior provides incentives for the candidates to make promises that are higher than can be met without running a business cycle. If candidates fear retribution at the polls for not keeping their promises, they will deliver a business cycle rather than not keep the promise. Since the voters do not initially know (in the version A experiments) whether or not they are risk averse, it can initially be rational behavior for the voters to behave in this way. And, once such a pattern is established, it can be difficult to get rid of it. This type of behavior is evident in experiments 2A and 3A (figs. 5 and 6). In these experiments, which use the same group of subjects, the voters in experiment 2A consistently vote for the candidate making the higher promise on consumption (66.7 percent or 30 of 45 votes) through the first six elections. In the second experiment, having seemingly learned that the cycle is not good for them, the voters vote in every election except election 7 for the candidate making the *lower* promise on consumption (73.2 percent or 41 of 56 votes). However, since the incumbent consistently promises less, there is no turnover in incumbency until election 6, when the challenger promises 0, and subsequently delivers a cycle just like their opponent. With the candidates seemingly unable to interpret the signals being sent by the voters, the cycles continue unabated.

A third feature of the data concerns the tendency of the candidates to keep their promises (see table 4). We say that a candidate keeps a promise when he or she delivers at least as much investment and consumption as had been promised in the last period of his or her term of office. By this measure, the winning candidate only keeps his or her promise 55 percent of the time. On the other hand, notice that the winning candidate keeps his or her promise

TABLE 4. Frequency with which Candidates Keep Promise and the Probability of Reelection (version A)

Keep Promise			
Investment	Consumption	Frequency	Proportion Reelected
Yes	Yes	.554 (46)	.619 (26/42)
No	Yes	.253 (21)	.294 (5/17)
Yes	No	.048 (4)	.250 (1/4)
No	No	.145 (12)	.500 (5/10)
		83	.507 (37/73)

on consumption at least 80 percent of the time. The voters do seem to punish candidates for not keeping their promises, with an average of 62 percent reelection if candidates keep their promises versus 35 (11/31) reelection if they do not.

Version B

The version *B* experiments differ from the version *A* experiments in that there is less cyclical behavior by the candidates. Experiment 1B (fig. 14) is an exception to this pattern. Both experiments from the second group of subjects, experiments 2B and 3B (figs. 15 and 16), show rapid convergence to the equilibrium, with virtually no consumption in the first couple of periods, and then with the experiment sitting at the long-run equilibrium. Experiment 4B (fig. 17) shows a pattern of severe oscillations that does not coincide in period with the length of a term of office. Unfortunately, this experiment ended too quickly for us to determine if the policy proposals would have eventually stabilized around the equilibrium. This expectation of convergence is due to the fact that a second experiment with the same group, 5B (fig. 18), shows convergence to the optimal consumption level. The budget (and hence invest-

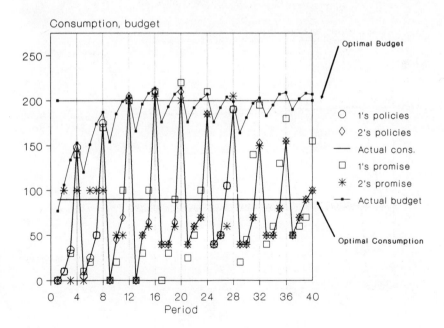

Fig. 14. Growth experiment 1B

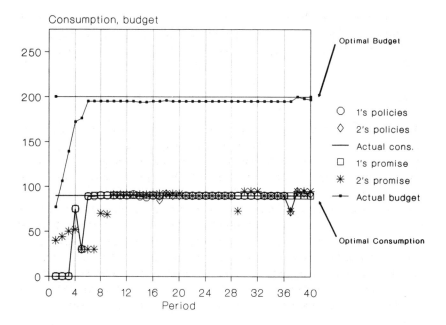

Fig. 15. Growth experiment 2B

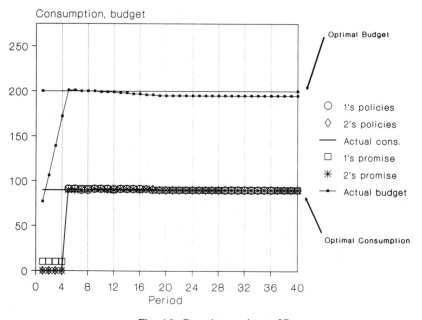

Fig. 16. Growth experiment 3B

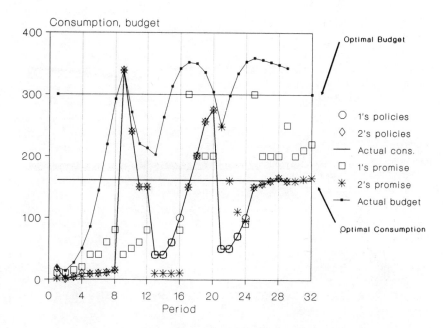

Fig. 17. Growth experiment 4B

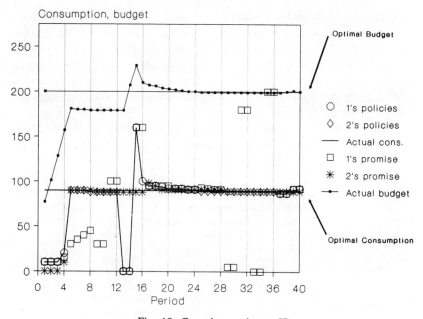

Fig. 18. Growth experiment 5B

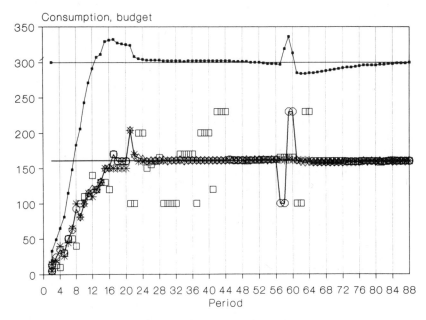

Fig. 19. Growth experiment 6B

ment) is initially below the predicted level, then stabilizing, after period 16, to a level above the predicted value. Finally, in the last experiment, 6B (fig. 19), we see convergence to the optimal consumption. There is one election in which the incumbent deviates from the optimal path and delivers a business cycle. But after this brief shock, the incumbent is thrown out of office, and the challenger begins building up the capital stock again to a level that sustains a budget above the optimal level.

Despite these different patterns, the notable feature of the version *B* experiments is that there is only one experiment that exhibits a business cycle.

TABLE 5. Frequency with which Candidates Keep Promises and the Probability of Reelection (version *B*)

	Frequency	Proportion Reelected
Keep	.725 (50)	.533 (24/45)
Break	.275 (19)	.611 (11/18)
	69	.556 (35/63)

Thus, overall, these experiments follow the optimal path more closely than the version *A* experiments. In addition, we see a greater tendency to keep promises in the version *B* experiments than in the version *A* experiments (see table 5). Promises are broken only 19 out of 69 times, and in only two cases is the total deviation from the promised consumption over the four periods of the term in office greater than ten units of consumption. There also does not seem to be any tendency of voters to punish candidates for breaking promises.

6. Voter Behavior

While the candidates' behavior seems to exhibit considerable regularity, that of the voters seems much less susceptible to a simply described pattern. Recalling that each experiment consists of a finite number of terms of office, where a term consists of four periods followed by an election, we call the jth period of term t period (j; t), and refer to the election at the end of term t as election t. Let $i(t)$ be the incumbent during term t, and $c(t)$ be the challenger (the losing candidate in election $t - 1$). For $1 \leq j \leq 4$, let $Z_{tj} = (C_{tj}, I_{tj})$ be the policy adopted by the incumbent in period j of term t, and $Y_{tj} = C_{tj} + I_{tj}$ be the real income, or budget, in that period. $Z_{tj}^k = (C_{tj}^k, I_{tj}^k)$ denotes the campaign promise made by candidate k in period j of election t. The type of promises differ in the version *A* and version *B* experiments. In the version *A* experiments, the candidates make promises about the level of consumption and investment they will deliver in the fourth period of their term of office, while in the version *B* experiments, the candidates make promises about the consumption stream they will deliver over their entire term of office. So for the version *A* experiments, promises in election t are of the form $Z_{t4}^k = (C_{t4}^k, I_{t4}^k)$. This is the campaign promise made by candidate j about what that candidate plans to accomplish by period 4 of term $t + 1$. For the version *B* experiments, on the other hand, promises are of the form $(C_{t1}^k, C_{t2}^k, C_{t3}^k, C_{t4}^k)$.

To evaluate the promises from the version *A* experiments, we must determine an associated consumption path. Unfortunately, if the promise is feasible, there are typically multiple paths that can support it. A particular consumption path that supports it can be constructed as follows: The candidate attempts to achieve the implied total output $Y_{t4}^{*k} = C_{t4}^k + I_{t4}^k$ as quickly as possible. If this occurs before the fourth period, this output is maintained until the fourth period, after which the candidate delivers the promised value of consumption and investment in the fourth period. If the promise is not feasible, we assume that the candidate chooses a consumption path that gets as close as possible: In the first three periods the candidate attempts to get the output as close as possible to Y_{t4}^k. Since equality cannot be achieved in the fourth period, and in all our data the consumption promise is infeasible, we assume that the candidate keeps his or her investment promise, and violates the consumption promise (in our data this always leads to a feasible path). More specifically, we invert G in equation 2.6 to obtain I_{tj}^k as a function of Y_{tj}^k and the desired $Y_{t(j+1)}^k$. Thus, we set

$$G^{-1}(y_t, y_{t+1}) = \frac{1}{b}\left[(1 - \lambda)\ln(1 - \frac{1}{a}y_t) - \ln(1 - \frac{1}{a}y_{t+1})\right].$$

For $0 \le j \le 3$, we set

$$I_{tj}^k = \max\{0, \min[Y_{tj}^k, G^{-1}(Y_{tj}^k, Y_{t4}^{*k})]\},$$

$$C_{tj}^k = Y_{tj}^k - I_{tj}^k,$$

and

$$Y_{t(j+1)}^k = G(I_{tj}^k, Y_{tj}^k).$$

For $j = 4$, we set I_{tj}^k to be the promised value, and $C_{tj}^k = Y_{tj}^k - I_{tj}^k$.

Using this procedure, we can construct an implied consumption path in the version A experiments that has the same form as the consumption promises in the version B experiments. For our econometric analysis of the version A experiments, we assume that all voters assess the promise according to this consumption path.

We now describe how utility is assigned to a given four-period consumption promise. Let $C_t^k = C_{t1}^k, C_{t2}^k, C_{t3}^k, C_{t4}^k)$ denote a four-period promise by candidate k, and let $K(C_t^k)$ be the capital that is implied by this promise in period 1 of election $t + 1$. This can be computed by successive application of equations 2.1–2.3. Let $C_t^{k*} = (C_{t1}^{*k}, C_{t2}^{*k}, C_{t3}^{*k}, \ldots)$ be the optimal path of consumption for the median voter starting from an initial capital stock of $K(C_t^k)$. Next, define

$$UC_{kt}^i = \sum_{j=1}^{4} \delta^{t-1} u_i(C_{tj}^k)$$

$$UK_{kt}^i = \delta^4 \sum_{j=1}^{\infty} \delta^{t-1} u_i(C_{tj}^{*k})$$

$$U_{kt}^i = UC_{kt}^i + UK_{kt}^i$$

$$DUC_t^i = UC_{1t}^i - UC_{2t}^i$$

$$DUK_t^i = UK_{1t}^i - UK_{2t}^i$$

$$DU_t^i = U_{1t}^i - U_{2t}^i.$$

Thus, UC_{kt}^i is the present value of the utility obtained by the median voter during the tth term if k is elected and keeps his or her promise.

UK_{kt}^i is the present value of the capital stock that will be left by candidate k if that candidate keeps his or her promise for term t, and then in all successive terms, the incumbent reverts to the optimal path of consumption for the voter with median discount rate.

U_{kt}^i is the expected utility of candidate k's promise.

DUC_t^i, DUK_t^i, and DU_t^i are simply the differences between the two candidates of the corresponding components of the utility of the promises.

In addition to these variables, let V_t^i be the vote of voter i in election t, defined to be 1 if the voter votes for candidate 1, and 0 otherwise. Table 6 shows an analysis of this data using a probit model of voter decision making:

$$Pr(V_t^i = 1) = 1 - \Phi(\beta_1 DU_t^i), \tag{6.1}$$

where $\Phi(x)$ is the cumulative normal density function $N(0, 1)$. We analyse the aggregate data, thus forcing all voters to have the same coefficients. Note that if voters pay attention only to promises, and vote based on the basis of the best promise, then in cases where the candidates promises are different, our statistical model should explain all of the voting behavior in the version B experiments. Errors could be expected in the version A experiments due to the ambiguity of the promises, and the artificial way we construct a consumption path from the promise. Despite these theoretical expectations, the model explains less than 50.0 percent of the voting behavior in the version A experiments and only 55.6 percent of the voting behavior in the version B experiments.

There are at least two explanations for our model's poor performance. First, even though we attempt to induce the same discount rate for all voters, it

TABLE 6. Estimates of Equation 6.1

	Version A	Version B
β_1	−.000774 (.000563)	.000978 (.00148)
N of observations	704	541
Percent predicted	49.4	55.63

Note: Standard errors in parentheses.

is possible that we are not successful, and voters actually have different subjective values of δ_i. To get a rough indication of whether this is a factor, we can proceed as follows. With individualized discount rates, the utility U_{kt}^i would be

$$U_{kt}^i = \sum_{j=1}^{4} \delta_i^{t-1} u_i(C_{tj}^k) + \delta_i^4 \sum_{j=1}^{\infty} \delta_i^{t-1} u_i(C_{tj}^{*k}).$$

If we are close to equilibrium, so that the consumption streams $(C_{t1}^k, C_{t2}^k, C_{t3}^k, C_{t4}^k)$ $(C_{t1}^{*k}, C_{t2}^{*k}, C_{t3}^{*k}, \ldots)$ are each approximately constant, then we can rewrite

$$U_{kt}^i \simeq u_i(C_{t1}^k) \sum_{j=1}^{4} \delta_i^{t-1} + u_i(C_{t1}^{*k}) \delta_i^4 \sum_{j=1}^{\infty} \delta_i^{t-1}$$

$$= \frac{1 - \delta_i^4}{1 - \delta_i} u_i(C_{t1}^k) + \frac{\delta_i^4}{1 - \delta_i} u_i(C_{t1}^{*k})$$

$$= \left(\frac{1 - \delta_i^4}{1 - \delta_i} \right) \left(\frac{1 - \delta}{1 - \delta^4} \right) \left(\frac{1 - \delta^4}{1 - \delta} \right) u_i(C_{t1}^k)$$

$$+ \left(\frac{\delta_i^4}{1 - \delta_i} \right) \left(\frac{1 - \delta}{\delta^4} \right) \left(\frac{\delta^4}{1 - \delta} \right) u_i(C_{t1}^{*k})$$

$$= \left(\frac{1 - \delta_i^4}{1 - \delta_i} \right) \left(\frac{1 - \delta}{1 - \delta^4} \right) UC_{kt}^i + \left(\frac{\delta_i^4}{1 - \delta_i} \right) \left(\frac{1 - \delta}{\delta^4} \right) UK_{kt}^i$$

$$= \beta_{1i} UC_{kt}^i + \beta_{2i} UC_{kt}^i$$

where

$$\frac{\beta_{1i}}{\beta_{2i}} = \left(\frac{1 - \delta_i^4}{\delta_i^4} \right) \left(\frac{\delta^4}{1 - \delta^4} \right).$$

Thus $\beta_{1i} > \beta_{2i} \Rightarrow \delta_i < \delta$, and $\beta_{1i} < \beta_{2i} \Rightarrow \delta_i > \delta$. We thus estimate the model

$$Pr(V_t^i = 1) = 1 - \Phi(\beta_{1i} DUC_t^i + \beta_{2i} DUK_t^i), \tag{6.2}$$

allowing different coefficients for each subject. For subjects who participated in two experiments, we pool the data. Our results, summarized in table 7, are improved in terms of the percent of voting behavior predicted correctly, but

**TABLE 7. Summary of Individualized Estimates
of Equation 6.2**

	Version *A*	Version *B*
Average β_1	.184 (0.5420)	.678 (4.980)
Average β_2	.335 (1.050)	.919 (7.130)
Average δ_i	.813 (0.354)	.942 (0.171)
N of subjects	49	33
Percent predicted	.660	.631
Vote	483/732	351/556

Note: Standard deviation in parentheses.

the estimates of the individual coefficients are seldom significant. Note that the estimates of δ_i indicate that voters are acting as if they have lower discount rates than the induced factor of .97. Thus, voters are placing more weight on current consumption and less on the value of the capital stock than they should. This makes the candidate behavior even more perplexing.

7. Conclusions

Candidate behavior in our experiments exhibits considerable regularity, with the candidates converging toward the point that optimizes long-run, steady state sustainable consumption. However, the candidates tend to overinvest. In addition, political business cycles appear frequently, although, with the exception of one experiment, the amplitude of the cycle seems to moderate as each experiment proceeds. These cycles occur with more regularity in the version *A* experiments, which incorporate more uncertainty about preferences.

We find that there is no support in our experiments for the idea that political processes lead to suboptimal investment plans because of the shortsightedness of the candidates. On the contrary, we do not find optimal investment, but only because the candidates tend to overinvest. Regarding political business cycles, we find that they are indeed a feature of the experimental data. Moreover, we find them in models that have none of the features that are required to generate cycles in the theoretical models of Nordhaus, Alesina, or Rogoff. Given the differences between the version *A* and version *B* experiments, we are tempted to attribute the business cycles to incomplete information and to ambiguities in the messages of the candidates. However, we know of no model that has been able to theoretically derive cyclical behavior in such contexts.

We are much less successful, on the other hand, at discerning patterns in voter behavior, and it is somewhat of a puzzle why, in this context, the candidates act so predictably. Certainly, voters send only weak signals to the candidates regarding the policies they prefer. We cannot, then, exclude the possibility that candidates ignore voters and, instead, approach their task as a problem-solving exercise.

We conclude that there is some experimental support that political systems of two-party competition can achieve consumption paths that approximate those that would be chosen by a central planner. However, in the experiments that did not incorporate complete information, we found more evidence of consistent business cycles. In contrast, then, to the explanations offered by Nordhaus, Hibbs (1977), and Rogoff, these findings suggest that such phenomena may be characteristic of incomplete information rather than of the myopia of the voters.

APPENDIX

General Information

There will be two experiments. After the first experiment is completed, the second experiment will begin. It will the same as the first, except that between each experiment, both voters and candidates will be shuffled. This means that the candidates may (or may not) be relabeled, and the voter income functions will be changed. The voters will remain voters, and the candidates will remain candidates.

After the two experiments have been completed, the session will be complete, and subjects will be paid on the basis of the earnings they have accrued. To compute your total payment, add the amount you have earned from each of the two experiments, and multiply by the exchange rate, which is listed on your record sheet. Enter this amount in the final column of your record sheet, and submit it to the experimenter to receive your payment.

Are there any questions?

Experiment Instructions

General Instructions:
This experiment is part of a study of elections. You are being paid in cash for your participation; the amount of your payment depends on your decisions, the decisions of others, and chance. The incomes in the experiment are not necessarily fair, and we cannot guarantee that you will earn any specified amount. However, if you are careful, and make good decisions, you can generally expect to make a substantial amount of money.

The experiment consists of a series of elections in which some of you will be candidates, some of you will be advisers to candidates, and most of you will be voters. Candidates, with the help of their advisers, will make promises to the voters. Voters will then vote, and the winning candidate will become the incumbent, who will serve a four-period term in office. If you want, you can think of each period as a year in office. In each period, the incumbent must select a policy and, as in public opinion polls reported in the media, voters can indicate their approval or disapproval of this policy. At the end of the incumbent's term of office, we will hold the next election.

The experiment will take place through a network connecting computer terminals. All interaction between you will take place through these terminals, and you are not allowed to communicate in any other way. If any difficulty arises, raise your hand, and an experimenter will come to assist you.

Before beginning the actual experiment, we will have an instruction session so that you can familiarize yourself with the terminals, the information they display, and with the sequence of events. After the instruction session there will be a brief quiz. It is important that you pay close attention to the instructions, since you must pass the quiz to participate. Any questions you have should be addressed to me, and I will repeat the answer for everyone to hear.

At this point, one of the experiments will give each of you an envelope. A card inside the envelope will tell you your role in the experiment. Will the experimenters please pass out the envelopes.

[ENVELOPES PASSED OUT]

Now that you all know your roles, we are ready to proceed with the instruction session. Will the candidates and advisers please sit at the terminals to my left, and will the voters sit at the terminals in the center of the room. A candidate and his or her adviser should share one terminal. Voters each get their own terminal.

Candidate Advisers:
Both candidates have their own campaign adviser. The role of a candidate is demanding, and an adviser's purpose is to assist the candidate. Candidates should discuss their actions with their advisers. If a candidate and his or her adviser disagree on strategy, the candidate has the final say as to what action will be taken.

Computer Instruction:
Turn on your terminal now by pressing the key labeled "master" directly below the screen. When the terminal asks for your name, please type in your name, then hit "Enter."

[SUBJECTS ENTER THEIR NAMES]
[MASTER: ENTER INSTRUCTIONAL DATA SET]

[WAIT FOR EXPERIMENT SCREEN TO APPEAR]

Voter and candidate screens are different, but have some similarities. The top part of all screens keeps a record of what has happened previously, while the bottom part tells you what is happening now. The first column on all of the screens is labeled ELECT and tells you which election in the sequence you are in. It is currently election number 1. The second column tells which period you are in. It is currently period E of election 1, which means that it is time to hold an election.

[SUBJECTS LOOK AT SCREEN]

Each experiment consists of a series of elections. In each election, the voters will vote for one of the two candidates, called A and B. The vote is then tallied, and that candidate obtaining the largest number of votes will be declared the winning candidate, and will serve a four-period term of office.

Before describing the sequence of events, we want to tell you about the way candidates affect how much voters earn in the experiment. You should think of this experiment as corresponding to a situation in which you are like an island society that exists, for the most part, off of the tropical fruit of Mangoes. Each year, Mango trees produce fruit, some portion of which can be consumed (eaten). The remainder of the year's crop, which is not eaten, may be invested (planted) to produce more trees in the future. If all of the year's fruit is consumed (eaten), the old trees will slowly age and die, producing less fruit each year; whereas if all the fruit is planted (invested), living standards may be low initially, but more fruit is produced in the future. In your society, it is the government that owns the land and the trees, and must decide how much may be consumed by the voters each year, and how much is invested (planted). In this experiment, government decisions are made by the incumbent candidate, whom the voters elect. The incumbent's investment decision in one period, then, determines the budget (total crop of Mangoes) in the next period.

Because the way in which resources grow or decline as a function of investment is complicated, we would like you to refer now to the chart that we have given each of you. This chart tells you how resources change as a function of an incumbent's decisions. Suppose that the incumbent starts with a budget of 100 units an that 10 units are invested and 90 consumed. To see what the budget in the next period will become, locate 100 on the vertical axis, and locate 10 on the horizontal axis. Notice that the corresponding point on the grid, (10, 100) falls approximately on the curve marked 80. Thus, investing 10 of 100 units means that the total budget available next period drops to 80. On the other hand, suppose 75 out of 100 units are invested. Since the corresponding point (75, 100) falls on the curve marked 120, investing 75 increases the budget in the next period to 120. Of course, this policy requires that voters consume less and be paid less in the current period.

For points falling between two curves, you should interpolate to estimate the effects of a particular investment. For example, if the investment is 50, then the next period budget is about one third of the way between the 100 and 120 curves, so the next period budget would be about 107.

On your screens now, you see that the budget for the first period is 77. This is the amount that will be available for consumption or investment in the first period of the experiment.

Candidate promises:
In an election, both candidates must make promises. These promises tell voters how much consumption (C) and investment (I) they intend to choose, if elected, by the last (fourth) period of their term in office.

During the actual experiment, candidates will make these decisions on their own. For now, the candidates should make the promise $I = 40$ and $C = 40$. To make this promise, type in 40, and press enter, then type 40, and press enter again. Candidates will be asked to confirm their promise, they can do so by typing "Y" then enter. If candidates make a mistake in typing in their promise, they can correct it by typing "N."
[CANDIDATES ENTER PROMISE]

First Election:
Voters, when I instruct you, please vote in election 1. The promises are displayed on the bottom of your screen. Pressing "Enter" will move the promises to the top part of your screen. To vote for candidate A, type "A," then hit "Enter." To vote for candidate B, type "B," then hit enter. Please vote for candidate A in election 1 now by entering "A" at your terminal. Wait for further instructions before doing anything else.
[SUBJECTS VOTE IN ELECTION 1]

As you can see, candidate A has won the election, because a majority of you voted for that candidate. To see the election result, look in the last column, which is labeled "Vote." This column shows the vote for A followed by the vote for B. Notice that all of the information you receive about elections will be in red.

Candidate and Adviser Income:
Candidates, notice on the right side of your screen, the column labeled "INCOME." Since candidate A won the election, candidate A will see that he or she has 100 pounds, while Candidate B will see that he or she has zero pounds. These pounds can be exchanged for dollars at the end of the experiment at a fixed exchange rate. Candidates and advisers are paid for participating in the experiment based on the number of elections they win. Both candidate and adviser earn 100 pounds each for an election victory, but earn nothing for each election they lose. The total income for both candidates and

advisers is kept track of at the bottom of the candidates' screens.

[SUBJECTS LOOK AT SCREEN]

After each election, there will be a term of office during which the winning candidate is the incumbent. You can find who the incumbent is by looking in the third column.

[SUBJECTS LOOK AT SCREEN]

The incumbent's term of office is divided into four periods. The current period is indicated in the second column on your screen. It is currently period 1 of candidate A's term in office.

Incumbent's Policies: (To candidates)

Candidates, after you win an election, you must choose policies which consist of the amount of consumption (C) and investment (I) for the first period of your term in office. The amount of C and I you can choose depends on your budget.

The budget, located in the bottom left corner of your screens, is the total amount available for consumption or investment during your first period of your term in office. How the budget is divided between C and I and from period to period is up to you and your adviser.

Voter Income:

The policy you choose will determine, according to the function on the graph you have been provided, the income for each voter that period. This function will be different for different voters, but they all share one characteristic: The higher the value of C in a period, the higher all voters' incomes.

At this time, will the incumbent, candidate A, please enter the policy $I = 0$, thus consuming the whole budget. When asked to confirm this policy, please do so by pressing "Y," then "Enter."

[INCUMBENT ENTERS POLICY]

To Voters:

Pressing the "Enter" key will move the record of this policy to the top of the screen in the column labeled "POLICY." Each voter's income from the policy appears in the column labeled "INCOME." Your income is computed in "Pounds," which you will exchange for dollars at the end of the experiment at a prespecified exchange rate. In this instruction session, all of the voters will receive the same income. Your income from the incumbent's policy should equal 8.77 pounds. In the real experiment, a given policy will give each voter a different income.

[SUBJECTS SHOULD CHECK SCREENS]

Your total income in each experiment is kept track of by the computer under the heading "CUMULATIVE INCOME," which is at the bottom of your screen in green.

[SUBJECTS SHOULD CHECK SCREENS]

Polls:
After the incumbent chooses a policy and its value is reported to each voter, there will be an opinion poll. Thus, there will be four polls taken between each election. In the poll, the voters are asked their opinion of the way the candidate is performing his or her duties in office, and voters indicate that they approve or disapprove.

The polls do not affect the candidate or voter incomes, and do not determine if the incumbent remains in office (he or she does remain in office regardless of the poll result). The poll is simply informative, and can be used by the candidates to adjust their subsequent policy positions.

When I instruct you, type "A," then "Enter" if you approve of the incumbent's policy. Type "D," then "Enter" if you disapprove. How you make this decision is up to you. Please enter "A" or "D" in election 1, period 1, now.

[SUBJECTS ENTER THEIR CHOICE]

The first poll in election 1 has been completed. You can find out the results of the poll by looking in the column labeled "Poll." The first number in the column tells how many voters approved of the incumbent's performance, the second number shows how many disapproved. Both the voters and candidates see the poll and election results, but no one will ever learn how specific voters voted or who approved and disapproved of the policies.

Notice, in the bottom left hand corner of your screen, the letters "PC," followed by a number which is less than 1 but greater than zero. "PC" is short for "Probability of Continuing" and is the probability that the experiment will continue at the end of this period. Currently "PC" is .9999. "PC" is updated after each period so that the number on your screen is the current probability of continuing. During the real experiment, you will be given a table that includes the value of "PC" for every period of the experiment.

Instruction Session Continues:
The incumbent must now enter another policy. Candidates will notice that the computer keeps track of their budget at the bottom of their screen. Since the incumbent began with a budget of 77 and the first policy was $I = 0$, $C = 77$, the second period budget is 56, as you could determine from the chart. Remember, the policy C and I that you choose in a given period determines the next period budget according to the handout you have been provided. Will the incumbent please enter the policy $I = 21$.

[INCUMBENT ENTERS POLICY]

As before, voters should now indicate whether they approve or disapprove of the incumbent's performance.

[VOTERS RESPOND TO POLL]

Notice that the probability of continuing, "PC," is now .9989.

The same sequence as we have just completed will continue for each of the four periods of the incumbent's term of office. We will now proceed with the remaining two periods of A's term in office. After the fourth poll, wait for further instructions. Will the incumbent please enter the policy $I = 15$ as his or her third policy and $I = 52$ as his or her fourth policy when prompted by the computer to do so. When prompted, will the voters please participate in periods 3 and 4 of election 1.

[SUBJECTS PLAY PERIODS 3 AND 4 OF ELECTION 1]

The policy adopted by the incumbent in period 4 was $I = 52$, and $C = 0$. Notice that this breaks the promise of $I = 40$, $C = 40$, that was made by the candidate, because C is less than the promised value of $C = 40$.

At this point, voters can see that they have accumulated a total of £21.08 in income. In a real experiment, this would represent your total earnings during candidate A's term in office, and at the end of the experiment would be converted to dollars at the prespecified exchange rate.

Candidates will notice that the upcoming budget equals 75. This represents the amount that will be available in the first period of your term of office, if you are elected.

Election # 2:

After four periods, the incumbent's term of office ends, and an election takes place. Will both candidates please enter the promise $I = 30$, $C = 25$, now. Confirm this promise, if correct, when asked to do so. [PAUSE] Voters can now see the promises of the candidates in the lower part of their screen. Voters, please press "Enter" and then vote for candidate B. After voting, wait for further instructions.

[SUBJECTS PARTICIPATE IN ELECTION 2]

You can now verify that candidate B has won election 2 by checking the last column of your screen. [PAUSE] As before, candidate B will serve four periods in office. Since candidate B is now the incumbent, I will ask that he or she submit the policy, of $I = 25$. Please confirm that the promise on your screen is the correct promise by pressing "Y," then "Enter." [PAUSE] Voters, when I instruct you, approve or disapprove of the policy of the incumbent. At the end of the fourth poll, wait for further instruction. Please participate in periods 1–4 of election 2 now by typing in "A" or "D."

Will the incumbent enter $I = 2$ as the second, $I = 53$ as the third, and $I = 50$ as the fourth policy.

[PAUSE BETWEEN EACH POLICY FOR VOTER POLL]

The policy adopted by the incumbent in the fourth period was $I = 50$, $C = 27$. This satisfies the promise of $I = 50$, $C = 25$, as both I and C are at least what the candidate promised they would be.

Election # 3:
It is time for election 3 of the instruction session. Will the candidates please enter their promises and, when asked to do so, will the voters vote for either candidate A or candidate B. How you decide to vote in this election is totally up to you. After voting, wait for further instructions. Please vote in election 3 now. Don't forget to hit "Enter" after choosing your candidate.
    [SUBJECTS SHOULD VOTE IN ELECTION 3]
    Candidate _____ has won the third election, which completes the instruction session.

The Quiz:
It is now time for a brief quiz. Please do not touch your terminal until I tell you to. It will be necessary for you to pass this quiz in order to participate in the experiment. The quiz is on things which we have already discussed. If you have any questions about the content of your screen or the structure of the experiment, please ask them now.
    [EXPERIMENTERS HAND OUT QUIZZES]
    You have four minutes to complete this quiz, please begin, now.
    [SUBJECTS ANSWER QUIZ, EXPERIMENTERS CORRECT]

REFERENCES

Alesina, A. 1987. "Macroeconomic Policy in a Two-Party System as a Repeated Game," *Quarterly Journal of Economics* 102:651–78.
Boylan, R., J. Ledyard, and R. D. McKelvey. 1990. "Political Competition in a Model of Economic Growth: Some Theoretical Results." California Institute of Technology. Mimeo.
Harris, M. 1987. *Dynamic Economic Analysis*. New York: Oxford University Press.
Hibbs, D. A., Jr. 1977. "Political Parties and Macroeconomic Policy." *American Political Science Review* 71:146–87.
Nordhaus, W. D. 1975. "The Political Business Cycle." *Review of Economic Studies* 42:169–90.
Rogoff, K. 1990. "Equilibrium Political Budget Cycles." *American Economic Review* 80:21–36.
Rogoff, K., and A. Sibert. 1988. "Elections and Macroeconomic Policy Cycles." *Review of Economic Studies* 55:1–16.

The Explanation and Prediction of Presidential Elections: A Market Alternative to Polls

Robert Forsythe, Forrest Nelson, George Neumann, and Jack Wright

1. Introduction

The explanation and prediction of presidential election outcomes has been of longstanding interest to both political scientists and economists. Curiously, the explanations that fit best, after years of research, are those that have little or nothing to do with campaigns themselves. Election outcomes are explained best by general economic conditions prior to the election, by the division of voters' partisan preferences, and by voters' evaluations of the incumbent president or his party. Candidates' choices of running mates, campaign statements, and the general ebb and flow of the campaign are typically assigned little importance or are overlooked altogether in academic models.

One reason that campaign events are discounted is that it is difficult empirically to assess which events play upon the fortunes of the candidates, and when. Polling is often too sporadic, and public opinion often too volatile, to provide a reliable gauge. As an alternative to public opinion polls, in early 1988 we designed and implemented an experimental market, known as the Iowa Presidential Stock Market (IPSM). This market was designed to yield predictions of the expected vote shares of the presidential candidates in 1988. Participants bought and sold shares of stock in the presidential candidates, with payoffs determined by the final popular vote totals. Because the market operated continuously from June 1 through election day, it provided a com-

The support of the Summer Grant Program, College of Business, University of Iowa; the University House Interdisciplinary Research Grant Program, University of Iowa; and the National Science Foundation is gratefully acknowledged.

plete record of how and when specific campaign events affected the standing of the presidential candidates.[1]

One might be skeptical about a market approach on two grounds. First, if campaign events really have little to do with outcomes, then a market that encourages traders to make use of information about campaign events will reveal nothing new. Various statistical models yield relatively good forecasts without taking into consideration campaign activities (e.g., Brody and Sigelman 1983; Lewis-Beck and Rice 1984; Hibbs 1978; Fair 1978 and 1988). In 1984, campaign events "mattered little" according to Frankovic (1985, 41); according to Rosenstone (1985, 32), the outcome in 1984 was determined by conditions that were "in place well before the campaign even began." In the face of these claims, however, Markus (1988, 152) suggests that campaign events are relevant to election outcomes, even though they probably account for a relatively small proportion of the total vote.

A second concern with a market approach is that of judgment bias—the tendency for people to see events and situations as they wish to see them. Research in both economics and political science is replete with evidence that individuals often do not, or perhaps even cannot, perceive circumstances objectively. Voters routinely report an overrating of the electoral chances of their preferred candidate, while underrating the chances of other candidates (Bartels 1985 and 1987). Feelings of partisan loyalty act as a "cognitive filter" to bias voters' perceptions of the issue positions of candidates and parties (Campbell et al. 1960). In security markets, there occur waves of buying and selling—sometimes described as "herd" effects—that cannot be accounted for objectively by changes in earnings announcements. And in wager markets on sporting events, a person's preferences across the contenders may influence or bias his or her assessment of the likely outcome of the event.[2] The presence of widespread judgment bias raises the possibility that market prices may reflect only the underlying partisan preferences of the traders.

We assess the performance of the IPSM on both of these grounds. An

---

1. The idea of using of markets to predict presidential outcomes is not original. We are aware of similar markets run during the 1988 campaign at the University of Rochester, California Institute of Technology, Princeton University, The Wharton School of the University of Pennsylvania, and the Brookings Institution. The IPSM, however, appears to be the first and only market set up strictly as a research venture.

2. The Triple Crown of horse racing provides one example. Easy Goer, a horse from New York, lost the Kentucky Derby and the Preakness to Sunday Silence, a California horse, before finally prevailing in the Belmont. Simultaneous pari-mutuel betting in California (Santa Anita) and New York (Belmont) revealed the California horse to be thought more likely to win among California bettors and the New York horse was considered more likely to win among New York bettors. Moreover, when the race was held at a neutral site (Lexington, Ky., and Baltimore, Md.) the odds on either horse at the neutral site always fell between the odds established at the partisan tracks. For similar examples involving cross-track betting see Hausch and Ziemba 1990.

experimental market is useful for studying campaigns only if it provides new information, or at least better information, than the current technology. Equilibrium prices in the market should predict the outcome, and the change of prices in response to particular campaign events should contribute to an explanation of the outcome in terms of campaign-related events. In our analysis, we examine whether the IPSM predicted the election any better than polls and statistical models. We consider, as well, the extent to which market prices responded to the release of polling information. Importantly, we examine market prices to determine which campaign events, if any, constituted "news" in terms of price adjustments. Finally, we report on the nature and extent of judgment bias in the market. Because individuals' perceptions of political events—perhaps more so than any other events—are avowedly clouded by personal predilections, the IPSM provides a unique, and particularly strong, test of the consequences of judgment bias.

The remainder of the paper is organized as follows. In section 2, we discuss how markets as well as polls may predict election outcomes, and in section 3 we describe the organization and operation of the IPSM in particular. Section 4 presents results about how well the market predicted the outcome, the relationship between poll results and market prices over the course of the campaign, and an analysis of judgment bias in trading behavior. A summary is given in section 5.

2. Using Polls and Market Prices to Predict Outcomes

One of the problems with using a market to predict political events is that individuals are often uninterested in politics and have little political information. Voters often have difficulty identifying candidates' issue positions, and when asked which candidate is likely to win, voters demonstrate prescience only in lopsided elections (Lewis-Beck and Skalaban 1989). However, not all voters are apathetic and ignorant. Some voters are reasonably well informed, and thus the problem is not that voters uniformly lack information, but that voters are differentially informed.

An analogous problem exists in economics where traders are differentially informed about the future value of some asset. The dominant hypothesis in economics for how markets operate under this condition is the rational expectations (RE) hypothesis. Simply put, this hypothesis states that agents will condition their beliefs on some publicly observable signal—for example, a market price or a poll—to make correct inferences about other agents' information. Quite naturally, this hypothesis can lead to an RE equilibrium in which the signal aggregates and disseminates information. In particular, when the signal is a sufficient statistic for the collective information of all agents, the RE model predicts that, in equilibrium, all agents will be fully informed.

In an RE market model, the value of an asset depends on the probability distribution of future prices which is not, in general, independent of today's price. Consider the market of some vintage wine that is sold well in advance of when it is to be consumed. While no one knows the eventual quality of the wine, some potential buyers will have better information than others. To compensate for that, uninformed (or poorly informed) buyers might attempt to judge quality by the wine's price. Thus, by inferring information from price and acting upon these inferences, the equilibrium price will be affected.

To illustrate this, suppose there is a single asset being traded whose future value depends on which one of three possible states of the world occurs, S_i, $i = 1, 2, 3$. Suppose each state is equally likely and that there are two types of traders, type 1 and type 2, who differ in their values for holding the asset in the future. All traders are assumed to know each type's state-contingent future valuation of the asset as displayed in table 1. Finally, suppose all traders possess some information about which future state will obtain—half of each trader type knows one of the states that will not occur and the other half knows the other state that will not occur. Collectively, then, traders know which future state will occur. The question is whether market prices will reveal this collective information to the individual traders.

To see how prices can reveal information, suppose traders, given their private information, are initially willing to pay up to their expected value for the asset. These conditional expected values are also given in table 1. Suppose, first, that S_3 is the true future state. Then, traders of type 1 who have the "not S_1" information should bid the price of the asset up to 185, and all other traders who have lower expected values should be willing to sell at that price. Alternatively, if the true future state is either S_1 or S_2, traders of type 1 who have the "not S_3" information will, using only their private information, bid the price to 225. These would be the equilibrium prices in an ordinary model of supply and demand where traders do not make any attempt to infer other traders' information from market prices. But if the market equilibrated at these prices, it would be surprising if some traders, upon seeing a price of 185, did not infer that the true state was S_3 since the price in that state differs from the prices in the other state. Similarly a price of 225 should reveal that some traders have the "not S_3" information. Acting on the basis of this, traders

TABLE 1.   Traders' Valuations for an Asset

Trader Type	Valuation in State			Expected Value Given Information		
	S_1	S_2	S_3	not S_1	not S_2	not S_3
1	120	330	40	185.0	80	225.0
2	205	90	125	107.5	115	147.5

with the other bit of information will become fully informed and the prices will react accordingly.

In an RE model more generally, each trader is assumed to have a "model" of the relationship between other traders' nonprice information and the market price. However, the actual relationship depends on each trader's behavior, which, in turn, depends on each trader's model. An RE equilibrium results when no trader has an incentive to alter his or her beliefs or behavior when the price is revealed. Thus, in equilibrium, the individual models are identical to the true model, and each trader correctly perceives the relationship between the nonprice information received by all traders and the equilibrium market price that prevails.

As should be apparent, the RE model puts much larger information processing demands on traders than does the ordinary model of supply and demand in which traders condition their beliefs only on their private information. The RE model, however, requires far more of traders. As Radner (1982, 942) notes, "this approach seems to require of the traders a capacity for imagination and computation far beyond what is realistic." Further, for agents to acquire information from public signals, they must know the relationship between other agents' private information and the signals. As Jordan (1985) points out, the issue of how this knowledge is acquired is commonly ignored in the theoretical literature on rational expectations. On the other hand, it is difficult to believe in the adequacy of any equilibrium model that assumes agents naively ignore the information conveyed in public signals.[3]

The RE hypothesis has been applied to polls and elections in a series of articles by McKelvey and Ordeshook (1984, 1985a, 1985b) and Ordeshook (1987). In their model, two candidates hold positions on a single issue and voters are divided into informed and uninformed sets. Each voter has an "ideal" point that represents his or her preferred stand on the issue, and a voter's utility for a candidate is given by the distance between the preferred candidate's position and the voter's ideal point. A voter is also assumed to know the position of his or her ideal point relative to all other voters, as well as the ordering of the candidates—that is, which candidate is farthest left on the issue. The informed voters know the candidates' stands on the issue while the uninformed voters do not, and thus the problem for uninformed voters is to determine which candidate is closest to their ideal points.

In this framework, McKelvey and Ordeshook are able to demonstrate the existence of a rational expectations equilibrium in which *all* voters are fully informed about the candidates' positions. To illustrate how such an equi-

---

3. When contrasted with models where traders use only their exogenous private information, the RE model has found some support in the experimental literature. See, for example, Forsythe, Palfrey, and Plott 1982; Plott and Sunder 1982 and 1988; and Forsythe and Lundholm 1990.

librium might be achieved, they consider a dynamic process in which voters report their preferences in a sequence of polls. In each poll, voters are assumed to act rationally on the basis of the information reported in the previous poll. In particular, each poll provides uninformed voters with an estimate of the position of the candidates relative to their ideal points. If uninformed voters use these estimates when responding to the next poll, this sequence will converge monotonically to the election outcome that would result if all voters had full information about both candidates' positions on the issue. This scenario suggests that polls should be expected to exhibit some volatility over the course of the campaign, with the pollster's prediction becoming more accurate as election day approaches.

Rational expectations, as applied to the IPSM, offers an explanation for how stock prices might successfully predict the election outcome when some—perhaps many—traders are initially uninformed. In the IPSM, traders were given a financial incentive to collect information about the voting intentions in the national electorate, and, as they conditioned their demands on this information, the prices of a candidate's shares were affected. The RE hypothesis states that traders were aware of this process and attempted to infer each other's information from market prices. In equilibrium, the RE hypothesis predicts that all traders are equally informed about the election outcome.

Assuming traders are capable of inferring information about the relative standing of the candidates from market prices, rational expectations is a leading hypothesis for how the IPSM aggregates information. However, the RE hypothesis states only that traders will infer political information from prices such that, in equilibrium, no trader will unilaterally revise his or her beliefs about the election outcome after observing the equilibrium market price. The RE hypothesis does not specify any particular dynamic for achieving the equilibrium, and thus it does not state exactly when the equilibrium price will be reached. How far in advance the market actually "called" the election can only be determined from observing the behavior of stock prices. We discuss these stock price histories in the next section, but first, we describe how the IPSM basically operated.

3. The Iowa Presidential Stock Market

Market Description

The IPSM was initiated in April, 1988, and the market opened for trading on June 1.[4] Aspiring traders were sold basic portfolios of shares in candidates at

---

4. Specific details of the IPSM can be found in Forsythe et al. 1990; here we summarize only the essential details.

$2.50 each, with each basic portfolio consisting of one share in each of the major candidates in the campaign. The slate of candidates included George Bush, Michael Dukakis, Jesse Jackson, and a candidate labeled "Rest-of-Field." Shares were given value by the dividends paid after the election, with the dividend on each share determined as the candidate's fraction of the popular vote times $2.50. Since "Rest-of-Field" covered all third-party candidates who earned votes in the election, the vote shares summed to one across the four candidates and the total dividend paid on a basic portfolio of one share in each candidate just matched the fee charged for that basic portfolio. This investment/payoff rule was adopted for the IPSM because it provides a direct translation of market prices into estimates of vote shares,

Expected Vote Share = Price/$2.50,

and thus offers a prediction of not only the election winner but also the margin of victory.[5]

The IPSM operated as a double auction market on a mainframe computer at the University of Iowa. Upon payment of a portfolio investment fee and posting of a deposit to a cash account, each trader was assigned an individual computer account. Logging in to this account enabled the participant to trade in the market. Except for brief maintenance periods and mainframe down times, the market operated around the clock from the open of the market on June 1, until its close at 9:00 A.M. on November 9, 1988, the day after the election. The portfolio investment fee was an integer multiple of $2.50. For each $2.50, a participant received a newly issued block of stocks consisting of one share in each candidate on the slate. This new stock issue operated similarly to the issuance of new shares in an open-end mutual fund. But separate markets operated in each of the components (candidates) of a new issue and investors unbundled their purchases, trading each component separately. In addition to the portfolio investment, each new trader was required to deposit some amount in a cash account. This account provided the liquidity for stock transactions—purchases of shares were charged to it, and sales of shares were credited to it. New traders were allowed to enter the market at any time, and existing traders could purchase new $2.50 portfolios (each consisting of 1 share in each candidate on the current slate) or make additions to their

---

5. An all or nothing rule—a fixed payoff of, say, $2.50 to shares in the election winner with zero payoffs to shares in losers—is perhaps the most obvious example of the many possible alternative designs. But this all or nothing rule would have provided only a prediction of the probability of winning. And in a runaway election, the expected convergence of prices to $2.50 and $0 with little or no subsequent price movement might well have stifled continuing interest in the market.

cash account at any time. In addition, the conversion of cash account deposits into shares or share blocks into cash were allowed at any time. No withdrawals from cash accounts were allowed prior to the close of the market on November 9.

By June 1, the IPSM opening date, enough convention delegates were committed to George Bush to guarantee him the Republican nomination. On the Democratic side, only Jesse Jackson and Michael Dukakis remained as viable candidates. To account for all possible minor party candidates and to allow for the emergence of new, major candidates, a fourth entry, Rest-of-Field, was included on the slate. Throughout the operation of the market, the slate included the four candidates: Bush, Dukakis, Jackson, and Rest-of-Field. Though it was never invoked, the contingency for the admission of new candidates to the slate was an integral part of the market description and may have been a factor in the Rest-of-Field pricing decisions by traders. Had a new, major candidate emerged, say from a brokered convention or the premature withdrawal of a major party nominee, each Rest-of-Field share would have been split into a continuing Rest-of-Field share and a new "Named-Candidate" share.

The popular vote totals used for determining payoffs were obtained from News Election Service—a consortium of the major news services under the management of the Associated Press. Field reporters collected and phoned in election results to AP, and AP then distributed the results to members of the consortium. The popular vote results reported to us on Tuesday, November 22, and the resulting dividends were as follows.

	Total Votes	Percentage of Vote	Dividend Payment
Bush	48,138,478	53.208	$1.33
Dukakis	41,114,068	45.444	$1.14
Rest-of-Field	1,219,240	1.348	$0.03
Total	90,471,786	100.000	$2.50

Since Rest-of-Field included all third-party candidates who received at least 200 votes and Jackson was not one of these candidates, there was no dividend payment on Jackson shares.

Participants traded in the double auction market by issuing offers to buy (bids) or offers to sell (asks). There could be many bid and ask prices in the system at any time; they were maintained in bid and ask queues ordered first by offer price and then by time of issuance. When an offer was entered into the bid or ask queue, it remained there until one of these events occurred: (a) it was withdrawn by the bidder, (b) it reached the top of the bid queue (bottom of the ask queue) and was found to be infeasible, as described below, or (c) it reached the top of the bid queue (bottom of the ask queue) and was subsequently matched with an opposing offer. The actual transactions were executed by the system when it found overlapping bid and ask prices in the respective queues. Note, too, that the system did not check the identities of the traders when overlapping bid and ask prices resulted in a trade, so that a trader could sell stock to himself or herself.

The computerized market provided facilities for obtaining information about the trader's account and the market, as well as for issuing bids and offers. Available account information included the number of shares held in each candidate, the balance in the cash account, a list of outstanding offers, and a list of recent transactions. Available market information included current high bid, low ask, and last transaction prices, and a record of the previous day's activity including opening and closing bid and ask prices, the last transaction price, the average transaction price, and the number of shares traded in each candidate. As on most stock markets, information on the depth of the bid and ask queues was never revealed. Traders were shown only current market quotes—the maximum of all the bid prices and the minimum of all the ask prices in the system at that time.

Short sales and purchases on margin were disallowed by the system; offers to buy with insufficient funds in the cash account of the buyer or offers to sell when the sellers portfolio contained no shares in that candidate were ruled infeasible. But checks for feasibility were made only when an offer reached the top of its queue (high bid or low ask). If an offer failed the feasibility check, the entire offer was withdrawn from the queue and a note to that effect was placed in the trader's transactions log. Thus, the system accepted offers that were not feasible at the time of issuance. The intention was to enrich the set of strategies a trader might adopt, while at the same time preventing the market itself from becoming a net creditor. Since only the high bid and low ask prices were revealed to traders, the system also avoided giving false information; traders were guaranteed that at least one share was available at quoted prices.

When a new feasible bid was entered with a price equal to or exceeding the current minimum price in the ask queue, the system recorded a trade at the ask price. Likewise, if a new ask was entered with a price equal to or less than the current maximum price in the bid queue, a trade was recorded at that bid price. Such trades were executed one share at a time, regardless of the number of shares bid or asked, with renewed checks for feasibility of both the bid and the ask after each one-share transaction. The recording of a transaction included notes in the transactions logs of the two traders involved, a credit to the cash account of the seller, a debit to the cash account of the buyer, and a transfer of the share of stock from the seller's portfolio to that of the buyer. The principles followed for the execution of trades were (*a*) offers to buy were processed "high-prices first"; (*b*) offers to sell were processed "low-prices first"; (c) in the case of ties (two offers at the same price), the earliest offer to arrive on the market was processed first; and (d) when an overlap between bid and ask prices was found, the trade was executed at the price of the older of these two offers.

The rules of the market, particularly the investment/payoff rule, made the IPSM a "zero-sum game"—all funds invested were returned in the form of dividends, and gains by one trader were exactly offset by losses of other traders. This structure raises the question of what motivated traders to participate in the IPSM. The zero-sum nature of the IPSM makes it resemble markets for futures contracts, except that an important motive for the existence of futures contracts is the transfer of risk from one party to another. In a large-scale presidential stock market there might conceivably be a transfer of risk—arms makers might enter the market to buy shares in a pacifist candidate as a hedge against the loss of future income should that candidate win the election, for example. But such risk transfers could hardly be the motive for trading in the 1988 IPSM. That leaves four reasonable motives—a novelty factor, confidence in one's knowledge about the election and its likely outcome relative to the knowledge of other traders, confidence in one's talents as a trader, and risk-seeking behavior.

We expected these differing motivations to attract a diverse group of traders to the market. Our expectations were correct. Besides differing in their motives for participating in the market, traders varied considerably in their demographic characteristics, in their partisan and ideological preferences, and in their investments and earnings.

The Traders

Participation in the IPSM was voluntary. Ideally, enrollments would have been unrestricted, but University of Iowa attorneys expressed concern over the possible violation of laws governing either or both gambling and stock exchanges. Cost aside, the time required to obtain necessary exemption from state and federal securities laws would have thwarted plans to conduct the market during the 1988 election year. Thus, we opted to operate under the provisions of Chapter 99B.12 of the Iowa State Code, which allows betting pools within employee groups. This meant restricting participation to members of the University of Iowa community. A total of 190 traders enrolled in the market; those traders held a total of 1,462 shares in each candidate. The total investment in stock portfolios was $3,655, and $1,312 was posted to traders' cash accounts, yielding an average individual investment of roughly $25. The smallest investment was $5 ($N = 7$), and the largest was $420 ($N = 1$).

During the third week of September, we asked existing traders to complete a brief mail survey in an effort to collect descriptive information about their political preferences and demographic characteristics. Subsequently, new traders were asked to complete the survey when they enrolled in the market. The full text of the survey form is included in Forsythe et al. 1990. Using the data from traders registered as of September 27, table 2 compares the traders' presidential preferences, partisan orientations, and frequency of voter registration with comparable figures from a CBS/*New York Times* national poll conducted during the same week.

IPSM traders were slightly more supportive of George Bush, more Republican, and less independent in the partisan leanings. Except for the undecided voters, preferences of the IPSM traders were well within the margin of sampling error for the national poll. However, in direct contrast with the national tendency in partisanship where the Democrats still claim the largest share of identifiers, the traders professed a noticeably higher affinity for the Republican party. Moreover, the traders were clearly less independent than voters nationally. The traders also appeared to be more politically active than the average citizen, with 80.4 percent claiming to be registered to vote as compared with only 67.0 percent in the national sample. That IPSM traders tended to be relatively conservative and politically active is consistent with the demographic makeup of the group. In general, the traders were predominantly male, white, well-educated, and among the middle and upper income categories. Students comprised the largest category of traders, and the largest share of these students were business majors. One-third of the traders had at

TABLE 2. Political Characteristics of Traders, in Percentage

	Market Survey	CBS/*New York Times* Survey
Presidential preference[a]		
Bush	50.0	46
Dukakis	41.3	40
Other	2.2	0
Undecided	6.5	14
Party identification		
Republican	45.7	31
Democrat	31.5	36
Independent	21.7	33
Other	1.1	
Registered to vote	80.4	67

Note: The CBS/*New York Times* poll was conducted September 21–23. See the *New York Times*, September 25, 1988.

[a] Presidential preference was recorded only for those respondents planning to vote.

TABLE 3.   Traders' Preferred Candidates

	Bush	Dukakis	Other	Undecided
Pre–Debate 1	47.0 (47)	42.0 (42)	2.0 (2)	9.0 (9)
Debate 1	43.1 (53)	47.2 (58)	0.8 (1)	8.9 (11)
Debate 2	45.8 (65)	45.1 (64)	2.1 (3)	7.0 (10)
Debate 3	50.0 (68)	41.1 (56)	1.5 (2)	7.4 (10)
Election night	46.7 (56)	50.8 (61)	2.5 (3)	

Note: Table entries are the fraction of the responding traders who favor a given candidate. The actual frequencies are given in parentheses.

least a college degree, more than 90 percent were white, 71 percent were male, and more than 70 percent placed themselves in the middle or upper end of the income distribution.

Besides the initial enrollment survey, we also conducted telephone surveys of our traders immediately following each debate and another telephone poll on election night to ask traders which candidate they had voted for if they had voted, or which candidate they now preferred if they had not voted. These results are summarized in table 3.[6] Whether and how the political and demographic characteristics of our trader population affect investment strategies is unclear. Theoretically, of course, we expect that these factors should have little bearing on individuals' efforts to maximize the return on their investments. Yet, individuals' backgrounds and preferences may affect their selection of information and perceptions of a candidate's viability and, in turn, affect their trading behavior.

Final payouts were made following the election. The largest profit earned in the market was $13.54 on an investment of $250.00, while the largest loss was $22.48 on an investment of $95.00. Since investment levels varied across traders, and traders entered the market at different times, an annualized rate of return may be a more informative measure of market gains and losses.[7] By this measure, one trader realized an annualized gain of 65.8 percent while the biggest loser suffered an annualized loss of 659.0 percent. One-fifty of the traders earned an annualized rate of return of more than 10.0 percent, while 36 of the 190 traders incurred annualized losses of more than 10.0 percent. In

---

6. The entries in the first row of table 3 are different than those reported in table 2—here they include all respondents, while the previous table only included information on those who said they were planning to vote.

7. This annualized rate is computed as 365 × profit/(investment dollar days), where "investment dollar days" is the weighted sum of investments, with the weight being the number of days remaining on the market at the time of the investment.

short, traders did have something at stake. This was necessary, of course, if the IPSM was to perform any differently than public opinion polls. The results of the IPSM, to which we now turn, do indeed reveal clear differences with polls.

4. Results

In our analysis of results, we first examine the behavior of stock prices during the campaign; we then consider the relation between stock market prices and results of public opinion polls; and finally, we analyze trading patterns and trader preferences. One obvious question about stock price histories is how well the market predicted the final vote shares of the candidates. Viewed simply in terms of how well prices matched up with actual vote shares, the market worked extraordinarily well. Using the last price a share traded at the night before the election, the comparison between the actual outcome and the market prediction is as follows.

	Percentage of Vote	Market Prediction[8]
Bush	53.2	53.2
Dukakis	45.4	45.2
Rest-of-Field	1.4	2.0

On the eve of the election, the IPSM perfectly predicted George Bush's share of the popular party vote, and it forecast within two-tenths of a percentage point the actual difference in vote shares between the two major candidates. Even more impressively, prices in the IPSM began to converge to these results long before election eve. We now examine the process of convergence of prices during the last days of the campaign and determine when the IPSM effectively "called" the election.

Aside from predicting the election outcome, stock price histories are useful for determining which events of the campaign constituted "news." Campaign events such as gaffes, strokes of brilliance, and exogenous incidents may have affected the election outcome, but, unfortunately, a definitive census (e.g., an actual election) cannot be conducted immediately after each event to judge its importance. Unlike sporadic opinion polls, which typically are conducted only after major events, the IPSM operated continuously. Thus, to the extent that it accurately measures the "pulse" of the electorate, move-

---

8. To obtain the market prediction of a candidate's vote share, the price of a candidate's shares are divided by $2.50. The predicted vote shares on each security sum to more than one. This is an artifact of using the last trading price in the day, since not all shares trade simultaneously.

ments in market prices can be taken as a measure of the impact of an event. In the subsequent section, Stock Price Histories, we examine the responses of the market and the polls to several major events during the campaign: the selection of vice presidential candidates, the announcement of Jesse Jackson not to run as a third-party candidate, and the two presidential and one vice presidential debates.

Comparing the response of the market to the response of public opinion polls at "big" events, even when possible, does not provide a full comparison of these two very different ways of eliciting public opinion. Accordingly, in the sections on "Opinion Poll Histories" and "Polls and Markets," we compare the behavior of stock prices and opinion polls over the entire course of the campaign. We consider how well the market predicted relative to the polls, we compare the volatility of polls and the market, and we inquire into whether poll results "drove" the market.

Finally, we have a wealth of data, gathered by surveying the participants in the IPSM, about trader preferences for political candidates and their assessment of certain events—the presidential debates. We have merged this information with each trader's portfolio data, and thus we assess how personal preference and personal opinion affects market trading. The results of our analysis of these data are reported below under "Judgment Bias." We turn first, however, to the stock price histories.

Stock Price Histories

The IPSM opened on June 1, 1988, to considerable fanfare and also to considerable uncertainty for the small number of traders. Prices were initially not defined, and traders moved warily in setting out bids and asks. At the close of the market day (arbitrarily chosen as 3:00 A.M.) on June 3, prices were Bush 124, Dukakis 129, Jackson 1, and Rest-of-Field 2. Prices are recorded in pennies. A total of 41 shares had traded in the first two days of operation.

The weekly trading volume history of the market is given in table 4. A simple characterization of this data is that trading started slowly, but by June 20, the market activity was sufficient to produce meaningful (i.e., approximately continuous) changes in prices. The month of July, which includes the Democratic convention (July 18–21), shows relatively thick markets also, but trading drops off precipitously in August. This period covers the end of the summer term at the University of Iowa, and is a popular time for vacations by faculty, staff, and students. Since the market required computer access, the departure of traders from the area had an obvious and pronounced effect on market activity. Unfortunately, this period includes the Republican convention (August 15–18), and so we have nothing to say about the effect of Bush's selection of Quayle as the Republican vice presidential candidate. Thinness of

TABLE 4. Weekly Market Activity

	Week	Number of Shares Traded	Cumulative Number of Trades
June	1–5	46	46
	6–12	31	77
	13–19	34	111
	20–26	241	352
	27–July 3	68	420
July	4–10	86	506
	11–17	183	689
	18–24	90	779
	25–31	41	820
August	1–7	4	824
	8–14	8	832
	15–21	3	835
	22–28	34	869
	29–Sept. 4	190	1,059
September	5–11	1,625	2,684
	12–18	1,302	3,986
	19–25	1,075	5,061
	26–Oct. 2	1,503	6,564
October	3–9	1,656	8,220
	10–16	4,087	12,307
	17–23	783	13,090
	24–30	1,349	14,324
	31–Nov. 6	1,342	15,666
November	7–9	832	16,498

the market during August also precludes identification of the source of information leading to an increase (five cents) in Bush's price by late August. These gaps in the market are a noticeable consequence of the restriction of participation to members of the University of Iowa community.

Figures 1 and 2 show the history of prices for Bush and Dukakis, and for Jackson and Rest-of-Field, respectively, from June 1 to November 9. Superimposed on the graphs are horizontal lines representing the share-price equivalent of the vote tally of November 22, as provided by the News Election Service, with vertical lines and bars at interesting dates during the campaign. Market thinness problems plagued the IPSM for about two weeks, as traders were slowly added to the system. This resulted in several large, discrete jumps in price.[9] For example, Bush stock fell from 124 on June 2, to 115 on

9. A reference to *price* will mean the last traded price as of a particular day. When trading is thin, as it was in the first month, this price may be the result of a transaction one or more days in the past.

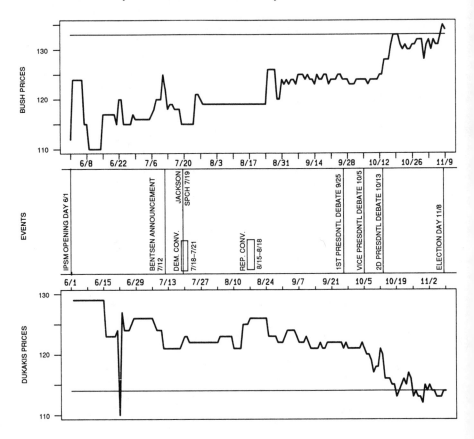

Fig. 1. Price histories for Bush and Dukakis stock

June 7 (due to the trade of only 2 shares of Bush stock), and to 110 on June 9 (due to the trade of 5 shares of Bush stock). This thinness prevents us from making strong conclusions about events in the early stages of the market's operation. By late June, market volume was sufficient to allow meaningful interpretation of price movements, and indeed certain events in July appear to have been "news," judging from the price responses. The first such event was the selection of Lloyd Bentsen as the Democratic vice presidential candidate. Dukakis's price peaked at 127 on July 6, and then dropped to 121 after the Bentsen announcement. At the same time, Bush's price rose from 117 to 125. Apparently, the uncertainty about the meaning of Bentsen was short-lived, as both stocks retreated to positions closer to July 1 levels within a week.

The next event that had a noticeable effect on market prices was Jesse

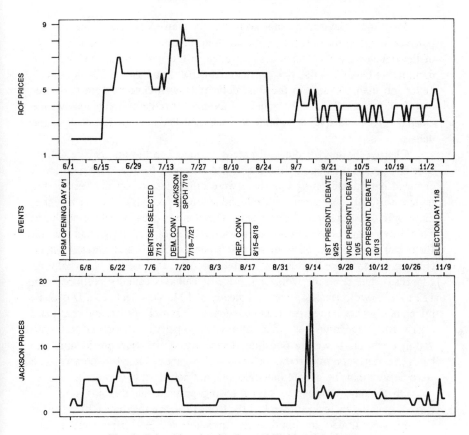

Fig. 2. Price histories for Rest-of-Field and Jackson

Jackson's speech (July 20) at the Democratic convention where he promised to support the Democratic nominee by announcing that he would not run a third-party campaign. Understandably, Jackson's stock fell to a penny (the smallest unit in the market). However, Dukakis's price did not increase and Bush's price actually fell. This is surprising if one believes that Jackson supporters would either vote for Dukakis or not vote.[10]

___

10. After Jackson's speech, his stock became essentially worthless, and traders in the market paid little attention to it—i.e., the bid and ask queues emptied. Nonetheless, a dedicated group of traders wanted to "send a message to Jesse" and periodically bought and sold shares at 2 cents. When the bid and ask queues were empty, traders could trade with themselves and thus determine any price they wanted at no cost. "Trades with self" have been omitted from the price

The three televised debates were widely viewed ex ante as having the potential to affect the outcome of the election. Press and opinion poll coverage of the debates gave Dukakis a slight edge in the first debate, had Bentsen dominating Quayle in the vice presidential debate, and showed Bush doing a better job than Dukakis in the final debate. How important were these debates? Did they influence the beliefs of the market traders? Table 5 shows the closing prices and trading volume in Bush and Dukakis around each of the debates.

Clearly, the market did not see any "winner" in the first debate. In the four-day period surrounding the event, 216 shares of Bush and Dukakis stock changed hands, indicating that there were differences of opinion among the traders (a result consistent with telephone survey results), but, on balance, these opinions were split fairly evenly. The Bentsen-Quayle debate produced even fewer changes of opinion, as measured by trading activity, than the first Bush-Dukakis debate. A total of 100 shares of Bush and Dukakis stock changed hands in the four days around this debate. Despite the overwhelming consensus that Bentsen "won," the price of Dukakis actually declined from 122 to 120 while Bush's price held steady at 124. This decline in Dukakis's price does not seem to be related to the debate. It started earlier, and continued afterward, suggesting that other information—perhaps reports of key-state voting intentions—was responsible. Evidently, either vice presidential debates are not very important, or expectations about Quayle's performance were so low that the debate outcome was not news.

On Sunday, October 9, strong selling pressure on Dukakis stock occurred, pushing the price down to 118 (from 121). On that day, 670 shares of Dukakis were traded, and on the next, an additional 299 shares were traded. On Tuesday and Wednesday, October 11 and 12, the price of Dukakis rebounded as traders took positions for the upcoming presidential debate. A total of 488 shares of Dukakis changed hands, compared to 211 shares of Bush. Thus, immediately before the third debate, the market was still predicting a close race: Bush at 124, Dukakis at 121. But unlike the first two debates, the third produced an immense volume of trading. Bush share rose only a penny right after the debate, but on a volume of 1,196 shares. Dukakis's price fell one cent, but on a volume of only 4 shares traded. By the end of the trading day on October 14, the margin had widened to 128–116, although it

histories of figs. 1 and 2, but they were not omitted when "last transaction price" was reported to all traders. This accounts for the sometimes anomalous behavior of Jackson prices throughout the campaign and particularly the "Jackson bubble" near mid-September. For example, when self-trades are included, the average transaction price of Jackson stock was 9 cents on September 11, while on September 12, it was 94 cents. The profit potential this occasioned attracted the attention of serious traders and the ask queue filled up quickly. Thereafter, the price of sending a message was not zero.

TABLE 5. Presidential Debates and Stock Prices

	Shares Traded	Price of Bush	Shares Traded	Price of Dukakis
		Debate 1: Sunday, September 25		
Day before	124	40	122	49
Debate day	125	13	122	13
One day later	124	41	121	31
Two days later	124	24	122	5
		Debate 2: Wednesday, October 5		
Day before	124	0	122	16
Debate day	124	26	121	26
One day later	124	12	120	11
Two days later	124	1	120	8
		Debate 3: Thursday, October 13		
Day before	124	189	121	130
Debate day	125	1196	121	4
One day later	128	173	116	114
Two days later	128	0	116	0

had been as wide as 131–115 during the day. Clearly, there was information in the third debate.

After the third debate, the price series did not show any other event to have been "news." The lead in the market—determined as (Bush's price − Dukakis's price)/2.50—rose steadily to 8 points by October 20, and thereafter bounced around a little from day to day, remaining in the range 6.8–8.0 from November 2 on. Thus, the market had effectively called the election by October 20. In fact, from that time on, the price of Bush stock varied only between 1.28 and 1.34, with a modal price of 1.31. This modal price implies a vote share of 52.4 percent for Bush.

Opinion Poll Histories

Unlike stock market prices, opinion polls have no obvious beginning—"trial heats" between potential candidates are run steadily at least one year before the election—and results are reported by many different polling organizations. To provide order to the plethora of polling results, we focus on poll results from March, 1988, to the election eve in November, and we consider results only from the major polling organizations—ABC/*Washington Post* (ABC/*WP*), CBS/*New York Times* (CBS/*NYT*), Gallup, Harris, NBC/*Wall Street Journal* (NBC/*WSJ*), and Gordon Black for CNN/*USA Today*

(CNN/*USA*). Together, these six polling organizations accounted for seventy-five polls, and they were frequently in the field at the same time, which allows us to compare results across polls.[11] The survey methods used by the six pollsters are similar. All are telephone polls and employ sample sizes in the range 750 to 2500, yielding "margins of error" in the range of 2 percent to 4 percent. The earliest surveys for most of them included all adults; however, by about May they began reporting results only for registered voters, and they restrict their reports further to "likely voters" by late summer or early fall, though the timing of these changes does vary slightly across organizations. In all cases, the results reported are in response to a question about the interviewee's candidate preference on the day of the poll. The wording of the Gallup Poll question used after the conventions, for example, was "If the presidential election were held beginning today, would you vote for the Republican ticket of George Bush and Dan Quayle or for the Democratic ticket of Michael Dukakis and Lloyd Bentsen?" (*Gallup Report,* November, 1988).

Table 6 presents a summary of the poll results for the 1988 campaign. This table reports the dates that each poll was in the field, the proportion of individuals who stated a preference for Bush (Bush percentage) or Dukakis (Dukakis percentage), and the marginalized lead for Bush. By marginalized lead we mean (Bush percentage − Dukakis percentage)/(Bush percentage + Dukakis percentage), that is the difference in the fraction of the two-party vote. For each month, the table also shows the average marginalized lead across the six polls and its associated standard error. In March, the situation was fluid with Bush having a large lead in the Gallup poll, but mixed support in the other polls. In May and June, the polls uniformly showed Dukakis in the lead by 12 points. Prior to the Democratic convention (July 18–21), Dukakis's lead had shrunk to about 6 points, but later in the month, after the convention, a pronounced "halo" effect was evident: Dukakis's lead rose to 17 percent, with NBC/*WSJ* placing it as high as 20 points. The Republican convention was held August 15–18, and polls taken shortly thereafter showed the Dukakis lead had disappeared, being replaced by a small lead for Bush. Actually, because the CNN/*USA* poll in August was taken before the end of the Republican convention and thus may not have reflected a Republican "halo" effect, excluding this poll from the average may provide a better estimate of the Bush lead of about 6 percent. Bush's lead in the polls grew from September through early November, although not uniformly in any particular poll. On election eve, as the last entry in table 6 indicates, Bush's lead in the polls ranged from 4.2 percent to 11.6 percent, averaging 8.5

---

11. We followed national polling results from twenty-three organizations over the 1988 campaign. Some of these polls were available only at sporadic intervals, and, in the interest of comparability, we have focused on the six major polling organizations.

TABLE 6. Bush's Lead as Reported by the Major Polls, March–November, 1988

	Poll	Date	Bush Percentage	Dukakis Percentage	Marginalized lead	Average (SE)
March						2.62 (6.75)
	ABC/*WP*	17–21	45	50	−5.26	
	CBS/*NYT*	19–22	46	45	1.10	
	Gallup	10–12	52	40	13.04	
	Harris	9–13	47	50	−3.09	
	CNN/*USA*	9	44	38	7.32	
May						−12.57 (3.61)
	ABC/*WP*	19–26	40	53	−13.98	
	CBS/*NYT*	9–12	39	49	−11.36	
	Gallup	13–15	38	54	−17.39	
	Harris	5–10	43	50	−7.53	
June						−12.15 (4.64)
	ABC/*WP*	15–19	39	51	−13.33	
	Gallup	10–12	38	52	−15.56	
	Harris	1–6	44	49	−5.38	
	NBC/*WSJ*	9–12	34	49	−18.07	
	CNN/*USA*	7–9	38	45	−8.43	
July (pre–Democratic convention)						−5.80 (4.92)
	ABC/*WP*	7–11	42	48	−6.67	
	CBS/*NYT*	5–8	39	47	−9.30	
	Gallup	8–10	41	47	−6.82	
	Harris	7–12	47	50	−3.09	
	NBC/*WSJ*	8–11	36	46	−12.20	
	CNN/*USA*	6–10	47	44	3.30	
July (post–Democratic convention)						−17.52 (3.24)
	CBS/*NYT*	31–8/3	34	50	−19.05	
	Gallup	22–24	37	54	−18.68	
	Harris	22–25	39	57	−18.75	
	NBC/*WSJ*	23–25	34	51	−20.00	
	CNN/*USA*	20–21	40	50	−11.11	
August (post–Republican convention)						3.19 (6.93)
	ABC/*WP*	17–23	48	40	9.09	
	CBS/*NYT*	19–21	46	40	6.98	
	Gallup	19–21	48	44	4.35	
	Harris	19–22	49	47	2.08	
	NBC/*WSJ*	20–22	47	40	8.05	
	CNN/*USA*	17–18	35	44	−11.39	
September						4.28 (1.65)
	ABC/*WP*	21–10/1	49	46	3.16	
	CBS/*NYT*	21–23	46	40	6.98	
	Gallup	27–28	47	42	5.62	
	Harris	24–29	49	46	3.16	
	NBC/*WSJ*	16–20	45	41	4.65	
	CNN/*USA*	5–8	48	46	2.13	

(*continued*)

TABLE 6—*Continued*

Poll	Date	Bush Percentage	Dukakis Percentage	Marginalized lead	Average (SE)
October					7.15 (5.29)
ABC/*WP*	12–18	52	45	7.22	
CBS/*NYT*	8–10	47	42	5.62	
Gallup	7–9	49	43	6.52	
Harris	6–10	50	48	2.04	
NBC/*WSJ*	14–16	55	38	18.28	
CNN/*USA*	8–10	48	45	3.23	
November (final)					8.53 (2.74)
ABC/*WP*	2–5	54	44	10.20	
CBS/*NYT*	2–4	48	40	9.09	
Gallup	3–6	53	42	11.58	
Harris	2–5	50	46	4.17	
NBC/*WSJ*	1–5	48	43	5.49	
CNN/*USA*	3–6	52	42	10.64	

percent.[12] The marginalized outcome of the popular vote was a lead for Bush of 7.9 percent (= [48,138,478 − 41,114,068]/[48,138,478 + 41,114,068]).

Polls and Markets

An obvious question about markets such as the IPSM is, how do they compare to opinion polls? Several comparisons are of particular interest, but the most obvious is accuracy: does the market "forecast" the election results more accurately than opinion polls? While this is an obvious comparison to make, some would argue that it is inappropriate. One view, prominent among poll-sters, is that a poll should be interpreted as a reading of how the electorate would vote if an election were held that day, and not as a forecast of an election sometime in the future. Indeed, the polling question usually asked is a variant of "If the election were held today, who would you vote for?" Nevertheless, it is difficult to see why this invalidates the use of poll results as forecasts. Suppose, for example, that a poll asked two questions: (1) "If the election were held today, who would you vote for?" and (2) "In the election to be held on November 8th, who do you think you will vote for?" The results of

---

12. Several organizations reported poll results, or subsets of poll results, for periods later than we have indicated in table 6. For example, CBS, without the *New York Times*, reported a Bush lead of 9.5 percent from polls taken on November 6 and 7, while Gallup reported leads of 9 percent and 8 percent over a similar period. We have used the announced final polling results for each of the six organizations because the reporting procedures of these last minute results are unclear.

the second question would surely be interpreted as a forecast, and, yet, it is difficult to imagine the circumstances under which truthful revelation of preferences would produce a different answer to the two questions. Of course, new information may arrive that leads an individual to actually vote differently than he or she previously thought he or she would, but this just reflects the obvious fact that forecasts are not 100 percent accurate.

A deeper objection to the comparison of the market's predictions with the polls arises in the work of McKelvey and Ordeshook (1984, 1985a, 1985b), Ordeshook (1987), and Bowden (1978 and 1989). In rational expectations models of voting with informed and uniformed voters, polls can convey information about candidates and about the electorate's preferences. Consequently, the publication of a poll may induce uninformed voters to change their stated voting intentions. It is only after repeated announcement of poll results, that is, when an invariant point in the space of poll results and beliefs has been reached, that polls can be regarded as forecasts of election outcomes. Although the outcome of a poll would be an unbiased estimator of what the vote would be if the election were held today, in general it will not be an unbiased estimator of the election outcome in the future as long as there are more polls to be conducted (Bowden 1989, 118). Under this view, it should not be surprising that opinion polls are faulty predictors of election outcomes. While this argument may have some descriptive value in explaining why polls may be volatile, particularly in the early stages of a campaign, the same arguments suggest that a market would also be volatile. Put differently, it is difficult to imagine how the results of a market and a poll would differ, given that participants in each have the same information set. For this reason, it is of interest to compare their performance.

Based on just one observation, the forecasting accuracy of the IPSM is impressive. One observation clearly does not tell us much; however, the operation of the market does provide information about other aspects of polls. For example, does information from opinion polls drive market trading, much like news about weather conditions affects the price of orange juice futures? If opinion polls contained genuine news, then one would expect their publication to affect the price of a candidate's stock. An alternative view argues that polls are simply one noisy measure of voting intentions, and that more reliable direct readings are available from other sources. In this view, polls do not convey news at all, but at best merely confirm what a knowledgeable observer could glean from other sources. In this section we provide empirical evidence on the behavior of polls and markets. The evidence, in the main, is largely supportive of the view that polls do not contain news.

The overall performance of the market relative to polls can be seen in figures 3 and 4, which show Bush's lead in the popular vote as implied by the stock market prices and as revealed by the Gallup and CBS/*New York Times*

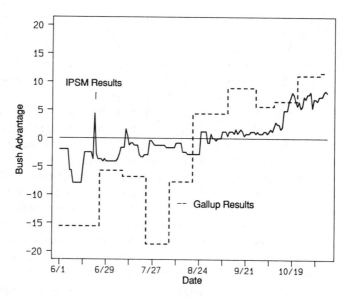

Fig. 3. Bush's lead in the IPSM and the Gallup poll

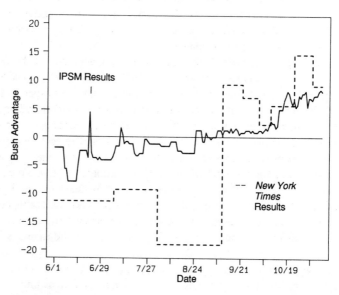

Fig. 4. Bush's lead in the IPSM and the CBS/*NYT* poll

opinion polls, two polls that are representative of the set of public opinion polls announced in 1988. Stock market prices reveal information about the share of the popular vote that a candidate is expected to receive, because the payoff to holding a share is a function of the vote share. Thus, if George Bush were expected to get 56 percent of the vote and Michael Dukakis were expected to get 40 percent, the no-arbitrage prices would be 140 (= 250 × .56) and 100 (= 250 × .40). The difference in prices divided by 250 ([140 − 100]/250 = .16) reveals the market assessment of Bush's lead in the popular vote. The lead implied by an opinion poll is computed in a straightforward manner; it is the difference between the percent favoring Bush and the percent favoring Dukakis, as revealed by the poll. There is a slight complication introduced by the fact that more than two candidates are in the race. In the IPSM, Rest-of-Field shares paid off on the combined third-party vote share. Public opinion polls lump voters who intend to vote for a third-party candidate in with the undecided voters. To make the comparison between the market and the polls, therefore, we normalize by the Bush-Dukakis total. Thus, the lead revealed by the market is calculated as (price of a Bush security − price of a Dukakis security)/(price of a Bush security + price of a Dukakis security), and the lead from the polls is calculated as (percentage favoring Bush − percentage favoring Dukakis)/(percentage favoring Bush + percentage favoring Dukakis).

The Gallup and CBS/*New York Times* polls are selected to illustrate the general behavior of polls during the campaign. In figures 3 and 4 the lead indicated by the polls is shown by the step-function that changes values at discrete intervals—usually about a month apart—occasioned by the release of a new poll. The lead implied by the market is shown by the continuous series. Inspection of both figures suggests that opinion polls are excessively volatile, certainly more so than can be attributed to sampling error alone. For example, after the Democratic convention, Bush's lead fell to −17 percent, and yet in two weeks—after the Republican convention—it increased to +7 percent. Stated differently, if we were to believe these numbers it would imply that 25 percent of the U.S. voters changed their minds in a short, uneventful two-week period. In contrast, the lead implied by the market changed little over this period.

Volatility per se is not bad, however. If the underlying public opinion is volatile, then large fluctuations in poll results are to be expected. But if polls measure public opinion only with error—error apart from that due to sampling—the observed volatility may simply be due to the infirmities of polling, rather than to fluctuations in public opinion. Of course, it is impossible to examine this question using data from polls alone. A natural way to examine this issue is to compare the volatility of the IPSM to opinion polls. In general, this is a difficult task because the IPSM prices are recorded daily, while polls are recorded at much coarser intervals, typically a month in the early stages of the campaign. This coarseness in sampling public opinion makes it difficult to separate true movements in public opinion from excess volatility.

Fortunately, in the 1988 campaign the American Political Network (APN) sponsored a daily public opinion poll from September 3 to November 8. Approximately 300 interviews were conducted per day, and the results were reported using overlapping three-day panels. Thus, the sample gathered on day 20 would be one-third of the sample reported on the day 20, day 21, and day 22. Because of the serial correlation induced by this overlapping of responses, the apparent variability of this series will be less than its true variability.[13]

As figure 5 shows, the volatility in APN data appears to be greater than that of the IPSM during the same period. One measure of volatility is the sample variance of each series. For these data, the sample variance of Bush's lead in the IPSM was 7.33, while that of the APN poll was 9.33. This is an underestimate of the volatility of each series, partly because of the serial correlation problem in the APN data, and, more importantly, because the variance for each series is computed about the sample mean, which may not be the appropriate estimate of the expected value of the lead on any date. In other words, the lead might well be changing. If we assume that the lead is varying smoothly over time, first differencing the two series will effectively remove the mean effects. For the first differences of the lead, the IPSM sample variance is 0.675, while the APN sample variance is 4.345, over 6 times larger. Thus, unless day-to-day changes in public opinion are large, polls are evidently a noisy measuring rod for determining voting outcomes.

Apart from volatility, a second question about the relation between polls and the market is whether polls "drive" the market. A number of colleagues predicted that participants in the IPSM would get their information about likely voting intentions from polling data, and hence the market prices would be determined by the latest poll results. This view, while superficially plaus- ible, ignores a very important feature of polling data: which poll do you believe? At any moment there were a substantial number of polls being conducted—the APN poll, for example, was conducted daily—and as a comparison of figures 3 and 4 shows, there is a difference, often a substantial difference, between the results of seemingly comparable polls. Direct com- parison of individual polls with the market, such as depicted in figures 3 and

---

13. The autocorrelation induced by three-day averaging of responses to a poll is due to use of the same answer from a participant for each of the three days. In contrast, while IPSM traders were the same each day (ignoring new entrants to the market), they were free to alter their offers from one day to the next. Thus, the influence of any one trader on the day's closing price represents a new observation on the beliefs of that trader.

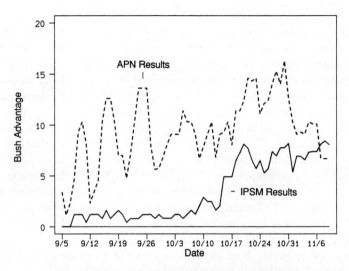

Fig. 5. Bush's lead in the IPSM and the APN poll

4, did not suggest any obvious case where a poll was seen to be driving the market. But this is essentially an "eyeballing the data" test, and it may not be very powerful.

To proceed further in examining the question of whether opinion polls drive the market we collected data on all polls that we could find. In total, we obtained 193 polls from fifteen polling organizations, excluding the daily poll results of the APN.[14] Of these polls, 86 were independent polls that occurred during the time that the IPSM was in operation.[15] For each of the polls we were able to obtain the dates when the poll was conducted and the release date of the poll. Typically the data was gathered over a three-day interval, and the results were publicly reported two days after the last day in the field. Actually, it is difficult to know precisely when the results were publicly announced, particularly in the cases where a poll is sponsored by one member of the print media and one member of the broadcast media. For our purposes, we focus on the last date that the polling organization was in the field, because we can then safely assume that the results of the polls were not known to the traders in the IPSM at that time.

---

14. The polling organizations, with the number of polls used in parentheses, were: ABC/*WP* (14), Bruskin (3), CBS/*NYT* (12), CNN/*USA Today* (10), Gallup (17), Harris (12), *Los Angeles Times* (7), NBC/*WSJ* (9), and *Time*/Yankelovich, Clancy, and Schulman (YCS) (2).

15. By *independent* we mean that the polls were not a subset of some other poll—for example, ABC would sometimes report on one day's panel of a three-day poll that was jointly produced by ABC and the *Wall Street Journal*.

If polls are an important source of news, possession of advance information about the results would have enabled one to make money on the IPSM. To test whether one could have done so, we perform an event-history of these stock market returns. For each poll, we know the last date that it was in the field, and we consider what would happen if an individual had access to the poll results on this date and could trade in the IPSM. We consider a seven-day period from the polls' last day in the field and inquire whether knowledge of the poll results would have been profitable. In order to examine the gains from having knowledge of the poll results, we need to have a decision rule for an investor. One strategy would be to compute the price of, say, Bush stock implied by the poll results and, if this price is higher than the current market price, buy a share of Bush stock, otherwise buy a share of Dukakis stock. Call this trading rule 1. Because the polls had different characteristics, for example, in how they report undecided voters, it is not clear that this rule can be meaningfully compared across polls. As an alternative, we considered the trading rule of buying Bush stock if the new poll is favorable news for Bush, relative to the last poll by the same polling organization. This strategy, call it trading rule 2, amounts to assuming that the poll conveys the direction of change in a candidate's support, but does not say much about the actual level.

Note that an event study of this sort tests only whether polls provide information about the eventual outcome, but does not test whether the IPSM was efficient. The information being considered here is private information— by construction it was not available to market participants. Under a rational expectations equilibrium, the release of the poll results would affect stock prices if it were news. In contrast, if the information being considered were publicly available and traders could make profits based on it several days after it became available, that would be a rejection of market efficiency.

Table 7 contains he results of applying each trading rule to the poll data. Neither trading strategy consistently makes money. Having knowledge of the poll results in advance, buying one share of the appropriate candidate, and holding it for one day leads, on average, to a statistically insignificant gain of 0.02 cents following strategy 1, and 0.07 cents following strategy 2. The largest average gain was achieved by pursuing a three-day buy and hold strategy following trading rule 2. Even in this case, the only gain significant by customary standards, 0.71 cents, is practically meaningless. Note that the sample minimum and maximum of daily trading gains indicates that there was money to be made if a trader knew which way the market was going to move. The small gains registered by knowing the outcome of a poll in advance suggests that this information had already been discounted by the market.

Taken together, the comparisons of individual polls with the market and the results of the stock market events-history study suggest that the market was not driven by polls. In this sense, polls are not "news" to traders who

TABLE 7. Returns to Buy and Hold Trading Strategies

	Day 1	Day 2	Day 3	Day 4	Day 5	Day 6
Trading rule 1						
Mean	−0.02	0.36	0.37	0.43	0.20	0.21
SD	0.21	0.25	0.35	0.32	0.35	0.34
T-statistic	−0.11	1.44	1.07	1.33	0.57	0.62
Minimum	−9	−9	−14	−14	−14	−14
Maximum	7	7	7	7	7	9
Trading Rule 2						
Mean	0.07	0.40	0.71	0.59	0.30	0.35
SD	0.22	0.27	0.33	0.34	0.36	0.35
T-statistic	0.31	1.44	2.18	1.74	0.84	1.00
Minimum	−9	−9	−14	−14	−14	−14
Maximum	7	7	7	7	7	9

Note: The reported statistics are for the gain in cents per share. The *t*-statistics report tests of the null hypotheses that the mean gain is zero.

have an incentive to seek out information from other sources. This does not mean that the market does not react to news events. Indeed, events like the naming of Lloyd Bentsen as a vice presidential candidate, Jesse Jackson's announcement that he would not run on a third-party ticket, and the outcomes of the presidential debates had predictable effects on the stocks of the candidates. In each of these cases, the market reacted quickly to the events, but not to the poll results about the event.

Judgment Bias

Studies of polling data have documented two types of judgment bias where a voter's individual preference for a candidate colors that voter's objective view of the campaign. For example, among voters who have already indicated an intention to vote for a particular presidential candidate, those intentions serve as a screen influencing judgments of which candidate "won" a debate (see, for example, Sigelman and Sigelman 1984). An additional bias has also been demonstrated using polling data to demonstrate that people distort their perception about an election's outcome in the direction of their own preferred candidate (Lazarsfeld, Berelson, and Gaudet 1944; Carroll 1978; Brown 1982; Granberg and Brent 1983; Uhlaner and Grofman 1986). Some evidence of this latter bias is documented in table 8, which reports the relationship between preference and expectation for eight presidential elections. For example, even in a very close election year like 1976, over 80 percent of the supporters of each candidate thought their candidate would win. Although the

TABLE 8. Relation between Preference and Expectation in Ten U.S. Presidential Elections

	Democrat/Republican	Percentage of Respondents Intending to Vote Democratic Who Expect Democrat to Win	Percentage of Respondents Intending to Vote Republican Who Expect Republican to Win
1988	Dukakis/Bush	51.7	94.2
1984	Mondale/Reagan	28.8	99.0
1980	Carter/Reagan	87.0	80.4
1976	Carter/Ford	84.2	80.6
1972	McGovern/Nixon	24.7	99.6
1968	Humphrey/Nixon	62.5	95.4
1964	Johnson/Goldwater	98.6	30.5
1960	Kennedy/Nixon	78.4	84.2
1956	Stevenson/Eisenhower	54.6	97.6
1952	Stevenson/Eisenhower	81.4	85.9
Average		65.2	84.7

Source: Granberg and Brent (1983), who use survey data collected by the Survey Research Center/Center for Political Studies of the University of Michigan.
Note: Entries for 1984 and 1988 were obtained from correspondence with Professor Granberg.

size of the bias reported in these studies is truly large, the evidence is not entirely convincing because of inaccuracies in polls themselves—inaccuracies due, perhaps, to the fact that participants have no incentive to reveal their true beliefs. Thus, it is not clear whether these are simply isolated instances of the lack of political objectivity, or whether the consequences of judgment bias are truly significant.

To the economist there is compelling theoretical justification for believing that the consequences of judgment bias are insignificant in the efficient operation of markets. When studying markets, the economist analyzes the behavior of the marginal trader; however, biases of the type documented in table 8 all have to do with the behavior of some *average* respondent. If market prices are to provide an accurate forecast of an election outcome, the behavior of the average trader is unimportant; it is the behavior of the *marginal* trader that matters. The market may well perform successfully, therefore, even if most traders exhibit some form of judgment bias. All that is required for efficient operation of the market is that there are a few traders in the market who are aware that others exhibit biases and trade accordingly. In the remainder of this section we look for the presence and impact of judgment biases on average trading behavior, and we examine the effects of these biases on marginal trading behavior.

From our market data, we can document both kinds of judgment biases—bias involving judgments about which candidate won a debate and bias in perceptions of the electoral success of one's preferred candidate. First, from the postdebate surveys of our traders, we show that traders' beliefs about which candidate won the debate were influenced by their individual partisan preferences, and, further, that traders backed these beliefs with cash. Second, we document that Bush supporters were more likely to buy Bush stock and to sell Dukakis stock at any price than were Dukakis supporters. Similarly, Dukakis supporters were more likely to buy Dukakis stock and sell Bush stock at each price than Bush supporters. This is consistent with the earlier polling evidence that voters overrate the chances of their preferred candidate while underrating those of the opposition. These findings of judgment bias on the part of traders in the market raises the question of how the market could have worked so well. We present some evidence on this question at the end of this section.

The nature of the first type of judgment bias observed in the IPSM was as follows.[16] When we studied trading behavior, we observed that traders appeared to be maximizing income. For example, while female participants exhibited a gender bias in preferences roughly similar to that detected in national polls (an 8–11 percent preference advantage for Dukakis over Bush), their trading behavior was indistinguishable from that of males.[17] But when we examined political preferences, we found a different result. Trading behavior around the presidential debates was affected by beliefs about the outcome of the debate in the direction consistent with expected income maximization—individuals who thought that Dukakis had won the debate bought shares of Dukakis and/or sold shares of Bush, while those who thought Bush had won bought Bush and/or sold Dukakis. Judgment bias arose because traders who expressed preferences for a candidate were significantly more likely to believe that their candidate had won the debate. For example, 80.4 percent of the Dukakis supporters thought Dukakis did better than Bush in the third debate, while only 22.2 percent of the Bush supporters shared that view. While our observation of such a phenomenon is not unique, the distinctive result from the IPSM is that traders were willing to back their disparate opinions with cash. Table 9 shows the changes in the proportion of Bush shares held (number of Bush shares held / [number of Bush shares +

---

16. In the psychology literature this bias is known as the assimilation-contrast effect (Sherif and Hovland 1961; Parducci and Marshall 1962). Simply put, it states that an individual's preference for an outcome biases his or her interpretation of information about the likelihood of the outcome occurring.

17. Similar results were found for other demographic variables, for example income level, education, and religious preference. It is noteworthy that participants in the IPSM were not a representative sample of either the U.S. or Iowa electorates—they are too well educated, too white, too well off, and too liberal, even by Iowa standards.

TABLE 9.   Portfolio Composition by Perceived Debate Outcome after Each Debate: Change in Proportion of Major Candidate Shares Held in Bush Stock

	Candidate Thought to Have Won			
	Bush	Dukakis	No One	All Other Traders
Debate 1	4.8	−4.0	0.0	1.0
	(2.3)	(2.2)	—	(1.0)
Debate 2	1.5	−1.6	0.0	−1.2
	(1.6)	(0.7)	—	(1.7)
Debate 3	2.2	−0.9	0.0	−2.8
	(3.4)	(1.0)	—	(1.8)

Note: Entries in parentheses are standard errors.

number of Dukakis shares]) categorized by which candidate was perceived to have won the debate. In the table it can be seen that those traders who believed that the Bush team won increased their holdings in Bush stock consistently, while those who believed Dukakis won the debate consistently reduced their holdings of Bush stock after the debate. Interestingly, those who thought that there was no winner in the debate—twenty-three traders in debate 1, ten traders in debate 2, and sixteen traders in debate 3—acted consistently with those beliefs and did not trade the two days after the debate.

Evidence of the second type of bias can also be observed in the IPSM data.[18] With this bias, traders who prefer Bush should anticipate a larger share of the popular vote for their candidate, and, accordingly, they should demand more shares of Bush stock at each price than traders who prefer Dukakis. Similarly, traders who prefer Bush should also be willing to sell fewer shares of Bush stock at each price than traders who prefer Dukakis. This is illustrated with hypothetical, constituent-specific demand and supply curves in figure 6. Demand and supply curves for the Bush and Dukakis constituencies appear in panels *a* and *b,* respectively, and the solid line at price = 125 represents the market equilibrium. Assuming that all trades take place at the market clearing price, Bush supporters should buy more Bush stock than they sell, while Dukakis supporters should sell more Bush stock than they buy. By analogous reasoning, Dukakis supporters should buy more Dukakis stock than they sell, while Bush supporters should sell more Dukakis stock than they buy.

18. This bias is known as the false consensus effect in the social psychology literature (Ross, Greene, and House 1977; Brown 1982). It states that individuals tend to overestimate the extent to which their views are representative of the population. Such a phenomena has been documented in the literature investigating behavior in experimental games (Kelley and Stahleski 1970; Dawes, McTavish, and Shaklee 1977).

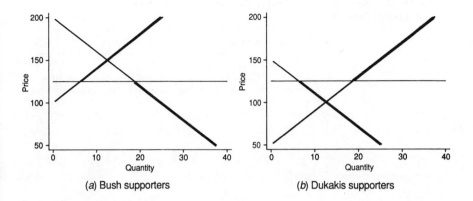

(*a*) Bush supporters   (*b*) Dukakis supporters

These biases are evident in the data of table 10. The basic data used for this table consists of purchases and sales of the stock of each candidate by trader and by day. We identified traders' candidate preferences from their survey responses and then computed net purchases by day (purchases minus sales) across all traders within the Bush and Dukakis constituencies. The second row of table 10 contains the mean value of such net purchases across all days in the market with active traders from the respective constituency, while rows three and four provide counts of the number of days in which purchases by the constituency exceed sales. Test statistics, including a *t*-ratio for testing the difference between means for row 2, and a chi-square statistic for testing independence with the count data of rows 3 and 4, suggest significant differences in trading behavior between the two constituencies. These differences could have been generated by a small number of traders with deep pockets, but that was not the case. Rows 6 and 7 of the table, which contain means of the proportion of traders in a constituency who were net buyers and net sellers respectively, reveal that, on average, for example, 62 percent of the Bush supporters bought more Bush stock than they sold, while only 31 percent of the Dukakis supporters bought more Bush stock than they sold. Again the difference across support groups is statistically significant in the direction suggested by judgment bias—Bush supporters revealed a higher valuation on Bush stock relative to Dukakis supporters by buying significantly more of it, and Dukakis supporters likewise bought relatively more of the stock in their candidate. Finally, the differences are not attributable merely to new and naive traders. Rows 9 and 11 contain the daily mean net purchases of stock by a constituent group as in row 2, but this time including only trades undertaken by a trader during the first seven days of entry in the market (row 9) and only after the first seven days (row 11). Again, all the differences between constituent group are in the direction suggested by judgment bias, and all but one

TABLE 10. Measures of Quantity Differences between Bush and Dukakis Supporters

	Transactions in Bush Stock			Transactions in Dukakis Stock		
	By Bush Supporters	By Dukakis Supporters	Test Statistic	By Bush Supporters	By Dukakis Supporters	Test Statistic
(1) Days with active trade in either candidate	92	80		92	80	
(2) Average of net purchases across active days	1.12 (1.11)	−1.59 (0.96)	1.85 [170]	−2.26 (0.90)	2.01 (0.86)	−3.43 [170]
(3) Days in which purchases > sales	43	21	8.88 [1]	24	46	14.72 [1]
(4) Days in which purchases < sales	30	42		46	20	
(5) Average across active days of number of traders in this candidate	2.41 (0.20)	1.53 (0.15)		1.67 (0.17)	2.00 (0.19)	
(6) Average proportion of traders with net purchases > 0	0.62 (0.038)	0.31 (0.048)	5.06 [146]	0.39 (0.044)	0.68 (0.045)	−4.61 [143]
(7) Average proportion of traders with net purchases < 0	0.37 (0.038)	0.68 (0.048)	−5.06 [146]	0.60 (0.044)	0.31 (0.044)	4.66 [143]
(8) Days with active new traders	51	45		51	45	
(9) Average of net purchases across active days by new traders	1.63 (0.58)	−0.20 (0.49)	2.41 [94]	0.49 (0.56)	2.09 (0.46)	−2.21 [94]
(10) Days with active *old* traders	82	66		82	66	
(11) Average of net purchases across active days by old traders	0.24 (1.23)	−1.79 (1.12)	1.22 [146]	−2.84 (1.01)	1.01 (1.00)	−2.71 [146]

Note: Entries in parentheses are standard errors; entries in square brackets are degrees of freedom.

would be judged significant. Interesting trade patterns emerge here. Apparently, traders are net buyers of their favorite candidate during the first week of participation on the market, and they become net sellers of the opposition candidate after the first week.

In spite of these judgment biases, the market provided an extremely accurate prediction of the final outcome. To explain this anomaly we have three competing hypotheses. The first is that we were simply lucky and that other markets will perform more poorly. A test of this hypothesis must await further elections. The second hypothesis is that we had a representative sample of traders in the market in terms of their presidential preference. In this case, traders who engage in market activities in accord with their (theoretically irrelevant) preferences could well lead the market to successfully predict the final outcome. Note that this hypothesis is at odds with current economic theory, which assumes that as long as traders are financially well motivated, they will trade objectively. To investigate this second hypothesis, we examine the relationship between the election and market outcomes and the reported preferences of IPSM participants. As reported in table 11, of the traders responding to questions on the enrollment survey and on the postelection telephone poll, the share expressing support for Dukakis was relatively high as compared with the market and election outcomes. These measures seem to contradict the hypothesis of offsetting biases—the market outcome favored Bush even though a majority of market participants expressed preferences for Dukakis. Still, even with this configuration of preferences, the market could have been successful in spite of judgment bias if Bush supporters, for example, had larger investments, on average, in the market. Markets, after all, operate under a one dollar, one vote rule rather than a one man, one

TABLE 11. Comparison of Market and Election Outcomes with Trader Preferences, in Percentages

	Bush	Dukakis	Other	IPSM Traders Represented
Popular vote in national election	53.2	45.4	1.4	—
Market forecast on election eve	53.2	45.2	2.0	—
Preference of traders according to IPSM enrollment survey	48.1	49.6	2.3	70
Preference and/or vote of IPSM traders according to exit poll	46.7	50.8	2.5	63
Share of total market value controlled by enrollment day supporters	55.2	40.6	4.2	70
Share of total market value controlled by election day supporters	49.7	47.9	2.4	63

vote rule. Indeed a one dollar, one vote rule swings the balance toward the market outcome, but the swing is either not far enough (49.7 percent for Bush in the election day survey), or else too far (55.2 percent for Bush in the enrollment survey). Thus, evidence from the market of how the judgment biases of Bush and Dukakis supporters might have offset each other to produce the realized market outcome remains inconclusive. Nevertheless, it seems unlikely such an offset could have been so precise so as to yield market prices as accurate as those achieved in the IPSM.

A third hypothesis for the success of the market is that there were a few traders in the market who knew that other traders exhibited judgment bias and profited by acting as arbitragers. In other words, they bought Dukakis stock from (biased) Bush supporters and sold it to (biased) Dukakis supporters, and they bought Bush stock from (biased) Dukakis supporters and sold it to (biased) Bush supporters. Theoretically, this would require arbitragers to have sufficient information about the other traders in the market. In particular, they would have to know the extent of the judgment bias exhibited by traders of each political preference and they would have to know the fraction of traders that preferred each candidate. While it seems implausible that any trader in the IPSM had such information, perhaps some had a sufficient intuitive grasp to successfully play the arbitrager's role.

To test this third hypothesis, we construct empirical counterparts to the extramarginal portions of the preference-specific demand and supply curves of figure 6. The extramarginal bid and ask curves are the offers to buy or sell that were not consummated in the market during this period, and they are anchored at the average price and the actual quantity at which trade did occur. We examined these curves following each of the three debates. At these times, both forms of judgment bias are present in the data on quantity traded, so any effect of these biases on market prices should be magnified. Normally, an observer sees only a point on the demand and supply curves, but here we have direct observations on portions of the demand and supply curves themselves, and thus there is no identification problem (at least not of the usual sort) in disentangling the effects of demand and supply. As a practical matter, we could construct the entire demand and supply schedules—both infra- and extramarginal—but this raises the question of what the bid and ask offers reveal when trading occurs. For example, if an individual actually is willing to bid $1.00 for a stock and when he comes to the market sees that the current price is $0.50, will he or she submit a bid of $0.50 or $1.00? To avoid this issue, we focus here on the extramarginal portions of the demand and supply curves.

Executed trades and the offers in the bid and ask queues are separated according to the preference of the trader involved, and these are used to construct preference-specific, extramarginal bid and ask functions. Specifically, outstanding bids and asks are used to construct step functions representing slopes, and executed trades are used to locate their positions. Such constructions for market activity occurring after each of the three debates appear in figures 7 through 9. For example, the two step-functions in the upper right panel of figure 7 are constructed from the offers made for Bush stock by Dukakis supporters after the first debate, and they represent an empirical measure of the illustrative demand and supply curves in panel *b* of figure 6. Each dot on the curves represents an individual offer; the distance between dots indicates the number of units in that offer. The dominant feature of these bid and ask functions is their flatness near the equilibrium price. Most distinctly for the Bush supporters, but for Dukakis supporters as well, the implied demand and supply curves are highly elastic in a region near the market price. Such behavior is consistent with the presence of marginal traders in both camps who remain unaffected by judgment bias and act to arbitrage away the differences in bid and ask prices coming from the two camps.

Evidence consistent with the presence of marginal traders in the market acting as arbitragers provides an explanation for why the market successfully

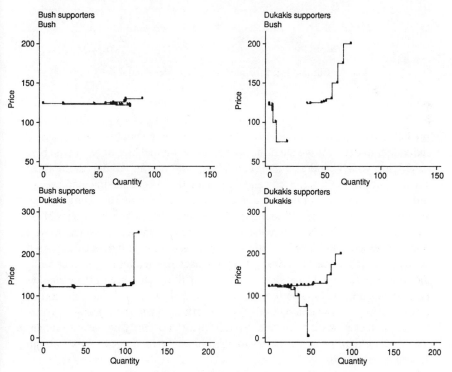

Fig. 7. Bid and ask functions after first presidential debate

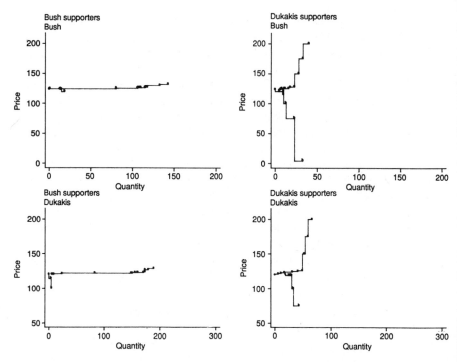

Fig. 8. Bid and ask functions after vice-presidential debate

predicted the outcome in spite of the evidence of judgment bias on the part of individual traders. As we have shown, traders exhibited bias of two sorts: bias in judging which candidate won the debates and bias in judging the relative standing of the one's preferred candidate. That traders entered the market with different expectations of the election outcome might not be surprising to even ardent members of the rational expectations school; however, it should be surprising that differences in revealed preference for shares correlated so well with professed candidate preferences, and that those differences persisted beyond the first week of trading. If these biases showed up in prices as well, then the market would be successful only if the preferences of the market participants reflected the preferences of the underlying electorate. This sort of distortion in prices would naturally be very damaging to the rational expectations hypothesis. As it turns out, though, price apparently conveys sufficient information to allow some traders to equilibrate the market correctly through arbitrage operations.

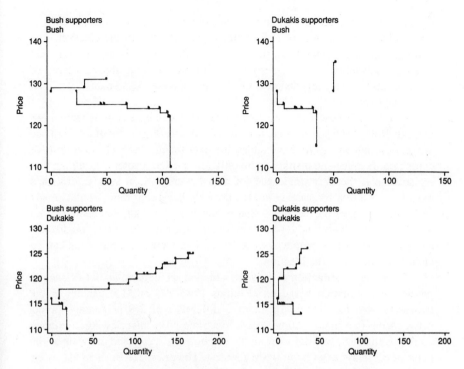

Fig. 9. Bid and ask functions after second presidential debate

5. Summary

Future studies of presidential elections can benefit from experimental markets like the IPSM in several ways. First of all, the IPSM forecast the outcome of the 1988 presidential election with impressive accuracy. The market provided a much better election eve forecast than public opinion polls, and over the course of the campaign, market prices were much less volatile than poll results. The market was able to anticipate and adjust to information contained in public opinion polls well before poll results were released. In this sense, market prices were not determined by the release of new polling information.

The predictive success of the IPSM also surpasses the performance of prominent statistical forecasting models. A model recently proposed by Erikson (1989), for example, predicts the incumbent presidential party's percentage of the two-party vote as a function of just two variables, one economic and one political. The economic variable, drawn from the work of Hibbs

(1982), is the cumulative weighted average of annual percentage change in per capita disposable income over the fifteen quarters prior to the election. The political variable, drawn from the work of Tufte (1978), is the average "net candidate advantage," derived from the National Election Study's survey of respondents' likes and dislikes of the presidential candidates' personal characteristics.

Combining these two variables for ten presidential elections from 1948 through 1984, Erickson's model accounts for nearly 90 percent of the variance in election outcomes. We have added the data for the 1988 election, but we computed the likes and dislikes score only for registered voters, assuming that registration is the best single cue for actual voting. As it stands, Erikson's model is not a true forecasting model, not only because it relies on data made available only after the election—that is, the candidate likes and dislikes from the National Election Study—but also because the candidate likes and dislikes are computed for the sample of major party voters only, a sample that can be identified only after the election.[19]

From our reestimation of Erikson's model, we derived an out-of-sample prediction (estimation based on elections 1948–84) of 51.4 percent of the two-party vote for George Bush, or a difference of 2.8 percentage points between the two major candidates.[20] Since the NES interviewing continued until November 6, two days before the election, we have used that date as the point of comparison with the IPSM forecast. The prices for Bush and Dukakis on November 6 imply a difference of 7.4 percentage points between the two candidates, compared with the actual outcome of a 7.8 percentage point difference. For the 1988 election, the IPSM performed far better in this election than the hybrid Tufte-Hibbs model touted by Erikson.

In addition to its predictive value, a market approach contributes to the explanation of election outcomes. Because a continuously operating market such as the IPSM is potentially instantaneous in its adjustment to new information, it is a unique tool for assessing the impact of specific campaign events on the relative standing of the candidates. Public opinion polls, in contrast, almost always involve a substantial lag, perhaps of a week or more, before new results can be observed. The IPSM identified three campaign events in

---

19. Basing the likes-dislikes score on registered, rather than actual, voters makes a big difference in the point estimate for 1988. The out-of-sample prediction for Bush's share of the vote is 53.0 when actual voters are used for the candidate variable. See n. 20 for estimation results.

20. For the likes and dislikes variable, C, in 1988, we used a value of .140; for the economic variable, E, a value of 2.1; and for the vote share, V, a value of 53.9. Our estimation using data from all presidential elections from 1948–88 yielded the following results.

$$V = 44.96 + 2.71E + 6.59C \qquad R^2 \text{ (adjusted)} = .89 \qquad N = 11$$
(t-statistics)   (1.21)   (5.48)   (4.63)   Root MSE = 2.08

1988 as having an impact on the candidates' fortunes: Dukakis's selection of Lloyd Bentsen as a running mate, Jesse Jackson's announcement at the Democratic convention that he would not run a third-party campaign, and the second presidential debate. Thus, evidence from the IPSM contradicts the conventional wisdom that campaign events had no explanatory relevance during the 1988 campaign.

Finally, the IPSM verified what political scientists have observed for some time—voters' judgments about political events are biased by their ideological and partisan preferences. What is noteworthy about the IPSM experiment is that this bias persists even when individuals are given financial incentives to behave otherwise. However, it is also noteworthy that the market predicted the final outcome of the election quite accurately in spite of this bias. Thus, while judgment bias exists on average, it seems to have no impact on the marginal traders who arbitraged away any existing bias.

The explanation for the predictive success of the IPSM is partially consistent with a rational expectations hypothesis, where traders infer information about the outcome from market prices. This is an encouraging result for the success of experimental markets in future elections—the theoretical success of the IPSM was no fluke. The viability of a market approach is especially important, given the pervasiveness of judgment bias. Such bias makes the analyses of political events through individual opinion surveys, for example, highly problematic. For this reason alone, a financial market is a promising alternative to polls.

REFERENCES

Bartels, Larry M. 1985. "Expectations and Preferences in Presidential Nominating Campaigns." *American Political Science Review* 79:804–15.
Bartels, Larry M. 1987. "Candidate Choice and the Dynamics of the Presidential Nominating Process." *American Journal of Political Science* 31:1–30.
Bowden, Roger J. 1987. "Repeated Sampling in the Presence of Publication Effects." *Journal of the American Statistical Association* 82:476–84.
Bowden, Roger J. 1989. *Statistical Games and Human Affairs: The View from Within.* Cambridge: Cambridge University Press.
Brody, Richard, and Lee Sigelman. 1983. "Presidential Popularity and Presidential Elections: An Update and Extension." *Public Opinion Quarterly* 47:325–28.
Brown, Clifford E. 1982. "A False Consensus Effect in 1980 Presidential Preferences." *Journal of Social Psychology* 118:137–38.
Campbell, Angus, Phillip E. Converse, Warren E. Miller, and Donald E. Stokes. 1960. *The American Voter.* New York: Wiley.
Carroll, John S. 1978. "The Effect of Imagining an Event on Expectations for the Event: An Interpretation in Terms of the Availability Heuristic." *Journal of Experimental Social Psychology* 14:88–96.

Dawes, Robyn M., Jeanne McTavish, and Harriet Shaklee. 1977. "Behavior, Communication, and Assumptions about Other People's Behavior in a Commons Dilemma Situation." *Journal of Personality and Social Psychology* 35:1–11.

Erikson, Robert S. 1989. "Economic Conditions and the Presidential Vote." *American Political Science Review* 83:567–73.

Fair, Ray C. 1978. "The Effect of Economic Events on Votes for President." *Review of Economics and Statistics* 60:159–73.

Fair, Ray C. 1988. "The Effect of Economic Events on Votes for President: 1984 Update." *Political Behavior* 10:168–79.

Forsythe, Robert, Forrest Nelson, George Neumann, and Jack Wright. 1990. "Forecasting the 1988 Presidential Election: A Field Experiment." In *Research in Experimental Economics,* ed. R. M. Isaac. Vol. 4. In press.

Forsythe, Robert, and Russell J. Lundholm. 1990. "Information Aggregation in an Experimental Market." *Econometrica* 58:309–48.

Forsythe, Robert, Thomas R. Palfrey, and Charles R. Plott. 1982. "Asset Valuation in an Experimental Market." *Econometrica* 50:537–67.

Frankovic, Kathleen A. 1985. "The 1984 Election: The Irrelevance of the Campaign." *Political Science* 18:39–47.

Granberg, Donald, and Edward Brent. 1983. "When Prophecy Bends: The Preference-Expectation Link in U.S. Presidential Elections." *Journal of Personality and Social Psychology* 45:477–91.

Hausch, Donald B., and William T. Ziemba. 1990. "Arbitrage Strategies for Cross-Track Betting on Major Horse Races." *Journal of Business* 63:61–78.

Hiobs, Douglas A., Jr. 1982. "President Reagan's Mandate from the 1980 Elections." *American Politics Quarterly* 10:387–420.

Hibbs, Douglas A., Jr. 1987. *The American Political Economy: Macroeconomics and Electoral Politics.* Cambridge, Mass.: Harvard University Press.

Jordan, James S. 1985. "Learning Rational Expectations: The Finite State Case." *Journal of Economic Theory* 36:257–76.

Kelley, Harold H., and Anthony J. Stahelski. 1970. "Social Interaction Basis of Cooperators' and Competitors' Beliefs about Others." *Journal of Personality and Social Psychology* 16:66–91.

Lazarsfeld, Paul F., Bernard R. Berelson, and Helen Gaudet. 1944. *The People's Choice: How a Voter Makes Up His Mind in a Presidential Campaign.* New York: Columbia University Press.

Lewis-Beck, Michael S., and Tom W. Rice 1984. "Forecasting Presidential Elections: A Comparison of Naive Models." *Political Behavior* 6:39–51.

Lewis-Beck, Michael S., and Andrew Skalaban 1989. "Citizen Forecasting: Can Voters See into the Future." *British Journal of Political Science* 19:146–54.

Markus, Gregory A. 1988. "The Impact of Personal and National Economic Conditions on the Presidential Vote: A Pooled Cross-sectional Analysis." *American Journal of Political Science* 32:137–54.

McKelvey, Richard D., and Peter C. Ordeshook. 1984. "Rational Expectations in Elections." *Public Choice* 44:61–102.

McKelvey, Richard D., and Peter C. Ordeshook. 1985a. "Elections with Limited Information: A Fulfilled Expectations Model Using Contemporaneous Poll and

Endorsement Data as Information Sources." *Journal of Economic Theory* 36:55–85.

McKelvey, Richard D., and Peter C. Ordeshook. 1985b. "Sequential Elections with Limited Information." *American Journal of Political Science* 29:480–512.

Ordeshook, Peter C. 1987. "Public Opinion Polls and Democratic Processes: A Comment." *Journal of the American Statistical Association* 82:486–91.

Parducci, Allen, and Louise M. Marshall. 1962. "Assimilation vs. Contrast in the Anchoring of Perceptual Judgments of Weight." *Journal of Experimental Psychology* 63:426–37.

Plott, Charles R., and Shyam Sunder. 1982. "Efficiency of Experimental Security Markets with Insider Information: An Application of Rational Expectations Models." *Journal of Political Economy* 90:663–98.

Plott, Charles R., and Shyam Sunder. 1988. "Rational Expectations and the Aggregation of Diverse Information in Laboratory Security Markets." *Econometrica* 56:1085–1118.

Radner, Roy. 1982. "Equilibrium under Uncertainty." In *Handbook of Mathematical Economics,* ed. K. J. Arrow and M. D. Intriligator. Vol. 2. Amsterdam: North-Holland.

Rosenstone, Steven J. 1985. "Explaining the 1984 Presidential Election." *Brookings Review* 4:25–32.

Ross, Lee, David Greene, and Pamela House. 1977. "The 'False Consensus Effect': An Egocentric Bias in Social Perception and Attribution Processes." *Journal of Experimental Social Psychology* 13:279–301.

Sherif, M., and C. I. Hovland. 1961. *Social Judgment: Assimilation and Contrast Effects in Communication and Attitude Change.* New Haven, Conn.: Yale University Press.

Sigelman, Lee, and Carol K. Sigelman. 1984. "Judgments of the Carter-Reagan Debate: The Eyes of the Beholders." *Public Opinion Quarterly* 48:624–28.

Tufte, Edward R. 1978. *Political Control of the Economy.* Princeton, N.J.: Princeton University Press.

Uhlaner, Carole J., and Bernard Grofman. 1986. "The Race May Be Close But My Horse Is Going to Win: Wish Fulfillment in the 1980 Presidential Election." *Political Behavior* 8(2): 101–29.

Candidate Convergence and Information Costs in Spatial Elections: An Experimental Analysis

Kenneth C. Williams

The fundamental result of the traditional spatial model of candidate competition (Downs 1957; Davis and Hinich 1966; Enelow and Hinich 1984) is that, in equilibrium, candidate positions on issues converge to the median voter's ideal point. This result has been rejected outright by some political scientists because of the severe and unrealistic assumptions about the information that candidates and voters possess. The assumptions that candidates know the preferences of voters, and voters know their own preferences as well as the candidate's position on salient issues, seems at odds with empirical investigations that suggest the opposite. Survey and public opinion polls consistently point to the low levels of information that voters have about political candidates and issues (Berelson, Lazarsfeld, and McPhee 1954; Campbell et al. 1960; Kinder and Sears 1985). One reason voters are uninformed is because the cost of gathering, processing, and evaluating information is high (Downs 1957). Also, since the market for information is imperfect, much of the information that voters need to make informed decisions is not available (Page 1977; Ferguson 1983).

However, full information is not a prerequisite for making informed decisions. A rational ignorance hypothesis suggests that voters do not need to be fully informed to make political choices in limited information systems (Downs 1957; Popkin et al. 1976; Denzau and Munger 1986; McKelvey and Ordeshook 1986; Roberts 1989). Instead, voters can rely on costless cues that are endogenous in the system, such as retrospective signals from the candidates or parties, when deciding which candidate to vote for. Empirical evi-

The author would like to thank Paul Abramson, Allen Brierly, and Rick Wilson for their helpful comments on earlier drafts. The author would also like to thank the Labor and Industrial Relations department at Michigan State University who through a grant by the IBM corporation allowed me access to their computer lab.

dence, in fact, shows that voters do tend to vote retrospectively, considering only the policies and actions of the previous incumbent (Key 1966; Fiorina 1981; Abramson, Aldrich, and Rohde 1990). Thus, what appears to be ignorance on the part of voters is, in fact, a rational response to shortcut high information costs.

Using this rationale, contemporary formal models of elections have weakened the information conditions for candidates and voters, and the results show that candidate positions still converge to or near the median (Calvert 1985; Ferejohn 1986; Coughlin 1986; Ledyard 1989). One approach takes a rational expectations model of markets and applies it to elections. McKelvey and Ordeshook (1985 and 1986) show that even if candidates and voters are uninformed, they can learn from each other, and eventually their actions will resemble those taken under conditions of full information. Thus, in a sequential election game where candidates do not know the location of the median, and voters do not know the exact position candidates take on issues, as long as both actors behave rationally, candidates will locate the median and voters will vote for the candidate who best serves their self-interest.

To test the robustness of this result, experiments that model limited information spatial elections (McKelvey and Ordeshook 1984; Collier et al. 1987) have been conducted. In these experiments, candidate subjects compete against each other by selecting strategies in a n-dimensional policy-space, where strategies selected by an incumbent translate into a monetary payoff for voter subjects based on an assigned utility function. Voters then vote for candidates based on their welfare for the corresponding payoff. An incomplete information game exists because candidates are unaware of the distribution of the voter's utility functions; thus, they do not know the location of the median position. Voters do not observe the current position of the incumbent, but have alternative incomplete information sources that they can use to estimate this position. In the McKelvey and Ordeshook experiment, voters observe contemporaneous poll information and an interest group endorsement that relates the left-right orientation of the candidates, and, in the Collier et al. experiment, voters observe only retrospective information about the incumbent's payoff. The experiments show that these incomplete information sources are sufficient for voters to send the appropriate signals to candidates, and, in general, candidates locate the median and incumbent strategies converge to it. However, one problem with these studies is that voters do not have the option to be informed and are forced to use the information source provided by the experimenter.

The purpose of the study reported here is to extend previous results by examining candidate convergence when voters are uninformed and given the option to purchase contemporaneous information. The design is related to, but different from, one reported elsewhere in which voters were charged a nominal fee (three cents) for information about the challenger's promised position—a position challengers promise to adopt if they are elected (Collier, Ordeshook, and Williams 1989). The main difference is that their study did not examine candidate convergence, since the major emphasis was whether voters shortcut high information costs by relying on retrospective evaluations. Consequently, to concentrate on voter behavior, human candidate subjects were not used and candidate positions were chosen from a predetermined series. To examine candidate convergence, the experiments reported here use human candidate subjects.

In these experiments, two trials are conducted in which the cost of information is varied. By increasing the level of costs it is possible to examine the degree to which candidate convergence is dependent on the full information assumption. Raising the cost of information from a low to a high level (three cents to nine cents) should affect consumption of information, producing two electorates in which voters are relatively more informed in one than the other. If previous experimental findings are not spurious, then increasing the cost should have no effect on the rate in which candidates converge to the median, even though the behavior of subjects may differ. For example, according to a rational ignorance hypothesis, we would expect that voters who confront high information costs will rely more on cues from the incumbent (since this is free information), while cues from both the incumbent and challenger will be more important for voters who confront low information costs. Thus, even though voters use different decision rules, there will be enough correct voting (in terms of individual welfare) so that candidate strategies will converge to the median of the electorate at approximately the same rate in both trials.

Sections 1 and 2 of this paper describe the spatial model that the experiment replicates and the experimental procedures. Section 3 reports on the results of the experiments, and the last section presents some concluding remarks.

1. Experimental Model

The standard spatial model of candidate competition includes a set of candidates $K = \{A, B\}$, a set of n voters, N, and an n-dimensional Euclidean issue-space $X \subseteq R^n$ (for the experiment $n = 2$). Candidates A and B compete by selecting strategies in the set $S_k \in X$ for all $k \in K$, where $S_k = S_1 \times S_2$, and a strategy choice by candidate A is $s_A = (s_1, s_2) \in S_k$. Candidate strategies can either be a policy that an incumbent adopts once in office, or it can be a campaign pledge that a candidate commits to adopt if elected. We let s_k denote the policy position of the incumbent and w_k denote the campaign commitment where $w_k = (w_1, w_2) = s_k = (s_1, s_2) \in S_k$.

Each voter $i \in N$ has a utility function $u_i : X \to R^2$ with an ideal point at y_i. Utility functions are assumed to be of the form:

$$u_i(s_k) = u(s_k, y_i) = -|s_k - y_i|. \tag{1.1}$$

This utility function defines preferences so that strategies closer to y_i are preferred to positions farther away, and voter i prefers s_A to s_B iff:

$$|s_B - y_i| > |s_A - y_i|. \tag{1.2}$$

If the two sides of the inequality are equal, then voter i is indifferent between the alternatives. Let $f(g)$ be a symmetric density function describing voters ideal points in X, which has a median at y^*, where $y^* = (y_1, y_2)$. Consider a game where candidates pick $w_k = (w_1, w_2)$, which gives the voter a promised payoff of $u_i(w_k)$. Voters observe $u_i(w_A)$ and $u_i(w_B)$ before election period t, and use this information about payoffs to vote for one of the two candidates. Define plurality as: $V_k(w_A, w_B) = \#[u_i(w_A)] - \#[u_i(w_B)]$, where $\#[u_i(w_A)]$ is the number of voters who prefer the utility from candidate A using decision rule 1.2. Candidate A then has the following payoff function:

$$V_A(w_A, w_B) = \begin{cases} 1 & \text{if } \#[u_i(w_A)] > \#[u_i(w_B)] \\ 0 & \text{otherwise.} \end{cases} \tag{1.3}$$

Thus, candidates choose w_k to maximize V_k, taken the other candidate's platform as given. They have no policy preference. Voters are assumed to vote for candidates who select strategies closer to their ideal point or maximize $u_i(w_k)$. Thus, it is a two-stage game with candidates selecting (w_A, w_B), and voters then voting for the closest candidate. In a full information game with no abstention, candidates know $f(g)$ and the location of y^*, and voters know $u_i(w_k)$, then an equilibrium to this game is $w_A = w_B = y^*$. Thus, both candidates pick the median, all voters receive the same payoff from each candidate, and the election outcome will be decided by a random draw.

A modified version of this election game is a more complex sequential game of incomplete information where, in the first stage, candidates campaign against each other by selecting promise positions $w_k^t = (w_1, w_2)$. In the next stage, voters have an option to purchase information about $u_i(w_k^t)$ for a fixed fee, c. After this stage, an election is held where the voters vote for one of the two candidates, and the winner is determined by the candidate's function described in equation 1.3. In the last stage, the winning candidate selects a position $s_k^t = (s_1, s_2)$ possibly with $s_k^t \neq w_k^t$, giving the voters a payoff of $u_i(s_k^t)$. After $u_i(s_k^t)$ is revealed to each voter, candidates select w_k^{t+1}. This process continues in a sequential manner, where voters and candidates do not know when the last election will be held. Candidates do not observe $f(g)$, so they do not know the location of y^*, and have knowledge only of $V_k^{t-1}, \ldots,$ V_k^{t-n} (the plurality in past elections), $s_k^t, \ldots, s_k^{t-n}$ (the current incumbent's position and past positions), and $w_k^{t-1}, \ldots, w_k^{t-n}$ (a stream of past campaign promises). Voters know $u_i(s_k^{t-1})$, the incumbent's past payoff, but must purchase information about $u_i(w_k^t)$ by investing c. Thus informed, voters observe $u_i(s_k^{t-1}), \ldots, u_i(s_k^{t-n})$ (a stream of past payoffs from the incumbent), $u_i(w_k^t)$ (the set of the candidates current campaign pledges), and $u_i(w_k^{t-1}), \ldots,$ $u_i(w_k^{t-n})$ (a stream of past campaign pledges [if the set is not empty]). Uninformed voters do not observe $u_i(w_k^t)$.

This election game, then, is a very complicated sequential game of incomplete information where candidates do not know $f(g)$ and some voters are informed about current candidate promises while others are not. Grossman and Stiglitz (1980) show that there may not be an equilibrium to this game since everyone can free ride on the information of everyone else, and nonexistence occurs if no one purchases information. In lieu of this, as long as we can assume that enough voters purchase information, then we can use a rational expectations equilibrium to solve the game (McKelvey and Ordeshook 1985). An equilibrium can be defined if no candidate, given his or her beliefs about the median, and no voter, given his or her beliefs about candidate positions, has a unilateral incentive to defect once all strategies are revealed. To illustrate an equilibrium of this sort, first assume d_k represents candidates beliefs about the median position, and their strategies are a function of their beliefs so that $w_A = w_A(d_A)$ and $w_B = w_B(d_B)$. Also assume that e_n represents all voters' beliefs about candidate positions, and voter strategies are a function of their beliefs so that $e_n = e_n(v_n)$, where v_n is the voting strategy of all voters. Hence, beliefs are a function of the strategies that voters and candidates choose, so that $d_k = d_k(v_n, w_A, w_B)$ and $e_n = e_n(v_n, w_A, w_B)$. If d_k^* and e_n^* are equilibrium beliefs and v_n^*, w_A^*, w_B^* are equilibrium strategies, then an equilibrium exists if:

$$w_A^* = w_B^* = y^*, \text{ and}$$

$$d_k^* = d_k(v_n^*, w_A^*, w_B^*)$$

$$e_n = e_n(v_n^*, w_A^*, w_B^*)$$

Thus, in equilibrium, everyone behaves as if they were fully informed. By making behavioral assumptions about beliefs, the equilibrium of this incomplete information game resembles the equilibrium of the full information game, in which candidates adopt the median as their election strategy.

The cost variable allows us to test the robustness of equilibrium in this game. By varying c from a low to a high level it is possible to determine the extent to which candidate convergence is dependent on contemporaneous information. If voters do, in fact, respond appropriately when c is high, then candidate convergence should be unaffected. The next section describes a procedure to experimentally replicate the spatial game depicted above.

2. Procedures

This experiment was designed to examine the behavior of voters and candidates in limited information settings. To study this question, subjects, who play the roles of candidates and voters, participate in a series of elections in which two candidates compete to be elected. As in the game specified above, candidates first select promise positions that the voters have an option to purchase for a fixed fee. After the decision to purchase information has been made, voters then cast their votes for one of the two candidates. The candidate who receives a majority of the votes is declared the winner and becomes the incumbent for that period. The incumbent then selects a position that becomes the voters' payoff. After their payoffs are revealed, the two candidates select promise positions, and the process repeats itself.

The subjects were undergraduate students at Michigan State University who were recruited by an advertisement placed in the student employment office. Two candidate subjects and three or five voter subjects were used for each experimental session. The experiment took place in a computer lab equipped with IBM PS/2 model 80 computers connected by a Token Ring local area network. Except for the reading of the instructions, all interaction in the experiment was conducted via computer terminals.

Before the experiment begins, two subjects are assigned to be candidates while the remaining subjects are voters. Candidates are instructed to pick positions from a $1,000 \times 1,000$ issue-space, where positions selected translate into monetary payoffs for voters. They are told that, during the preelection period, both candidates select positions. However, these positions are only campaign promises that relate a monetary amount that they promise to pay voters if they are elected. Candidates are informed that, after the election, only the winner selects a position to give each voter a payoff for that period. The experimenter instructs the candidates that the program perturbs the incumbent's position randomly (plus or minus seven units) so that the position chosen may or may not be the actual position selected. For example, if the incumbent selects (450, 500) as his or her position, then the actual position that pays the voters may be (452, 503). The program displays only the perturb position. Consequently, candidates may not be able to deliver the exact position they had promised. Candidates are not informed about the relationship between positions and payoffs, or how much the program perturbs the incumbent's position.

The program assigns each voter a quadratic utility function that converts candidate positions into monetary payoffs and has the following form:

$$u_i(s) = [m - h \times (s_1 - y_i^*)^2 + (s_2 - y_i^*)^2]^{1/2} \qquad (2.1)$$

where $m = 500$ and $h = 1$.

During the experiment, subjects were paid in francs that they could exchange for dollars at the end of the experiment at an exchange rate of .0014 per franc. Thus, the maximum the voter subjects could receive in an election period was 500 francs or seventy cents. Candidates were paid one dollar for each election they won. Subjects were not informed about the existence of utility functions or the maximum payoff they could receive. Two preference configurations were used that map voter ideal points into the $1,000 \times 1,000$ issue-space. The first configuration is series 1 with a median at (400,400) and the second configuration is series 2 with a median at (700,700). Figure 1 contains the two preference configurations and table 1 contains the voter ideal points and the median for each series. Each experimental session consists of running series 1 followed by series 2. Subjects were told before the experiment began that they would participate in two experiments.

Each subject is assigned to a terminal that is positioned to prevent sub-

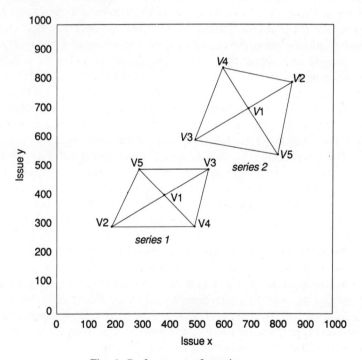

Fig. 1. Preference configurations

TABLE 1. Ideal Points

Voter	Series 1	Series 2
1	400,400	700,700
2	300,200	800,850
3	500,600	600,550
4	300,500	850,600
5	500,300	550,800

jects from seeing the screens of other subjects. To begin the experiment the program randomly picks an initial incumbent. The incumbent selects a strategy that gives each voter a payoff. This amount is revealed on the voters' screens and the strategy is displayed on the candidates' screens. A two-stage election game is then held with a campaign period followed by an election. During the campaign period both candidates select a position from the issue-space that is their pledge or a position they promise to adopt if they are elected. Again these strategies are displayed on the candidates' screens. Voters have the option to purchase this information about campaign pledges for a fixed fee. Those voters who purchase information have the promised payoffs displayed on their screen. After the voters see the promises, an election is held and they vote for one of the two candidates. The winner of the election and the vote margin then appear on all the subjects' screens. In addition, the candidates see the number of voters who purchased information. The incumbent then selects a policy to provide voters with a payoff for that election period. If a voter purchased information, then the program automatically deducts that amount from his or her payoff. This process repeats itself for a specified time limit, but subjects are not told in advance when it will end.

Using this design, two different trials that varied the cost of information were conducted. Trial 1 is a low-cost information experiment where information cost each voter three cents. Trial 2 is a high-cost information experiment and information cost nine cents. In each trial, voters were informed that they had the option to purchase information and they were under no obligation to purchase it.

Overall, twenty experiments were conducted, ten trial 1 experiments and ten trial 2. Within each trial, five experiments were conducted using series 1 and five using series 2. The length of each experiment was determined randomly and the number of election periods varied from twenty-one to thirty-three rounds with an average of twenty-eight rounds. Each experimental session lasted approximately two hours. Voters were paid, on average, $0.37 per round or $20.00 per experimental session.

3. Results

The results confirm the conjecture that varying the cost of information affects the rate of consumption. In trial 1, where information cost three cents, information was purchased, on average, 70 percent of the time (with a standard deviation of .195), and in trial 2, where information cost nine cents, it was purchased, on average, 44 percent of the time (with a standard deviation of .286). Figure 2 graphically displays the trends of information purchasing between the two trials. As illustrated, raising the cost substantially reduced the demand for information, and the negative trend indicates that information was purchased less as the experiment proceeded. Consequently, varying information costs has the desired effect of producing two electorates in which voters are relatively more informed in one than the other.

Candidate Convergence

It is clear from the results that candidates converge to or near the median in nearly every case. However, there are differences among the experiments in the rate and accuracy of convergence. Figure 3 contains the incumbent positions for six experiments. Experiments 1 and 2 are examples where incumbent strategies converge rather rapidly to the median and remain there for the duration of the experiment. The next two experiments, 3 and 4, illustrate series where incumbent strategies slowly converge to the med-

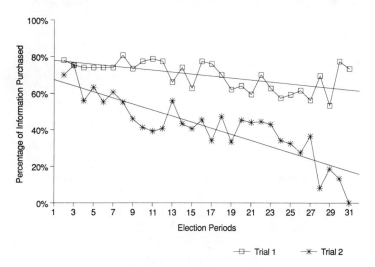

Fig. 2. Percentage of information purchased

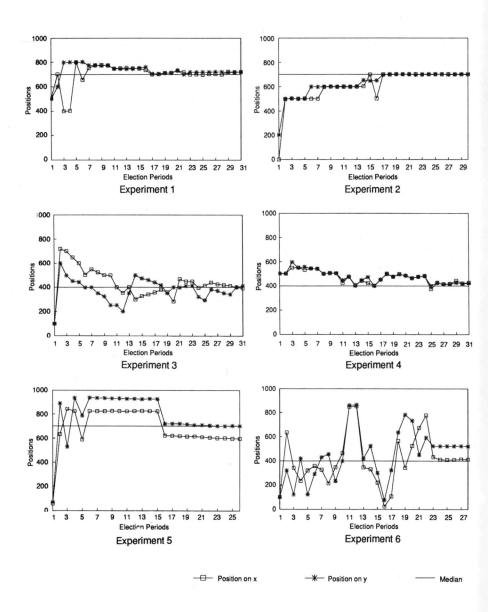

Fig. 3. Incumbent positions

ian. The final two experiments, 5 and 6, are cases where incumbents locate the median on one dimension but fail to find the median on the second dimension.

To examine the rate at which incumbent positions converge to the median, the data are analyzed first on an aggregate level where an observation is the average of periods across elections. Table 2 contains the average distance from the median for the first five rounds, the antepenultimate five rounds, the penultimate five rounds, and the ultimate five rounds. The combined results show that distance from the median decreases as the experiment proceeds. The table also contains average distances for trial 1 and trial 2. It is interesting that these two trials are similar until the last five election periods where trial 1 converges substantially more than trial 2. To differentiate the convergence rates of the two trials, the aggregated data of the trends of convergence are graphically displayed in figure 4. Notice that the trend for the low information cost experiment converges to the median at a slightly faster rate than the high-cost information series. To test the significance of the differences in convergence rates, we regress the distance incumbent positions are from the median against the number of election periods. Formally, the following log-linear model is first estimated on the aggregate data set:

$$\delta_t = \alpha e^{\beta t}, \tag{3.1}$$

where

$$\delta_t = \sum_{t=1}^{n} [(s_{1t} - y_1)^2 + (s_{2t} - y_2)^2]^{1/2}$$

and

$$\delta_t = 0 = y_i^*.$$

TABLE 2. Average Distance from Median

	Grouping of Rounds			
	First	Antepenultimate	Penultimate	Ultimate
Trial 1	189.08	148.20	123.03	79.72
Trial 2	224.19	176.73	126.99	123.69
Combined	206.63	162.46	125.01	101.70

Note: Rounds are presented in groups of five; the total rounds in each trial were not equal.

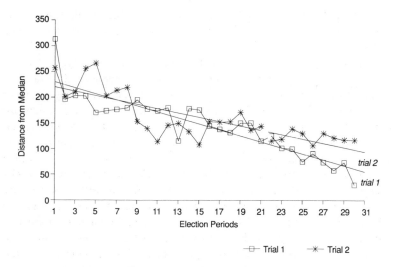

Fig. 4. Rates of convergence

The regression results in table 3 show that the direction of convergence is as expected ($\beta < 0$) for both trials. The comparable constant terms and negative beta coefficients guarantee eventual convergence. The results show that the beta coefficient for trial 1 is twice the magnitude of the beta coefficient for trial 2. The R^2 is also higher for trial 1. To further test the differences in

TABLE 3.   Estimates of Incumbent Convergence

	α	β	Corrected R^2	N
		Aggregate Results		
Trial 1	5.59 (61.38)	−0.04 (−9.47)	.76	30
Trial 2	5.38 (80.0)	−0.02 (−6.34)	.58	29
		Individual Results		
Trial 1	5.41 (48.73)	−0.05 (−7.81)	.18	279
Trial 2	5.44 (33.63)	−0.05 (−5.91)	.11	267

Note: Figures in parentheses are *t*-ratios.

TABLE 4. Combined Results with Information Costs Dummy

	α	β	Dummy (t-ratio)	Corrected R^2	N
Trials 1 and 2	2.14	−4.55	10.20	.134	548
	(22.34)	(−9.19)	(1.25)		

convergence rates between trials, the model was estimated using a disaggregated data set where each election period is an observation. These results are also contained in table 3. The estimated beta coefficients are both negative and significant, indicating convergence for both trials. However, the beta coefficient for trial 2 is the same magnitude as the coefficient for trial 1, suggesting that there is no significant difference in the rate of convergence. To further test the effect of information costs on convergence, regression equation 3.1 was run on the individual-level data for both trials with a dummy variable for level of costs. Notice in table 4 that the *t*-statistic for the dummy variable indicates that it is not significantly different from zero.

These results show that candidate convergence was not affected by varying information costs. Convergence occurs in both trials at approximately the same rate. In the next section I examine the behavior of voters and candidates to determine the extent to which raising information costs influenced decision making. This is important because it is predicted that, if both voters and candidates behave accordingly, then convergence to the median is assured. The behavior of these actors is analyzed by seeing how well their choices fit simple decision models.

Behavior of Actors

Aside from the differences in the amount of information purchased, there is evidence that subjects were reacting to information costs. First, to examine the behavior of voters, a simple voting model is estimated in which voters compare the promise positions of the incumbent, c_t, with the challenger, z_t, and vote for the candidate who offers the highest payoff. Formally, a voter uses the following decision rule:

$$\text{if } (w_z^t - y_i) \geq (w_c^t - y_i), \text{ then vote for the incumbent;} \qquad (3.2)$$

otherwise vote for the challenger.

This decision rule, of course, assumes that voters are fully informed of the issues that candidates adopt. Overall, 82 percent of all decisions are consistent with this voting rule. In the first trial, 85.5 percent of all voting decisions fit this model, while in the second trial 78.0 percent of all voting decision fit. Even though this model implies full information by assuming that voters observe w_k each election period, in trial 2, where less than half the electorate is uninformed on average, 78 percent of the subjects vote as if they have full information. Table 5 divides subjects within each trial to examine the consistency of voting decisions for subjects who purchased information and those who did not purchase it. Notice that in trial 1, 92 percent of informed subjects and 71 percent of uninformed subjects voted correctly, while in trial 2, 93 percent of informed voters and only 65 percent of uninformed voters voted correctly. Hence, when information was cheap and more readily available, uninformed voters made better decisions. Notice, also, that in both trials between 7 percent and 8 percent of voters who were informed voted against their self-interest. This may be due to the reputation of the candidates, and voters who attempt to punish candidates who reneged on their promises. Recall that candidates were under no obligation to keep their promises, and, in fact, incumbents were limited in their ability to do so since their selected positions were perturbed. As a result, there were instances where the incumbent made a promise that appealed to voters and selected the same position as his or her policy; the perturb position, however, actually yielded lower payoffs than the voters expected. Thus, even though voters purchased information and saw that one candidate was promising higher payoffs, they may not have had confidence that the candidate would deliver his or her promise due to past experience. Another candidate may promise lower payoffs, but voters vote for him or her because he or she has consistently delivered higher payoffs than the other candidate.

Candidate performance is estimated by seeing how well candidates fit a

TABLE 5. Vote Consistency and Information Procurement, in Percentages

	Trial 1		Trial 2	
	Consistent	Not Consistent	Consistent	Not Consistent
Combined	85.5	14.5	78.0	22.0
	(1013)	(171)	(858)	(248)
Bought information	92.0	8.0	93.0	7.0
	(755)	(66)	(464)	(34)
No information	71.0	29.0	65.0	35.0
	(258)	(105)	(394)	(214)

Note: The number of subjects are included in parentheses.

simple model in which the candidate whose campaign pledge is closest to the median wins. Let W be the set of winning candidates; then

$$K_A \in W \text{ if } |w_B - y^*| > |w_A - y^*| \tag{3.3}$$

and

$$K_B \in W \text{ if } |w_A - y^*| > |w_B - y^*|.$$

Estimating this model reveals that 77.5 percent of all candidate actions are consistent with this simple decision rule. Comparing the trials show that 81 percent of the subjects fit the model in trial 1, while 74 percent fit the model in trial 2. By using these two simple models of voter and candidate behavior, 80 percent of all decisions can be explained. Candidates and voters, however, both performed better when information costs are low and their behavior more closely approximates the behavior expected under conditions of full information.

To examine factors that may explain the differences in the behavior of subjects, I estimate two Probit models using a disaggregated data set where each election period for each voter is an observation. The first Probit model examines voting behavior and seeks to determine which information variables increase the likelihood of a voter voting for the candidate whose promise is closest to their ideal point. The model incorporates both contemporaneous and retrospective information variables to determine which, if any, are correlated with voting decisions. The dependent variable is $VCOR_t$, which is 1 if a voter's decision is consistent with voting rule 3.2 and 0 otherwise. The model to be estimated is:

$$\Pr(VCOR_t = 1) = 1 - \Phi(\beta_0 + \beta_1 IC_t + \beta_2 IZ_t + \beta_3 VOT_{t-1} + \beta_4 \Delta P_t), \tag{3.4}$$

where $\Phi(x) = \int_{-\infty}^{x} \frac{1}{2\pi} e^{-t^2/2} \, dt$ is the cumulative normal density function.

Also IC_t indicates, if a voter purchased information, the value of the incumbent's promise (if purchase information, then $u_i(w_c^t)$; 0 otherwise), and IZ_t indicates, if a voter purchased information, the value of the challenger's promise (if purchase information, then $u_i(w_z^t)$; 0 otherwise). VOT_{t-1} is whether a voter voted for the incumbent in election period $t - 1$ (1 if yes, 0 otherwise). ΔP is the difference in payoffs from the incumbent in election period t to period $t - 1$ or the variance in a voter's payoff $(u_i[s_c^t] - u_i[s_c^{t-1}])$.

The results of the estimation for the two trials are presented in table 6. First, notice that the coefficients for the contemporaneous information variables, IC_t and IZ_t, are significant and have the correct directions in both trials. Thus, information increases the likelihood that voters will vote correctly, and information from the incumbent is positively related while the challenger's position is negatively related. The next two variables, VOT_{t-1} and ΔP_t, are measures of retrospective evaluations. Interestingly, these variables are only significant in trial 2, when information consumption is low, indicating that voters rely on these retrospective sources to shortcut high costs. Thus, the tendency toward incumbency voting and variance in payoffs increases the likelihood that voters will vote correctly when information costs are high.

To evaluate the chances of a candidate getting reelected, a second Probit model is estimated to explain $REELECT_t$, the likelihood that the incumbent is reelected in election period t. This variable is 1 if the incumbent is reelected and 0 otherwise. The model to be estimated is:

$$\Pr(REELECT_t = 1) = 1 - \Phi(\beta_0 + \beta_1\delta_t + \beta_2 c\delta_t + \beta_3 DIFF_t + \beta_4 UTIL_t + \beta_5 INFO_t) \tag{3.5}$$

In the equation, δ_t is the distance the incumbent's policy is from the median in election period t. Variable $c\delta_t$ is the distance the challenger's promise is from the median in election period t; $DIFF_t$ is the difference in the distance the incumbent's and challenger's promises are from the median ($[w_c^t - y^*] - [w_z^t$

TABLE 6. Probit Estimates of Voter Decisions

Variable	Trial 1	Trial 2
Constant	.093	.066
	(.091)	(.086)
IC_t	.005**	.004**
	(.0006)	(.0007)
IZ_t	-.002**	-.001*
	(.0006)	(.0007)
VOT_{t-1}	.175	.237*
	(.095)	(.094)
ΔP_t	.0002	.001*
	(.0005)	(.0004)
Log Likelihood	-279.82	-161.51
N	1,184	1,106

Note: Standard errors are in parentheses.
$*P = .05.$ $**P = .001.$

$- y^*$]). This variable will be negative when the incumbent's promise position is closer to the median than the challenger's. UTIL$_t$ is the positive increase in a voter's payoff from election period $t - 1$ to t ($u_i[s_c^t]$ if $u_i[s_c^t] \geq u_i[s_c^{t-1}]$; 0 otherwise). Finally, INFO$_t$ is whether or not a voter purchased information in election period t (1 if purchased information; 0 otherwise).

The results of the estimation are contained in table 7. Notice that in both trials the coefficients for δ_t are negative and significant, indicating that the likelihood of reelection increases, the closer the incumbent's policy is to the median. Next, UTIL$_t$ is significant and negative in both trials. Thus, small changes or stability in voter's payoffs, rather than large positive changes in payoffs, increase the likelihood of reelection for the incumbent. This suggests that incumbents who find a winning position increase their chances of reelection by not deviating from positions that won in the past.

The next two variables, $c\delta_t$ and DIFF$_t$, measure the significance of the challenger's position. In trial 1, when information costs are low, the challenger's distance from the median is significant and positively related, while in trial 2 this variable is significant and negatively related. This same trend is found with DIFF$_t$, which is significant in both trials but positive in trial 1 and negative in trial 2. Thus, when information costs are low, the probability of reelection for the incumbent increases the further the challenger is from the median. That is, stark differences between the candidates matter when voters are informed about both candidates. However, when voters are

TABLE 7. Probit Estimates of Reelection

Variable	Trial 1	Trial 2
Constant	.691**	1.12**
	(.090)	(.090)
δ_t	−.002**	−.001*
	(−.0004)	(.0005)
$c\delta_t$	.002**	−.002**
	(.0005)	(.0006)
DIFF$_t$	.002**	−.002**
	(.0005)	(.0006)
UTIL$_t$	−.004**	−.008**
	(.0006)	(.0008)
INFO$_t$	−.208**	−.002
	(.086)	(.029)
Log Likelihood	−128.45	−146.17
N	1,184	1,106

Note: Standard errors are in parentheses.
*$p = .05$.   **$p = .001$.

relatively uninformed, more voting errors are committed, and even though the challenger may perform well, more voters are unaware of this fact. Hence, when information costs are low, voters have access to information about the challenger and can more readily judge his or her performance. Conversely, when costs are high, this information is scarce, and challengers who adopt winning positions often lose. Finally, the coefficient for $INFO_t$ is negative and significant in trial 1 and not significant in trial 2. This confirms the conjecture that when information costs are low, information acquisition decreases the chances of reelection for the incumbent. However, when information costs are high, this variable is not significant, indicating that the incumbent's performance is a major determinant of reelection.

To further examine the effect of information acquisition on the incumbent's reelection chances, table 8 divides the trials into instances when the incumbent was reelected and instances when information was purchased and not purchased. Incumbents did slightly better in trial 1 than trial 2 (70 percent compared to 69 percent), however, the importance in these tables is revealed by examining the differences between reelection rates when subjects purchased and did not purchase information. In both cases, the reelection rate of the incumbent increased when information was not purchased; from 67 percent to 75 percent in trial 1 and from 65 percent to 71 percent in trial 2.

These result show that incumbents have an advantage when the electorate consists of uninformed voters. That is, uninformed voters are more likely to vote for the incumbent than informed voters. Thus, in general, when voters are relatively uninformed, retrospective signals from incumbents are more important in determining election outcomes, and when voters are relatively more informed, the challenger's performance becomes an important determination.

TABLE 8.   Reelection and Information Procurement, in Percentages

	Trial 1		Trial 2	
	Reelected	Not Reelected	Reelected	Not Reelected
Combined	70	30	69	31
	(823)	(361)	(758)	(348)
Bought information	67	33	65	35
	(552)	(269)	(324)	(174)
No information	75	25	71	29
	(271)	(92)	(434)	(174)

Note: The number of subjects are included in parentheses.

4. Discussion

The traditional spatial model of candidate competition predicts that if voters and candidates are fully informed, then, in equilibrium, candidate strategies will converge to the median voter's ideal point. This study experimentally demonstrates that, if we weaken the information conditions for the actors, then candidate convergence still occurs. In the experiment, candidates do not know the distribution of voter ideal points, and voters have only retrospective information about the incumbent's past payoff, thus they do not know the current position that the candidates adopt. However, in each election period, candidates select promise positions that the voters can purchase for a nominal fee. In order to examine the behavior of candidates and voters operating within two different electorates (relatively informed and uninformed), the cost of information was varied from three cents to nine cents.

The result show that varying the cost of information has no effect on the rate at which candidates converge to the median. However, there were differences in voting behavior between the trials. When information costs are low, information from both the incumbent and challenger is significant; when information costs are high, retrospective cues from the incumbent are more significant. A similar trend was found when evaluating the reelection chances of the incumbent. When voters are relatively more informed, a poor performance by the challenger increases the likelihood of reelection for the incumbent; when voters have less information, the challenger's performance becomes less important. In other words, when information costs are high, the incumbent may offer less attractive payoffs in a current election period. However, uninformed voters are unaware of this fact, and simply vote for the incumbent based on past performance. In fact, the Probit analysis provided evidence that information decreases the chance of reelection for the incumbent. This result is consistent with that found in Collier et al. 1987, in which reelection was also found to be a function of the incumbent's performance. Recall in those experiments, voters were given access only to retrospective information about the incumbent's payoff. Consequently, the present experiments show that incumbents increase their chances of winning when the electorate confronts high costs and is relatively uninformed.

Considering the objections to the traditional spatial model of candidate competition, these results show that candidate convergence is not dependent on the full information assumption. Even though more errors were committed by voters in the high-cost trial, there was enough correct voting so that candidates could identify and select winning strategies. These experiments provide evidence that voters and candidates can learn from the actions of each other in limited information settings.

APPENDIX

Instructions

This experiment is a study of voting in elections. As subjects you will each be assigned to be either a voter or a candidate, and you will each be paid for your participation on the basis of the decisions that you make. If you are careful and make good decisions, you can make a substantial amount of money. However, the payoffs in the experiments are not necessarily fair. Your payoff depends partly on your decisions, partly on the decisions of others, and partly on chance. The experiment uses computer terminals, and when we begin you will each be assigned to a terminal. The entire experiment will take place through a network connecting the terminals.

In this experiment, there are two candidates, A and B, and the rest of you are voters. The experiment is divided into a number of election periods, and each period consists of two steps. The first step consist of a campaign, where each candidate makes a campaign promise. I will explain the meaning of campaign promises later, but for now just think of promises as a method candidates use to convince voters to vote for them. After candidates have made their promises, voters will have the option to have these promises revealed to them for a fixed cost. In the second stage, an election takes place where you vote for one of the two candidates. The winning candidate then provides the voters with a payoff. After voters receive payoffs, the candidates will again make a campaign promise, and an election will be held. This process repeats itself for an unspecified time period.

To begin the experiment, in the first period an initial incumbent is chosen randomly. The incumbent then picks a position that translates into payoffs for each voter. This payoff will be revealed to you on the computer monitor. After payoffs are revealed, voters all vote whether to elect candidate A or B—that is, whether to make A or B the incumbent for that period. The vote is tallied and announced, and the winning candidate becomes the "incumbent" for that period. After the winner has been announced, an election campaign will follow. In this stage, both the incumbent and the challenger each choose an election strategy. These are positions the candidates promise to adopt if they are elected. Again, think of these positions as a stance candidates adopt on a particular issue. After candidates have chosen positions, voters are allowed to purchase this information about the candidates' campaign promise for a fee of three (nine) cents. Those voters who purchase information will be told the monetary amount associated with the incumbent's and challenger's promise. After you learn this information, you vote for one of the two candidates. After the election, the candidate who is elected selects a policy that becomes your payoff for that period. This payoff is presented in "francs," and can be exchanged for dollars at the end of the experiment.

Summarizing events then, an election period consists of: (1) selection of promised positions by the incumbent and the challenger, (2) the voter's decision whether or not to purchase information about the challenger's or incumbent's promise, (3) revelation of this information to those who purchase it, (4) voting, (5) announcement of winner, and (6) the incumbents selection of policy for payment.

Voters. All voters have the option to purchase information about the candidates' promised positions. Whether or not you purchased information, you must then vote for one of the two candidates. I would like to emphasize that you have the option to purchase information, you are under no obligation to actually purchase it if you do not want to. This information is only provided to help you select candidates.

Candidates. All candidates pick promised positions during the campaign period. After the campaign period is over, the winner of the election picks a position that translates into payoffs for voters. Then, both candidates again pick promised positions. Voters decide whether or not to purchase information, and vote. The winner is announced, and the winner picks a position to pay the voters.

Candidates are paid based on the number of elections they win (one dollar for each election they win), and voters are paid based on the positions chosen by incumbents. Voter payoffs will be in "francs" during the experiment and will be converted to dollars after the experiment ends (I will show you an example later).

Note that a voter's payoff in a given period does not depend on who that person voted for, but only on the policy adopted by the current incumbent. Thus, if *A* is elected, and if *A* adopts a policy that gives you a certain amount of money, then you receive that amount regardless of whether you voted for *A* or *B*—less, of course, the cost of information if you chose to purchase information. Your vote can affect who is elected, but once that candidate is elected, you have no further control over your payoff. Your payoff in a given period depends entirely on the policy that the incumbent decides to adopt after he or she is elected.

One important rule of this experiment is that once we begin, *no one is allowed to talk to anyone else.* The only communication permitted is the communication that occurs over your computer terminals.

Again, the candidates are paid for their participation in the experiment on the basis of the number of elections that they win. Thus, each time a candidate is elected as the incumbent, he or she receives a fixed payoff. This will be displayed on the candidate's screen, and added to his or her cumulative total.

The payoffs of voters, as we have already stated, depend on the policy of the incumbent. No one, including the candidates, will be told, however, the relationship between policy and payoffs. Different voters may have different functions relating payoffs to policy. Thus, a particular policy may greatly benefit one voter but be strongly disliked by another. Voters will also not be told the maximum payoff possible in a period.

The process I have described will continue for a fixed number of periods, or until a given time has elapsed. At that point, the first experiment will end, and you should each record your cumulative payoff on the sheet provided. Then, a second experiment will begin, which will be similar to the first, except that the function relating each voters' payoff to the incumbent's policy may be different than in the first experiment. Between each experiment, voters may be shuffled and the candidates may be relabeled. So, for example, if candidate *A* wins many more elections in the first experiment, you should not suppose that letting *B* win more in the second will equalize payoffs—it may benefit the same person.

We will have a five-period trial session where the experimenter will explain the information that will appear on your display. You will not be paid for the trial session, although the payoffs you would receive if this were a real session will be computed. After the trial session, please ask questions. I would like to emphasize that the number of rows on the screen should not be interpreted as limiting the number of periods in an actual experiment, since data on the screen can scroll up and off the screen to make room for as many periods as we choose.

REFERENCES

Abramson, Paul R., John H. Aldrich, and David W. Rohde. 1990. *Change and Continuity in the 1988 Elections.* Washington, D.C.: Congressional Quarterly Press.
Berelson, Bernard, Paul F. Lazarsfeld, and William McPhee. 1954. *Voting: A Study of Opinion Formation in a Presidential Election.* Chicago: University of Chicago Press.
Calvert, Randall L. 1985. "Robustness of the Multidimensional Voting Model: Candidate Motivations, Uncertainty, and Convergence." *American Journal of Political Science* 29:69–95.
Campbell, Angus, Philip E. Converse, Warren E. Miller, and Donald E. Stokes. 1960. *The American Voter.* New York: Wiley.
Collier, Kenneth E., Richard D. McKelvey, Peter C. Ordeshook, and Kenneth C. Williams. 1987. "Retrospective Voting: An Experimental Study." *Public Choice* 53:101–30.
Collier, Kenneth E., Peter C. Ordeshook, and Kenneth C. Williams. 1989. "The Rationally Uninformed Electorate: Some Experimental Evidence." *Public Choice* 60:3–29.

Coughlin, Peter J. 1986. "Elections and Income Distribution." *Public Choice* 50:27–91.

Davis, Otto. A., and Melvin J. Hinich. 1966. "A Mathematical Model of Policy Formation in Democratic Society." In *Mathematical Applications in Political Science*, ed. Joseph Bernd. Vol. 2. Dallas: Southern Methodist University Press.

Denzau, Arthur T., and Michael C. Munger. 1986. "Legislators and Interest Groups: How Unorganized Interests Get Represented." *American Political Science Review* 80:89–106.

Downs, Anthony. 1957. *An Economic Theory of Democracy.* New York: Harper and Row.

Enelow, James, and Melvin J. Hinich. 1984. *The Spatial Theory of Voting: An Introduction.* Cambridge: Cambridge University Press.

Ferejohn, John. 1986. "Incumbent Performance and Electoral Control." *Public Choice* 50:5–25.

Ferguson, Thomas. 1983. "Party Realignment and American Industrial Structure: The Investment Theory of Parties in Historical Perspective." In *Research in Political Economy*, ed. P. Zarembka. Vol. 6. Greenwich: JAI Press.

Fiorina, Morris P. 1981. *Retrospective Voting in American National Elections.* New Haven: Yale University Press.

Grossman, Sanford, and Joseph Stiglitz. 1980. "On the Impossibility of Information Efficient Markets." *American Economic Review* 70:393–408.

Key, V. O., Jr. 1966. *The Responsible Electorate: Rationality in Presidential Voting, 1936–1960.* Cambridge, Mass.: Harvard University Press.

Kinder, Donald R., and David O. Sears. 1985. "Political Psychology." In *The Handbook of Political Psychology*, ed. G. Lindzey and E. Aronson. New York: Random House.

Ledyard, John O. 1989. "Information Aggregation in Two-Candidate Elections." In *Models of Strategic Choice in Politics*, ed. Peter C. Ordeshook. Ann Arbor: University of Michigan Press.

McKelvey, Richard D., and Peter C. Ordeshook. 1984. "Rational Expectations and Elections: Some Experimental Results Based on a Multidimensional Model." *Public Choice* 44:61–102.

McKelvey, Richard D., and Peter C. Ordeshook. 1985. "Elections with Limited Information: A Fulfilled Expectations Model Using Contemporaneous Poll and Endorsement Data as Information Sources." *Journal of Economic Theory* 36:55–85.

McKelvey, Richard D., and Peter C. Ordeshook. 1986. "Information, Electoral Equilibrium, and the Democratic Ideal." *Journal of Politics* 48:910–37.

Page, Benjamin. 1976. *Choices and Echoes in Presidential Elections.* Chicago: University of Chicago Press.

Popkin, Samuel, John W. Gorman, Charles Phillips, and Jeffrey A. Smith. 1976. "What Have You Done for Me Lately: Toward an Investment Theory of Voting." *American Political Science Review* 20:779–805.

Roberts, Brian E. 1989. "Voters, Investors, and the Consumption of Political Information." In *Models of Strategic Choice in Politics*, ed. Peter C. Ordeshook. Ann Arbor: University of Michigan Press.

Part 2
Committee Decision Making

An Experimental Test of a Stochastic Game Model of Committee Bargaining

Richard D. McKelvey

1. Introduction

There have been numerous solution concepts proposed for cooperative games over the past couple of decades. Most of these solutions were initially developed for games with sidepayments, and then extended to nontransferable utility games. Besides the core and the von Neumann–Morgenstern solution, there is the bargaining set (Peleg 1963; Aumann and Maschler 1964; Asscher 1976), the competitive solution (McKelvey, Ordeshook, and Winer 1978), and the aspiration bargaining set (Bennett 1983; Bennett and Zame 1988).

Despite the plethora of solution concepts, all of them are essentially ordinal in nature. This presents some problems in applying the solutions to experimental data. First, the solution concepts only make set-valued predictions. Second, in any two profiles that are ordinally equivalent, a given solution concept should make equivalent predictions. Regarding the first point, the experimental data seem to show consistent patterns in which alternatives are adopted with different probabilities, and set-valued predictions would not be able to predict such a phenomenon. Regarding the second point, there is strong experimental evidence that the actual utility values matter. It is not hard to construct profiles that are ordinally equivalent but cardinally different, which leads to consistently different experimental outcomes.

In this article, I investigate the usefulness of modeling finite cooperative nontransferable utility games as a stochastic noncooperative game. The model used here is the same as a model recently studied by Baron and Ferejohn (1987), and uses ideas originally introduced by Rubinstein (1982). Namely, it

This is a revision of a paper that was originally presented at the International Conference on Coalition Theory and Public Choice, Fiesole, Italy, May 25–29, 1987. The work was supported, in part, by NSF grant SES-86-04384 to the California Institute of Technology. I thank Richard Boylan for his comments on previous drafts, and for his help in running the experiments.

is assumed that bargaining can be modeled as an infinitely repeated game in which one individual makes an offer, and the remaining individuals decide whether or not to accept the offer. The game ends when an offer is accepted, and each individual has time preferences represented by a discount factor. As in Baron and Ferejohn, I assume that the proposer is selected randomly each period, and that a proposal is accepted when a majority vote to accept it.

The model is developed here only for a finite alternative situation, and specific computations are only made for a three-voter example. However, in the cases analysed, the model has a unique, stationary, subgame perfect equilibrium that makes specific predictions about the probability that various alternatives will be the final outcome agreed on. The theoretical probabilities that alternatives are chosen is a function of the cardinal utility values assigned to them by the players. So the model has the potential of providing an explanation for the observed relation in experimental data between the cardinal utility values of alternatives and their probability of occurrence. The model also makes predictions about the probability that the selected proposer will propose a given alternative, about the probability an alternative will be accepted by a majority given that it has been proposed, and about how long the bargaining will last. Unlike the Rubinstein model, the equilibrium involves mixed strategies and does not necessarily predict that the first proposal is accepted.

This article computes the stationary solution of the stochastic model for some simple three-person, three-alternative examples, and I then conduct experiments under the exact extensive form specified by the model. I also conduct experiments in which a fair alternative is added to the basic three-alternative cycle and find that the data from my experiments is not explained well by the stationary solution.

2. Previous Experiments

There are two phenomena that occur consistently in the experimental literature on bargaining in committee settings that cannot be explained by existing solution theories for cooperative games. The first is the fact that, in given experimental designs in which various solution theories make only set-valued predictions, the experimental data show that different alternatives within the solution set occur with significantly different relative frequencies. The frequency with which the alternatives occur is sensitive to the cardinal utilities attached to the alternatives. The simplest example of this occurs in experiments that have been done in finite alternative settings. McKelvey and Ordeshook (1983), for example, have run experiments with three voters and three alternatives in which the alternatives are in a majority-rule voting cycle, as in figure 1. Here, the entries represent von Neumann–Morgenstern utility

	1	2	3
A	1	a	0
B	0	1	b
C	c	0	1

Fig. 1. Normalized three-alternative cycle

values, and a, b, and c are numbers strictly between 0 and 1. These experiments are run as characteristic function form games, where any majority coalition is effective for any outcome. When any majority can agree on the final outcome, they can then terminate the experiment by signing for the proposal they agree to. The games are run without any possibility of sidepayments or transferable utility. The outcomes of these experiments show that, with different values of a, b, and c, the frequency distribution of the final outcomes is different. Thirteen experiments were run with the values $a = .5$, $b = .8$, $c = .2$, yielding the following distribution of final outcomes: $A = 2$, $B = 9$, $C = 2$. A whole series of experiments on five-person committees run by McKelvey and Ordeshook (1979) and by Gretlein (1981) show similar tendencies for the outcomes not to be uniformly distributed over the solution set.

The second phenomenon that is observed in experimental data is the persistent occurrence of "fair" outcomes. The frequency with which the "fair" outcomes occurs seems related to the "perceived fairness" of the alternatives—that is, to the utility values attached to the outcomes. Thus, Miller and Oppenheimer (1982) have run experiments using the preference orders of table 1. In these experiments, alternative D is a "fair" alternative whose cardinal utility is varied from \$2.10 to \$12.00. The results from the Miller and Oppenheimer experiments are reported in table 2.

Note that changing the utility assigned to D does not change the ordinal rankings of any of the players. Further, note that alternative D is not predicted by any of the standard solution theories of cooperative game theory. In fact, it is majority beaten by all of the other alternatives, so it is not even in the top

TABLE 1. Preference Orders for the Miller-Oppenheimer Experiments

Value	Player 1	Player 2	Player 3	Player 4	Player 5
14.25	F	C	B	E	A
\$13.30	C, B	E, F	A, F	A, C	E, B
V(D)	D	D	D	D	D
\$0.75	A	B	E	F	C
\$0.00	E	A	C	B	F

TABLE 2. Outcomes of the Miller-Oppenheimer Experiments (D/All Others)

V(D)	Outcomes
$12.25	5/0
$8.50	4/1
$6.72	4/1
$4.20	4/1
$2.10	1/4

cycle set. Yet D is chosen quite frequently, and the frequency with which it is chosen is related to the utility value that is associated with it. Experiments by McKelvey and Ordeshook (1983) have shown similar results to those of Miller and Oppenheimer, that is, one can obtain universalistic, or fair, outcomes by varying the utility values of the outcomes in ways that do not change the ordinal rankings.

While existing solution theories cannot predict the occurrence of fair alternatives, it is not hard to see why "rational" individuals might, in some circumstances, settle for alternative D. Note that all outcomes except D (let us call them the coalition outcomes) are good for a winning coalition, but bad for the remaining two players. If the committee were to reject D, then all of the coalition outcomes are unstable, and there is no way of telling which one will occur. If one assumes that each of the possible coalition outcomes will occur with equal probability, then the expected value to each individual from a coalition outcome is $8.32. On the other hand, if the utility from D is greater than this value, then all subjects should prefer the "fair" alternative D to the lottery between the coalition outcomes. This argument was first put forward by Klingaman (1969), and has been used by Weingast (1979) to explain universalistic outcomes in a legislative setting. Unfortunately, while the argument has been around for awhile, and has intuitive appeal, it has not been incorporated into any formal coalition theory.

3. Definitions and Notation

In this section, I define an infinitely repeated bargaining game that will be used to model the committee bargaining process. This model has the same structure as that used by Baron and Ferejohn (1987) to model bargaining in legislatures. Rather than the infinite divide-the-dollar space that they consider, only finite alternative spaces are considered here.

Assume that there is a set $N = \{1, 2, \ldots, n\}$ of players, a finite set X of alternatives, and a utility profile, $u : X \rightarrow \mathfrak{R}^n$ representing an n-tuple of von

Neumann–Morgenstern utility functions for player i over the set of alternatives. The ith component of u, u_i: $X \to \mathfrak{R}$, is the utility function for player i. Define $N_0 = N \cup \{0\}$, where "0" denotes a nonstrategic player, nature, and let T be a finite set of states. We now let $\{\Gamma^t: t \in T\}$ be a collection of game elements, $\Gamma^t = (S^t, \pi^t)$, where $S^t = \Pi_{i \in N_0} S_i^t$ is an $(n + 1)$-tuple of strategy sets and $\pi^t: S^t \times [X \cup T] \to \mathfrak{R}$ is a transition function that specifies for each $s^t \in S^t$ a probability distribution, $\pi^t(s^t, \cdot)$ on $\Delta^{\{X \cup T\}}$, which determines a probability of terminating at any outcome in X or proceeding to any other game element.

Let $S = \Pi_{t \in T} S^t$ be the set of collections of strategy $(n + 1)$-tuples, one for each game element, and $S_i = \Pi_{t \in T} S_i^t$. Then define, for any $\tau \geq 0$, $H^\tau = \Pi_{1 \leq t \leq \tau} S$ to be the set of histories of length τ and $H = \cup_{\tau=0}^{\infty} H^\tau$ to be the set of all histories. Then the set Σ_i of strategies for player i is the set of all functions $\sigma_i: H \to S_i$, and write $\Sigma = \Pi_{i \in N} \Sigma_i$ for the set of all strategy profiles. For any $\sigma \in \Sigma$, write $h^1(\sigma) = \sigma(\varnothing) \in H^1$, and $h^\tau(\sigma) = [h^{\tau-1}(\sigma)]$, $\sigma[h^{\tau-1}(\sigma)] \in H^\tau$. Given a strategy, $\sigma \in \Sigma$, define the τ round transition function, $\pi_\tau^t(\sigma, \cdot)$ on $\Delta^{\{T \cup X\}}$ inductively as follows: For any $t \in T$, and $r \in T \cup X$,

$$\pi_1^t(\sigma, r) = \pi^t[\sigma(\varnothing), r],\tag{3.1}$$

$$\pi_\tau^i(\sigma, r) = \sum_{y \in T} \pi_{\tau-1}^t(\sigma, y)\pi^y\{\sigma[h^{\tau-1}(\sigma)], r\}.$$

The value function, $v^t: \Sigma \to \mathfrak{R}^n$, can then be defined by

$$v^t(\sigma) = \sum_{\tau=0}^{\infty} \sum_{x \in X} \pi_\tau^t(\sigma, x)u(x).\tag{3.2}$$

Setting $M(\sigma) = v^0(\sigma)$, then the pair $\Gamma = (\Sigma, M)$ defines a stochastic game.

A strategy n-tuple, $\sigma \in \Sigma$, is said to be a Nash equilibrium if $M_i(\sigma_i', \sigma_{-i}) \leq M_i(\sigma)$ for all $\sigma_i' \in \Sigma_i$. A strategy n-tuple, $\sigma \in \Sigma$, is said to be stationary if $\sigma[h^\tau(\sigma)] = [h^{\tau-1}(\sigma)]$ for all τ. In this case, we can write, with some abuse of notation, $s = s(\sigma) = \sigma(\varnothing) = \sigma[h^\tau(\sigma)] \in S$ for all τ.

For a stationary strategy,

$$v^t(s) = \sum_{t=0}^{\infty} \sum_{x \in X} \pi_\tau^t(s, x)u(x),\tag{3.3}$$

where

$$\pi_\tau^t(s, r) = \sum_{y \in T} \pi_{\tau-1}^t(s, y)\pi^y(s, r),\tag{3.4}$$

and applying Bellman's optimality principle, a stationary Nash equilibrium can be characterized by a set $\{v^t\}_{t \in T} \subseteq \mathfrak{R}^n$ of values for each game element Γ^t, and a strategy $(n+1)$-tuple $s \in S$ such that for all $t \in T$, s^t is a Nash equilibrium to the game with payoff function:

$$v^t(s^t) = \sum_{x \in X} \pi^t(s^t, x)u(x) + \sum_{y \in T} \pi^t(s^t, y)v^y, \tag{3.5}$$

and also, for all t,

$$v^t(s^t) = v^t. \tag{3.6}$$

The states for our particular problem can now be defined. Let $T = N_0 \cup X$ be the set of states. The strategy sets and transition functions for the game elements are defined as follows:

$$\text{For } t = 0: \qquad S_i^t = \begin{cases} N & \text{if } i = 0 \\ \{0\} & \text{if } i \in N, \end{cases} \tag{3.7}$$

$$\pi^t(s^t, \Gamma^{s_0^t}) = 1.$$

$$\text{For } t \in N: \qquad S_i^t = \begin{cases} \{0\} & \text{if } i \in N_0 - \{t\} \\ X & \text{if } i = t, \end{cases} \tag{3.8}$$

$$\pi^t(s^t, \Gamma^{s_t^t}) = 1.$$

$$\text{For } t \in X: \qquad S_i^t = \begin{cases} \{0\} & \text{if } i = 0 \\ \{0,1\} & \text{if } i \in N, \end{cases} \tag{3.9}$$

$$\pi^t(s^t, t) = 1$$

if $\sum_{i \in N} s_i^t > \dfrac{n}{2}$

otherwise $\pi^t(s^t, \Gamma^0) = \delta$, $\pi^t(s^t, x^0) = 1 - \delta$.

Here, $0 < \delta < 1$ is a fixed discount rate, and $x^0 \in X$ is a fixed alternative satisfying $u_i(x^0) = 0$ for all $i \in N$. Thus the game Γ^0 is a game in which only nature has any moves, and it is assumed that nature moves according to a probability distribution assigning equal probability to all of its strategy choices. In the game Γ^t, for $t \in N$, only player t has any moves, and that player may choose any alternative in X for consideration by the remaining voters. Finally, in the game Γ^t, for $t \in X$, all players except chance have a move in which they can either approve or disapprove of the alternative under consideration. If a majority approve of the alternative under consideration, then the process ends, with alternative t being the final alternative adopted by the committee. However, if a majority does not approve of the alternative under consideration, then one returns to game Γ^0, and all payoffs are discounted by a factor of δ.

In this stochastic game, probabilities of movement from one game element to another are determined by the strategy choices of the players. The game has positive probability of termination each time one is in Γ^t for $t \in X$, and there are no absorbing sets not passing through such a Γ^t. Hence, it follows from the results of Sobel (1971) that a stationary Nash equilibrium strategy n-tuple exists. Further, as Sobel argues, any stationary strategy for the game will also be a Nash equilibrium in the space of unrestricted strategies (that is, where strategies in any game element at a given time may depend on the evolution of the play up until that time). It should also be noted that a stationary equilibrium is also subgame perfect, since the analysis at any time period is the same.

4. Three Voters and Three Alternatives

In this section, I solve the game of the previous section for the special case where there are three voters and three alternatives in a majority cycle. Thus $N = \{1, 2, 3\}, X = \{A, B, C\}$, and assume $u(A) = (1, a, 0), u(B) = (0, 1, b)$, and $u(C) = (c, 0, 1)$, where $0 < a < 1, 0 < b < 1$, and $0 < c < 1$. Let $v^0, v^1, v^2, v^3, v^A, v^B$, and v^C represent the values to the games $\Gamma^0, \Gamma^1, \ldots, \Gamma^C$, respectively, and write $v = v^0$. For any strategy that yields a positive probability of eventually stopping at least two different outcomes in X, we must have $0 < v < 1$. It then follows that in the games Γ^A, Γ^B, and Γ^C, two players always have dominant strategies, as follows:

$$\Gamma^A: s_1^A = 1, s_3^A = 0, \tag{4.1}$$

$$\Gamma^B: s_2^B = 1, s_1^B = 0, \quad \text{and}$$

$$\Gamma^C: s_3^C = 1, s_2^C = 0.$$

Assume that players always adopt these dominant strategies. Hence the only players with nontrivial strategy choices in these games are

$$\Gamma^A: \text{player 2}, \tag{4.2}$$

$$\Gamma^B: \text{player 3}, \quad \text{and}$$

$$\Gamma^C: \text{player 1}.$$

Let q_A, q_B, and q_C denote the probability of players 2, 3, or 1 adopting s_i

= 1 in game Γ_A, Γ_B, or Γ_C, respectively. Further, for $i \in N$, let p_{iA}, p_{iB}, and p_{iC} denote the probability, in game element Γ^i that player i adopts strategy A, B, or C, respectively. Then, using the optimality principle of equations 3.5 and 3.6, the following equalities must be satisfied:

$$v = \frac{1}{3}(v^1 + v^2 + v^3), \tag{4.3}$$

$$v^1 = p_{1A}v^A + p_{1B}v^B + p_{1C}v^C,$$

$$v^2 = p_{2A}v^A + p_{2B}v^B + p_{2C}v^C,$$

$$v^3 = p_{3A}v^A + p_{3B}v^B + p_{3C}v^C,$$

$$v^A = q_A u_A + (1 - q_A)\delta v,$$

$$v^B = q_B u_B + (1 - q_B)\delta v, \quad \text{and}$$

$$v^C = q_C u_C + (1 - q_C)\delta v.$$

Solving for v, we get

$$v = \frac{1}{3}\{(p_{1A} + p_{2A} + p_{3A})[q_A u_A + (1 - q_A)\delta v](p_{1B} + p_{2B} + p_{3B})$$

$$\times [q_B u_B + (1 - q_B)\delta v](p_{1C} + p_{2C} + p_{3C}) \tag{4.4}$$

$$\times [q_C u_B + (1 - q_C)\delta v]\},$$

which implies that v is equal to

$$\frac{(p_{1A} + p_{2A} + p_{3A})q_A u_A + (p_{1B} + p_{2B} + p_{3B})q_B u_B + (p_{1C} + p_{2C} + p_{3C})q_C u_C}{3 - [(p_{1A} + p_{2A} + p_{3A})(1 - q_A) + (p_{1B} + p_{2B} + p_{3B})(1 - q_B) + (p_{1C} + p_{2C} + p_{3C})(1 - q_C)]\delta}$$

$$\tag{4.5}$$

We solve here for the case when $0 < q_A < 1$, $0 < q_B < 1$, and $0 < q_C < 1$, identifying the region of the space of parameters for which a solution satisfying these conditions exists. The appendix solves for the other cases. Note that

$$0 < q_A < 1 \Rightarrow \delta v_2 = u_2{}^A = a, \tag{4.6}$$

$$0 < q_B < 1 \Rightarrow \delta v_3 = u_3{}^B = b, \quad \text{and}$$

$$0 < q_C < 1 \Rightarrow \delta v_1 = u_1{}^C = c.$$

So $\delta v = (c, a, b)$. But then

$$v^A = q_A u^A + (1 - q_A)\delta v = [q_A + (1 - q_A)c, a, (1 - q_A)b], \quad (4.7)$$

$$v^B = q_B u^B + (1 - q_B)\delta v = [(1 - q_B)c, q_B + q(1 - q_B)a, b], \quad \text{and}$$

$$v^C = q_C u^C + (1 - q_C)\delta v = [c, (1 - q_C)a, q_C + (1 - q_C)b].$$

But

$$v_1^A > v_1^C > v_1^B \Rightarrow p_{1A} = 1, p_{1B} = p_{1C} = 0, \quad (4.8)$$

$$v_2^B > v_2^A > v_2^C \Rightarrow p_{2B} = 1, p_{2A} = p_{2C} = 0, \quad \text{and}$$

$$v_3^C > v_3^B > v_3^A \Rightarrow p_{3C} = 1, p_{3A} = p_{3B} = 0.$$

Thus, equation 4.5 reduces to

$$v = \frac{q_A u_A + q_B u_B + q_C u_C}{3 - [(1 - q_A) + (1 - q_B) + (1 - q_C)]\delta}, \quad (4.9)$$

or, using $\delta v = (c, a, b)$,

$$\delta v = (c, a, b) = \frac{\delta}{3(1 - \delta) + \delta(q_A + q_B + q_C)} \quad (4.10)$$

$$\times (q_C c + q_A, q_A a + q_B, q_B b + q_C).$$

This yields the following equations:

$$\frac{(1 - c)}{c} q_A - q_B = \frac{3(1 - \delta)}{\delta}, \quad (4.11)$$

$$\frac{(1 - a)}{a} q_B - q_C = \frac{3(1 - \delta)}{\delta}, \quad \text{and}$$

$$-q_A + \frac{(1 - b)}{bq_C} = \frac{3(1 - \delta)}{\delta}.$$

Solving for q_A, q_B, and q_C, we get

$$q_A = 3\rho\left(\frac{1 + \beta + \beta\alpha}{\alpha\beta\gamma - 1}\right), \quad (4.12)$$

$$q_B = 3\rho \left[\frac{1 + \gamma + \gamma\beta}{\alpha\beta\gamma - 1} \right], \quad \text{and}$$

$$q_C = 3\rho \left[\frac{1 + \alpha + \alpha\gamma}{\alpha\beta\gamma - 1} \right],$$

where we define $\alpha = \dfrac{1 - a}{a}$, $\beta = \dfrac{1 - b}{b}$, $\gamma = \dfrac{1 - c}{c}$, and $\rho = \dfrac{1 - \delta}{\delta}$.

For this to be a solution, we need $0 < q_A$, $0 < q_B$, and $0 < q_C$, which holds if

$$\alpha\beta\gamma > 1 \Leftrightarrow abc < (1 - a)(1 - b)(1 - c). \tag{4.13}$$

Also, we need $q_A < 1$, $q_B < 1$, and $q_C < 1$, which holds if

$$3\rho(1 + \beta + \beta\alpha) < \alpha\beta\gamma - 1 \Leftrightarrow abc + 3\rho[abc + c(1 - b)]$$
$$< (1 - a)(1 - b)(1 - c), \tag{4.14}$$

$$3\rho(1 + \gamma + \gamma\beta) < \alpha\beta\gamma - 1 \Leftrightarrow abc + 3\rho[abc + a(1 - c)]$$
$$< (1 - a)(1 - b)(1 - c), \quad \text{and}$$

$$3\rho(1 + \alpha + \alpha\gamma) < \alpha\beta\gamma - 1 \Leftrightarrow abc + 3\rho[abc + a(1 - a)]$$
$$< (1 - a)(1 - b)(1 - c).$$

Clearly, equations 4.14 imply 4.13. So the inequalities in equations 4.14 characterize the set of values of a, b, and c that will yield an equilibrium satisfying $0 < q_A < 1$, $0 < q_B < 1$, and $0 < q_C < 1$.

Assuming that a, b, and c satisfy the inequalities of equations 4.14, let us characterize some aspects of the equilibrium. First, the probability of termination in any round (where a round is considered to be a pass through one of the game elements Γ^t, with $t \in X$), will be

$$q_T = \frac{q_A + q_B + q_C}{3} = 3\rho\frac{(3 + \alpha + \beta + \gamma + \alpha\beta + \alpha\gamma + \beta\gamma)}{\alpha\beta\gamma - 1},$$

with the expected number of rounds before termination being $\dfrac{1}{q_T}$. It follows that

$$\frac{\partial q_T}{\partial \delta} = -\frac{3(3 + \alpha + \beta + \gamma + \alpha\beta + \alpha\gamma + \beta\gamma)}{\delta^2(\alpha\beta\gamma - 1)} < 0,$$

and

$$\frac{\partial q_T}{\partial a} = \frac{3\rho}{a^2(\alpha\beta\gamma - 1)^2}[3\beta\gamma + \beta^2\gamma + \beta\gamma^2 + \beta^2\gamma^2 + 1 + \beta + \gamma] > 0.$$

Similarly $\frac{\partial q_T}{\partial b} > 0$, and $\frac{\partial q_T}{\partial c} > 0$. The probability of eventually terminating

at outcomes A, B, and C can be written q_A^*, q_B^*, and q_C^*, where $q_A^* = \frac{q_A}{3q_T}$,

$q_B^* = \frac{q_B}{3q_T}$, and $q_C^* = \frac{q_C}{3q_T}$. Setting $K = 3 + \alpha + \beta + \gamma + \alpha\beta + \beta\gamma + \alpha\gamma$, we have

$$q^* = (q_A^*, q_B^*, q_C^*)$$

$$= \frac{1}{K}(1 + \beta + \beta\alpha, 1 + \gamma + \gamma\beta, 1 + \gamma + \gamma\beta, 1 + \alpha + \alpha\gamma).$$

Note that q^* is independent of the discount rate, δ. But

$$\frac{\partial q_A^*}{\partial a} = \frac{(1 - \beta)(1 + \gamma + \gamma\beta)}{a^2 K^2} \quad \begin{cases} < 0 \quad \text{if} \quad b < \frac{1}{2} \\ > 0 \quad \text{if} \quad b > \frac{1}{2}, \end{cases}$$

$$\frac{\partial q_B^*}{\partial a} = \frac{(1 + \gamma + \gamma\beta)(1 + \beta + \gamma)}{a^2 K^2} > 0, \quad \text{and}$$

$$\frac{\partial q_C^*}{\partial a} = -\frac{2 + 3\gamma + \gamma^2}{a^2 K^2} < 0.$$

Symmetric formulas can be found for $\frac{\partial q^*}{\partial b}$ and $\frac{\partial q^*}{\partial c}$. Recall that the majority cycle proceeds from A and B to C and back to A. Raising the value of a increases the probability of eventual termination at B (the next element of the cycle) and decreases the probability of eventual termination at B (the preceding point in the cycle). Whether the probability of ending at A is raised or lowered depends on the strength of B (the next point in the cycle). If B is "strong" ($b > 1/2$), then q_A^* increases as a increases. If B is "weak," then q_A^* decreases as a increases.

It should be emphasized that these conclusions are only valid for situations that satisfy the inequalities of equations 4.14. The appendix solves for other cases. Another notable case occurs when $q_A = q_B = q_C = 1$. This case occurs when $a > \dfrac{\delta}{3 - \delta}$, $b > \dfrac{\delta}{3 - \delta}$, and $c > \dfrac{\delta}{3 - \delta}$. We have $p_{1A} = p_{2B} = p_{3C} = 1$, and, in this situation, the game ends on the first round, with the randomly selected individual proposing his or her most preferred alternative, and the pivotal voter voting for it with probability one. The value of the game for this case is $v = \dfrac{2}{3}(c, a, b)$.

5. Fair Alternatives

A "fair" alternative will not necessarily emerge as a result of a stationary equilibrium of the game described in section 3. For example, consider the case of three voters with four alternatives $X = \{A, B, C, D\}$ where $u(A) = (1, a, 0)$, $u(B) = (0, 1, b)$, $u(C) = (c, 0, 1)$, and $u(D) = (d, d, d)$. Assume $a = b = c = .8$, and $d = .7$. The unique stationary solution to this game yields $q_A = q_B = q_C = q_{D1} = q_{D2} = q_{D3} = 1, p_{1A} = 1, p_{2B} = 1, p_{3C} = 1$, and $v = (.6, .6, .6)$. The resulting probabilities of eventually terminating at the outcomes are $q_A^* = q_B^* = q_C^* = \frac{1}{3}$, and $q_D^* = 0$. Thus, even though d exceeds the value of the continuation game for all three players, none of them will ever propose D since, if they are selected to propose an alternative, they can insure their best alternative.

   While D does not emerge as an outcome from any stationary equilibrium, it is the outcome of a trigger strategy: all players, if they are selected, propose D. If D is proposed, they vote for D. If any other alternative is selected, everyone votes against it. On the first deviation from such a strategy n-tuple, players revert to the stationary equilibrium. This is a subgame perfect Nash equilibrium which results in achieving the "fair" outcome, D.

   By this line of reasoning, one can support any outcomes that are Pareto preferred to the value of the game resulting from stationary strategies. In fact, this might provide a good definition of what is meant by "fair" alternatives. Unfortunately, while this argument rationalizes the occurrence of fair alternatives, it opens up a whole can of worms—namely, the problems of multiple equilibria. In the case of multiple equilibria, we have no good theories for predicting which, if any, of the equilibria will be selected. Hence, we cannot make any predictions as to the frequency with which each equilibrium will occur. Second, while the preceding argument can be used to explain the occurrence of alternatives that are Pareto preferred to the outcome from the stationary equilibrium, it also may be used to justify the occurrence of alternatives whose utility is less than the value of the game for some players. Baron and Ferejohn (1987) show that if the alternative space is the unit simplex, then any outcome can be supported as the result of subgame perfect strategy n-tuple using appropriate punishment strategies. While I have not investigated this question, the same result may be true here.

6. Experiments

To test my theory, I conducted a number of experiments, using undergraduates from the California Institute of Technology as participants. In each experiment, one participant was selected to serve as an observer/assistant, and the remaining individuals participated as subjects. The number of subjects differed from experiment to experiment, varying from six to fifteen (see table 3). The role of the observer/assistant was to generate the random numbers for the experiment by rolling dice. The observer/assistant was paid a fixed amount ($15.00) for participating in the experiment. The remaining subjects were paid a fixed fee of $3.00 for showing up, plus whatever payoff they accumulated during the experiment.

All of the experiments were conducted on a computer network in the Caltech Experimental Economics and Political Science Laboratory, with all communication between the subjects taking place through the computer network. Each experiment consisted of a short instruction period, in which subjects could familiarize themselves with the computers, followed by twelve experimental sessions.

In each experimental session the n subjects were first matched by a prespecified matching rule into $k = n/3$ groups of three subjects each. Each of the k groups then participated in a random recognition voting game like that described in the preceding sections. A payoff table (see fig. 2) was displayed at the top of each subject's computer screen during each session.[1] The payoff table told the subject number, what the "stake" was, and, for each outcome and each subject, it gave a number between 0 and 1, representing the odds that the subject had of winning that stake. The stake is the maximum amount the subject could earn in the session. The odds told the subjects, for each outcome, the chance that they had of winning their stake if the final outcome selected by the committee was that indicated in the table. Subjects were paid in lotteries in order to induce von Neumann–Morgenstern utility functions and avoid risk preferences. To generate the lotteries, at the termination of the session, the assistant rolled two, ten-sided dice to obtain a number between 0 and 99. If the number the assistant rolled was strictly less than the odds associated with the chosen alternative, the subject won the stake for the

---

1. On the computer screen, the row corresponding to the subject's payoffs was highlighted in a different color. Once a proposal was made, the letter corresponding to the proposed alternative and the subject's own payoff for that alternative were also highlighted in a different color.

TABLE 3.   Summary of Stochastic Game Experiments

Experiment	Number of Subjects	Games per Subject	Total Games	Sequence
1	6	12	24	1
2	6	12	24	2
3	9	12	36	1
4	15	12	60	2

session; if the number rolled was greater than or equal to the odds, the subject lost, and was not paid anything for participating in that session.

Each session proceeded in a series of identical rounds. At the beginning of each round, the observer/assistant spun a fair die to pick a subject number. The subject who was selected then made a proposal; that subject could pick any of the alternatives, A, B, or C, as their proposal. This proposal was then announced to the other subjects, and all three subjects voted whether to accept the proposal or reject it. If a majority (two or more) of the subjects voted to accept the proposal, then that was the final outcome of the committee, and the session ended. If, on the other hand, a majority did not accept the proposal, then the session proceeded to the next round. However, at the beginning of each new round after the first, the stakes of all subjects were decreased by 5 percent. The second and subsequent rounds of each session were identical to the first round: A subject was picked randomly, that subject made a proposal, and the proposal was voted on by all subjects. The session proceeded in this fashion, with stakes decreasing by 5 percent each round, until a majority of the subjects accepted the proposal that was made. At that point, the session

Payoff Table

Subject	A	B	C
1	.90	.10	.50
2	.66	.90	.10
3	.10	.18	.90

You are subject #2

Your stake: $2.00

Fig. 2. Sample payoff table for experiments

ended, and the subjects wrote down the outcome selected by the committee, their stake, and their odds for the selected outcome on the record sheet that was provided. The assistant then rolled the dice to determine the subjects' payoff from the session.

After each session, the subjects were reshuffled, and a new session with a different payoff table began. After the last session, all subjects were paid, in cash, the total amount they had accumulated in all the sessions, plus their participation fee. In all the experiments reported here, we used an initial stake of $2.00, and a discount rate of 5 percent.

The entire structure of the experiment was made common knowledge, at least as much as possible in an experimental setting. In other words, the instructions were read to all subjects in the presence of the other subjects. All subjects were shown not only their own payoffs, but the payoffs of the other subjects. They were also told the procedure by which random numbers would be generated. The subjects were also told that subjects would be shuffled between each session, although they were not told the matching rule by which subjects were shuffled. During each round of the experiment, subjects in each group were informed which subject had been selected to make the proposal, and after the vote, they were told how each of the subjects voted. At the termination of the session, a lottery (as previously described) was conducted for each subject in accordance with the odds assigned to that subject for the outcome the committee selected. The subjects learned the outcome of the lottery before they began the subsequent session.

To test the stochastic game theory, we used three basic preference configurations, labeled X, Y, and Z. Configurations X and Y each had two versions, labeled X and $\overline{X}$, and Y and $\overline{Y}$, respectively. In all of these preference configurations, there were three alternatives, labeled A, B, and C, with utility functions of the form shown in figure 1. Thus, all configurations had a majority cycle in which A was defeated by B, B was defeated by C, and C was defeated by A. The only differences in the configurations were in the assignment of a, b, and c, the utilities to the second-ranked alternatives. The values of a, b, and c are given in table 4. The configurations in table 4 were chosen because they allowed us to test some fairly subtle, but important predictions

TABLE 4. Parameters Used for
Three Alternative Experiments

	X	$\overline{X}$	Y	$\overline{Y}$	Z
a	.7	.7	.1	.3	.9
b	.1	.5	.3	.1	.4
c	.5	.1	.5	.5	.4

of the stochastic theory. Namely, they allowed us to test the prediction that the location of alternatives in the cycle matters. Thus, configurations X and $\overline{X}$ are identical; both configurations have an alternative with utilities (from best to worst) of (1.0, 0.5, 0.0), one with utilities (1.0, 0.1, 0.0), and one with utilities (1.0, 0.7, 0.0). The only difference is in where the second-ranked utilities are in the cycle. Yet, as seen in table 5, this difference has major implications for the predicted probabilities of the various outcomes. Similarly, Y and $\overline{Y}$ are identical; both configurations have an alternative with utilities of (1.0, 0.5, 0.0), one with utilities (1.0, 0.3, 0.0), and one with utilities (1.0, 0.1, 0.0). Again, the only difference is in where the second-ranked utilities are in the cycle. Finally, configuration Z has two alternatives, B and C, that give the same payoffs (1, 0.4, 0.0), but the stochastic solution predicts that these alternatives will occur with different probabilities because of their location in the cycle.

Table 5 gives the predicted and actual behavior for the five configurations of preferences. The first level of the table gives the predicted probabilities q_x^* that the experiment will terminate at each of the outcomes, x. The second level gives the conditional probabilities, q_x that a majority will vote for x given that it has been proposed. Since two subjects always have dominant strategies at this stage, this is the probability that the subject with x as its second-ranked alternative will vote for x. The third level of the table gives the probability p_{ix} that subject i will propose its top-ranked alternative, x, when i has been selected as the proposer.

The most obvious deviation from the predicted behavior is in the p_{ix}'s. Here we see a consistent reluctance, across all of the configurations, to propose an alternative in which the coalition partner gets a low payoff. Thus, in configuration X, alternative B is proposed only 25 percent of the time by subject 2, and in $\overline{X}$, C is never proposed by player 3. In Y, player 1 only proposes A 10 percent of the time, and in $\overline{Y}$, subject 2 never proposes B. In all these cases, the behavior predicted by the stochastic solution is that that alternative should always be proposed.

The second feature of the data is that proposals that are made are accepted with a higher probability than they should be. Thus, with one exception, whenever there is a significant difference between the predicted and observed q_x's, the observed values are higher than the predicted values. We do not get enough observations on the q_x's associated with the low-utility alternative to know whether they are accepted with different probability than expected. If they were accepted with lower probability than expected, this would make the deviations in the proposal behavior more understandable.

The stochastic solution also yields a prediction on the duration of the experiment. Namely, it can be predicted that the experiment will last $1/q_T$ rounds on average. The last row of table 5 reports this statistic. The experi-

TABLE 5. Data from Three Alternative Experiments

	X		$\bar{X}$		Y		$\bar{Y}$		Z	
	Predicted	Actual	Predicted	Actual	Predicted	Actual	Predicted	Actual	Predicted	Actual
q_A^*	0.519	0.706	0.092	0.316*	0.510	0.059*	0.650	0.526	0.405	0.682*
q_B^*	0.412	0.000*	0.715	0.684	0.091	0.059	0.231	0.000*	0.543	0.318
q_C^*	0.070	0.294*	0.193	0.000	0.399	0.882*	0.119	0.474*	0.052	0.000
		(17)		(19)		(17)		(19)		(22)
q_A	0.766	1.000*	0.129	0.833*	0.192	0.333	0.245	1.000	1.000	0.938*
		(12)		(6)		(3)		(10)		(16)
q_B	0.608	0.000	1.000	1.000	0.034	0.200	0.087	—	1.000	1.000
		(2)		(13)		(5)		(0)		(8)
q_C	0.103	0.556*	0.271	—	0.150	1.000	0.045	1.000*	0.196	1.000*
		(9)		(0)		(15)		(9)		(6)
p_{1A}	1.000	1.000	1.000	1.000	1.000	0.100*	1.000	0.800*	1.000	1.000
		(6)		(3)		(10)		(5)		(10)
p_{2B}	1.000	0.250*	1.000	0.778	1.000	0.500*	1.000	0.000	1.000	0.333*
		(8)		(9)		(4)		(6)		(12)
p_{3C}	1.000	1.000	1.000	0.000*	1.000	0.750	1.000	1.000	0.666	0.375
		(8)		(7)		(8)		(8)		(8)
$\dfrac{1}{q_T}$	2.030	1.350	2.140	1.000	7.980	1.350	7.960	1.000	1.020	1.330
		(17)		(19)		(17)		(19)		(22)

Note: The number of observations is in parentheses.
*$p = .05$.

ments consistently end much sooner than predicted. The subjects seem to be behaving as if they are risk averse, even though I attempted to control for this by paying them in lotteries.

In addition to the three alternative experiments, I ran some four-alternative experiments in which a fourth alternative, D, is added to the same underlying cyclical structure as that in the three-alternative configurations. Thus, I set $a = b = c = .8$, and added an alternative with utility of $d = u_1(D) = u_2(D) = u_3(D)$. Three different versions of the four-alternative experiment, which differed only in the value of d, were run. The experiments are called W_5, W_6, and W_7. In W_5, $d = .5$, in W_6, $d = .6$, and in W_7, $d = .7$. The outcomes of these experiments are reported in table 6. It is clear from the results of these experiments that there is no support for the proposition that higher values of d lead to higher a probability of choosing the fair alternative. In fact, these experiments are fairly consistent in that subjects never propose the fair alternative. The only configuration in which the fair alternative was proposed was W_5, which is exactly the reverse of what would be expected.

TABLE 6.   Data from Four Alternative Experiments

	W_5		W_6		W_7	
	Predicted	Actual	Predicted	Actual	Predicted	Actual
q_A^*	0.333	0.157	0.333	0.500	0.333	0.411
q_B^*	0.333	0.473	0.333	0.166	0.333	0.235
q_C^*	0.333	0.263	0.333	0.333	0.333	0.353
q_D^*	0.000	0.105	0.000	0.000	0.000	0.000
		(17)		(19)		(17)
q_A	1.000	1.000	1.000	0.857*	1.000	1.000
		(3)		(7)		(7)
q_B	1.000	1.000	1.000	0.667*	1.000	1.000
		(9)		(3)		(4)
q_C	1.000	1.000	1.000	0.800*	1.000	1.000
		(5)		(5)		(6)
q_D	1.000	1.000	1.000	—	1.000	—
		(2)		(0)		(0)
p_{1A}	1.000	0.750*	1.000	1.000	1.000	1.000
		(4)		(3)		(7)
p_{2B}	1.000	0.900*	1.000	0.600*	1.000	1.000
		(10)		(5)		(4)
p_{3C}	1.000	1.000	1.000	0.500*	1.000	1.000
		(5)		(6)		(6)
$\dfrac{1}{q_T}$	1.000	—	1.000	—	1.000	1.000
		(17)		(19)		(17)

Note: The number of observations is in parentheses.
*$p = .05$.

7. Conclusions

The stationary solution of the stochastic model does not do a terribly good job of explaining observed experimental data. In the three alternative experiments, there is a tendency to offer too much to the coalition partner, and to accept proposals with a higher probability than predicted. In the four-alternative experiments with a fair alternative, there is no evidence that subjects choose the fair alternative. What explanations can be offered for the failure of the stochastic model? The three-alternative experiments can be explained, perhaps, by the consideration that subjects may be trying to find a nonstationary equilibrium. Subjects may offer too much to a disadvantaged coalition partner because of a fear of retaliation in successive rounds, if the proposal does not attain a majority vote. Nevertheless, such explanations seem to be inconsistent with the behavior demonstrated in the four-alternative experiments, in which subjects seem to explicitly shy away from fair alternatives.

APPENDIX

To be a stationary equilibrium, the following equality must hold:

$$3v = [p_{1A}(1 - q_A) + p_{1B}(1 - q_B) + p_{1C}(1 - q_C)]\delta v +$$
$$p_{1A}q_A u_A + p_{1B}q_B u_B + p_{1C}q_C u_C$$

$$+ [p_{2A}(1 - q_A) + p_{2B}(1 - q_B) + p_{2C}(1 - q_C)]\delta v +$$
$$p_{2A}q_A u_A + p_{2B}q_B u_B + p_{2C}q_C u_C$$

$$+ [p_{3A}(1 - q_A) + p_{3B}(1 - q_B) + p_{3C}(1 - q_C)]\delta v +$$
$$p_{3A}q_A u_A + p_{3B}q_B u_B + p_{3C}q_C u_C,$$

where $v = (v_1, v_2, v_3)$, $u_A = (1, a, 0)$, $u_B = (0, 1, b)$, and $u_C = (c, 0, 1)$. There are twenty-seven cases.

Case 1: $a < \delta v_2$, $b < \delta v_3$, $c < \delta v_1$.
Here, $q_A = q_B = q_C = 0 \Rightarrow 3v = \delta v + \delta v + \delta v = 3\delta v >=<$.

Case 2: $a < \delta v_2$, $b < \delta v_3$, $c = \delta v_1$.
Here, $q_A = q_B = 0 \Rightarrow p_{2C} = 0$, $p_{3C} = 1 \Rightarrow 3v = [p_{1A} + p_{1B}$
$+ p_{1C}(1 - q_C)]\delta v + p_{1C}q_C u_C + (p_{2A} + p_{2B})\delta v + (1 - q_C)\delta v + q_C v_C$
$< 3\delta v + (1 + p_{1C})q_C u_C \Rightarrow 3v_2 < 3\delta v_2 >=<$.

Case 3: $a < \delta v_2$, $b < \delta v_3$, $c > \delta v_1$.
Here, $q_1 = q_B = 0$, $q_C = 1 \Rightarrow p_{1C} = 1$, $p_{2C} = 0$, $p_{3C} = 1 \Rightarrow 3v = \delta v + 2u_C \Rightarrow 3v_2 = \delta v_2 \gtreqless$.

Case 4: $a < \delta v_2$, $b = \delta v_3$, $c < \delta v_1$.
As in case 2, $\gtreqless$.

Case 5: $a < \delta v_2$, $b = \delta v_3$, $c = \delta v_1$.
Here, $q_A = 0 \Rightarrow p_{1B} = 0$, $p_{2B} = p_{3C} = 1 \Rightarrow 3v = [p_{1A} + p_{1C}(1 - q_C)]\delta v + p_{1C}q_Cu_C + (1 - q_B)\delta v + q_Bu_B + (1 - q_C)\delta v + q_Cu_C \Rightarrow 3v_1 = [p_{1A} + p_{1C}(1 - q_C)]\delta v_1 + p_{1C}q_Cc + (1 - q_B)\delta v_1 + (1 - q_C)\delta v_1 + q_Cc = \delta v_1 + (1 - q_B)\delta v_1 + \delta v_1 < 3v_1 \gtreqless$.

Case 6: $a < \delta v_2$, $b = \delta v_3$, $c > \delta v_1$.
Here, $q_A = 0$, $q_C = 1 \Rightarrow p_{1C} = p_{2B} = p_{2C} = 1 \Rightarrow 3v = 2u_C + (1 - q_B)\delta v + q_Bu_B$

$$\Rightarrow v = \frac{2u_C + q_Bu_B}{3 - (1 - q_B)\delta}$$

$$\Rightarrow v_1 = \frac{2c}{3 - (1 - q_B)\delta} , \quad v_2 = \frac{q_B}{3 - (1 - q_B)\delta} ,$$

$$v_3 = \frac{2 + q_Bb}{3 - (1 - q_B)\delta} .$$

But $b = \delta v_3 \Rightarrow 3b - (1 - q_B)\delta_b = 2\delta + q_Bb\delta \Rightarrow b = \frac{2\delta}{3 - \delta}$. So if

$b = \frac{2\delta}{3 - \delta}$, this case can occur.

Case 7: $a < \delta v_2$, $b > \delta v_3$, $c < \delta v_1$.
Here, $q_A = q_C = 0$, $q_B = 1 \Rightarrow p_{1B} = 0$, $p_{2B} = p_{3B} = 1$. As in case 3, $\gtreqless$.

Case 8: $a < \delta v_2$, $b > \delta v_3$, $c = \delta v_1$.
Here, $q_A = 0$, $q_B = 1 \Rightarrow p_{1B} = 0$, $p_{2B} = 1$, $p_{3B} = 0 \Rightarrow 3v = [p_{1A} + p_{1C}(1 - q_C)]\delta v + p_{1C}q_Cu_C + p_{2B}u_B[p_{3A} + p_{3C}(1 - q_C)]\delta v + p_{3C}q_Cu_C \Rightarrow 3v_1 = [p_{1A} + p_{1C}(1 - q_C)]\delta v_1 + p_{1C}q_C\delta v_1 + [p_{3A} + p_{3C}(1 - q_C)]\delta v_1 + p_{3C}q_C\delta v_1 = 2\delta v_1 \gtreqless$.

Case 9: $a < \delta v_2$, $b > \delta v_3$, $c > \delta v_1$.

Here, $q_A = 0$, $q_B = q_C = 1 \Rightarrow p_{1C} = p_{3C} = p_{2B} = 1 \Rightarrow 3v = 2u_C$
$+ u_B \Rightarrow v_1 = \frac{2}{3}c$, $v_2 = \frac{1}{3}$, and $v_3 = \frac{2 + b}{3}$. But $a < \delta v_2 \Leftrightarrow a <$
$\frac{\delta}{3}$, $b > \delta v_3 \Leftrightarrow b > \frac{2\delta}{3 - \delta}$, and $c > \delta v_1 \Leftrightarrow c > 0$.

So, if $a < \frac{\delta}{3}$, $b > \frac{2\delta}{3 - \delta}$, $3 > 0$, then this case can occur.

Case 10: $a = \delta v_2$, $b < \delta v_3$, $c < \delta v_1$.
Here, $q_B = q_C = 1 \Rightarrow p_{1A} = 1$, $p_{3A} = 0$. As in case 4, $>=<$.

Case 11: $a = \delta v_2$, $b < \delta v_3$, $c = \delta v_1$.
Here, $q_B = 0 \Rightarrow p_{1A} = 1$, $p_{2C} = 0$, $p_{3C} = 1$. As in case 5, $>=<$.

Case 12: $a = \delta v_2$, $b < \delta v_3$, $c > \delta v_1$.
Here, $q_B = 0$, $q_C = 1 \Rightarrow p_{1B} = 0$, $p_{2C} = 0$, $p_{3C} = 1$. As in case 8, $>=<$.

Case 13: $a = \delta v_2$, $b = \delta v_3$, $c < \delta v_1$.
Here, $q_C = 0 \Rightarrow p_{1A} = p_{2B} = 1$, $p_{3A} = 0$. As in case 5, $>=<$.

Case 14: $a = \delta v_2$, $b = \delta v_3$, $c = \delta v_1$.
Here, $p_{1A} = p_{2B} = 1$, $p_{3C} = 1$

$$\Rightarrow 3v = (1 - q_A)\delta v + q_A u_A + (1 - q_B)\delta v + q_B u_B + (1 - q_C)\delta v$$

$$+ q_C u_C = [3 - (q_A + q_B + q_C)]\delta v + (q_A u_A + q_B u_B + q_C u_C)$$

$$\Rightarrow v = \frac{q_A u_A + q_B u_B + q_C u_C}{3(1 - \delta) + (q_A + q_B + q_C)}$$

$$\Rightarrow v_1 = \frac{q_C c + q_A}{3(1 - \delta) + (q_A + q_B + q_C)},$$

$$v_2 = \frac{q_A a + q_B}{3(1 - \delta) + (q_A + q_B + q_C)}, \text{ and}$$

$$v_3 = \frac{q_B b + q_C}{3(1 - \delta) + (q_A + q_B + q_C)}.$$

$$\Rightarrow q_A = \frac{3\rho(1 + \beta + \beta\alpha)}{\alpha\beta\gamma - 1}, q_B = \frac{3\rho(1 + \gamma + \gamma\beta)}{\alpha\beta\gamma - 1},$$

$$q_C = \frac{3\rho(1 + \alpha + \alpha\gamma)}{\alpha\beta\gamma - 1}, \text{ where}$$

$$\alpha = \frac{1-a}{a}, \beta = \frac{1-b}{b}, \gamma = \frac{1-c}{c}, \rho = \frac{1-\delta}{\delta}.$$

This case can occur if $(1 + 3\rho)abc < [(1 - a)(1 - b)(1 - c)] - \max[c(1 - b), a(1 - c), b(1 - a)]$.

Case 15: $a = \delta v_2$, $b = \delta v_3$, $c > \delta v_1$.
Here, $q_C = 1$, $p_{1B} = 0$, $p_{2B} = p_{3C} = 1 \Rightarrow 3v = p_{1A}(1 - q_A)\delta v + p_{1A}q_A u_A$
$+ p_{1C}u_C + (1 - q_B)\delta v + q_B u_B + u_C$. So $3v_1 = p_{1A}(1 - q_A)\delta v_1 + p_{1A}q_A$
$+ p_{1C}c + (1 - q_B)\delta v_1 + c$. There are three subcases:

Subcase 15.1: $p_{1A} = 1$.

Then $(1 - q_A)\delta v_1 + q_A \geq c \Rightarrow v_1 \geq \dfrac{c - q_A}{(1 - q_A)\delta}$.

Here, $3v = (1 - q_A)\delta_v + q_A u_A + (1 - q_B)\delta v + q_B u_B + u_C$,

$$v = \frac{q_A u_A + q_B u_B + u_C}{3 - (2 - q_A - q_B)\delta}, v_1 = \frac{q_A + c}{3 - (2 - q_A - q_B)\delta},$$

$$v_2 = \frac{q_A a + q_B}{3 - (2 - q_A - q_B)\delta}, v_3 = \frac{q_B b + 1}{3 - (2 - q_A - q_B)\delta}.$$

So

$$a = \delta v_2 \Rightarrow 3a - 2\delta a + q_B \delta a = q_B \delta \Rightarrow q_B = \frac{a(3 - 2\delta)}{\delta(1 - a)},$$

$$b = \delta v_3 \Rightarrow 3b - 2\delta b + q_A \delta b = \delta \Rightarrow q_A = \frac{\delta + 2b\delta - 3b}{\delta b},$$

$$c > \delta v_1 \Rightarrow 3c - 2\delta c + q_A \delta c + q_B \delta c > q_A \delta + c\delta$$

$$\Rightarrow q_A \delta(c - 1) + q_B \delta c > 3c\delta - 3c \Rightarrow q_A(c - 1)$$

$$+ q_B c > 3c\frac{(\delta - 1)}{\delta},$$

$$q_B < 1 \Leftrightarrow a < \frac{\delta}{3 - \delta}, 0 < q_A < 1 \Leftrightarrow \frac{\delta}{3 - \delta} < b < \frac{\delta}{3 - 2\delta} .$$

This case can occur when $a < \dfrac{\delta}{3 - \delta}$ and $\dfrac{\delta}{3 - \delta} < b < \dfrac{\delta}{3 - 2\delta}$.

Subcase 15.2: $0 < p_{1A} < 1$.

Then $(1 - q_A)\delta v_1 + q_A = c \Rightarrow v_1 = \dfrac{c - q_A}{(1 - q_A)\delta}$, and

$$3v_1 = 2c + (1 - q_B)\delta v_1 \Rightarrow v_1 = \frac{2c}{3 - (1 - q_B)\delta} . \text{ But } a = \delta v_2,$$

$b = \delta v_3$

$$\Rightarrow \begin{cases} 3a - p_1 a\delta + p_1 q_A a\delta - a\delta + q_B a\delta = \delta p_1 q_A a + \delta q_B \\ 3b - p_1 b\delta + p_1 q_A b\delta - b\delta + q_B b\delta = \delta q_B b + 2\delta - p_1\delta \end{cases}$$

$$\Rightarrow \begin{cases} q_B \delta(1 - a) + p_1 a\delta = a(3 - \delta) \\ p_1\delta(1 - b) + p_1 q_A b\delta = 2\delta - b(3 - \delta) \end{cases}$$

$$\Rightarrow q_B c\delta - q_B q_A\delta + q_A[\delta + 2c\delta - 3] = 3c(\delta - 1).$$

$$p_{1A} = \frac{a(3 - \delta) - q_B\delta(1 - a)}{a\delta},$$

$$q_A = \frac{2\delta - b(3 - \delta) - p_1\delta(1 - b)}{p_{1A} b\delta} , \text{ and}$$

$$q_B = \frac{3c(\delta - 1) - q_A[\delta + 2c\delta - 3]}{(c\delta - q_A\delta)} .$$

But $p_{1A} < 1 \Rightarrow q_B > \dfrac{a(3 - 2\delta)}{\delta(1 - a)} .$

Subcase 15.3: $p_{1A} = 0$

Then $(1 - q_A)\delta v_1 + q_A < c \Rightarrow v_1 < \dfrac{c - q_A}{(1 - q_A)\delta} .$

Here, $3v = 2u_C + (1 - q_B)\delta v + q_B u_B$

$$v = \frac{2u_C + q_B u_B}{[3 - (1 - q_B)\delta]}$$

$$v_1 = \frac{2c}{3 - (1 - q_B)\delta}, \; v_2 = \frac{q_B}{3 - (1 - q_B)\delta}, \; v_3 = \frac{2 + q_B b}{3 - (1 - q_B)\delta}.$$

So

$$a = \delta v_2 \Rightarrow 3a - \delta a + q_B \delta a = q_B \delta \Rightarrow q_B = \frac{a(3 - \delta)}{\delta(1 - a)},$$

$$b = \delta v_3 \Rightarrow 3b - \delta b + q_B \delta b = 2\delta + q_B b \delta \Rightarrow b = \frac{2\delta}{3 - \delta}, \text{ and}$$

$$c > \delta v_1 \Rightarrow 3c - \delta c + q_B \delta c > 2c\delta \Rightarrow q_B > \frac{3(\delta - 1)}{\delta} = 3\left(1 - \frac{1}{\delta}\right).$$

This case can occur when $b = \dfrac{2\delta}{3 - \delta}$, and $a < \dfrac{\delta}{3}$.

Case 16: $a = \delta v_2$, $b > \delta v_3$, $c < \delta v_1$.

Here, $q_B = 1$, $q_C = 0 \Rightarrow p_{1A} = p_{2B} = p_{3B} = 1$,

$$3v = 2u_B + (1 - q_A)\delta v + q_A u_A,$$

$$v = \frac{2u_B + q_A u_A}{3 - (1 - q_A)\delta}.$$

Same as case 6. Occurs if $a = \dfrac{2\delta}{3 - \delta}$.

Case 17: $a = \delta v_2$, $b > \delta v_3$, $c = \delta v_1$.

Here, $q_B = 1 \Rightarrow p_{1A} = p_{2B} = 1$, $p_{3A} = 0$

$$3v = p_{3C}(1 - q_C)\delta v + p_{3C} q_C u_C + p_{3B} u_B$$

$$+ (1 - q_A)\delta v + q_A u_A + u_B.$$

Same as case 15 (three subcases):

Subcase 17.1: $p_{3C} = 1$.

Here, $q_A = \dfrac{c(3 - 2\delta)}{\delta(1 - c)}$, $q_C = \dfrac{\delta + 2a\delta - 3a}{\delta a}$.

This case can occur when $c < \dfrac{\delta}{(1 - \delta)3}$ and $\dfrac{\delta}{3 - \delta} < a < \dfrac{\delta}{3 - 2\delta}$.

Subcase 17.2: $0 < p_{3C} < 1$.

Here, $p_{3C} = \dfrac{c(3 - \delta) - q_A\delta(1 - c)}{c\delta}$,

$q_C = \dfrac{2\delta - a(3 - \delta) - p_{3C}\delta(1 - a)}{p_{3C}a\delta}$, and

$q_A = \dfrac{3b(\delta - 1) - q_C(\delta + 2c\delta - 3)}{b\delta - q_C\delta}$.

Subcase 17.3: $p_{3C} = 0$.

Here, $q_A = \dfrac{c(3 - \delta)}{\delta(1 - c)}$.

This case can occur when $a = \dfrac{2\delta}{3 - \delta}$, and $c < \dfrac{\delta}{3}$.

Case 18: $a = \delta v_2$, $b > \delta v_3$, $c > \delta v_1$.

Here, $q_B = q_C = 1 \Rightarrow p_{1B} = 0$, $p_{2B} = p_{3C} = 1$.

$$3v = p_{1A}(1 - q_A)\delta v + p_{1A}q_A u_A + p_{1C}u_C + u_B + u_C$$

$$v = \frac{p_{1A}q_A u_A + u_B + (1 + p_{1C})u_C}{3 - p_{1A}(1 - q_A)\delta}$$

Subcase 18.1: $p_{1A} = 1 \Rightarrow (1 - q_A)\delta v_1 + q_A > c$.

Here, $3v = (1 - q_A)\delta v + q_A u_A + u_B + u_C$.

$$v = \frac{q_A u_A + u_B + u_C}{3 - (1 - q_A)\delta}$$

$$a = \delta v_2 \Rightarrow a = \frac{\delta}{3 - \delta}$$

$$b > \delta v_3 \Rightarrow q_A > \frac{2b\delta + \delta - 3b}{\delta b}$$

$$c > \delta v_1 \Rightarrow q_A < \frac{c(3 - 2\delta)}{\delta(1 - c)}.$$

So $\dfrac{2b\delta + \delta - 3b}{\delta b} < q_A < \dfrac{c(3 - 2\delta)}{\delta(1 - c)} \Rightarrow (2b\delta + \delta - 3b)(1 - c) <$

$bc(3 - 2\delta) \Rightarrow 2b\delta + \delta - 3b - 2bc\delta - c\delta + 3bc < 3bc - 2bc\delta \Rightarrow$

$b < \delta(1 - c)/(3 - 2\delta)$. Also, $\dfrac{2b\delta + \delta - 3b}{\delta b} < q_A < 1 \Rightarrow b >$

$\dfrac{5 - 2\delta}{\delta}$, and $0 < q_A < \dfrac{c(3 - 2\delta)}{\delta(1 - c)} \Rightarrow c > 0$.

This case can occur if $a = \dfrac{\delta}{3 - \delta}$, $\dfrac{5 - 2\delta}{\delta} < b < \dfrac{\delta(1 - c)}{(3 - 2\delta)}$, $c > 0$.

Subcase 18.2: $0 < p_{1A} < 1$.

Then $v_{A1} = (1 - q_A)\delta v_1 + q_A = c = v_{C1}$, $3v_1 = c + 0 + c \Rightarrow v_1 =$

$\dfrac{2c}{3} \Rightarrow q_A = \dfrac{(3 - 2\delta)c}{(3 - 2\delta c)}$, and $3v_2 = p_{1A}(1 - q_A)v_2 + p_{1A}q_A a + 1$.

But $a = \delta v_2 \Rightarrow p_{1A} = 3/\delta - 1/a$. So $0 < p_{1A} < 1 \Rightarrow \dfrac{\delta}{3} < a < \dfrac{\delta}{3 - \delta}$,

and $0 < q_A \Rightarrow 0 < c$.

This case can occur if $\dfrac{\delta}{3} < a < \dfrac{\delta}{3 - \delta}$, and $0 < c$.

Subcase 18.3: $p_{1A} = 0$

Then $(1 - q_A)\delta v_1 + q_A < c$, $3v = 2u_C + u_B$

$$\Rightarrow v_1 = \frac{2}{3}c, \quad v_2 = \frac{1}{3}, \quad v_3 = \frac{2 + b}{3}, \text{ and}$$

$$b > \delta v_3 \Rightarrow b > \frac{2\delta}{3 - \delta}.$$

This case can occur if $a = \frac{\delta}{3}$, and $b > \frac{2\delta}{3 - \delta}$.

Case 19: $a > \delta v_2$, $b < \delta v_3$, $c < \delta v_1$.
  Here, $q_B = q_C = 0$, $q_A = 1 \Rightarrow p_{1A} = p_{2A} = 1$, $p_{3C} = 0$. Same as case 3 $>=<$.

Case 20: $a > \delta v_2$, $b < \delta v_3$, $c = \delta v_1$.
  Here, $q_A = 1$, $q_B = 0 \Rightarrow p_{1A} = p_{2B} = p_{3C} = 1$.

$$3v = 2u_A + (1 - q_C)\delta v + q_C u_C, \text{ and}$$

$$v = \frac{2u_A + q_C u_C}{3 - (1 - q_A)\delta}.$$

Occurs if $c = \frac{2\delta}{3 - \delta}$. Same as cases 6 and 16.

Case 21: $a > \delta v_2$, $b < \delta v_3$, $c > \delta v_1$.

  Here, $q_A = 1$, $q_B = 0$, $q_C = 1 \Rightarrow p_{1A} = p_{2A} = p_{3C} = 1$.

$$3v = 2u_A + u_C, \text{ and}$$

$$v_1 = \frac{2 + c}{3}, \; v_2 = \frac{a}{3}, \; v_3 = \frac{1}{3}.$$

This case occurs if $b < \frac{\delta}{3}$, and $c > \frac{2\delta}{3 - \delta}$. Same as case 9.

Case 22: $a > \delta v_2$, $b = \delta v_3$, $c < \delta v_1$. Same as cases 8 and 12, $>=<$.

Case 23: $a > \delta v_2$, $b = \delta v_3$, $c = \delta v_1$.
  Here, $q_A = 1 \Rightarrow p_{1A} = 1$, $p_{2C} = 0$, $p_{3C} = 1$.
    $3v = p_{2B}(1 - a_B)\delta v + p_{2B}q_B u_B + p_{2A}u_A + (1 - q_C)\delta v + q_C u_C + u_A$.
  Same as cases 15 and 17, three subcases:

Subcase 23.1: $p_{2B} = 1$.

  Here, $q_C = \frac{b(3 - 2\delta)}{\delta(1 - b)}$, $q_B = \frac{\delta - 2c\delta - 3c}{\delta c}$.

This case can occur when $b < \dfrac{\delta}{(1 - \delta)3}$, and $\dfrac{\delta}{3 - \delta} < c < \dfrac{\delta}{3 - 2\delta}$.

Subcase 23.2: $0 < p_{2B} < 1$.

$$(1 - q_B)\delta v + q_B = a$$

$$\Rightarrow p_{2B} = \frac{b(1 - \delta) - q_C \delta(1 - b)}{b\delta},$$

$$q_B = \frac{2\delta - c(3 - \delta) - p_{2B}\delta(1 - c)}{p_{2B}c\delta}, \text{ and}$$

$$q_C = \frac{3a(\delta - 1) - q_B[\delta + 2a\delta - 3]}{\delta - q_B\delta}.$$

Subcase 23.3: $p_{2B} = 0$.

Here, $q_C = \dfrac{b(3 - \delta)}{\delta(1 - b)}$.

This case can occur when $c = \dfrac{2\delta}{3 - \delta}$, and $b < \dfrac{\delta}{3}$.

Case 24: $a > \delta v_2$, $b = \delta v_3$, $c > \delta v_1$.
  Here, $q_A = q_C = 1 \Rightarrow p_{1A} = 1$, $p_{2C} = 0$, $p_{3C} = 1$. Same as case 18.

Case 25: $a > \delta v_2$, $b > \delta v_3$, $c < \delta v_1$.
  Here, $q_A = q_B = 1$, $q_C = 0$. Same as cases 9 and 12.

Case 26: $a > \delta v_2$, $b > \delta v_3$, $c = \delta v_1$. Same as cases 18 and 24.

Case 27: $a > \delta v_2$, $b > \delta v_3$, $c > \delta v_1$.
  Here, $q_A = q_B = q_C = 1$, $p_{1A} = p_{2B} = p_{3C} = 1$.

$$3v = u_A + u_B + u_C, \text{ and}$$

$$v_1 = \frac{1 + c}{3}, v_2 = \frac{1 + a}{3}, v_3 = \frac{1 + b}{3}.$$

$$a > \delta v_2, b > \delta v_3, c > \delta v_1 \Rightarrow a > \frac{\delta}{3 - \delta}, b > \frac{\delta}{3 - \delta}, c > \frac{\delta}{3 - \delta}.$$

REFERENCES

Asscher, N. 1976. "An Ordinal Bargaining Set for Games without Sidepayments." *Mathematics of Operations Research* 1:381–89.

Aumann, R. J., and M. Maschler. 1964. "The Bargaining Set for Cooperative Games." *Annals of Mathematical Studies* 52:443–76.

Baron, D., and J. Ferejohn. 1987. "Bargaining in Legislatures." *American Political Science Review* 83.

Bennett, E. 1983. "The Aspiration Approach to Predicting Coalition Formation and Outcome Distribution in Sidepayment Games." *International Journal of Game Theory* 12:1–28.

Bennett, E., and W. Zame. 1988. "Bargaining in Cooperative Games." *International Journal of Game Theory* 17:279–300.

Gretlein, R. 1981. "Ordinal Theories of Group Choice." Ph.D. diss. Carnegie-Mellon University.

Klingaman, D. 1969. "A Note on a Cyclical Majority Problem." *Public Choice* 6:99–101.

McKelvey, R. D., and P. C. Ordeshook. 1979. "An Experimental Test of Several Theories of Committee Decision Making under Majority Rule." In *Applied Game Theory*, ed. S. J. Brams, A. Schotter, and G. Schwodiauer. Wurzburg: Physica Verlag.

McKelvey, R. D., and P. C. Ordeshook. 1983. "Some Experimental Results that Fail to Support the Competitive Solution." *Public Choice* 40:281–91.

McKelvey, R. D., P. C. Ordeshook, and M. Winer. 1978. "The Competitive Solution for *N*-Person Games without Sidepayments." *American Political Science Review* 72:599–615.

Miller, G. J., and J. A. Oppenheimer. 1982. "Universalism in Experimental Committees." *American Political Science Review* 76:561–74.

Peleg, B. 1963. "Bargaining Sets of Cooperative Games without Sidepayments." *Israel Journal of Mathematics* 1:197–200.

Rubinstein, A. 1982. "Perfect Equilibria in Bargaining Models." *Econometrica* 50:97–109.

Sobel, Matthew J. 1971. "Noncooperative Stochastic Games." *Annals of Mathematical Statistics* 42:1930–35.

Weingast, B. 1979. "A Rational Choice Perspective on Congressional Norms." *American Journal of Political Science* 23:245–62.

Costly Agendas and Spatial Voting Games: Theory and Experiments on Agenda Access Costs

Roberta Herzberg and Rick Wilson

Introduction

All collective choices are costly, requiring the expenditure of time, information, and political resources. While few would disagree with such an assertion, most models of collective choice processes ignore these costs in favor of general models of the aggregation process.[1] Such models assume a frictionless decision-making process whereby actors bear no costs of moving from one policy to another. This focuses the theorist's attention on policy alternatives preferred by a winning coalition and assumes that any preferred policy, even those resulting in only an epsilon-improvement for members of the coalition, will be chosen. Assuming a world of no transaction costs for decision making has contributed enormously to an understanding of preference-induced equilibrium. But, by the same token, these models yield theoretical predictions at variance with empirical observations. We contend that at least part of the gap between theoretical prediction and empirical observation can be accounted for by the assumption that collective decision making is costless. We propose an extension to one class of "chaotic" spatial voting models by explicitly incorporating a form of transaction costs into the model. We find that, in certain cases, these costs are sufficient to induce an equilibrium. This equilibrium concept is then subjected to empirical testing by using laboratory experimental data.

We gratefully acknowledge the support of the Workshop in Political Theory and Policy Analysis and the National Science Foundation (SES 87-21250). Neither bear any responsibility for the conclusions reached in this paper. Thanks are due to Robert Brown and Dean Dudley for their often cheerful assistance in conducting these experiments. Helpful comments were provided by a number of people, including Lin Ostrom, Tom Palfrey, and Jerry Wright. An early version of this paper was presented at the Economic Science Association Meetings, October 28–29, 1989, Tucson.

1. A notable recent exception is Baron and Ferejohn 1989.

The costs of decision making can be characterized in a variety of ways. At one end of a spectrum are those decision costs that are endogenous to the decision process. These costs are privately borne and they can be folded neatly into an individual actor's utility function. A typical example of such endogenous costs are the opportunity costs of decision making in which individual actors have different opportunity sets and regard those costs under purely private calculations. Exogenous costs to the decision process anchor the opposite end of the spectrum. Such costs are externally derived and are often imposed by a set of institutional rules defining the collective choice process. Exogenous costs are akin to what Buchanan and Tullock (1962) call "decision costs"—the transaction costs to building a decisive coalition. For example, imposing extraordinary majority rule on the collective choice process generates greater decision costs than simple majority rule. As political scientists, our concern is with these exogenous costs of decision making. The question we pose is whether institutionally imposed decision costs affect the strategic behavior of actors, and, if so, whether the joint play of those strategies yields predictable outcomes.

In our discussion, we focus on *agenda access costs* as a constraint on strategic choice. Agenda access costs are characterized as the transaction costs borne by actors seeking to change an existing policy. In a collegial collective choice setting like the U.S. Congress, proposing a successful amendment entails considerable transaction costs for the winning coalition. These costs include staff research efforts in putting together the amendment, staff efforts in building a winning coalition through the inclusion or exclusion of subsidiary issues, and, finally, the lobbying efforts of the chief sponsors in pushing the legislation. All of these "efforts" can be viewed as the transaction costs borne by legislators' staffs when building a decisive coalition. These expenditures of effort are nothing more than part of the finite resources every legislator holds. Clearly these resources could just as well be transferred to (other) valued activities such as casework. While agenda access costs are only one form of transaction cost for the collective choice process, our results are suggestive of how decision costs can affect majority-rule outcomes more generally.

This paper is split into two parts. In the first we outline a spatial voting model of agenda access costs. Using a comparative statics approach, we contrast the equilibrium outcomes under costs with the expected outcomes under a no-cost, institution-free process. In the second part of the paper, we use laboratory experimental methods to test the robustness of the agenda access cost model. These experiments provide empirical content for our theoretical discussions and also point toward new avenues for theoretical explanation.

Theoretical Structure

In this section we begin with the results of other researchers showing that, when employing a binary choice procedure under majority rule, the decision process can wander anywhere.[2] Consistent (equilibrium) outcomes emerge from such processes only when actors' preferences meet highly restrictive conditions. This has led at least one prominent scholar to characterize political science as "the dismal science" (Riker 1980). We show that introducing agenda access costs into this setting induces an equilibrium set with no restrictions on the distribution of actors' preferences. In turn, incorporating these costs into the decision process brings stability to collective choices.

Definitions and Assumptions

Let $N = \{1,2, \ldots , n\}$ be the n-membered (odd) set of decision makers charged with selecting a single alternative, x, from a compact, convex policy-space $X \subseteq R^m$. Each member $i \in N$ has a strictly quasi-concave binary preference relation (type 1 preferences). Utility declines as a function of distance away from i's ideal point, x^i, so that the set of alternatives preferred to x by player i is defined as $P_i(x) = \{x' \in X | \, \|x^i - x'\| < \|x^i - x\|\}$.

For simple majority-rule games, we define the *set of winning coalitions* in N as $S = \{S_1, S_2, \ldots , S_k\}$ where $S_j \in S$ if and only if $|S_j| > \frac{n}{2}$. An alternative, x', is *socially preferred* if it is preferred by all members of any S_j $\in S$ or $x' \in \beta_j(x)$ where $\beta_j(x) = \underset{i \in S_j}{\cap} P_i(x)$. The set of all socially preferred alternatives is defined as the win set of x or $W(x) = \underset{S_j \in S}{\cup} \beta_j(x)$. We define the existing policy, or the status quo, as x^o.

For most distributions of voters preferences and most alternatives, $x \in X$, $W(x)$ will be nonempty, which implies that x can be beaten in pairwise comparison. In particular, Cox (1987) has shown that majority-rule spatial games under the preference assumptions used here result in an empty win set at some x if and only if x is "a median on all lines."[3]

---

2. For the clearest statements of this point, see McKelvey 1976 and 1979 and Schofield 1978. Also see McKelvey 1986 for a restatement and refinement of the process, as well as Ordeshook and Schwartz 1987 for characteristics of different agenda processes.

3. A median on all lines is simply the median of the induced ideal points on all lines

Agenda Access Costs

The standard findings hold that equilibrium in multidimensional choice-spaces only occur under highly restrictive conditions. Rather than imposing limiting conditions on the distributions of actors' preferences, we turn toward the effect of decision costs on collective choices. Specifically, we characterize a single type of decision cost, *agenda access costs,* whereby voters are assessed a fixed fee each time the status quo is amended. We define this cost for an individual as c^i and measure it in terms of utility units. A change from the status quo to an alternative x results in a value for i of $v^i(x) = u^i(x) - c^i$, or the utility of alternative x minus the access costs assessed to achieve that alternative. We assume that the decision cost is the same for all individuals and therefore drop the superscript, or $c^i = c, \forall i \in N$.

The introduction of decision costs imposes a powerful constraint on this spatial voting game. Costs constrain decision making by reducing the size of an individual's preferred set by an amount relative to the cost imposed. In particular, i's cost-induced preferred set, defined here as $P_i^c(x^o) = \{x \in X| \ u^i(x^o) < v^i(x)\}$, can easily be shown to be a subset of $P_i(x^o)$ whenever $c > 0$:

LEMMA 1. If $c > 0$, then $P_i^c(x^o) \subset P_i(x^o)$.

In order to understand how costs affect an individual's choices among alternatives, we define an individual's cost contour relative to x^o as $C^i = f(x^o,c)$. The upper bound of C^i is represented as i's indifference contour through x^o. The lower bound is defined by first defining a distance $z = \|c\|$.[4] Then from any point, x^o, we define i's lower cost bound as the indifference curve exactly z units inside the curve through x^o. C^i is z units wide whenever x^o is greater than z units from x^i. If $\|x^i - x^o\| < z$, then C^i is the set of all alternatives inside the indifference curve through x^o. When costs are zero, C^i collapses to the indifference contour through x^o.

The cost contour provides an important dividing point for i's decision making relative to x^o. Every point inside the lower bound of C^i is strictly preferred by i to x^o with or without costs and every point outside the upper bound is strictly inferior regardless of costs. Choices over alternatives within the contour change as a function of the imposed costs. For all $x \in C^i(x^o)$,

---

containing that point. For further discussion of the restrictiveness of this condition, see Cox 1987, sec. 2 (in particular, theorem 1).

4. Using a mapping of utility into distance, we can define the cost of changing the agenda in terms of distance in the space. Since we assume linear preferences, and since costs are measured in terms of utility units, the distance associated with a given decline in utility, c, can be calculated as z and measured from any point in the space.

xR_ix^o when costs are absent but x^oP_ix when costs are included. The cost contour, therefore, represents the set of i's decisions over alternatives affected by the introduction of costs equal to c. With costs included, i's preferred set shrinks to incorporate only those points interior to the lower bound of C^i or $P_i^c(x^o) = \{x \in X | \, \|x^i - x\| < \|x^i - x^c\|\}$ where x^c is a point on the lower bound of C^i.

The full set of alternatives affected by the introduction of costs is defined as the social cost set, $D = \bigcup_{i \in N} C^i$. For each $x \in D$ there is at least one $i \in N$ whose vote in the binary choice between x and x^o changes as a function of cost. The cost-induced win set is simply the union of all winning coalitions' cost-induced preferred-to sets or $W_j^c(x^o) = \bigcup_{Sj \in S} B_j^c(x^o)$. The cost-induced win set relates to the win set in the following way:

LEMMA 2. If $c > 0$, then $W^c(x^o) \subset W(x^o)$.

By lemma one, $\forall \, S_j \in S, \; B^c(x^o) \subset B(x^o)$

$$\Rightarrow \bigcup_{S_j \in S} B_j^c(x^o) \subset \bigcup_{Sj \in S} B_j(x^o) \Rightarrow W^c(x^o) \subset W(x^o).$$

Q.E.D.

Introducing agenda access costs constrains the decision process and limits moves previously preferred by a majority. A comparison of $W(x^o)$ and $W^c(x^o)$ for the three-person example shown in figure 1 suggests how costs limit the process. Without decision costs, majorities support any move from x^o into one of the three shaded petals shown. For example, the move from x^o to y results in a higher utility for players 1 and 3 and, thus, y is part of $W(x^o)$. When costs are introduced, however, many previously preferred outcomes, including y, no longer yield sufficient utility to compensate for the agenda costs. The cost-induced win set for this example is shown as the smaller, interior, cross-hatched petal $B_{23}^c(x^o)$. No alternatives are preferred to x^o by player 1 in the face of costs. Only if an alternative within the cross-hatched region is proposed will a further move away from x^o be made in the face of costs. The introduction of costs forces actors to think in terms of moves significant enough to compensate for the costs of change.

We define x as a cost-induced equilibrium, denoted $x \in E^c$, if $W^c(x) = \emptyset$. We can compare the sets $W^c(x^o)$ and $W(x^o)$ beginning with the general results for majority-rule processes. Under most preference conditions, $W(x^o) \neq \emptyset$ for all $x^o \in X$. For every point there exists a majority-preferred alterna-

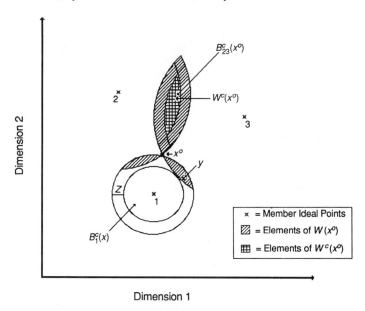

Fig. 1. Example of $W(x^o)$ and $W^c(x^o)$ in two dimensions

tive so that there is no particular point at which the decision process is expected to stop. By contrast, the presence of costs can result in predictable and stable decisions. If all winning alternatives relative to x^o under a no-cost condition improve the utility of one member of each winning coalition by a value less than the cost, then, once costs are included, that status quo will be an equilibrium. To see this, consider the following result.

THEOREM 1. If $c > 0$, $x \in E^c$ if and only if $W(x) \subset D$.

Proof: Sufficiency. we show that for any x' where $x' \in W(x)$ and $x' \in D$, if x' $\notin W^c(x)$ then $x \in E^c$. Assume the contrary, $x \notin E^c$, but $W(x) \subset D$. Then if x $\notin E^c$, there exists an $x' \in W^c(x)$. By lemma 2, $x' \in W(x)$. With strictly quasi-concave preferences, $x' \in W(x)$ implies $x' \in B_j(x)$ for some S_j. Then for all i $\in S_j$, $\|x^i - x'\| < \|x^i - x\|$. By definition of D and the strictly quasi-concavity of member's preferences, $x' \in D$ implies that for some $i \in S_j$, $\|x^i - x\| < \|x^i$ $- x'\| - z$, which implies $x \, P_i^c \, x'$ for some $i \in S_j$. But then $x' \notin B_j^c(x)$ for any S_j containing i. Then $x \notin W^c(x)$ contrary to our assumption. Therefore, $x \in E^c$.

Necessity. We show that if $x \in E^c$, then $W(x) \subset D$. Let $x \in E^c$. If $x \in E^c$, then either $W(x) = \varnothing$ or $W(x) \neq \varnothing$, but $W^c(x) = \varnothing$. If $W(x) = \varnothing$, then trivially $W(x)$ is a subset of D. Thus, consider the case in which $W^c(x) = \varnothing$ but $W(x) \neq$ $\varnothing$. Assume $x' \in W(x)$, but $x' \notin D$. Since $x \in E^c$, $x' \notin W^c(x)$. By definition of

$W^c(x)$, if $x' \notin W^c(x)$ then $x\, R_j^c x'\; \forall\, S_j \in S$. Then either $x\, R_j\, x'$, contradicting the assumption that $x' \in W(x)$, or $x' \in D$ contradicting the assumption $x' \notin D$. Thus, $x \in E^c$ only if $W(x) \subset D$.   Q.E.D.

When costs cover all majority preferred movements from a given status quo, x^o, that status quo is an equilibrium. Without costs, any point in the win set results in a higher utility for all members of a winning coalition, and, under institution-free theories, that move is assumed to occur. Access costs, however, introduce sufficient friction in the agenda process to prevent previously preferred moves. Small moves will not be made under such a condition, and, where only small moves are possible, that status quo is in equilibrium. In Herzberg and Wilson 1989, we address a variety of conditions relating to the size of costs sufficient to yield an equilibrium. As we show, obtaining a cost-induced equilibrium is contingent on the distribution of voters' ideal points, the size of majorities, and the level of costs borne. The interesting finding is that, for most distributions of preferences, even small transaction costs can still yield an equilibrium.

Our model shows that introducing transaction costs to the agenda can yield an equilibrium in spatial voting games. By contrast, where these costs are absent, even if the same voting and agenda mechanisms remain, an equilibrium does not exist. This comparative statics finding yields sharp predictions. In a costless setting, actors will continue to form and reform winning coalitions, generating an agenda that wanders throughout the policy-space and results in outcomes scattered throughout that space. Where there are costs of changing policies, the agenda will not wander throughout the policy-space. Instead, if a choice is made that falls in the cost-induced equilibrium set, the agenda will stop. It is important to note that this cost-induced equilibrium is only retentive and not attractive. That is, an agenda trajectory will not necessarily lead into that equilibrium. The model simply predicts that if a policy is chosen that falls into the equilibrium, rational actors will not move from it. Consequently, collective choices will be located in the cost-equilibrium.

Observing the presence of these decision costs is obviously problematic in natural settings. While it may be possible to infer that such costs exist, characterizing their size requires much more sophisticated measurement tools than are currently available. Even if these cost-based measurement difficulties could be overcome, serious problems remain with inferring individual's preferences and reconstructing the policy-space. Consequently, a direct test of this model in a natural setting is quite difficult. However, the laboratory experimental setting provides an ideal mechanism for testing the robustness of this model.[5] In the next section we turn toward a description of a laboratory

---

5. For clear expositions concerning the merits of laboratory experiments for testing formal theories see Plott 1979 and Wilson 1989.

experiment that implements a spatial voting committee to test the effects of agenda access costs on collective choices.

Experiments

In this section we report the results of two different experimental series, each of which includes several different experimental manipulations. Our primary concern in each series is with comparing the collective choices made when decisions are costly and when they are not. The first experimental series, series *A*, is comprised of experiments with a fully open agenda. The series *B* experiments introduce constraints on the agenda process intended to provide a crisper test of the model. Both experimental series share the same generic structure. Where there are differences in design, these are separately noted.

The experimental design used here is based on five-person committee experiments conducted by Fiorina and Plott (1978), McKelvey, Ordeshook, and Winer (1978), and Wilson (1986b).[6] Only "naive" participants were allowed in the experiment—individuals who had not previously participated in a spatial voting experiment. All participation in these experiments took place at computer terminals that were physically separated. Players could not see one another's terminals, and their identities were randomized and kept anonymous during the experiments. This minimized the possibility that groups of players successfully colluded using prearranged coalition strategies.

Participants were given instructions designed to familiarize them with the experiment and test their comprehension.[7] Upon completing these instructions, individuals participated in a practice period for which they were not paid. During practice, participants were urged to try all the options until they were familiar with the experiment. Participants were cautioned that, once they completed the practice session, their earnings depended solely on the collective choice that was reached.

In the experiment, participants were to collectively choose an alternative from a two-dimensional policy-space. Alternatives were represented as Cartesian coordinates from orthogonal dimensions labeled *X* and *Y*. At the outset of the experiment, a fixed status quo was introduced by the experimenter. Any subject was able to propose an amendment to the status quo, thereby calling a vote. All amendments were treated as an amendment in the nature of a substitute. When voting, subjects were asked only to consider whether to

---

6. Unlike the committee experiments by Fiorina and Plott (1978) and McKelvey, Ordeshook, and Winer (1978) that were conducted in face-to-face settings, these experiments used computer controlled settings to mediate all player interaction. The experiments were conducted on Macintosh computers connected over a local area network. Source code for these computer programs is available from the second author.

7. These instructions are available from the authors upon request.

retain the status quo or substitute the amendment for the status quo. If a simple majority of the committee (three out of five) voted in favor of retaining the status quo, the experiment continued, with the floor open to new amendments. If a majority voted for the amendment, it became the (amended) status quo, and the floor was opened to amendments to this new status quo. The experiment continued in this fashion until a subject made a motion to adjourn the committee meeting. If a simple majority voted to adjourn, then that decision period came to an end and subjects were paid their value for the current status quo. If a majority voted against adjournment, the experiment continued, with the floor open to further amendments to the status quo. It was up to a majority of the committee to decide when to end the decision period.[8]

Each individual was assigned an ideal point in this two-dimensional space and was given a preference function. In these experiments, member preferences are represented as circles, with utility linearly decreasing with distance from the member's ideal point. The utility functions varied across experimental manipulations and are summarized in table 1. By using an abstract policy-space (made up of X and Y axes) and by inducing player's valuation for points in the space, we sought to avoid problems associated with participants adopting different subjective valuations for the policy-space. All calculations for a subject were handled by the microcomputer. The computer terminal displayed the alternative space, the member's ideal point, representative indifference curves, and the ideal points of all other members (but not their utility functions). The current status quo and all proposals currently on the floor were also represented on this alternative space. In addition, members had before them menus from which they could select a number of actions. This screen is displayed in figure 2.

Pilot experiments showed that there were statistically significant differences in the amount of time subjects spent in the experiment under the different cost conditions. When costs are imposed, subjects spend about half as much time in the experiment and far less time examining the dominance relations among proposals. In order to control for this difference and to ensure that subjects had sufficient time to consider a variety of points in the alternative space, a motion to adjourn was not allowed until fifteen minutes had

---

8. The earliest of the series *A* experiments had a single decision period. In later experiments, subjects participated in two distinct decision periods. While the second period used the same preference configuration as the first, two adjustments were made so that subjects treated these as independent decisions. First, participants were randomly assigned to new ideal points and identities at each decision period. Second, the ideal points of all players were rotated 90 or 180 degrees around the center of the alternative space. All outcomes reported here have been normalized to the same space. The evidence is consistent with the supposition that subjects treated these decisions as independent. Subjects were told the number of decision periods in which they would participate.

TABLE 1. Parameters Used in Experiments

Member	Ideal Points	Maximal Value	Loss Function	Agenda Cost
		Series A, Low Cost		
1	(22,214)	22.00	0.07	0.00
2	(171,290)	22.00	0.07	0.00
3	(279,180)	22.00	0.07	0.00
4	(225,43)	22.00	0.07	0.00
5	(43,75)	22.00	0.07	0.00
1	(22,214)	25.00	0.07	0.75
2	(171,290)	25.00	0.07	0.75
3	(279,180)	25.00	0.07	0.75
4	(225,43)	25.00	0.07	0.75
5	(43,75)	25.00	0.07	0.75
		Series A, High Cost		
1	(22,214)	25.00	0.14	0.00
2	(171,290)	25.00	0.14	0.00
3	(279,180)	25.00	0.14	0.00
4	(225,43)	25.00	0.14	0.00
5	(43,75)	25.00	0.14	0.00
1	(22,214)	28.00	0.14	1.50
2	(171,290)	28.00	0.14	1.50
3	(279,180)	28.00	0.14	1.50
4	(225,43)	28.00	0.14	1.50
5	(43,75)	28.00	0.14	1.50
		Series B		
1	(22,214)	25.00	0.14	0.00
2	(171,290)	25.00	0.14	0.00
3	(279,180)	25.00	0.14	0.00
4	(225,43)	25.00	0.14	0.00
5	(43,75)	25.00	0.14	0.00
1	(22,214)	28.00	0.14	1.50
2	(171,290)	28.00	0.14	1.50
3	(279,180)	28.00	0.14	1.50
4	(225,43)	28.00	0.14	1.50
5	(43,75)	28.00	0.14	1.50

Note: Utility for any X and for the ith member's ideal point, X_i, is given by: $U_i =$ (Maximal Value) $- [(\|X - X_i\|) \times$ Loss Function].

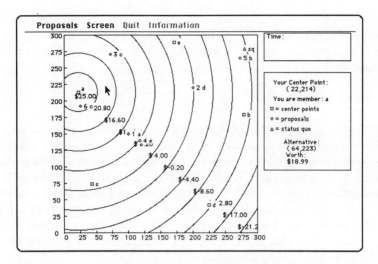

Fig. 2. Main screen for committee experiments

passed. This was the average amount of time subjects spent in the pilot experiments without costs. The time was displayed in the upper right corner of the subjects' computer terminals and included only time that had passed during proposal making, not voting.

In these experiments a participant could lose money. To compensate for this possibility, individuals were instructed that they would participate in a separate, initial experiment where they could earn money. This "preexperiment" required that a participant choose a point from a line ranging from 1 to 100. In turn, the computer selected a point from a known, normal distribution. A subject was then paid based on the distance of his or her choice from that selected by the computer. Once a subject accumulated $5.00 or more, the "preexperiment" ended. This approach was used instead of giving subjects $5.00, since experimental evidence points out that subjects treat an endowment differently than money they perceive they earn (Hoffman and Spitzer 1985).

We ran two distinct experimental series to test the effects of agenda access costs on collective outcomes. The series *A* experiments used an open agenda procedure in which proposing alternatives, voting, and adjourning was governed under a modified version of *Robert's Rules of Order*. This setting is closely related to the models presented previously using compact, convex, multidimensional policy-spaces. Participants could choose from a dense, two-dimensional space made up of 300 × 300 points. The series *B* experiments greatly simplified the task by limiting subjects to a finite set of alternatives.

They were still free to structure the agenda in any manner they pleased. These limited alternatives were chosen to test several competing solution concepts. Each experimental series is sufficiently different that they are analyzed separately.

Series *A*

All experimental conditions under the series *A* experiments relied on "forward-moving," open-agenda rules (see Wilson 1986a). This meant that any participant could bring a proposal to the floor. Once a proposal was placed on the floor, it remained there throughout the decision period. However, no proposal was considered an amendment to the status quo unless "seconded" by another member. This had the effect of reducing the number of votes in these experiments and fits well with standard parliamentary procedure. Once a proposal was seconded, a vote was called, with the seconded proposal serving as an amendment to the status quo.

Costs were introduced into these experiments by assessing subjects a fee for *successful* amendments to the status quo. Corresponding with the theoretical construct developed here, members bore decision costs for making changes in the status quo. In these experiments, only subjects in the majority coalition, voting in favor of an amendment to the status quo, were assessed a fee.[9] In keeping with the theoretical model, costs were assessed at each agenda step. When voting between an amendment and the status quo, the member's value for the amendment and the status quo, the cost for the decision, and the resulting value of the amendment if it became the status quo were all displayed. In this way, each participant was fully informed of the result of his or her action. Costs were not directly subtracted following each vote, since earnings were totaled and carried over from decision periods. Instead, all assessed fees were represented as a decrease in a member's utility function. For instance, if the cost for making a decision was $.75 and a member's ideal point was initially $14.50, following the first successful amendment for which the member voted the member's ideal point was worth (and displayed as) $13.75. This continued with every successful amendment.

---

9. The theoretical model is silent about whether the full committee or a subset of the committee is assessed the decision costs. The only requirement under the model is that costs are sufficient for one or more members of a minimum winning coalition to prevent movement from the status quo. Clearly, in most natural settings, any vote on a motion requires that all bear the decision costs. However, in these experiments, we were concerned with confounding experimental effects, where participants might vote out of spite, knowing that, if the entire group was assessed a fee for changing the status quo, those in the minority would also bear the costs. To ensure a crisp test of the model, only those voting for the change were assessed the cost.

Throughout the experiment members were fully informed about their transaction costs.

In the series *A* experiments, four experimental conditions were introduced. The first two conditions were concerned with subjects' utility functions. A subject's utility was a decreasing linear function of distance of an alternative from his or her ideal point and two types of linear loss functions were used. In the first instance, characterized as a "low" loss rate, utility was decreased by $.07 per unit of distance in the alternative space. The second instance, a "high" loss rate, doubled the decrease in utility to $.14 per unit of distance. Varying these loss rates allowed us to vary the size of costs while preserving the same predicted solution. Table 1 provides a full listing of ideal points, maximal values, and loss rates for these experimental conditions.

The next two conditions fixed the size of the agenda access costs. In the first instance, costs were zero. This setting comports well with experiments conducted by Fiorina and Plott (1978) and Wilson (1986a). Such a setting lacks a majority-rule equilibrium and sets of predicted outcomes vary from the Copeland winner (Grofman et al. 1987) to the Yolk (McKelvey 1986). The second condition assessed costs to individuals for voting for a change to the status quo. Depending upon the type of loss function, individuals were assessed either $.75 or $1.50 for each change to the status quo. Corresponding to our model, these costs were sufficiently high to yield a set of equilibrium predictions. Moreover, since the agenda access costs were tied to subjects' utility functions, both the low- and high-access cost-parameters yield identical equilibrium sets. Consequently, we can examine whether the magnitude of the cost makes any independent difference, while maintaining comparable predicted solution sets.

Series A Results

Final outcomes from experiments conducted under low-loss functions are plotted in figure 3 and outcomes from experiments under high-loss functions are plotted in figure 4 (also see table 2). In each instance, the predicted equilibrium set for the cost conditions is contained in the irregularly shaped polygon in the center of the figure. From these figures there appears to be little difference in the distributions of outcomes, whether between the baseline condition and the cost condition, or across types of discount rates. First, none of the cost-based outcomes appear in the equilibrium set. Of eleven costly agenda access replications, only one is within a few units of the cost-induced equilibrium (under high costs).

To test whether there is any difference in the distribution of outcomes from the equilibrium set, we calculated the minimized distance of each out-

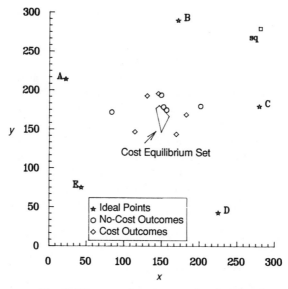

Fig. 3. Open agenda outcomes, low-loss function

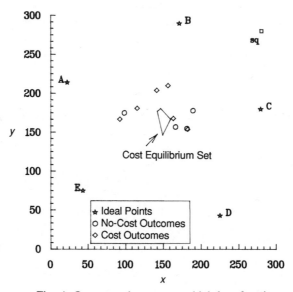

Fig. 4. Open agenda outcomes, high-loss function

TABLE 2. Outcomes for Series *A* Experiments

Experiment:Period	Outcome	Proposals	Agenda Steps	Cost Condition
		Low Loss		
A1:2	(83,172)	96	20	No Cost
A2:2	(152,179)	72	12	No Cost
A3:2	(201,180)	41	6	No Cost
A4:2	(149,194)	39	5	No Cost
A5:2	(156,175)	19	2	No Cost
A6:2	(130,193)	9	1	Cost
A7:2	(182,169)	28	2	Cost
A8:2	(114,147)	32	2	Cost
A9:2	(145,196)	71	5	Cost
A10:2	(169,144)	33	1	Cost
		High Loss		
A11:3	(181,155)	61	10	No Cost
A13:2	(98,175)	92	6	No Cost
A14:2	(166,157)	70	2	No Cost
A15:2	(189,178)	34	4	No Cost
A11:2	(156,210)	62	2	Cost
A12:2	(92,167)	82	3	Cost
A12:3	(182,154)	77	1	Cost
A13:3	(163,168)	80	3	Cost
A14:3	(141,204)	33	1	Cost
A15:3	(115,181)	40	3	Cost

come to the boundary of the equilibrium set. This distance of outcome was then regressed (using generalized linear model techniques) on a set of dummy variables, including whether utility loss functions were high or low, whether the outcome was part of a no-cost or cost condition, and an interaction term for these conditions. If the model has some predictive capacity, then outcomes under the cost condition should cluster around the equilibrium set. This means that the size of the discount rates should have no effect on the distribution of outcomes, while the cost condition should yield a negative parameter estimate. The interaction term should also be negligible.

Our parameter estimates are given by equation 1 (standard errors are in parentheses).

$$\text{DIST} = 25.286 + 2.652 \text{ LOSS} - 2.42 \text{ COST} + 2.496 \text{ INTER} \quad (1)$$
$$(11.328) \qquad (10.681) \qquad (15.261)$$

where:

$$\text{LOSS} = \begin{cases} 0 = \text{Low} \\ 1 = \text{High} \end{cases}$$

$$\text{COST} = \begin{cases} 0 = \text{No Cost} \\ 1 = \text{Cost} \end{cases}$$

$$\text{INTER} = \text{LOSS} \times \text{COST}.$$

Several points fall out from these estimates. First, the loss rate has an insignificant effect on outcomes. While high discount rates tend to result in choices further from the equilibrium set, the high standard error indicates that there is considerable variance in outcomes. Second, imposing decision costs results in outcomes somewhat closer to the equilibrium set, hence the negative sign for that estimate, but, again, the parameter estimate is not significantly different from zero. Finally, there is no evidence of an interaction between the presence or absence of costs and the type of discount rate. These estimates lead us to conclude that there is no difference between the cost and no-cost conditions— the estimates indicate that those outcomes could have been drawn from the same distribution.

Yet the distribution of final outcomes in these experiments fails to tell the entire story. There are important differences between agendas under the no-cost and cost conditions. Pooling the high- and low-loss function experiments, subjects make more than three times the number of changes to the status quo under the no-cost condition than where they are assessed costs. Under the baseline condition, this translates to an average of 7.67 agenda steps (with a standard deviation of 5.77) compared with 2.18 steps (and standard deviation of 1.25) under the cost condition. Clearly, participants are responding to constraints introduced by costs. The question remains, how should we interpret this pattern? Does it reflect committee members not carefully considering the proposals in the alternative space? Or does it illustrate that it is difficult to uncover an agenda path into the equilibrium set? The data tend to support the latter implication.

First, there is no statistically significant difference in the number of votes taken under either the cost or no-cost condition.[10] From this it is reasonable to infer that subjects are considering quite a number of proposals in the alterna-

---

10. Under a nonparametric test (Mann-Whitney) of rank sum differences, the null hypothesis that these conditions have the same number of votes cannot be rejected at even the .10 level of significance ($p = .148$). The absence of any difference holds whether one considers amendment or adjournment votes.

tive space. Second, participants under the cost condition are settling on about the best alternative available to them. Comparing the final choice by the committee with all proposals on the floor (including those not voted on), on average, only 7.6 percent of the available proposals represented an improvement for some majority coalition. By comparison, an average of 18.2 percent of the proposals in the no-cost condition represented an improvement over the final choice for a majority. The extent of differences between these two conditions is masked, however, by the fact that, in two of the cost experiments, participants settled on outcomes that could have been defeated by more than 20.0 percent of the proposals on the floor. In five of the eleven cost experiments, no proposal on the floor represented an improvement over the final outcome for a majority. As an example, in experiment A9:2, an experiment with low costs for each agenda step, only one of the seventy-one proposals represented an improvement over the final outcome, and it was not in the cost equilibrium. Figure 5 plots the agenda for this experiment and the sole proposal that represented an improvement for any coalition. A comparatively large number of agenda steps were taken in the experiment (five) as well as a large number of votes (forty-one). The general point here is that, even though a set of equilibrium outcomes exist, such points were seldom proposed in experiments with access costs.

Examining the agendas presents a very different picture than that gained from figures 3 and 4. Agenda access costs clearly generate a drag on the

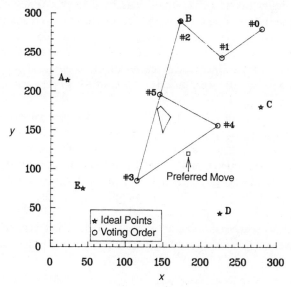

Fig. 5. Experiment A9:2 agenda trajectory

collective choice process. However, no clean separation among the outcomes exists. In part, this may be due to the difficulty that subjects have in building an agenda leading into the equilibrium set. After all, the agenda access cost equilibrium is only retentive, not attractive. Since it is costly to build an extensive agenda, and subjects seem attuned to these costs, it may be little surprise that points in the equilibrium are not selected. It is equally possible that subjects are confused by the complex structure of the experiment. Not only must subjects consider a large number of proposals, but subjects must also make proposals to the floor that are attractive to a majority coalition. In order to more precisely test the model of agenda access costs, we conducted a second series of experiments that simplified the proposing mechanism.

Series *B*

The series *B* experiments were designed to simplify the collective choice mechanism. A single, fundamental change was made in this series. Instead of subjects making proposals to the floor which could then be seconded as amendments to the status quo, a set of proposals were fixed by the experimenters. These alternatives were introduced at the outset of each decision period and subjects could second them in any order. In this way, we ensured not only that an alternative in the equilibrium set could be considered as an amendment, but we were able to test different solution concepts by judiciously selecting alternatives.

Only a single treatment condition was used in this series of experiments—the presence or absence of agenda access costs. Given that there was no statistical difference among outcomes across cost conditions when controlling for the size of the loss function, all series *B* experiments were run under the high-loss parameter. In replications under the cost condition, subjects voting for the amendment were assessed a fee of $1.50 for each successful change to the status quo.

Figure 6 displays the status quo and the sixteen alternatives that were placed on the floor in each replication. When subjects participated in multiple decision periods, each period subjects received new identities, were randomly assigned to new ideal points, and all ideal points and fixed alternatives were rotated either 90 or 180 degrees around the center of the alternative space. In addition, the numbering of the fixed proposals, but not their location, was randomly reset during each decision period.

Under the no-cost condition, alternatives 2, 3, 4, 5, and 6 are elements of the competitive solution (McKelvey and Ordeshook 1978).[11] The competitive

---

11. Because the points located in the space are integers, these points are not exact elements of the competitive solution. There is some small amount of rounding error. As well, the competi-

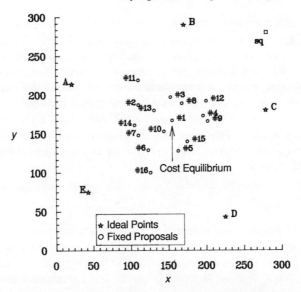

Fig. 6. Fixed proposals, series *B* experiments

solution is included since it has had reasonable success in predicting outcomes in committee games. Alternative 10 has several properties. It is a point lying inside the yolk (McKelvey 1986) and, for these alternatives, it is in the least alternative set (Packel 1981) and is the Copeland winner (Grofman et al. 1987). Finally, alternative 1 provides the group its maximum earnings in the experiment and is a point that Eavey (1989) focuses on in her discussions.[12] Under the no-cost replications, a large number of majority-rule voting cycles exist and no alternative is undominated.

The same alternatives are used in replications with a cost condition. In this instance, alternative 1 is a cost equilibrium, and for this set of alternatives, it is the only equilibrium. Thus, alternative 1 is the predicted outcome for collective choices under the cost condition. Introducing costs changes the

---

tive solution is not an appropriate prediction for these experiments, since it implicitly depends on a form of bargaining between coalition members. This element of bargaining is highly restricted in this experiment.

12. Alternative 10 is also a contender for the group maximum, since there is little difference between it and alternative 1. In some ways, alternative 10 might be a "fairer" alternative, in the sense that it has the least variance in subject payments of any of the alternatives and is quite close to providing the group maximum. However, it is unlikely that considerations of obtaining the group maximum are driving these experiments, since subjects have only private information about their own preferences and they are unable to communicate anything more than whether they wish to second an alternative.

dominance relations among the remaining proposals in two ways. First, the number of majority-rule cycles decreases and, second, it becomes increasingly difficult to uncover an agenda path leading to the equilibrium set. In the face of costs, the underlying preference relations between alternatives change. Any change to the status quo incorporates a cost of making that change. For an alternative to be preferred, it must be better than the status quo by an amount greater than the cost of changing the status quo. By incorporating these transaction costs, the dominance relations among alternatives change, with the consequence that the number of voting paths leading to any particular alternative is reduced.

Series *B* Results

The outcomes for the series *B* replications are shown in figure 7 and table 3. The results are less confusing than those under the series *A* replications, but, on first glance, do not draw a sharp distinction between the cost and no-cost conditions. While four of seventeen agenda cost outcomes appear at the predicted equilibrium, the remaining agenda cost outcomes are scattered among seven additional alternatives, including five outcomes located at two of the competitive solution points. By contrast, under the no-cost condition, only one of fifteen outcomes falls at alternative 1, while the modal number of

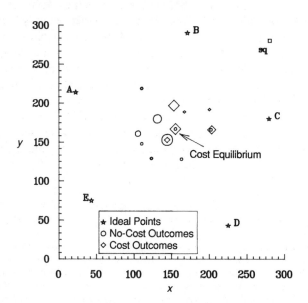

Fig. 7. Fixed agenda outcomes, series *B* experiments. Size of symbol indicates number of outcomes at the outcome point.

TABLE 3. Outcomes for Series *B* Experiments

Experiment:Period	Outcome	Agenda Steps	Votes	Cost Condition
B1:2	(163,128)	20	50	No Cost
B2:3	(155,167)	9	39	No Cost
B4:3	(105,161)	19	60	No Cost
B6:3	(110,219)	25	41	No Cost
B7:2	(105,161)	38	62	No Cost
B11:3	(110,148)	4	38	No Cost
B12:3	(131,180)	4	46	No Cost
B13:3	(144,153)	19	50	No Cost
B14:2	(144,153)	21	43	No Cost
B14:3	(131,180)	26	49	No Cost
B15:2	(144,153)	34	52	No Cost
B15:3	(202,166)	20	47	No Cost
B16:2	(131,180)	25	50	No Cost
B16:3	(123,129)	21	47	No Cost
B18:3	(144,153)	16	54	No Cost
B1:3	(203,166)	4	29	Cost
B2:2	(203,166)	9	51	Cost
B3:2	(200,192)	12	26	Cost
B3:3	(153,197)	1	41	Cost
B4:2	(203,166)	3	32	Cost
B5:2	(155,167)	2	47	Cost
B6:2	(167,189)	5	41	Cost
B7:3	(155,167)	2	43	Cost
B8:2	(110,219)	14	44	Cost
B8:3	(144,153)	2	45	Cost
B9:2	(144,153)	1	46	Cost
B9:3	(153,197)	4	57	Cost
B10:3	(155,167)	2	42	Cost
B11:2	(153,197)	1	29	Cost
B12:2	(153,197)	1	44	Cost
B13:2	(123,129)	3	63	Cost
B17:2	(155,167)	3	32	Cost

these outcomes falls at alternative 10, the least alternative point (or Copeland winner).

The difference in the number of agenda steps between conditions becomes even more striking here than it was under series *A*. On average, under the cost condition, 4.06 changes were made to the status quo. By comparison, an average of 20.07 steps were taken under the no-cost condition. The simplified task in this series of experiments largely accounts for the relatively greater number of agenda steps. No longer do participants make proposals, rather they second alternatives on the floor. The alternative set selected for these experiments induced a large number of voting cycles and it is clear that subjects voted accordingly.

Our theoretical model suggests that while the cost equilibrium may not be attractive, it should certainly be retentive. In thirteen out of seventeen cost replications, choices were made that were not at the equilibrium. Did the agenda move into the equilibrium and then away during the course of any replication? In only two of thirteen replications did the agenda path go into the cost equilibrium (alternative 1) and then move away. In one of these replications, experiment B8:2 this happened twice. However, in this experiment, subjects took fourteen agenda steps, and on average bore over $12.00 in agenda costs (far more than any individual earned in this experiment). This agenda is displayed in figure 8. What is clear from this particular decision period is that members had absorbed such great costs by steps 9 and 11 (when they abandoned the cost equilibrium) that the experiment was meaningless to them (they did not believe the experimenter would take money out of their own pockets, and that the worst that could be done is that they would lose any accumulated earnings for the experiment). The only other instance in which the equilibrium was reached and then abandoned occurred in experiment B9:3, in which subjects only moved four steps. After 36 consecutive votes attempting to change the status quo, two subjects voted to absorb losses of $1.84 and $0.24 to move from the equilibrium. Neither subject exhibited any peculiar voting patterns, so it may be that both regarded the committee at an

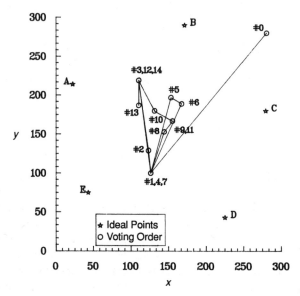

Fig. 8. Experiment B8:2 agenda trajectory

impasse and voted to break it. In the remaining twelve cases, the cost equilibrium was never reached.[13]

From examining the voting patterns of subjects as a whole, it is clear that subjects treat the cost conditions very differently from the no-cost conditions. Examining the percentage of "wrong" votes cast by committee members is illustrative. Considering a "wrong" vote as one that is contrary to the self-interest of a subject, less than 2.8 percent of the total votes cast under the no-cost condition could be considered wrong. On the other hand, 18.7 percent of the votes cast under the cost condition were contrary to a subject's self-interest. Almost uniformly these votes were cast by individuals whose position could have been improved by a movement from the status quo, yet they voted against such a move. We interpret this as meaning that subjects were concerned with the potential cumulative costs of changing the agenda. Consequently, they were very careful when making changes to the status quo, looking for large gains in utility rather than small marginal changes. We return to this point in our discussion of all the experimental results.

Results with a Core

In effect, these experiments point to costs imposing a drag on the agenda process. This translates to widely scattered outcomes in the policy-space under a cost condition as individuals anticipate the cumulative costs for continuing. To further tease apart this conjecture, four additional committees were brought together, each making two decisions. For each group, the first trial was under a cost condition, while the second was without costs. These trials replicate our fixed agenda experiments, except that five of the alternatives were removed (numbers 1, 3, 4, 6, and 9, see fig. 6). By removing five alternatives and retaining the same preference configuration as used in the other experiments, we were able to induce a Core. Alternative 10 is now a retentive equilibrium in the absence of costs. In addition, when costs are added to the agenda process, only alternative 10 is in equilibrium (it is not only the Core, but also the cost-induced equilibrium).

These final eight trials, then, attempted to observe the effect of agenda costs when a Core is present. If subjects are concerned with the potential cumulative costs for proceeding, the outcomes should be scattered around the Core. Meanwhile, when there are no transaction costs for changing the status quo, outcomes should fall in the Core. Our results are given in figure 9 and

---

13. It is worth noting that the dominance relations were such that, under the cost condition, proposal 1 was "reachable" via only four other alternatives. This meant that uncovering an agenda into the cost set remained difficult, even though the array of alternatives members considered was considerably reduced from the series *A* experiments.

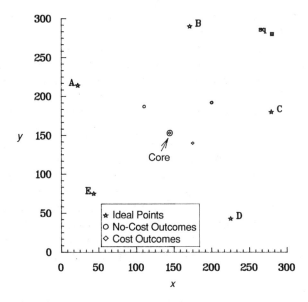

Fig. 9. Fixed agenda outcomes with a core. Size of symbol indicates number of outcomes at the outcome point.

table 4. In the absence of agenda access costs, two of four outcomes are at alternative 10. A third outcome was in the Core, but was moved out through the strategic actions of a single player.[14] The final outcome never included the Condorcet winner in the agenda. Outcomes with agenda access costs are quite revealing. One of the four outcomes fell into the Core, taking three agenda steps to arrive there. Two other outcomes were scattered in the space. The final outcome, from experiment B20:2, is perhaps the most interesting. Although 60 votes were taken in this experiment, all moves from the status quo were voted down. Subjects instead retained the initial status quo, even though some coalition always preferred a move.

These outcomes with a Core also point to the way in which costs have an effect on the agenda process. Again, when costs are present, subjects make far fewer agenda changes. Although subjects vote over almost all of the proposals, they are hesitant to make too many moves, anticipating the cost

---

14. In this experiment, an actor at position *C* on fig. 9 voted to move the status quo out of the Core, to a proposal even further from his ideal point. This vote passed. He subsequently amended the status quo with the alternative (200,192) that was closest to his ideal point. Following this, the subject used a variant of a filibuster tactic, calling for adjournment on the status quo. After 23 consecutive (and uninterrupted) votes against adjourning, a majority coalition ended the game. We regard this as a special case in which a player uncovered a strategy in the experiment allowing him to overturn an ordinarily powerful predictor.

TABLE 4. Outcomes for Series *B* Core Experiments

Experiment:Period	Outcome	Agenda Steps	Votes	Cost Condition
B19:2	(175,140)	1	60	Cost
B20:2	(280,280)	0	60	Cost
B21:2	(144,153)	3	63	Cost
B22:2	(200,192)	4	63	Cost
B19:3	(200,192)	8	70	No Cost
B20:3	(144,153)	2	52	No Cost
B21:3	(144,153)	4	47	No Cost
B22:3	(110,187)	16	49	No Cost

associated with changing the status quo. Nowhere is this clearer than in experiment B20:2 where subjects decided to adjourn and not bear the costs for changing the status quo. On the other hand, the Core provides a reasonable prediction for experiments without costs.

Discussion

Neither the series *A* nor series *B* experiments provide compelling evidence that the presence of agenda access costs yields predictable empirical outcomes. Yet both experimental series illustrate the importance of those costs for the collective choice process. In the first series of experiments, subjects were left to their own devices in proposing alternatives to the floor, making amendments to the current status quo, and choosing a stopping point. When agenda costs were imposed on these experiments, instead of converging to the (induced) cost equilibrium, choices were scattered around this equilibrium set. These choices appeared little different from outcomes selected in the absence of costs. Yet, when examining the agenda processes, important differences emerged between the cost and no-cost conditions. Under the former condition, far fewer agenda steps were taken and seldom did any proposal on the floor represent an improvement for some majority in the experiment.

With these points in mind, a second experimental series was designed with the intention of simplifying the experimental task and ensuring that an alternative exists that is an element of the cost-induced equilibrium set. With the series *B* experiments, we hoped to provide a crisper test of the theoretical model. The results were more encouraging in that a number of the outcomes fell at the cost equilibrium. Even so, subjects usually chose to adjourn the experiment well before uncovering an agenda path into the cost equilibrium. Further experiments with a Core highlight this pattern. Where the Core and cost equilibria coincide, subjects facing costs are less likely to reach these equilibria than subjects not facing costs. What continues to stand out in differentiating these cost conditions is the agenda process. The presence of agenda access costs places a noticeable drag on the collective choice process with subjects taking far fewer agenda steps when facing transaction costs for changing the agenda.

The nature of transaction costs imposed in the cost experiments results in subjects playing a game different from that modeled here. Instead of subjects making myopic vote choices concerned only with the costs attached to amending a status quo, they are much more attuned to the cumulative costs of decision making. Our theoretical model assumes that subjects continue to build an agenda based on marginal improvements over binary choices until they fall into the equilibrium. This model ignores the cumulative costs absorbed by subjects in taking a (potentially) large number of agenda steps. Indeed, in a handful of experiments, subjects took enough agenda steps to dissipate any earnings.

There is clearcut evidence that the voting calculus for subjects varies across experimental treatments. To illustrate this, we examined all 10,735 votes by individuals on amending the status quo. Focusing on whether an individual voted for or against the amendment, we calculated the gain (or loss) in utility, minus costs, for a move from the status quo to the amendment. We estimated, for each experimental series, a PROBIT model predicting vote, based on this change in utility for the amendment (minus costs), a dummy variable for the experimental manipulation (No Cost or Cost), and an interaction term for the change in utility and experimental manipulation. Our estimates for each of the experimental series are given in table 5.

The results for each series are consistent. An individual with a net positive gain in money (gains minus costs) for moving from the status quo to

TABLE 5. PROBIT Estimates for VOTE by Experimental Series

VOTE[a]	DIFF[b]	TRT[c]	DIFF × TRT	N	Percentage Predicted Correctly
Series A	.524	.753	.167	1,475	92.7
	(.035)	(.077)	(.042)		
Series B, no	.367	.466	.251	7,210	90.3
core	(.011)	(.024)	(.011)		
Series B,	.197	.741	.150	2,050	79.9
with core	(.010)	(.047)	(.011)		

Note: Standard errors are in parentheses.
[a]VOTE = 0 if vote for status quo (x^0), 1 if vote for amendment (x).
[b]DIFF = $[u_i(x) - \text{cost}] - u_i(x^0)$.
[c]TRT = 0 if no-cost condition, 1 if cost condition.

the amendment is more likely to vote for the amendment. However, where costs are present, subjects are *less* likely to vote for the amendment. The net gains must be much larger before subjects are willing to make a move and bear the costs for that move. In experiments without agenda costs, subjects consistently voted for the amendment, even though their net gain amounted to only pennies. In experiments with agenda access costs, even a net gain of a dollar would not result in most subjects voting for the amendment.

These PROBIT results are more clearly seen in figure 10. For each experimental series we calculated the probabilities for each subject's vote based on our estimates. These probabilities were then plotted by the dollar gains or losses for the vote. Under the series *A* experiments, votes in the no-cost manipulation illustrate how sensitive subjects were to small changes in value when voting. With the introduction of costs there are consistent deviations, with subjects less likely to vote for the amendment until the net gains are positive and large (in excess of $1.00). The same is true with subject's voting calculus in the two types of series *B* experiments. In these experiments without a Core, the deviations for the costly agenda experiments appear larger than those under the series *A* experiments. Nonetheless, the same pattern holds—subjects facing costs are more likely to vote for large, rather than small, positive gains. Finally, the odd-shaped plot for series *B* experiments with a Core and costs is primarily a function of experiment B20:2 where subjects took a large number of votes but failed to move from the initial status quo. Separate estimates excluding this experiment are consistent with the estimates obtained from series *B* experiments without a Core.

These data clearly support the idea that costs for making changes to the status quo place a drag on the agenda process over and above the costs for such changes. Subjects are clearly attuned to the cumulative costs they incur. They recognize the possibility that a large number of agenda steps can be taken, and that such action can be quite costly. Our theoretical model assumes that subjects continue to build an agenda until they fall into the equilibrium. Once there, no further movement is possible and rational decision makers stop. However, even in the series *B* experiments with a limited number of proposals, an agenda could consist of a large number of (costly) steps before reaching the equilibrium. In such a case, a subject could effectively squander his or her earnings long before settling on a point in equilibrium. Again, subjects appear to be concerned with finding an optimal stopping rule, given uncertainty about where the agenda can go and how many steps it can take to get there.

Faced with our experimental results, we might be tempted to conclude that costs make no difference, but such a conclusion is unwarranted. A careful analysis of the two experimental series indicates that costs do affect decision outcomes, but they do so in ways not captured by the equilibrium analysis

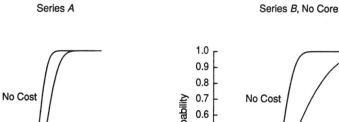

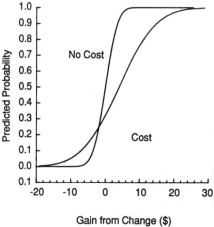

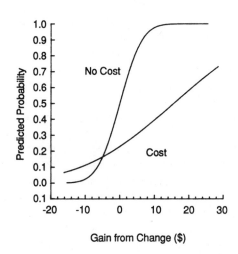

Fig. 10. Estimated probability of vote by dollar gain

used here. Instead of reacting myopically to each agenda change, subjects appear to consider the cumulative costs for continuing the decision process. Such a conjecture is supported informally by these experimental results. In each case, subjects took far fewer agenda steps under a cost condition than under a no-cost condition and often voted against proposals that left them marginally better off.

Conclusion

In this article, we have examined the effects of agenda access costs on the decision-making outcomes of a majority-rule spatial voting game. Theoretically, spatial voting games of the form we consider are generally characterized by a lack of predictable outcomes. Including agenda costs induces a nonempty equilibrium set and provides a predictive set for games incorporating such costs. Using this theoretical structure, we ran two experimental series, each designed to test differences in outcomes attributable to agenda access costs. Series *A* operated under an open agenda process in which subjects proposed alternatives, called votes on amendments, ordered an agenda, and decided collectively when the game would adjourn. Series *B* operated over a fixed set of alternatives where subjects called votes, ordered the agenda, and decided when to adjourn, but could not propose new alternatives. We assumed that the simplified task associated with series *B* would provide a crisper test of the model.

Neither the series *A* nor series *B* experiments provide compelling support for predictions of *outcomes* under our theoretical model. Yet the experiments clearly point to the salience of agenda costs for the collective choice *process*. With these mixed results we are forced to rethink the relationship between theory and empirical test in order to evaluate at what point our analysis might be improved. Several possibilities exist that might account for the limited predictive power of the model in its present form.

First, the initial contention that games with decision costs differ from games without costs may be wrong. Individuals may simply fail to incorporate such costs in their decision calculus. While the outcomes produced in our cost and no-cost experiments cannot completely refute such a contention, there are sufficient differences in the processes associated with each experimental condition to suggest that individuals react differently to these two manipulations. When confronted with agenda costs, actors behave as if they are far more deliberate in their choices, often voting against marginal gains and leaving behind a very constrained agenda. In the absence of costs, actors take a very myopic perspective, voting for marginal gains and, consequently, generating an agenda that wanders over a good deal of the policy space.

A second possibility concerns the relationship between equilibrium out-

comes and prediction. Our model establishes a retentive equilibrium set associated with the introduction of fixed agenda access costs. A nonempty equilibrium set can prove important in predicting final outcomes, but it depends on
other dynamic features of the game. Certainly, if an experiment were started
with a status quo located in the cost equilibrium set, our expectation would be
that, in the presence of costs, it would be the outcome. Alternatively, in the
absence of costs, an agenda would quickly move away from this set. When
the decision process starts outside this set, as is the case in our experiment, it
is less clear how successfully the equilibrium set will predict. Our model
ignores a good deal about the dynamic structure of the game. However, such a
process appears to be an important component of our results. Consequently it
may be useful to turn next to the relationship between process and retentive
equilibrium.

A final possibility asks whether a model based on myopic decisions at
each decision stage can account for a process in which individuals face cumulative costs as the agenda grows longer. While it is myopically rational to
continue mcvement until there exists no move that exceeds the access costs
for all members of a majority coalition, it may be rational in an expectations
sense to stop the process after a given number of decision stages regardless of
whether there exists an alternative that improves the coalition's position.

At this point we are not prepared to abandon our model of agenda access
costs. Certainly, costs matter when making collective choices. However, our
experiments indicate the static model we employ misses several key features
of this game. Incorporating a dynamic component, in which expectations held
by actors are taken into account in the model, may provide a fruitful direction
for additional research. We remain optimistic that models incorporating decision costs into the collective choice process will provide insight into the
stability of inherently unstable voting processes.

REFERENCES

Baron, David, and John Ferejohn. 1989. "Bargaining in Legislatures." *American
    Political Science Review* 83:1181–1206.
Buchanan, James, and Gordon Tullock. 1962. *Calculus of Consent.* Ann Arbor: Uni-
    versity of Michigan Press.
Cox, Gary. 1987. "The Uncovered Set and the Core." *American Journal of Political
    Science* 31:408–22.
Eavey, Cheryl. 1989. "Patterns of Distribution in Spatial Games." Working Paper.
    Florida State University.
Fiorina, Morris, and Charles Plott. 1978. "Committee Decisions under Majority Rule:
    An Experimental Study." *American Political Science Review* 72:575–98.
Grofman, Bernard, Guillermo Owen, Nicholas Noviello, and Amihal Glazer. 1987.

"Stability and Centrality of Legislative Choice in the Spatial Context." *American Political Science Review* 81:538–53.

Herzberg, Roberta, and Rick K. Wilson. 1989. "Effects of Agenda Access Costs in a Spatial Committee Setting." Working Paper no. 5. Rice University.

Hoffman, Elizabeth, and Matthew Spitzer. 1985. "Entitlements, Rights, and Fairness: An Experimental Examination of Subjects' Concepts of Distributive Justice." *Journal of Legal Studies* 14:259–97.

McKelvey, Richard. 1976. "Intransitivities in Multidimensional Voting Models and Some Implications for Agenda Control." *Journal of Economic Theory* 12:472–82.

McKelvey, Richard. 1979. "General Conditions for Global Intransitivities in Formal Voting Models." *Econometrica* 47:1085–1111.

McKelvey, Richard. 1986. "Covering, Dominance, and Institution-Free Properties of Social Choice." *American Journal of Political Science* 30:283–314.

McKelvey, Richard, and Peter Ordeshook. 1978. "Competitive Coalition Theory." In *Game Theory and Political Science*, ed. Peter Ordeshook. New York: New York University Press.

McKelvey, Richard, Peter Ordeshook, and Mark Winer. 1978. "The Competitive Solution for *N*-Person Games without Transferable Utility with an Application to Competitive Games." *American Political Science Review* 72:599–615.

Ordeshook, Peter, and Thomas Schwartz. 1987. "Agendas and the Control of Political Outcomes." *American Political Science Review* 81:179–99.

Packel, Edward. 1981. "A Stochastic Solution Concept for N-Person Games." *Mathematics of Operation Research* 6:349–62.

Plott, Charles. 1979. "The Application of Laboratory Experimental Methods to Public Choice." In *Collective Decision Making: Applications from Public Choice Theory*, ed. Clifford Russell. Washington, D.C.: Resources for the Future.

Riker, William. 1980. "Implications from the Disequilibrium of Majority Rule for the Study of Institutions." *American Political Science Review* 74:432–46.

Schofield, Norman. 1978. "Instability of Simple Dynamic Games." *Review of Economic Studies* 45:575–94.

Wilson, Rick K. 1986a. "Forward and Backward Agenda Procedures: Committee Experiments on Structurally-Induced Equilibrium." *Journal of Politics* 48:390–409.

Wilson, Rick K. 1986b. "Results on the Condorcet Winner: A Committee Experiment on Time Constraints." *Simulations and Games* 17:217–43.

Wilson, Rick K. 1989. "Decision Costs and Economic Rationality: Some Experimental Design Problems." Paper presented at the annual meeting of the American Political Science Association, Atlanta.

Sincere versus Strategic Voting Behavior in Small Groups

Amnon Rapoport, Dan S. Felsenthal, and Zeev Maoz

1. Introduction

Plurality voting (PV) is a voting system in which each individual casts a ballot for one alternative, and the alternative with most votes wins. Approval voting (AV) is another voting system for multicandidate elections (Brams and Fishburn 1983) that allows a voter to vote for as many alternatives as he or she wishes. Under AV an individual can cast no more than one vote per alternative (i.e., no cumulative voting), and the alternative with the most votes wins. It is well-known that PV is one of the most obviously manipulable of all voting systems. Manipulability is not an issue for AV if all voters have dichotomous preferences. But if at least some of the voters have nondichotomous preferences, AV is also likely to promote strategic voting (Niemi 1984).

As noted by Niemi and Frank (1982 and 1985), the topic of strategic voting does not readily lend itself to systematic investigation. This is the case where PV is concerned and, even more so—due to the ambiguity of "sincere" approval voting—where AV is concerned. Of course, we have Farquharson's (1969) algorithm of eliminating dominated strategies. However, as a descriptive model of voting behavior, his approach is seriously flawed by its complexity. We have little understanding of what would happen if voters tried to behave strategically in PV or AV elections when the group is small and the assumption of common knowledge of all preference orderings is tenable.

The present study continues the investigation of strategic voting in single-stage elections started by Farquharson (1969) and Niemi and Frank

This research was funded by grant # 84-00329 of the U.S.-Israel Binational Science Foundation (BSF) Jerusalem, Israel, in collaboration with Steven J. Brams. We wish to thank Thomas R. Palfrey for useful comments. We also wish to acknowledge the help of Ariel Cohen, who wrote the computer programs for the various voting tasks, and the assistance of Shmuel Ophir, Hamutal Pinnes, and Anat Toyster, who supervised the experimental sessions.

(1982 and 1985). It departs from these earlier studies in three major respects. First, the model that we propose to account for strategic voting relaxes the assumption, shared by these earlier studies, that blocs of voters act independently of one another. Although voters are assumed to vote secretly and anonymously, our model posits that they tacitly coordinate their actions. In this sense, we extend the assumption of tacit coordination, which Niemi and Frank (1982) used to justify bloc voting of voters sharing the same preference ordering, to interaction among blocs that do not have identical preferences. Second, we replace the a priori evaluation of the models of Farquharson (1969) and Niemi and Frank (1982 and 1985) by an experimental investigation designed to test these models competitively. Finally, our investigation includes both the PV and AV procedures.

Sincere voting is said to take place if and only if, whenever an individual votes for some candidate, he or she votes for all candidates preferred to that candidate (Brams 1982). For the PV procedure, this definition implies that the individual votes for his or her top preference. The implication of this definition for the AV procedure is ambiguous (Niemi 1984); we shall discuss it in section 3. It is important to note that, for both PV and AV, sincere voting does not require any consideration or even knowledge of the preference orderings of the other voters. In contrast, strategic voting—in the sense that we shall use it here—must take into consideration the preference orderings of the other voters. Therefore, we shall assume that strategic voting (in contrast to judgmental error) occurs only if the following two assumptions are satisfied: (1) each voter believes he or she knows how the other voters are likely to behave, and (2) each voter is willing and capable of performing all the necessary mental computations required to achieve his or her goal.

Both assumptions concern the cognitive system of the voter. Consequently, any model incorporating these two assumptions that attempts to describe rather than prescribe voting behavior is, in essence, a model about the belief system and mental ability of the individual voter. The first assumption concerns the voter's beliefs about the voting behavior of others. Even when these beliefs are based on common information (e.g., voting records of committee members) about preference orderings of the others, they may vary from one individual to another. For example, a voter in a small committee may have complete information about the preference orderings of the others and assume that they will all vote sincerely. Equipped with the same information, another voter may assume that some of the other voters who share a given preference ordering will vote sincerely, whereas another subset of voters with a different preference ordering will not.

The second assumption concerns mental calculations in the light of strategic (rather than environmental) uncertainty (Suleiman and Rapoport 1988). Political analyses of voting profiles and voting polls in national elections show that these calculations actually take place, and that they may become rather involved. Even in small committees, where the number of voters and number of candidates is small, strategic considerations may become so involved and the combinations so numerous as to exceed the mental capability of most voters. Voters who share the same information about the preference orderings of the other voters are likely to differ from one another in the "depth" of their strategic calculations. Therefore, modeling the mental steps that actually comprise these strategic calculations may prove to be a tedious and arduous task.

Modeling of voting behavior is considerably simplified if only admissible strategies are allowed. Relative to voter *i*, let us call a selection of strategies by each of the other voters a contingency (Dummett 1984). If voter *i* knows the contingency, he or she can calculate the effect of any strategy available to him or her, and then choose one defeated by no other. In general, the voter will not possess this information. Denote by M the set of strategies and by S, $S \in M$, a particular strategy. We say that strategy S_1 rivals another strategy S_2 for voter *i* if there is a contingency in which S_1 beats S_2. Of course, several strategies may rival each other depending on the contingency. Strategy S_1 is said to dominate S_2 if S_1 rivals S_2 but S_2 does not rival S_1. Finally, we call strategy S admissible for *i* if there is no other strategy S' that dominates it. Left to themselves, voters have no motive to adopt an inadmissible strategy. All of the models of voting behavior that we consider and test make the testable assumption that only admissible strategies will be chosen.

The frequency of strategic voting may depend on the number of alternatives (*m*), the number of blocs of voters (*n*), and the voting procedure under consideration. To simplify matters, the present study addresses the case $m = 3$. As noted by Niemi and Frank (1982, 152) "the case of three alternatives is sufficiently complicated to satisfy many a masochist." The study also assumes strict preferences, complete information about the preference orderings of others, no communication among voters, and bloc voting. For a discussion of these assumptions see Niemi and Frank (1982). Note that with the bloc voting assumption, PV or AV with three alternatives can be conceived of as non-cooperative games with no more than six players, since there are six different preference orderings when a bloc of voters sharing the same preference ordering is assumed to behave as a single player.

Our study has three major aims: (1) presenting and discussing a new model of voting behavior that allows for tacit cooperation among blocs of voters, (2) testing this model competitively against three other models of sincere or strategic voting, and (3) comparing voting behavior in small groups under the PV and AV procedures. The article is organized as follows. Section 2 briefly describes the two models of strategic voting proposed by Farquharson (1969) and Niemi and Frank (1982). Section 3 critically evaluates the independent-action assumption underlying these two models, and then introduces a new model. Sections 4, 5, and 6 report three experiments. The first is a three-alternative, five-person voting experiment conducted under the PV procedure. The second is a three-alternative, six-person experiment also conducted under the PV procedure. The third is a three-alternative, five-person experiment conducted under the AV procedure. Each of these experiments includes seven or eight different voting games with different preference orderings, different distributions of votes, and multiple iterations. Section 7 concludes with a general discussion of all three experiments.

2. Two Models of Strategic Voting

Two models of strategic voting have been proposed. The model of Niemi and Frank (1982)—hereafter referred to as model NF—was originally proposed for the case of three alternatives, strict preferences, and the PV procedure. Farquharson's (1969) model—which we call model F—has a more general scope. However, because the PV procedure is more common, and three alternatives are sufficient to induce strategic voting, model NF may be viewed as addressing the same basic issue of strategic voting.

Both models share the following assumptions.

1. Each voter has complete information regarding the preference orderings of all other voters.
2. Only a single alternative—the one with the largest number of votes—is elected.
3. Ties are broken randomly.
4. Voters with identical preference orderings over the m alternatives vote in the same way, that is, as a single bloc.
5. All voters (blocs) act independently of one another.
6. All voters (blocs) use only admissible voting strategies.

Farquharson's model views voting as the process of choosing one strategy over another. It relies on the observation that, by using the domination concept, participants in a noncooperative n-person voting game can successfully reduce the game without injuring their prospects.[1] First, no voter should choose a strategy that, regardless of how others vote, is dominated. Since this is common knowledge, every participant should eliminate all dominated strategies and focus on the resulting reduced game. After this first round of elimination, new strategies may become dominated, leading to a further reduction in the number of strategies. Each voter continues to eliminate domi-

---

1. It is assumed that voting is conducted simultaneously. For a characterization of inadmissible strategies under PV or AV see the discussion in sec. 3.

nated strategies under the assumption that all voters limit their choices to undominated strategies. Farquharson calls the successive application of this algorithm sophisticated voting, and the alternatives remaining after no further reductions are possible sophisticated voting strategies (Ordeshook 1986).

Model F was not originally proposed as a descriptive model of voting behavior. It has been noted that the algorithm it introduces of eliminating dominated strategies sequentially is cumbersome (e.g., Nurmi 1987). Voters may not be expected to implement the algorithm unless the number of voters or alternatives is small. To account for voting behavior, Niemi and Frank (1982, 157–58) proposed an alternative, simpler model involving the following steps.

1. Voters consider the current situation, a situation being a description of how all blocs vote and the outcome implied by that voting. At the beginning, the current situation is sincere voting by all blocs.
2. Each bloc determines whether it can improve the outcome by altering its own vote while assuming that all other votes remain the same.
3a. If no bloc can improve the outcome, the current situation is a Nash equilibrium, and the current situation contains the sophisticated strategy and the sophisticated outcome.
3b. If exactly one bloc can improve the outcome, each changes its vote accordingly, and the process reverts to step 1.
3c. If two voters can each obtain better outcomes than those obtained in step 1, they examine a 2 × 2, two-person game in normal form in which each of the two voters has two pure strategies—voting for one's top or second preference. The outcomes listed in the 2 × 2 payoff matrix are derived on the assumption that all the remaining voters will not change their strategies. In the 2 × 2 matrix, each of the two voters examines whether he or she has a dominant strategy. The voter(s) having dominant strategies are predicted to use them, and the process reverts to step 1. If neither of the two voters has a dominant strategy, the outcome is said to be indeterminate.

We (Felsenthal, Rapoport, and Maoz 1988) tested models F and NF experimentally in a series of seven four-person, three-alternative, noncooperative voting games under the PV procedure. Our results suggested that none of these models accounted satisfactorily for the voters' behavior. Consequently, we proposed a new model for three-alternative, n-person noncooperative games under the plurality voting procedure. Although the model outperformed models F and NF, we have recently concluded that one of its basic assumptions, which requires each voter to identify the Condorcet winner, is unrealistic.[2] The model presented in the following section maintains the assumption of tacit cooperation but no longer requires voters to identify Condorcet winners, if they exist.

3. Tacit Cooperation in Noncooperative Voting Games

The experimental evidence presented by us (Felsenthal, Rapoport, and Maoz 1988), is consistent with the assumption that voters tacitly coordinate their strategies and vote for the same alternative. The failure of models F and NF may be due, in part, to their common assumption that all voters act independently of one another. The following example, drawn from Niemi and Frank 1982 (163), illustrates the most obvious difficulty with model F and serves to motivate our proposed model.

Assume that there are twenty-nine voters operating under the PV procedure and having to choose one of three candidates, a, b, or c. The preference orderings are as follows: six voters (bloc A) have the preference ordering $a > b > c$, twelve voters (bloc B) have the preference ordering $a > c > b$, eight voters (bloc C) have the preference ordering $b > a > c$, and three voters (bloc D) have the preference ordering $c > a > b$. The social preference ordering in this example is $a > c > b$, and the Condorcet winner (a) constitutes the top preference of eighteen of the twenty-nine voters. Nevertheless, as shown in table 1, the outcome is indeterminate because, according to model F, none of the four blocs has a dominant strategy.

The reason for this indeterminacy is that, due to the inability of voters to communicate and reach binding agreements, model F requires each bloc to consider the possibility that each of the other three blocs may vote for any but its least preferred (and inadmissible) alternative. Indeed, when bloc A considers the possibility that bloc B will vote for its second preference (c), there is one contingency (compare outcomes of strategies 6 and 14 in table 1) where bloc A is better off by voting for its second preference (b). Similarly, when bloc B considers the possibility that bloc A will vote for its second preference, there is one contingency in which bloc B is better off by voting for its second preference (compare outcomes of strategies 9 and 13 in table 1). In a similar vein, neither bloc C nor bloc D have a dominant strategy in round 1. Consequently, no reduction in the number of strategy combinations is possible.

But is it reasonable, in this example, to require blocs A and B to determine their choices on the possibility that the other bloc will vote for its second

---

2. Condorcet winners do not always exist. If they exist, they are not necessarily unique. For example, two alternatives, x and y, constitute Condorcet winners if the number of voters preferring x to y is equal to the number preferring y to x, and if each of these two alternatives is preferred by an absolute majority of the voters to each of the remaining alternatives.

TABLE 1.   Voting Outcomes in Model F

Bloc	Voters	Preference Ordering	Admissible Strategies															
			1	2	3	4	5	6	7	8	9	10	11	12	13	14	15	16
A	6	$a > b > c$	a	a	a	a	a	a	a	a	b	b	b	b	b	b	b	b
B	12	$a > c > b$	a	a	a	a	c	c	c	c	a	a	a	a	c	c	c	c
C	8	$b > a > c$	b	b	a	a	b	b	a	a	b	b	a	a	b	b	a	a
D	3	$c > a > b$	c	a	c	a	c	a	c	a	c	a	c	a	c	a	c	a
Outcome		$a > c > b^a$	a	a	a	a	c	c	c	a	b	a	a	a	c	b	c	c

[a] This is the social preference ordering.

(rather than top) preference? We contend that an alternative way of modeling the voter's strategic considerations is possible. Although blocs A and B cannot communicate with each other and reach a binding agreement to vote for their top preference, they may realize that if they *tacitly* coordinate their actions and vote for their (identical) top preference, alternative a would be elected regardless of how blocs C and D vote. This tacit cooperation is quite straightforward, hardly requiring any mental effort on the part of the voters. Evidence that it actually takes place in other contexts has been provided by Schelling (1963). Niemi and Frank used tacit coordination to justify bloc voting: "Each voter is likely to see his interests as identical to those of all the voters who hold the same opinion as himself, and likewise for those holding other opinions, and as a consequence, presumably analyzes the strategic situation in terms of blocs (of known size) of like-minded individuals" (1982, 153). This reasoning is readily extended to our experimental investigation where bloc voting is experimentally induced.

This and other examples have motivated our present model of strategic voting, referred to as model RFM. In its present form, the model is applicable when preferences are strict, $m = 3$, and voters operate under the PV or AV procedure. Generalization to a larger number of alternatives is possible. Except for the independent-action assumption, the assumptions underlying model RFM are identical to those underlying models F and NF. Before describing the mental steps that the voter is assumed to follow, a few definitions are in order.

We denote the set of voters by N and the number of votes cast for alternative by i ($i \in M$) $v(i)$. Under PV, a voter is said to vote sincerely if he or she votes for his or her top preference, and to vote strategically if he or she votes for her second preference. Voting for the last preference is inadmissible. The same distinction between sincere and strategic voting under AV is ambiguous

(Niemi 1984). To illustrate this ambiguity, suppose that the voter has the preference ordering $x > y > z > w$. Surely, it would be insincere to vote for z and not to vote for x and y, because they are both preferred to z. Indeed, voting only for z (and only for y, for that matter) is inadmissible. But how should the voter express his or her preferences honestly, particularly—as is the case in our experiments—when the preference ordering is experimentally induced by rendering the payoff given to the subject contingent on the election of x, y, z, or w? Should the voter vote only for x? For x and y? For x, y, and z? "All of these votes satisfy the definition of sincere AV, but they are obviously not equivalent. Nor are they likely to lead to equivalent outcomes" (Niemi 1984, 953).

In attempting to resolve this ambiguity, we again considered the distinction between admissible and inadmissible strategies under AV. When $m = 3$, AV allows for seven voting strategies:

   a) voting for the first preference,
   b) voting for the second preference,
   c) voting for the third preference,
   d) voting for the first and second preferences,
   e) voting for the first and third preferences,
   f) voting for the second and third preferences,
   g) voting for all the three preferences.

Only strategies (a) and (d) are admissible; the other five are not (Brams and Fishburn 1983).

Because voting only for the top preference is: (1) identical with sincere voting under PV, and (2) seems to better reflect *honest* behavior, as it requires no calculations at all, we designate strategy (a) as sincere, and strategy (d) as strategic.

A winning set is a set $S \subseteq M$ of alternatives such that if all n voters vote sincerely (under PV or AV), then $i \in S$ implies that $v(i) \geq v(j)$ for all $j \neq i$.

A tacit coalition over alternative i is a set of voters $T(i)$, where $T(i) \subseteq N$ such that, for every member of $T(i)$:

   1. alternative i is the first preference, or
   2. alternative i is the second preference, and
       a) the last preference is included in the set S, if $i \notin S$, or
       b) the first preference is not included in the set S, if $i \in S$.

To illustrate these definitions, consider the following example. Assume that there are sixty voters operating under the PV procedure and having to choose one of three alternatives, x, y, or z. The preference orderings are as follows: eighteen voters (bloc A) have the preference ordering $x > z > y$, seven voters (bloc B) have the preference ordering $z > y > x$, twenty-one voters (bloc *C*) have the preference ordering $y > z > x$, one voter (bloc *D*) has the preference ordering $x > y > z$, and thirteen voters (bloc *E*) have the preference ordering $z > x > y$. If voting is sincere, then $v(x) = 19$, $v(y) = 21$, and $v(z) = 20$. The winning set is $S = \{y\}$, and the tacit coalitions are: $T(x) = \{A, D, E\}$, $T(y) = \{B, C, D\}$, and $T(z) = \{A, B, E\}$. $T(x)$ controls thirty-two voters, $T(y)$ controls twenty-nine voters, and $T(z)$ controls thirty-eight voters.

Each bloc (hereafter referred to as *voter*) is assumed by model RFM to go through the following steps.

Step 1.　Identify the winning set *S*.

Step 2.　Is there any alternative in *S* whose tacit coalition controls an absolute majority of the votes?

If yes, call such an alternative a *winner* and go to step 9 (vote sincerely).

If no, go to step 3.

Step 3.　Does the tacit coalition over the voter's first preference control more votes than the tacit coalition over his or her last preference?

If yes, go to step 4.

If no, go to step 7.

Step 4.　Does the tacit coalition over the voter's second preference control more votes than the tacit coalition over his or her last preference?

If yes, go to step 5.

If no, go to step 9 (vote sincerely).

Step 5.　Does the tacit coalition over the voter's first preference control more votes than the tacit coalition over his or her second preference, excluding his or her votes?

If yes, go to step 9 (vote sincerely).

If no, go to step 6.

Step 6.　Does the tacit coalition over the voter's first preference control exactly the same number of votes as the tacit coalition over his or her second preference, excluding his or her votes?

If yes, go to step 11 (the vote is indeterminate).

If no, go to step 10 (vote strategically).

Step 7.　Does the tacit coalition over the voter's second preference control more votes than the tacit coalition over his or her last preference?

If yes, go to step 8.

If no, go to step 11 (the vote is indeterminate).

Step 8.　Is the voter's first preference included in set *S?*

If yes, go to step 11 (the vote is indeterminate).

If no, go to step 10 (vote strategically).

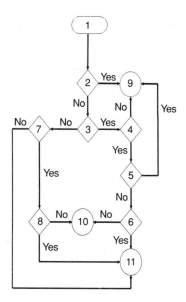

Fig. 1. Flow chart for model RFM

Step 9.   Vote sincerely.
Step 10.   Vote strategically.
Step 11.   The vote is indeterminate.

The steps of the model are depicted in figure 1.

To describe the different contingencies, assume (without loss of generality) that some voter has the preference ordering $x > y > z$. Denote the number of votes assigned to this voter by v, and the number of votes controlled by the three tacit coalitions $T(x)$, $T(y)$, and $T(z)$ by $t(x)$, $t(y)$, and $t(z)$, respectively.

There are three contingencies where model RFM predicts sincere voting for this voter (box 9 in fig. 1):

1. There exists a winner.
2. There exists no winner, $t(x) > t(z)$, and $t(z) \geq t(y)$.
3. There exists no winner, $t(x) > t(z)$, $t(y) > t(z)$, and $t(x) > t(y) - v$. In this case, if the focal voter joins the tacit coalition over his or her top preference, this coalition will defeat the two other tacit coalitions.

Strategic voting (box 10 in fig. 1) is predicted by model RFM in two cases:

1. There exists no winner, $t(x) > t(z)$, $t(y) > t(z)$, and $t(x) < t(y) - v$. Even if the focal voter joins the tacit coalition over his or her top preference, this coalition will be defeated by the tacit coalition over his or her second preference. Consequently, the voter joins the winners by voting strategically.
2. There exists no winner $t(z) \geq t(x)$, $t(y) > t(z)$, and $x \notin S$. In this case, the tacit coalition over the voter's second preference controls more votes than each of the other two tacit coalitions. In addition, the voters's top preference is not included in the winning set, thereby reducing the motivation to vote sincerely.

In three other cases (box 11 in fig. 1), model RFM leaves the choice between sincere and strategic voting indeterminate.

1. There exists no winner, $t(x) > t(z)$, $t(y) > t(z)$, and $t(x) = t(y) - v$. Because the two tacit coalitions over his or her first and second preference control the same number of votes, even when he or she casts his or her votes with the former coalition, the voter may vote either sincerely or strategically.
2. There exists no winner, $t(z) \geq t(x)$, and $t(z) \geq t(y)$. In this case, the tacit coalition over the voter's last preference is likely to win. Consequently, the voter is indifferent between sincere and strategic voting.
3. There exists no winner, $t(z) \geq t(x)$, $t(y) > t(z)$, and $x \in S$. In this case, the voter is supposed to have a conflict between voting for his or her top preference, which—under sincere voting—is included in the winning set, and voting strategically in support of the tacit coalition over the voter's second preference controlling the same or more votes than the other tacit coalitions. Model RFM leaves this conflict unresolved, making no prediction in this case.

Mental steps are not observable, but their implications are. To test model RFM competitively against models F, NF, and S (model S predicts sincere voting), we submitted all four models to carefully designed five- and six-person voting games in three different experiments. In none of these games are the predictions of all four models identical. The design and results of these experiments are described in the next three sections.

4. Experiment 1

Experiment 1 included seven different five-person voting games played under the PV procedure. All the games were played noncooperatively. Each involved the choice of one of three candidates.

Method

Subjects. Fifty male and female subjects participated in the experiment. The subjects were undergraduate students from the University of Haifa who volunteered to take part in a single-session, computer-controlled voting experiment with monetary reward contingent on performance.

Procedure. Ten groups of five subjects participated in a computer-controlled voting experiment. Each subject was seated in a separate, soundproof cubicle containing a computer terminal, paper, and pencil. Information about the voting game was displayed on a monitor, whereas the responses were typed on a computer keyboard. Communication among the subjects during the game was prohibited.

Written instructions informed the subjects that they were about to participate in a series of seven, five-person voting games, each of which iterated six times. Each game depicted a voting situation in which three candidates, labeled *a, b,* and *c,* compete in an election in which the one receiving the most votes is elected. Ties were to be broken randomly. Each subject was then presented (on the monitor) complete information, in tabular form, about (1) the payoff for each voter associated with the election of each of the three candidates, and (2) the number of votes assigned to each voter. Figure 2 presents the information displayed to the subjects in game 3.

Each voter was instructed to cast all of his or her votes on each iteration for one candidate only, thus maximizing his or her monetary gain. Voters were

GAME NUMBER 3

Iteration Number ____

You are player ____

				Payoffs
Player	No. of Votes	a	b	c
A	11	0.5	0	1
B	8	1	0	0.5
C	18	0	1	0.5
D	14	1	0.5	0
E	3	0	0.5	1

For which candidate do you wish to vote? ____

Fig. 2. Example of the computer display in experiment 1

informed that ties, if they occurred, would be broken randomly. A subject was paid IS 1.0, IS 0.5, or IS 0.0, if his or her first, second, or third most preferred candidate, respectively, was elected (IS 1 = $0.63).

Subjects were instructed to consider the information on the screen carefully before making their choice. Voting was conducted by pressing the appropriate key (*a, b,* or *c*) on the keyboard. The paper and pencil could be used for calculations or record keeping.

Each iteration ended after all five subjects registered their votes. At that point, the computer informed the subjects of the outcome of the election, presented the payoff gained by each of the subjects, and moved to the next trial.

At the end of the experiment (after completing 7 × 6 = 42 trials), the payoffs were totaled and displayed. The subjects were interrogated informally about their voting decisions, paid, and dismissed.

Experimental Games. In constructing the games, we required that at least one of the four models (F, NF, S, or RFM) predicts a different decision for at least one of the five voters. Additionally, the series of seven games included at least one game in each of the following categories.

1. Condorcet winner(s) exist(s), and model F predicts that the Condorcet winner(s) will be elected.
2. Condorcet winner(s) exist(s), but model F predicts an indeterminate outcome.
3. Condorcet winner(s) exist(s), but model F predicts that some other candidate will be elected.
4. The social preference ordering is cyclical.

Table 2 shows the seven voting games played in experiment 1. The games are labeled according to the sequence in which they were played. In each game, column 1 identifies the voter, column 2 presents the number of votes, and column 3 displays the preference ordering of the voter as induced by the payoffs associated with the election of each of the three candidates.

The predictions of each of the four models are presented in the four right-hand columns of table 2. For example, in game 1, model F predicts that voters *A, B, C, D,* and *E* would vote for candidates *a, c, b, a,* and *a,* respectively. The symbol *x−y* indicates a predicted indeterminacy between candidates *x* and *y*. In terms of the categories described previously, table 2 shows that game 2 falls in category 1, game 7 falls in category 2, game 3 falls in category 4, and the remaining four games fall in category 3.

Results

We first tested for possible learning effects within each game separately to determine whether the results of the voting might be collapsed over iterations.

TABLE 2. Results of Experiment 1

Player	Votes	Preference Ordering	Observed Frequencies					Model Predictions			
			a	a/b	b	b/c	c	F	NF	S	RFM
					Game 1						
A	18	$a > c > b$	15	—	5	—	40	a	a	a	a
B	7	$c > b > a$	0	—	12	—	48	c	c	c	c
C	21	$b > c > a$	1	—	35	—	24	b	b	b	$b–c$
D	1	$a > b > c$	25	—	33	—	2	$a–b$	a	a	$a–b$
E	13	$c > a > b$	14	—	4	—	42	a	a	c	c
Outcome		$c > a > b$	3	—	16	1	40	a	a	b	$b–c$
Del-value								.351	.252	.317	.476
					Game 2						
A	1	$a > b > c$	37	—	18	—	5	b	a	a	$a–b$
B	20	$b > a > c$	41	—	17	—	2	a	a	b	$a–b$
C	13	$a > c > b$	51	—	1	—	8	a	a	a	a
D	18	$c > a > b$	12	—	0	—	48	c	c	c	c
E	8	$c > b > a$	4	—	18	—	38	c	c	c	c
Outcome		$a > c > b$	43	—	3	—	14	a	a	c	$a–c$
Del-value								.455	.508	.429	.669
					Game 3						
A	11	$c > a > b$	15	—	3	—	42	c	c	c	c
B	8	$a > c > b$	42	—	1	—	17	a	a	a	a
C	18	$b > c > a$	5	—	36	—	19	c	c	b	$b–c$
D	14	$a > b > c$	42	—	17	—	1	a	a	a	a
E	3	$c > b > a$	1	—	16	—	43	c	c	c	$b–c$
Outcome		$a > b > c > a$	26	—	16	—	18	c	c	a	$a–c$
Del-value								.394	.394	.512	.614
					Game 4						
A	19	$b > c > a$	2	—	15	—	43	b	b	b	b
B	3	$c > a > b$	2	—	0	—	58	c	c	c	c
C	1	$a > b > c$	38	—	19	—	3	a	a	a	$a–b$
D	20	$a > c > b$	31	—	0	—	29	a	a	a	$a–c$
E	17	$c > b > a$	1	—	3	—	56	b	b	c	c
Outcome		$c > b > a$	4	—	3	—	53	b	b	a	?
Del-value								.288	.288	.456	.620
					Game 5						
A	1	$a > b > c$	17	—	30	—	13	b	b	a	$a–b$
B	17	$a > c > b$	20	—	0	—	40	a	c	a	a
C	21	$b > c > a$	0	—	28	—	32	b	b	b	$b–c$
D	14	$c > a > b$	7	—	0	—	53	a	c	c	c
E	7	$c > b > a$	0	—	4	—	56	c	c	c	c
Outcome		$c > a > b$	6	—	6	1	47	a	c	b/c	$b–c$
Del-value								.273	.414	.345	.547

TABLE 2—*Continued*

Player	Votes	Preference Ordering	Observed Frequencies					Model Predictions			
			a	*a/b*	*b*	*b/c*	*c*	F	NF	S	RFM
					Game 6						
A	10	$c > a > b$	4	—	7	—	49	*a*	*a*	*c*	*c*
B	10	$c > b > a$	0	—	7	—	53	*b*	*b*	*c*	*c*
C	3	$a > b > c$	42	—	18	—	0	*a*	*a*	*a*	*a–b*
D	18	$a > c > b$	41	—	0	—	19	*a*	*a*	*a*	*a*
E	19	$b > c > a$	0	—	17	—	43	*b*	*b*	*b*	*c*
Outcome		$c > a > b$	12	—	3	—	45	*a*	*a*	*a*	*c*
Del-value								.172	.172	.484	.656
					Game 7						
A	13	$c > a > b$	8	—	1	—	51	*a–c*	*a*	*c*	*c*
B	8	$b > a > c$	20	—	38	—	2	*b*	*b*	*b*	*a–b*
C	14	$b > c > a$	0	—	47	—	13	*b*	*b*	*b*	*b–c*
D	17	$a > c > b$	27	—	0	—	33	*a–c*	*a*	*a*	*c*
E	8	$c > b > a$	0	—	9	—	51	*c–b*	*b*	*c*	*c*
Outcome		$c > a \sim b$	5	3	9	2	41	?	*a/b*	*b*	*c*
Del-value								.724	.226	.549	.642

It may be recalled that, at the end of each trial, voters were not informed of the decisions of others; they were only informed of the outcome of the election. Consequently, although there was certainly a possibility of learning, we did not expect dramatic changes in voting patterns from one iteration to another.

Table 3 presents the frequency distributions of the votes cast by the subjects in experiment 1. The distributions are presented separately by game and iteration over all 50 voters. Inspection of table 3 suggests no systematic iteration effects. Statistical analyses of the data support this impression. We subjected the data of each separate game to a one-way ANOVA to test for iteration effect. None of the seven tests yielded significant results ($p > .05$).[3]

We therefore collapsed the votes in each game over iterations. The frequency distributions of the observed votes are presented in table 2 for each game and each player (*A, B, C, D,* and *E*) separately. Columns 4 to 6 (when there are no ties), 4 to 7 (when there is a single tie), or 4 to 8 (when there are

---

3. The ANOVA procedure was run by converting each strategy (sincere, strategic, inadmissible) into a binary variable that gets a value of 1 whenever a subject used this strategy, and zero otherwise. This results in a distribution for each iteration with a mean of *p* (with *p* being the proportion of subjects using the strategy at that iteration) and a variance of pq ($q = 1 - p$). We ran an ANOVA for each strategy and each subject type with the binary strategy variable as a dependent variable and the iteration as the independent variable.

TABLE 3. Frequency Distribution of Votes over Subjects in Experiment 1 by Game and Iteration

		Iteration						
Game	Strategy	1	2	3	4	5	6	Total
1	{*a*}	8	9	9	9	11	9	55
	{*b*}	16	16	16	16	14	11	89
	{*c*}	26	25	25	25	25	30	156
2	{*a*}	20	22	26	26	25	26	145
	{*b*}	9	10	9	8	12	6	54
	{*c*}	21	18	15	16	13	18	101
3	{*a*}	14	16	19	16	18	22	105
	{*b*}	12	13	13	11	13	11	73
	{*c*}	24	21	18	23	19	17	122
4	{*a*}	15	12	9	12	18	12	78
	{*b*}	6	3	7	7	7	7	37
	{*c*}	29	35	34	31	29	31	189
5	{*a*}	7	9	8	6	6	8	44
	{*b*}	9	10	11	13	9	10	62
	{*c*}	34	31	31	31	35	32	194
6	{*a*}	18	17	15	11	12	14	87
	{*b*}	8	6	6	10	9	10	49
	{*c*}	24	27	29	29	29	26	164
7	{*a*}	9	7	9	11	10	9	53
	{*b*}	19	15	14	14	15	18	95
	{*c*}	22	28	27	25	25	23	152

two ties) show the frequency with which each player voted for each of the three alternatives.

The outcome row in each matrix presents the social preference ordering, the observed frequency with which each of the three candidates was actually elected (including one or more ties), and the predicted outcome according to each of the four competing models. A hyphen between two letters indicates "or," a slash indicates a tie, and a question mark indicates an indeterminate outcome.

Dominated Strategies. All four models assume that initially dominated voting strategies will not be chosen. In the present experiment, this prediction means that no player will vote for his or her least preferred alternative. Table 2 confirms this prediction. Of a total of 2,100 votes cast in experiment 1 (fifty subjects by seven games by six iterations), initially dominated strategies were chosen only sixty-four times (3.05 percent), and were committed by only twenty-four of the fifty subjects.

Strategic Voting. Do voters always vote sincerely in accordance with their induced preference orderings? To answer this question, we compared, separately for each game, the frequency distribution of the observed votes to the alternative predicted by model S. For example, model S predicts that player A in game 1 will vote for candidate a. In actuality, as shown in table 2, only 15 of the 60 possible votes were cast for candidate a, whereas 40 votes were cast for the second preference (candidate c). The number of strategic votes summed over the five players in each group was 123, 97, 84, 96, 113, 91, and 83 in games 1 through 7, respectively. Overall, on 687 (32.7 percent) of 2,100 trials, the subjects in experiment 1 voted strategically.

Model Testing. The comparison of the four models to each other is complicated by the fact that model RFM and, to a greater extent, model F make many indeterminate predictions. However, an informal comparison of the observed and predicted voting distributions in table 2 reveals several findings that tend to favor model RFM over the other three models. All of these findings involve comparisons of frequencies of votes in a test between two competitive models. None of these comparisons considers inadmissible votes that disconfirm all the four models.

1. There are six instances in which models RFM and F make different and unique predictions with respect to the players' choices (see game 1, player E; 4, player E; 5, player D; 6, player A; 6, player B; and 6, player E in table 2 regarding the predicted votes). These six instances involve a total of 348 decisions, of which 296 (85.1 percent) are in accordance with model RFM and the remaining 52 (14.9 percent) in accordance with model F.
2. There are nine instances in which models RFM and NF make different, unique predictions with respect to the players' choices (see Game 1, player E; 4, player E; 5, player B; 6, player A; 6, player B; 6, player E; 7, player A; 7, player D; and 7, player E in table 2 regarding the predicted votes). These nine instances involve a total of 527 decisions, of which 398 (75.5 percent) are in accordance with model RFM and the remaining 129 (24.5 percent) in accordance with model NF.
3. There are two instances (player E in game 6 and player D in game 7) in which models RFM and S make different, unique predictions with respect to the player's choices. These two instances involve a total of 120 decisions, of which 76 (63.3 percent) are in accordance with model RFM and the remaining 44 decisions (36.7 percent) in accordance with model S.
4. Model RFM predicted an indeterminate decision in 13 cases. In most of these cases, the prediction corresponded to the high degree of variability in the votes (e.g., players C and D in game 1, player A in game 2, player C in game 3, players C and D in game 4, players A and C in game 5, and player B in game 7).

5. Table 2 shows that Condorcet winners—when they existed (in all games except game 3)—were elected more frequently than any of the other two candidates. Model RFM accounts for this finding as it always included the Condorcet winner in its set of predicted winners. This was not the case with the other three models (see the observed and predicted outcomes of models F, NF, and S in games 4, 6, and 7).

It is evident from these findings that model RFM outperforms the other three models. However, a competitive test of the models cannot rely solely on an inspection of frequency distributions of voting strategies, because event predictions typically differ on several dimensions. Hildebrand, Laing, and Rosenthal (1977) identified four major dimensions for evaluating prediction success: (1) accuracy—the extent to which predictions are correct (and errors are minimized); (2) scope—the proportion of cases for which it is possible for the prediction to be incorrect; (3) precision—a prediction specifying a unique state of the dependent variable is more precise than a prediction that an observation lies in any of several states of the dependent variable; and (4) differentiation—the extent to which different predictions are made for various states of the independent variable. They further developed a prediction logic, specified criteria for measuring prediction success, and proposed a unique measure for bivariate data, denoted ∇ (del), that satisfies these criteria.

For a $k \times n$ voting strategies[4] by voter table of cross classifications, ∇ is given by:

$$\nabla = 1 - \frac{\sum_i \sum_j w_{ij} P_{ij}}{\sum_i \sum_j w_{ij} P_{i.} P_{.j}} \quad i = 1, \ldots, k; j = 1, \ldots, n,$$

where w_{ij} is an error cell indicator ($w_{ij} = 1$ if a model predicts erroneously, otherwise 0), P_{ij} is the population probability of cases in cell (i, j), and $P_{i.}$ and $P_{.j}$ are the marginal probabilities. Alternative sampling models yield alternative equations for estimating ∇ from sample data (Hildebrand, Laing, and Rosenthal 1977, chap. 6). It can be shown that $\nabla \leq 1$, that $\nabla = 0$ if the variables are statistically independent, and that $\nabla = 1$ if no prediction errors are committed.

The measure del may be interpreted as the proportion of reduction in error attained by a given prediction, given knowledge of each observation's location on the independent variable, over that expected when the prediction is randomly applied according to the marginal distribution of the independent

---

4. As shown above, under PV $k = m$, whereas under AV $k = 2^m - 1$.

variable. As such, it seems to be appropriate for competitively testing models F, NF, S, and RFM.[5]

Inspection of the del values in table 2 shows that model RFM outperforms models S and NF in all seven games, and outperforms model F in all games except game 7.

Discussion

Our results show that, when $m = 3$, subjects tend not to choose their least preferred alternative. When given the opportunity to vote strategically, they exercise it frequently. The relative success of model RFM is taken as evidence for the tacit cooperation hypothesis. Other interpretations are possible; in particular, the possibility of constructing a model that may account for the observed results without assuming the formation of tacit coalitions may not be discarded.

The results presented here are limited, of course, to the voting procedure (PV) that we have used, the group size ($n = 5$) that we have employed, and the task parameters (vote distributions and preference orderings) that we have chosen to study. With regard to the effect of the number of blocs (n) on the prevalence of strategic voting, two hypotheses may be formulated. The first is based on the assumption that, as n grows larger, the mental computations involved in examining and comparing various voting configurations become more numerous, causing the task to become more demanding. Consequently—the first hypothesis states—strategic voting will decrease as n grows larger. An alternative hypothesis asserts that, given a fixed m, the number of blocs will have no effect on strategic voting. This hypothesis is consistent with the different cognitive processes assumed by models F, NF, and RFM.

To test these two hypotheses competitively, we compared the results of experiment 1 to the results of our earlier study (Felsenthal, Rapoport, and Maoz 1988) that used the same plurality voting procedure, the same population of subjects, and similar voting games. However, the electorate (n) in this

---

5. The del measure does not fully satisfy the precision criterion. In Hildebrand, Laing, and Rosenthal's (1977) terminology, the precision of the del-statistic is measured by U, the number of expected errors. However, the number of expected errors is a function of the marginal frequency distribution of the two variables, not of the number of cells in the table specified as error cells. This is very clear in table 2. A model that is highly specific (that is, a model that specifies a large number of error cells) will, generally speaking, yield a lower del-value than a model that has less specific predictions. We developed a modified del-value that is discounted by a ratio of the number of actual error cells specified by a model over the maximum number of error cells possible in a $k \times n$ contingency table—given by $n(k - 1)$. This discount reduces the del-values of model RFM somewhat but has no effect on the substantive conclusions. We refrain from presenting the results of the modified del analysis because we have as yet not tested the statistical properties of this modification.

earlier study consisted of four rather than five voters, rendering the task considerably easier. A reanalysis of the earlier results (reported in full in Felsenthal, Rapoport, and Maoz 1988, table 2) shows that, over all seven games, strategic voting was exercised in 556 out of 1,680 cases (33.1 percent). The percentages of strategic voting in both studies are very close to each other, in support of the second hypothesis. To determine whether these findings generalize to a larger number of voters, we conducted another voting experiment with the same voting procedure and $n = 6$.

5. Experiment 2

Method

Subjects. The subjects were sixty male and female undergraduate students from the University of Haifa. As in experiment 1, all the subjects were volunteers who responded to advertisements promising a monetary reward contingent on performance for participation in a single-session, computer-controlled voting experiment. None of the subjects who had participated in experiment 1 participated in this experiment.

    Procedure. The procedure of experiment 2 was identical to that of experiment 1 with two exceptions. First, each group consisted of six rather than five subjects. Second, each group played eight rather than seven voting games.

    Experimental Games. In constructing the voting games, we chose the vote distributions in accordance with the same principles that guided the design of experiment 1. First, we required that all four models would not yield identical predictions for all six players in the game. Second, we required that the sequence of eight games would include at least one game in each of the four categories specified earlier.

    Table 4 presents the eight voting games included in experiment 2. The games were played in the order listed in the table. In one game (game 2) a Condorcet winner exists and model F predicts that it will be elected. In three games (games 1, 4, and 5) either one or two Condorcet winners exist, but model F predicts an indeterminate outcome. In two other games (games 3 and 6) a Condorcet winner exists, but model F predicts that some other candidate will be elected. Finally, in the last two games (games 7 and 8) the social preference ordering is cyclical.

Results

As in experiment 1, we first tested for possible learning effects to determine whether the decisions might be collapsed over iterations. Table 5 presents the

TABLE 4.   Results of Experiment 2

Player	Votes	Preference Ordering	Observed Frequencies					Model Predictions			
			a	*b*	*a/b*	*c*	*b/c*	F	NF	S	RFM
					Game 1						
A	10	*a > b > c*	52	7	—	1	—	*a–b*	*a*	*a*	*a*
B	5	*a > c > b*	54	3	—	3	—	*a–c*	*a*	*a*	*a*
C	10	*b > a > c*	25	34	—	1	—	*b–a*	*a*	*b*	*a–b*
D	4	*b > c > a*	6	39	—	15	—	*b–c*	*c*	*b*	*b–c*
E	5	*c > a > b*	39	1	—	20	—	*c–a*	*c*	*c*	*a*
F	6	*c > b > a*	4	35	—	21	—	*c–b*	*c*	*c*	*b–c*
Outcome		*a ~ b > c*	37	15	6	2	—	?	*a*	*a*	*a,a/b*
Del-value								.867	.278	.417	.713
					Game 2						
A	1	*a > b > c*	41	16	—	3	—	*b*	*a*	*a*	*a–b*
B	13	*a > c > b*	34	0	—	26	—	*a*	*a*	*a*	*a*
C	19	*b > a > c*	34	20	—	6	—	*a*	*a*	*b*	*a–b*
D	1	*b > c > a*	0	24	—	36	—	*b*	*b*	*b*	*c*
E	18	*c > a > b*	13	0	—	47	—	*c*	*c*	*c*	*c*
F	8	*c > b > a*	2	9	—	49	—	*c*	*c*	*c*	*c*
Outcome		*a > c > b*	27	2	1	30	—	*a*	*a*	*c*	*a–c*
Del-value								.350	.432	.396	.567
					Game 3						
A	1	*a > b > c*	44	15	—	1	—	*a*	*a*	*a*	*a–b*
B	16	*a > c > b*	41	1	—	18	—	*a*	*a*	*a*	*c*
C	8	*b > a > c*	22	35	—	3	—	*b*	*b*	*b*	*a–b*
D	14	*b > c > a*	1	30	—	29	—	*b*	*b*	*b*	*b*
E	13	*c > a > b*	17	1	—	42	—	*a*	*a*	*c*	*c*
F	8	*c > b > a*	0	15	—	45	—	*b*	*b*	*c*	*c*
Outcome		*c > a ~ b*	12	11	—	33	4	*a/b*	*a/b*	*b*	*c*
Del-value								.285	.285	.488	.457
					Game 4						
A	1	*a > b > c*	44	16	—	0	—	*a–b*	*b*	*a*	*a*
B	3	*a > c > b*	35	0	—	25	—	*a–c*	*c*	*a*	*a*
C	27	*b > a > c*	30	30	—	0	—	*b–a*	*b*	*b*	*a–b*
D	1	*b > c > a*	1	32	—	27	—	*b–c*	*b*	*b*	*b–c*
E	27	*c > a > b*	13	0	—	47	—	*c–a*	*c*	*c*	*c–a*
F	1	*c > b > a*	0	10	—	50	—	*c–b*	*c*	*c*	*b–c*
Outcome		*a > c > b*	27	4	1	25	3	?	*c*	*b/c*	?
Del-value								.992	.337	.492	.737

(*continued*)

TABLE 4—*Continued*

Player	Votes	Preference Ordering	Observed Frequencies					Model Predictions			
			a	b	a/b	c	b/c	F	NF	S	RFM
			Game 5								
A	6	$a > b > c$	55	5	—	0	—	a–b	a–b	a	a–b
B	4	$a > c > b$	52	0	—	8	—	a–c	a–c	a	a
C	5	$b > a > c$	40	20	—	0	—	b–a	b–a	b	a–b
D	1	$b > c > a$	5	30	—	25	—	b–c	b–c	b	c
E	5	$c > a > b$	16	0	—	44	—	c–a	c–a	c	c
F	6	$c > b > a$	0	18	—	42	—	c–b	c–b	c	c
Outcome		$a > c > b$	41	4	—	14	1	?	?	c	a–c
Del-value								.958	.958	.513	.599
			Game 6								
A	1	$a > b > c$	42	18	—	0	—	a	a	a	b
B	14	$a > c > b$	33	0	—	27	—	a	a	a	a–c
C	14	$b > a > c$	20	40	—	0	—	b	b	b	b
D	9	$b > c > a$	2	36	—	22	—	b	b	b	b
E	9	$c > a > b$	7	0	—	53	—	a	a	a	a–c
F	13	$c > b > a$	0	6	—	54	—	b	b	c	b
Outcome		$c > b > a$	6	14	—	40	—	b	b	b	b–c
Del-value								.240	.240	.575	.534
			Game 7								
A	4	$a > b > c$	32	28	—	0	—	a–b	a	a	a
B	1	$a > c > b$	39	0	—	21	—	a–c	a	a	a–c
C	1	$b > a > c$	5	55	—	0	—	b–a	b	b	b
D	7	$b > c > a$	2	31	—	27	—	b–c	b	b	b
E	5	$c > a > b$	26	0	—	34	—	c–a	a	c	a–c
F	1	$c > b > a$	0	20	—	40	—	c–b	c	c	b
Outcome		$a > b > c > a$	23	18	3	16	—	?	a	b	a–b
Del-value								.983	.436	.463	.491
			Game 8								
A	4	$a > b > c$	43	17	—	0	—	a	a	a	a–b
B	2	$a > c > b$	55	0	—	5	—	a	a	a	a–c
C	1	$b > a > c$	4	56	—	0	—	b	b	b	b
D	8	$b > c > a$	1	49	—	10	—	b	b	b	b
E	4	$c > a > b$	45	0	—	15	—	a	a	c	a–c
F	1	$c > b > a$	0	37	—	23	—	b	b	c	a
Outcome		$a \sim b > c > a$	7	19	27	7	—	a/b	a/b	b	b,a/b
Del-value								.637	.637	.504	.766

TABLE 5. Frequency Distribution of Votes over Subjects in Experiment 2 by Game and Iteration

Game	Strategy	Iteration						Total
		1	2	3	4	5	6	
1	{a}	29	30	30	29	30	32	180
	{b}	20	19	19	19	22	20	119
	{c}	11	11	11	12	8	8	61
2	{a}	16	17	20	26	22	23	124
	{b}	13	12	10	10	10	14	69
	{c}	31	31	30	24	28	23	167
3	{a}	21	23	21	20	22	18	125
	{b}	17	17	19	14	14	16	97
	{c}	22	20	20	26	24	26	138
4	{a}	16	18	19	24	23	23	123
	{b}	17	16	16	11	15	13	88
	{c}	27	26	25	25	22	24	149
5	{a}	27	28	28	29	27	29	168
	{b}	6	13	14	13	15	12	73
	{c}	27	19	18	18	18	19	119
6	{a}	15	10	15	20	22	22	104
	{b}	19	21	18	14	14	14	100
	{c}	26	29	27	26	24	24	156
7	{a}	19	16	17	18	17	17	104
	{b}	27	23	22	19	21	22	134
	{c}	14	21	21	23	22	21	122
8	{a}	21	24	28	28	24	23	148
	{b}	29	29	24	24	25	28	159
	{c}	10	7	8	8	11	9	53

frequency distributions of votes over all sixty subjects in experiment 2 by game and iteration. There is some evidence for learning over iterations in games 2 and 7. In game 2, voter *B* displayed nearly significant iteration effects ($p = .06$). Likewise, significant iteration effects were found for voter *F* in game 7 ($p < .01$). In both of these games, the frequency of sincere voting increases over iterations, whereas the frequency of sophisticated voting decreases. The results of ANOVA show no significant iteration effect in each of the other six games. As a result—and in correspondence with the procedure in experiment 1—we decided to collapse the votes in each game over iterations.

Dominated Strategies. Although it should be more difficult for a player to decide whom to vote for in a six- rather than five-person voting game, the players chose initially dominated strategies in experiment 2 less often than in experiment 1. Out of a total of 2,880 decisions made in experiment 2, there were only 45 instances (1.6 percent) in which subjects voted for their least preferred candidate. These 45 strategic errors were committed by a total of 18 (out of 60) subjects. Of the 45 errors, 16 were committed in game 1.

Strategic Voting. We computed the number of strategic votes in experiment 2 by comparing, for each game and player, the candidate predicted by model S and the actual number of votes (out of 60) cast for the predicted candidate. The frequency of strategic votes (summed over the six players in each game) was 124, 134, 116, 121, 112, 100, 127, and 118 for games 1 through 8, respectively. Overall, the subjects voted strategically in 952 out of 2,880 instances. The overall percentage of strategic voting—33.05 percent— is remarkably similar to the percentages observed in our earlier four-person voting study (Felsenthal, Rapoport, and Maoz 1988) and in the five-person study in experiment 1.

Model Testing. Repeating the same comparisons as in experiment 1, several findings are pertinent for the comparison of model RFM with the other models. These comparisons, too, ignore inadmissible votes.

1. There are seven instances in which models RFM and F make different and unique predictions. Of a total of 417 instances, 242 (58 percent) support model RFM, compared to 175 (42 percent) that support model F.
2. There are eleven instances in which models RFM and NF make different and unique predictions. These eleven instances make a total of 656 decisions, of which 380 (57.9 percent) are in accordance with model RFM and the remaining 276 (42.1 percent) in accordance with model NF.
3. There are eight instances in which models RFM and S make different and unique predictions. However, model RFM does not exhibit the superiority it showed before. These eight instances involve a total of 472 decisions, of which only 222 (47 percent) are in accordance with model RFM, and the remaining 250 decisions (53 percent) are in accordance with model S.
4. In many of the instances where model RFM makes an indeterminate decision, the observed votes are actually split more or less evenly between the top and second preferences (see, e.g., the votes of players C and F in game 1, player C in game 2, player C in game 3, players C and D in game 4, player B in game 6, and player E in game 7).
5. As in experiment 1, Condorcet winners—when they existed—were always included in the predicted set of winners of model RFM. This was not the case with the other three models (see, e.g., the predicted outcomes of models F, NF, and S in games 3 and 6). Table 4 shows that when Condorcet winners existed (in all games except 7 and 8)

they were elected more often than any other candidate. (The single exception in game 2 is rather minor.)

Table 4 also lists the del-values for each model within each game. Inspection of the table shows that the del-values associated with model RFM exceeded the del-values associated with models F, NF, and S in four (games 2, 3, 6, and 8), seven (games 1, 2, 3, 4, 6, 7, and 8), and six (games 1, 2, 4, 5, 7, and 8) games, respectively.[6]

Discussion

The results of experiments 1 and 2 are similar in that (1) the subjects seldom chose their least preferred alternative, and (2) they divided their votes between their first and second preferred alternative in a ratio of approximately two to one. However, in comparison to its relative success in experiment 1, model RFM performed less well in experiment 2. In several cases (game 3, player B; 3, player D; 5, player D; 6, player A; 7, player F; and 8, player B) the discrepancy between observed and predicted decisions was sufficiently large to cast doubt on the assumptions of the model. As noted, the advantage that model RFM had over models F and NF in experiment 1 was maintained in experiment 2, but the advantage it had over model S was weakened.

The reduction in the descriptive power of model RFM may result from the difference in complexity between experiments 1 and 2. When the number of voters increases from five to six, the number of contingencies that each subject has to evaluate grows larger. As a consequence, some subjects may abandon the algorithm stipulated by model RFM in favor of some other algorithm.

Other algorithms may be invoked if the voting procedure is changed. To assess the generality of the cognitive process embodied in model RFM, experiment 3 was designed to extend the investigation from the PV to the AV procedure. Approval voting was chosen because of our interest in comparing PV to AV (Felsenthal, Maoz, and Rapoport 1986; Rapoport, Felsenthal, and

---

6. There are five cases where models F or NF predict that *each* of the six players will use *either* of his or her two admissible voting strategies (games 1, 4, 5, and 7 for model F and game 5 for model NF). As noted earlier, the percentage of voting for inadmissible strategies in experiment 2 was very low (1.6 percent). As a result, the del-values associated with models F and NF in these five cases are very close to unity. Clearly, if prediction is restricted to the set of admissible strategies only, models F and NF are devoid of any predictive power in these five cases. If these cases are eliminated, the relative advantage of model RFM over models F and NF is enhanced considerably.

Maoz, 1988a and 1988b), and because of the strong claim that it is "the most sincere and strategy-proof of all systems in which a voter can vote for, but not rank, candidates" (Brams and Fishburn 1983, 31).

6. Experiment 3

Experiment 3 was identical to experiments 1 and 2 with the exception that each voter could cast all of his or her votes for as many alternatives as he or she wished. The alternative with the most approval votes was the winner.

Method

Subjects. The subjects were 50 male and female undergraduate students from the University of Haifa. None of them had taken part in experiment 1 or 2. All of the subjects were recruited—as in the previous two experiments—by notices placed on bulletin boards promising a monetary reward contingent on performance for participation in a single-session, decision-making study.

    Procedure. The procedure of experiment 3 was identical to that of experiment 1 with the exception that subjects voted under the AV, rather than PV, procedure.

    Experimental Games. Table 6 presents the vote distributions and preference orderings for the seven games used in experiment 3. The games are labeled according to the sequence in which they were played. A comparison of tables 2 and 6 shows that game 5 in experiment 1 is identical to game 4 in experiment 3, and game 7 in experiment 1 is the same as game 7 in experiment 3. There are two games (games 1 and 4) where a Condorcet winner exists and model F predicts that it will be elected. There is one game (game 7) where a Condorcet winner exists, but model F predicts an indeterminate outcome. In three more games (games 2, 3, and 5), a Condorcet winner exists, but model F predicts that some other candidate will be elected. Finally, there is one game (game 6) where the social preference ordering is cyclical.

Results

Table 7 shows the frequency distributions of the seven possible voting strategies by game and iteration. The table shows no evidence that voters changed their voting strategies from one iteration of the game to another. One-way ANOVAs were conducted separately for each game. In each case the iteration effect was not significant. As a result, votes were collapsed over iterations as in experiments 1 and 2.

    Dominated Strategies. Table 8 reports the frequencies of the seven voting strategies for each game separately. The frequencies of the two admissible ({x}

TABLE 6. Results of Experiment 3

Player	Votes	Preference Ordering	Observed Frequencies							Model Predictions			
			a	b	c	ab	ac	bc	abc	F	NF	S	RFM
						Game 1							
A	28	c > a > b	6	1	39	1	9	4	0	c	c	c	c
B	3	a > c > b	19	3	0	26	10	2	0	a	a	a	a
C	27	b > a > c	17	5	4	17	14	3	0	ab	ab	b	b–ab
D	1	c > b > a	3	1	21	0	7	27	1	c	c	c	c
E	1	a > b > c	22	2	1	27	7	1	0	ab	a	a	a–ab
Outcome		a > c > b	33	7	17	0	3	0	0	a	a	c	a–c
Del-value										.238	.219	.208	.307
						Game 2							
A	16	c > a > b	7	7	20	14	11	1	0	ca	ca	c	c–ac
B	11	a > c > b	13	0	8	0	39	0	0	a	ac	a	a–ac
C	5	c > b > a	0	3	27	2	3	25	0	bc	bc	c	c
D	2	a > b > c	4	2	14	19	17	4	0	ab	ab	a	ab
E	26	b > c > a	3	20	5	2	3	27	0	b	b	b	b
Outcome		c > b > a	7	11	42	0	0	0	0	b	b	b	?
Del-value										.168	.243	.147	.320
						Game 3							
A	5	c > b > a	0	0	51	0	3	6	0	bc	bc	c	c
B	22	c > a > b	0	0	36	0	24	0	0	ac	ac	c	c
C	26	b > c > a	0	28	6	2	6	18	0	b	b	b	bc
D	5	a > c > b	2	0	20	0	38	0	0	a	a	a	ac
E	2	a > b > c	13	2	5	37	3	0	0	ab	ab	a	a–ab
Outcome		c > b > a	3	1	56	0	0	0	0	b	b	c	c
Del-value										.230	.230	.294	.519
						Game 4							
A	1	a > b > c	18	7	5	27	0	3	0	ab	ab	a	a–ab
B	21	b > c > a	1	11	15	0	1	32	0	bc	b	b	b–bc
C	17	a > c > b	26	0	1	0	32	1	0	a	ac	a	a
D	7	c > b > a	0	8	11	0	1	40	0	c	c	c	c
E	14	c > a > b	7	0	20	0	32	1	0	ac	c	c	c
Outcome		c > a > b	11	1	48	0	0	0	0	c	c	b/c	b–c
Del-value										.299	.221	.155	.333
						Game 5							
A	18	a > b > c	40	5	1	11	0	3	0	a	a	a	a
B	13	c > b > a	0	18	7	3	0	32	0	c	bc	c	c–bc
C	8	b > a > c	6	17	10	8	10	8	1	ab	ab	b	b
D	6	b > c > a	1	24	3	18	1	13	0	bc	bc	b	b–bc
E	2	c > a > b	8	6	11	3	18	14	0	ac	ac	c	ac
Outcome		b > a > c	15	37	8	0	0	0	0	a	a	a	?
Del-value										.158	.234	.190	.325

(continued)

TABLE 6—*Continued*

Player	Votes	Preference Ordering	Observed Frequencies							Model Predictions			
			a	b	c	ab	ac	bc	abc	F	NF	S	RFM
						Game 6							
A	8	$a > c > b$	35	2	0	1	19	3	0	a	a	a	a
B	11	$c > a > b$	9	0	23	0	28	0	0	c	c	c	c
C	14	$a > b > c$	18	0	0	38	3	1	0	a	a	a	a
D	14	$b > c > a$	0	15	0	3	0	42	0	bc	bc	b	b–bc
E	4	$c > b > a$	5	0	13	0	3	39	0	c	c	c	c–bc
Outcome		$a > b > c > a$	28	12	20	0	0	0	0	c	c	a	a–c
Del-value										.301	.301	.233	.481
						Game 7							
A	14	$b > c > a$	2	31	3	0	4	20	0	b–bc	b	b	b–bc
B	17	$a > b > c$	25	0	10	0	25	0	0	a–ac	a	a	ac
C	8	$b > a > c$	3	12	1	35	3	3	3	b–ab	b	b	b–ab
D	8	$c > b > a$	0	2	21	0	0	37	0	c–bc	bc	c	c
E	13	$c > a > b$	0	0	39	0	21	0	0	c–ac	ac	c	c
Outcome		$c > a \sim b$	12	3	42	0	2	1	0	?	a/b	b	c
Del-value										.825	.313	.302	.474

and $\{x,y\}$) and five inadmissible strategies are shown in the two right-hand columns of the table. The frequencies are presented separately for each game and then summed over games. Altogether, there are 2,100 instances. The symbols x, y, and z denote the three candidates a, b, and c after they are permuted so that x is preferred over y and y is preferred over z.

Inadmissible strategies were adopted in 480 (22.9 percent) instances. The percentage of initially dominated strategies adopted in experiment 3 is significantly higher than in each of the two previous experiments. We attribute this difference, in part, to the novelty and complexity of the AV procedure. When $m = 3$, the AV procedure increases the number of feasible strategies from three (under PV) to seven, and allows for new strategic considerations whose effect on the outcome of the voting is difficult to calculate.

A reasonable hypothesis is that many of the strategic errors committed by the subjects in experiment 3 resulted from the subjects' voting for their second preference. Recall that voting strategy y is admissible under PV but not AV. Subjects not familiar with AV may not be aware of this fact. Rather, they might well believe that voting strategies that are admissible under PV are also admissible under AV. This hypothesis was supported only in part. Voting for y was the most common strategic error. However, whereas 184 (38.3 percent) errors were committed by voting for the second-ranked candidate, the subjects also voted for their least preferred candidate (z) in 75 instances (15.6 percent)

TABLE 7. Frequency Distribution of Votes over Subjects in Experiment 3 by Game and Iteration

Game	Strategy	Iteration						Total
		1	2	3	4	5	6	
1	$\{a\}$	18	9	7	11	10	12	67
	$\{b\}$	2	2	2	1	4	1	12
	$\{c\}$	11	9	11	13	10	11	65
	$\{a,b\}$	8	12	12	12	13	14	71
	$\{a,c\}$	3	12	11	10	7	3	47
	$\{b,c\}$	8	5	7	3	5	9	37
	$\{a,b,c\}$	0	1	0	0	0	0	0
2	$\{a\}$	4	3	5	5	6	4	27
	$\{b\}$	6	7	5	6	5	3	32
	$\{c\}$	14	12	9	12	13	14	74
	$\{a,b\}$	6	7	6	5	7	6	37
	$\{a,c\}$	12	14	12	12	10	13	73
	$\{b,c\}$	8	7	13	10	9	10	57
	$\{a,b,c\}$	0	0	0	0	0	0	0
3	$\{a\}$	1	3	1	3	4	3	15
	$\{b\}$	6	6	5	4	4	5	30
	$\{c\}$	19	19	20	19	20	21	118
	$\{a,b\}$	7	6	7	6	7	6	39
	$\{a,c\}$	12	11	15	14	11	11	74
	$\{b,c\}$	5	5	2	4	4	4	24
	$\{a,b,c\}$	0	0	0	0	0	0	0
4	$\{a\}$	6	9	8	9	11	9	52
	$\{b\}$	6	6	2	3	5	4	26
	$\{c\}$	7	9	7	10	9	10	52
	$\{a,b\}$	3	5	6	4	4	5	27
	$\{a,c\}$	15	9	10	12	10	10	66
	$\{b,c\}$	13	12	17	12	11	12	77
	$\{a,b,c\}$	0	0	0	0	0	0	0
5	$\{a\}$	10	7	10	9	12	7	55
	$\{b\}$	4	10	10	16	15	15	70
	$\{c\}$	7	6	4	4	5	6	32
	$\{a,b\}$	7	10	9	5	5	7	43
	$\{a,c\}$	7	4	4	6	4	4	29
	$\{b,c\}$	15	13	13	10	8	11	70
	$\{a,b,c\}$	0	0	0	0	1	0	1
6	$\{a\}$	11	10	11	12	10	13	67
	$\{b\}$	1	6	1	2	3	4	17
	$\{c\}$	5	3	7	8	6	7	36
	$\{a,b\}$	8	7	7	7	6	7	42
	$\{a,c\}$	8	11	9	7	12	6	53
	$\{b,c\}$	17	13	15	14	13	13	85
	$\{a,b,c\}$	0	0	0	0	0	0	0

(*continued*)

TABLE 7—*Continued*

		Iteration						
Game	Strategy	1	2	3	4	5	6	Total
7	{a}	2	4	7	6	5	6	30
	{b}	7	9	8	7	8	6	45
	{c}	7	11	13	12	14	17	74
	{a,b}	7	5	7	4	6	6	35
	{a,c}	16	10	6	9	7	5	53
	{b,c}	11	10	9	11	10	9	60
	{a,b,c}	0	1	0	1	0	1	3

and for all but their most preferred candidate in 83 instances (17.3 percent).

Inadmissible voting strategies under AV may be chosen by some voters but not by others, as some voters may work out the strategic implications of AV and others may not. To assess the magnitude of individual differences, we counted, separately for each subject, the number of inadmissible voting strategies that he or she adopted in all seven games. These frequency counts are shown in table 9. Inspection of table 9 reveals large individual differences, with some subjects committing no strategic errors and other committing errors in twenty-eight of the forty-two trials. However, except for five subjects, all the remaining forty-five subjects adopted an initially dominated strategy at least once, and thirty-four of the fifty subjects adopted an initially dominated strategy at least five times.

Strategic Voting. Table 8 shows that subjects took advantage of the

TABLE 8. Analysis of Admissible and Inadmissible Voting Strategies in Experiment 3 by Game

Game	Voting Strategy							Admissible	Inadmissible
	{x}	{y}	{z}	{x,y}	{x,z}	{y,z}	{x,y,z}		
1	106	26	12	90	47	18	1	196	104
2	84	25	24	121	23	23	0	205	95
3	130	28	5	123	8	6	0	253	47
4	86	38	6	163	2	5	0	249	51
5	99	40	18	82	40	20	1	181	119
6	104	9	7	166	10	4	0	270	30
7	128	18	3	138	3	7	3	266	34
Total	737	184	75	883	133	83	5	1620	480
Percentage	35.10	8.76	3.57	42.05	6.38	3.90	0.24	77.14	22.86

TABLE 9. Frequency of Dominated Decisions in Experiment 3 by Player and Group

Player	Group										Total
	1	2	3	4	5	6	7	8	9	10	
A	3	1	0	1	6	7	11	13	13	28	83
B	4	2	26	0	12	10	19	10	6	7	96
C	4	19	4	1	10	16	12	14	17	17	114
D	0	3	8	12	18	12	8	12	16	17	106
E	3	2	23	0	7	6	24	6	10	0	81
Total	14	27	61	14	53	51	74	55	62	69	480

strategic possibilities afforded by the AV procedure. Unlike experiments 1 and 2, the frequency of strategic voting exceeded the frequency of sincere voting. Sincere voting occurred in 737 instances (35.1 percent), compared to strategic voting that occurred in 883 instances (42.1 percent). (The remaining 22.8 percent were inadmissible strategies.)

Model Testing. Because of the relatively large number of inadmissible voting decisions made in experiment 3, all four models[7] performed worse in comparison to their performance in experiments 1 and 2. Nevertheless, model RFM still outperformed the other three models. Comparison of the observed and predicted decisions in table 6 (which excludes inadmissible strategies) shows that:

1. Models RFM and F made different and unique predictions in seven instances. These instances involved 332 decisions of which 207 (62.3 percent) are in accordance with model RFM; the remaining 125 decisions (37.7 percent) are in accordance with model F.
2. There were ten instances in which models NF and RFM predicted that voters will adopt different and unique strategies. These ten instances involved a total of 506 decisions, of which 298 (59.9 percent) are in accordance with model RFM, whereas the remaining 208 decisions (41.1 percent) are in accordance with model NF.
3. There were five instances in which models RFM and S made different and unique predictions. These five instances involved a total of 188

---

7. Model S predicts that each voter will vote for his or her top preference. Although model NF was originally proposed for the PV procedure, its logic can be extended to the AV procedure with only one change: whenever model NF predicts that a voter will vote for his or her second preference under the PV procedure, it would predict that this same voter would vote for his or her first and second preferences under the three-alternative, AV procedure.

decisions, of which 118 (62.8 percent) are in accordance with model RFM; the remaining 70 decisions (37.2 percent) are in accordance with model S.

4. As in the previous two experiments conducted under the PV procedure, when Condorcet winners existed, they were always included in the predicted set of winners by model RFM. The three other models did not share this property (see the predicted outcomes of models F, NF, and S in games 2, 5, and 7). Table 6 shows that when Condorcet winners existed (in all games except game 6), they were elected by the voters more often than any other candidate.

Table 6 lists the del-values for each model within each game. It shows that in six of the seven games, the del-value associated with model RFM exceeded the del-values associated with the other three models. The only exception is game 7—where model RFM was outperformed by model F, which is completely indeterminate.

Discussion

Because AV offers more feasible voting strategies than PV, it might appear that it confuses voters by its large number of options. Brams and Fishburn (1983) argued that this conclusion is not justified because it is reasonable to assume that voters will entertain only admissible strategies. "Thus, the question of the number of options that a voter faces under different systems really turns on the number of admissible strategies and not on the number of feasible strategies" (1983, 26). In contrast to the assumption of Brams and Fishburn, our results suggest that voters may not restrict themselves to admissible strategies, even when the number of candidates is as small as three. In experiment 3, subjects chose inadmissible strategies in about one out of four instances. The relative frequency of inadmissible strategies did not decline over iterations. Nor was the choice of inadmissible strategies restricted to a minority of the subjects, who may have failed to understand the strategic implications of AV (see table 9). We have tested the hypothesis that inadmissible strategies resulted from voting for the second preference, because this strategy is admissible under PV but not AV. However, our results do not support this hypothesis, as approximately two-thirds of the dominated decisions resulted from entertaining some other strategy (see table 8).

We are not suggesting that these results discredit AV; the comparison between AV and other nonranked voting procedures is multidimensional. Moreover, we might have biased the results against AV by spacing the candidates at equal monetary intervals and disallowing indifference relations. Nevertheless, our results suggest that naive voters, who are not familiar with AV, may find it more confusing than the more familiar PV procedure.

7. General Discussion

Our research has been preceded by the work of Levine and Plott (1977), Plott and Levine (1978), and Eckel and Holt (1989) designed to study strategic voting in small committees choosing from a finite and typically small set of alternative outcomes. The focus of this earlier research was on multistage voting games, the dynamic structure of which is determined by an agenda specifying a sequence of choices to be made by a committee. It is known that the design of such agendas constitutes a powerful determinant of the committee's ultimate choice, and that if the preference orderings of all the committee members are common knowledge, strategic voting can mitigate the power of the agenda (Eckel and Holt 1989).

In contrast, our research has addressed the issue of strategic voting in static voting situations, where decisions are made simultaneously. Also, our focus has shifted from assessing the likelihood of strategic voting and determining the conditions (e.g., iteration of the game, changes in voting profiles over time) that foster strategic voting, to understanding the cognitive processes that voters go through in determining their votes. For this purpose, we have compared four models that differ from one another in their origin, purpose, and the assumptions they make about the cognitive system of the voter. Model S is the simplest of all models because it makes no requirements about the mental capability of the voter. It may well be applied when voters do not know others' preferences, or when the number of voters is large. Farquharson's model F is the most demanding; the algorithm it postulates for deleting dominated strategies would conceivably be adopted only when the number of alternatives and voters is very small. Models NF and RFM have been deliberately constructed to capture the cognitive stages that some, or possibly most, of the subjects go through in determining their votes.

Like model NF, model RFM supposes that each voter begins his or her deliberations by considering the outcome that results if all voters choose their top preference. Models NF and RFM then depart from each other in a very basic way. Whereas model NF requires the voter to find out whether he or she can independently obtain a more preferred outcome if he or she transfers his or her vote to his or her second preference, model RFM assumes a more complicated process whereby the voter is engaged in a sequence of pairwise comparisons between tacit coalitions. Another difference among models F, NF, and RFM concerns the treatment of individual differences. The indeterminateness in models F and NF is endogenous; it results if the algorithms specified by these models do not bring the election of a unique candidate. In contrast, the indeterminateness in model RFM reflects our inability, at this stage, to account for the large variability between subjects assigned the same role. We shall require more information about thought processes—possibly by using the "talking aloud" procedure—in order to determine why, under certain circumstances, some subjects resolve the strategic uncertainty about the other voters by voting for their most preferred alternative, whereas other subjects in the same situation vote for their second preference.

We have found that the voting situations in all three experiments generated a great deal of strategic voting. We have also found—perhaps not surprisingly, when inexperienced voters are involved—that voters are considerably more likely to employ dominated strategies when operating under the AV than the PV procedure. Yet another major finding is that model RFM outperforms the other three models. It accounts better for the observed distributions of votes and final outcomes. However, the success of model RFM is by no means unqualified. First, as shown in tables 2, 4, and 6, model RFM mispredicted the modal vote in several cases. Second, model RFM was always defeated by at least one of the other models when the social preference ordering was cyclical (see experiment 1, game 3; 2, game 7; 2, game 8; and 3, game 6). More information is needed about voting behavior in games that have no Condorcet winners in order to locate the deficiencies of all the models, including RFM.

Based on postexperimental interrogation of some of the subjects and our own introspection, we are quite convinced that subjects do not go through the laborious process of identifying and then voting for Condorcet winners, if they exist. However, the results of experiments 1, 2, and 3 show that, with a minor exception in experiment 2, game 2, when Condorcet winners exist, our subjects elected them more frequently than any other alternative. In all three experiments—in correspondence with these results—model RFM never excluded a Condorcet winner from its set of predicted winners, if a Condorcet winner actually existed. There remains the task of determining the generality of this result, as well as the more general task of accounting for the election of Condorcet winners without observing pairwise comparisons of preferences.

REFERENCES

Brams, S. J. 1982. "Strategic Information and Voting Behavior." *Society* 19:4–11.
Brams, S. J., and P. C. Fishburn. 1983. *Approval Voting.* Boston: Birkhauser.
Dummett, M. 1984. *Voting Procedures.* Oxford: Oxford University Press.
Eckel, C., and C. A. Holt. 1989. "Strategic Voting in Agenda-controlled Committee Experiments." *American Economic Review* 79:763–73.
Farquharson, R. 1969. *Theory of Voting.* Oxford: Basil Blackwell.
Felsenthal, D. S., A. Rapoport, and Z. Maoz. 1986. "Comparing Voting Systems in Genuine Elections: Approval-Plurality versus Selection-Plurality." *Social Behaviour* 1:41–53.
Felsenthal, D. S., A. Rapoport, and Z. Maoz. 1988. "Tacit Cooperation in Three Alternative Noncooperative Voting Games: A New Model of Sophisticated Behaviour under the Plurality Procedure." *Electoral Studies* 7:143–61.

Hildebrand, D. K., J. D. Laing, and H. Rosenthal. 1977. *Prediction Analysis of Cross Classifications.* New York: Wiley.

Levine, M. E., and C. R. Plott. 1977. "Agenda Influence and Its Implications." *Virginia Law Review* 63:561–604.

Niemi, R. G. 1984. "The Problem of Strategic Behavior under Approval Voting." *American Political Science Review* 78:952–58.

Niemi, R. G., and A. Q. Frank. 1982. "Sophisticated Voting under the Plurality Procedure." In *Political Equilibrium,* ed. P. C. Ordeshook and K. A. Shepsle. Boston: Kluwer-Nijhoff.

Niemi, R. G., and A. Q. Frank. 1985. "Sophisticated Voting under the Plurality Procedure: A Test of a New Definition." *Theory and Decision* 19:151–62.

Nurmi, H. 1987. *Comparing Voting Systems.* Dordrecht: D. Reidel.

Ordeshook, P. C. 1986. *Game Theory and Political Theory.* Cambridge: Cambridge University Press.

Plott, C. R., and M. Levine. 1978. "A Model of Agenda Influence on Committee Decisions." *American Economic Review* 68:146–60.

Rapoport, A., D. S. Felsenthal, and Z. Maoz. 1988a. "Microcosms and Macrocosms: Seat Allocation in Proportional Representation Systems." *Theory and Decision* 28:11–33.

Rapoport, A., D. S. Felsenthal, and Z. Maoz. 1988b. "Proportional Representation: An Empirical Evaluation of Single-Stage Nonranked Voting Procedures." *Public Choice* 59:151–65.

Schelling, T. C. 1963. *The Strategy of Conflict.* New York: Oxford University Press.

Suleiman, R., and A. Rapoport. 1988. "Environmental and Social Uncertainty in Single-Trial Resource Dilemmas." *Acta Psychologica* 68:99–112.

Part 3
Coordination and Cooperation

Testing Game-Theoretic Models of Free Riding: New Evidence on Probability Bias and Learning

Thomas R. Palfrey and Howard Rosenthal

1. Introduction

The free rider problem is endemic to political processes. Political activists bear organizational costs for the benefit of a large (free-riding) membership. Nonvoters can avoid bearing informational costs and transaction costs with little risk of affecting the outcome of an election. Legislators can avoid taking an unpopular stand on an issue (say, raising congressional salaries), if enough other legislators are willing to. In international politics, lesser powers can benefit from the policing activities of the mighty. At not quite so grand a level, professors who avoid onerous committee and teaching assignments benefit from these activities because some colleagues agree to serve.

All of these problems have the following features in common. There is a group, all members of which stand to benefit from the generous contributions of some subset of the group. They are all examples of *public good problems*. They have been studied extensively both theoretically and experimentally in most fields of social science. In this article, we present both theory and experiments about a particularly simple class of public good problems: voluntary contribution threshold games (Lipnowski and Maital 1983; Van de Kragt, Orbell, and Dawes 1983; Bliss and Nalebuff 1984; Palfrey and Rosenthal 1984, 1988, 1990; Rapoport 1985). In these games, a group benefit is produced if at least w of N players "contribute" their endowments. An individual

An earlier version of this paper was presented at the Conference on the Provision of Public Goods and Common Pool Resources at Indiana University, Bloomington, Indiana, May, 1990. We thank those participants, especially Roberta Herzberg, for helpful comments. We also thank participants in seminars at Carnegie-Mellon University, MIT, and Penn for their comments. John Ledyard provided very helpful feedback on several points. The research assistance of Jessica Goodfellow and Jeffrey Prisbrey is gratefully acknowledged, as is the financial support of the National Science Foundation. The authors are solely responsible for the contents.

obtains the highest possible payoff (when $w \neq N$) as a successful free rider—the good is produced without the individual having contributed.

Models of this kind of public goods problem that could eventually apply to natural settings should, we argue, incorporate some element of private information. Each individual will generally be incompletely informed about certain characteristics of other individuals. Here we model this uncertainty as pertaining to endowments. How much an individual values his or her own endowment, relative to the public good, is private information to the individual. Endowment values are randomly and independently assigned according to a probability distribution that is common knowledge. In the formal model of decision making, subjects are assumed to be risk neutral. The predicted outcomes under the assumption that players maximize expected earnings are provided by game theory.

Game theory makes "rational expectations" predictions about behavior. In our case, behavior reduces to a single binary decision—contribute the endowment or keep it. In order to make this decision, each player assesses the likely behavior of the other players. In our setting, the relevant assessment is of the likelihood that the other players will contribute. Players then optimize, given these expectations about the behavior of the other players.[1] An equilibrium of the game imposes the following rational expectations hypothesis: each player's optimization, given their probabilistic expectations, generates the probability distribution over behavior that everyone had been anticipating. This is called a *Bayesian-Nash Equilibrium* of the game of incomplete information. Corresponding to any equilibrium, there will be a dual prediction about (1) the probability distribution over outcomes, and (2) the decision rules adopted by the players.

This article presents findings from a large number of laboratory experiments and compares the behavior in these experiments with the predictions of the theory. We report three major findings.

First, the equilibrium predictions from game theory are very accurate, at least at an aggregate level. On a qualitative level, as we vary the treatments, the observed outcomes always move in the direction the theory would predict. On a quantitative level, the efficiency of actual public good provision almost exactly mirrors the numerical predictions of the theory. Furthermore, the level of voluntary contribution is usually very close to the predicted level of contribution. Moreover, once subjects gain familiarity with the rules of the game, we do not observe the kind of patently irrational behavior (violation of dominated strategies) often observed in other public good experiments.

Second, to the extent that we observe variations from the theoretical

---

1. Up to this point, our approach is the same as Rapoport's (1985) expected utility model of the Van de Kragt, Orbell, and Dawes experiments (1983). We impose game-theoretic equilibrium restrictions, which Rapoport does not do.

predictions, there is a relatively simple model that is very successful in accounting for the error. Specifically, for some treatments we observe over-contribution, while for others we observe undercontribution. For the most part, these deviations are consistent with subjects behaving approximately optimally, but assuming that other players are more "civic-minded" than they are. In other words, individuals underestimate the probability that others free ride. We compare this explanation of the variations from the theory to a variety of other possibilities, based on incomplete experimental control over utility functions. These alternative explanations fare poorly in comparison to the simpler model.

Third, we find little evidence that individuals update their inaccurate beliefs about the other subjects' inclinations to free ride. While we are unable to cleanly reject the hypothesis that individuals are learning about other individuals' behavior, we find the paucity of support for such a learning hypothesis surprising. Nevertheless, in spite of the apparent rigidity of beliefs, the data still are remarkably supportive of the equilibrium predictions from noncooperative game theory.

Thus, while we want to emphasize that we found mostly small deviations from the theory, the deviations do require further explanations. We chose to pursue two alternatives within the basic framework of our decision-making model.

One possibility is that the observations may have been measured badly. In particular, it is possible that some variables we thought we were controlling perfectly in the laboratory setting were, in fact, not perfectly controlled. For example, some players might not be risk neutral with respect to the dollar payoffs, but had a nonlinear utility function over the money outcomes, or have a utility function that depends on the payoffs to the other subjects.[2]

A second possibility is that the rational expectations hypothesis might be wrong. This would not necessarily mean that players did not maximize expected utility, but that their subjective assessments of the other players' behavior was inaccurate or even systematically biased. We propose one particular hypothesis about a systematic bias in players' expectations about the behavior of the other players:

H: Individuals overestimate the probability that others contribute.

Equivalently, individuals underestimate the probability that others do not contribute. In looser terms, individuals underestimate the probability that others will be tempted to either free ride or to avoid the potential loss of their

---

2. See, for example, Palfrey and Rosenthal's altruism model (1988) or, in the context of risk-averse behavior in sealed bid auctions, Cox, Roberson, and Smith 1982; and Cox, Smith, and Walker 1983.

endowment. Here the hypothesis has been stated verbally. A precise specification of the hypothesis that will allow us to investigate its validity with our experimental data is provided later.

H leads directly to predictions about how behavior will systematically deviate from the predictions of (risk-neutral) game theory. For example, if only 1 of N individuals need contribute to produce the public benefit, overestimation will lead to a reduced level of contribution. The reason is that, in any 1 of N game, raising the probability others contribute raises the expected utility of not contributing but leaves the expected utility of contributing unchanged. The reasoning is reversed in the N of N game. There, overestimation increases the expected utility of contributing, but leaves the expected utility of noncontributing unchanged. More generally, in some games, overestimation is predicted to increase individual contribution; in other games, the prediction is reversed.

We specifically chose experimental parameter values—in terms of w, N, and the distribution of endowments relative to the value of the public benefit—that lead to a prediction of increased contribution and those that lead to a prediction of decreased contribution. In section 3, we show that the predictions developed from overestimation of probabilities cannot be replicated by nonlinear utility models or by models of cooperative or altruistic behavior.

We were, in fact, led to develop the hypothesis of probability overestimation rather than nonlinear utility on the basis of a set of experiments conducted at the California Institute of Technology in 1987–88 and at Carnegie-Mellon University in early 1989. While game theory was reasonably successful in accounting for the outcomes of voluntary contribution games (without communication), there were some systematic departures from the predicted equilibrium rates of contribution. Depending on the experimental parameters, we found that sometimes there were significantly higher contribution rates than predicted and sometimes there were significantly lower rates than predicted. After developing our hypothesis, we designed several "critical" experiments with different parameter values than the original experiments. We also replicated the original parameter values. In some new experiments, overcontribution, relative to game theory, was predicted; in others, too little. The results of these new experiments, conducted at the California Institute of Technology in the summer of 1989, also strongly support **H**.

Finally, most adaptive expectations models or Bayesian learning models would predict that if an experiment is conducted repeatedly in a stationary environment with random groupings, then subjects will update their expectations about other players' behavior in light of information from early play in the experiment. In fact, there is a great deal of substantial evidence in favor of this elsewhere in the experimental literature (e.g., Forsythe, Palfrey, and Plott 1982; Camerer and Weigelt 1988; McKelvey and Palfrey 1989). This has implications for the data, as well. For example, in contrast to the nonlinear utility explanations for deviations from our predictions, the probability bias hypothesis, together with adaptive behavior, predicts that behavior will be closer to the Bayesian equilibrium predictions as the number of replications increases. We find some evidence supporting this, but it is very weak. Overall, there appears to be a great deal of persistence to the biased beliefs.

In section 2 of the article, we develop the game-theoretic model. In section 3, we outline the model of overestimation of probabilities and some alternatives to the model of risk-neutral, selfish behavior. In section 4, we present the experimental design and the results of the experiments. Concluding remarks appear in section 5.

2. The Equilibrium Model of Voluntary Contribution

A group consists of N persons. A group project requires at least w units of input. Each group member is endowed with one indivisible unit of input, which may be either "consumed" by the individual or "contributed" to the group project. The voluntary contributions game consists of a single simultaneous move in which each individual's choice set is the pair {contribute, not contribute}.

The project succeeds if and only if at least w units are contributed. The value of the project to any individual is normalized to equal 1. The private value of the endowed unit of input to an individual is denoted c_i. We refer to c_i as the "cost" of contribution for individual i, since this is how much i must forego when making a contribution. Each person knows his or her own c_i but only knows that the other players' c's are independent random draws from some common probability distribution with CDF $F(\cdot)$. Assume F is continuous and strictly increasing on $[0, \bar{c}]$, $\bar{c} > 0$, with $F(0) = 0$ and $F(\bar{c}) = 1$.

The payoff for player i with endowment (cost) c is given by:

$1 + c$ if i does not contribute and at least w others contribute,

c if i does not contribute and fewer than w others contribute,

1 if i contributes and at least $w - 1$ others contribute, and

0 if i contributes and fewer than $w - 1$ others contribute.[3]

No sidepayments are permitted.

---

3. Variations of the game with different payoff structures can be treated. Similarly, the model can be generalized to allow for a nonzero lower support to $F(c)$ and to $F(c)$ nonuniform. See Palfrey and Rosenthal 1987 and 1989. Here we introduce only parameters varied in the experiments reported below.

Individual rationality makes $c \leq 1$ a necessary condition for contribution.[4] Thus, if all costs were public information (complete information) and fewer than w players had $c \leq 1$, the only equilibrium is for everyone to not contribute. Indeed, total noncontribution is always an equilibrium unless $w = 1$.

If $k \geq w$ players had $c < 1$ in a game of complete information, there would be $\binom{k}{w}$ pure strategy equilibria where exactly w individuals contribute. One of these, where the w lowest cost individuals contribute, would be the "efficient" equilibrium. (If sidepayments were permitted, it would always be efficient for the w lowest cost individuals to contribute if $w\bar{c} < N$.) There are also be a multitude of equilibria where some or all of the players used mixed strategies (Palfrey and Rosenthal 1984).

Because communication among the players is ruled out in our environment, there is no direct way in which players can coordinate or correlate their strategies or arrive at an outcome similar to the complete information efficient outcome.[5] Moreover, since the asymmetries between the players—that is, their different endowments—remain private information, asymmetries cannot be used, even tacitly, as a coordinating mechanism.

It is natural, then, to assume that all individuals will use an identical rule when they make their contribution decisions independently and simultaneously. As shown in Palfrey and Rosenthal 1988, a *symmetric* Bayesian equilibrium to this game always has a particularly simple form. For any beliefs that player i has about the other players' decisions to contribute, there is a unique, best response strategy that is a *cutpoint rule*. A cutpoint rule is a simple rule of thumb according to which an individual contributes if and only if his or her cost c is less than some specified critical cost level. Therefore, a symmetric equilibrium is simply characterized by a critical cost level, call it c^*, such that contribution is optimal if $c_i < c^*$ and noncontribution is optimal if $c_i > c^*$. While there may be more than one equilibrium value of c^*, the mild regularity conditions imposed on $F(\cdot)$ guarantee existence of at least one such value.

To solve for an equilibrium cutpoint, we need to find a value of c^* at which an individual would be indifferent between contributing and not contributing. Everyone with a cost below c^* would be better off contributing and anyone with a cost above c^* would be better off not contributing. It is easy to show that, in our parameterization of the problem, an individual is indifferent

---

4. Since F is continuous and any specific c has zero measure, we will frequently simplify matters by being imprecise about knife-edge situations, in this case $c = 1$.

5. See Palfrey and Rosenthal 1991 for a theoretical and experimental analysis of the game when preplay communication is permitted.

between contributing and not contributing if and only if his or her c equals the probability that exactly $w - 1$ of the other $N - 1$ players are contributing (i.e., the probability that his or her contribution will put the group over the threshold). At the equilibrium c^*, the probability that a given player contributes equals $q^* = 1 - F(c^*)$. If an individual thinks the others will be contributing with probability q^*, then the probability that his or her contribution will make the difference is given by the binomial formula for the probability of $w - 1$ successes out of $N - 1$ trials when the likelihood of success is $q^* = 1 - F(c^*)$. Therefore the set of all equilibrium cutpoints is the set of all solutions (in c^*) to the following equation:

$$c^* = \binom{N - 1}{w - 1} \{F(c^*)^{w-1} [1 - F(c^*)]^{N-w}\} \qquad (1)$$

$$\equiv \text{Prob } (k = w - 1),$$

where k is the number of contributors other than i.

Reiterating, the interpretation of equation 1 is that a person with a private value of c faces an opportunity cost of contributing equal to c. In order for c^* to be an equilibrium, it must be that everyone with a cost below c^* has opportunity costs sufficiently low so as to be better off contributing, given others are using the c^* decision rule and everyone with private costs greater than c^* have too high an opportunity cost. Therefore, individuals with a cost of exactly c^* must be indifferent between contributing and not contributing. Since the value of the group benefit was normalized to one, indifference implies that the cost of contribution must equal the probability of being pivotal to the success of the group project. This probability is Prob($k = w - 1$).

As an example of how an equilibrium would be computed, suppose that $N = 3$, $w = 2$, $\bar{c} = 1.5$, and F is the uniform distribution on $[0,1.5]$. Then equation 1 becomes: $c^* = (c^*/1.5)[1 - (c^*/1.5)]$. Solving for c^* gives $c^* = 0.375$. Since $\bar{c} = 1.5$, this implies $q^* = 0.25$.

The possibility of multiple solutions to equation 1 poses a potential problem in evaluating the data from the experiments. However, for the experiments that we conducted, it turns out that there is a natural concept of stability of equilibrium that nearly always generates a unique equilibrium prediction with our range of parameters. We say that a Bayesian equilibrium is *expectationally stable* if the following *tâtonnement* process converges to the equilibrium c^*.

Let c_0 be some initial cutpoint in the open interval $(0,\bar{c})$. Suppose everyone started out using c_0 as their cutpoint rule. Then, on average, players will observe a frequency of contribution $q_0 = F(c_0)$. Next suppose that this results in each of the players having expectations q_0 about the likelihood that a randomly selected opponent will contribute. One could imagine this, for example, as the outcome of a learning process after many repetitions with opponents using c_0. Then the best response under these expectations (q_0) is to use a cutpoint c_1 satisfying:

$$c_1 = G(c_0) = \binom{N-1}{w-1} \{F(c_0)^{w-1}[1 - F(c_0)]^{N-w}\}.$$

We say that c^* is an *expectationally stable equilibrium* (ESE) if there exists an interval $C^E(c^*) \subset [0,\bar{c}]$ containing c^* such that, for all $c_0 \in C^E(c^*)$, $[c_0 - G(c_0)](c_0 - c^*) > 0$ if $c_0 \neq c^*$. We define c^* as being a *globally expectationally stable equilibrium* (GESE) if it is an ESE relative to the open set $(0,\bar{c})$. Thus, a Bayesian-Nash equilibrium to our game is GESE if the adjustment process moves in the direction of the equilibrium from any initial cutpoint that is above 0 or below the maximum possible cost, $\bar{c}$.

In the experiments we report here, F is always uniformly distributed between 0 and $\bar{c}$ so there is always at least one ESE, and with one exception, there is always a unique GESE. The exception occurs when $w = N$ and $\bar{c} \leq 1$. In that case, both $c^* = 0$ and $c^* = \bar{c}$ are ESE and there is also an unstable equilibrium, c°, between 0 and $\bar{c}$. For $c_0 < c^\circ$, $c^* = 0$ is the limit point of the adjustment process $G(c_t)$ while $c^* = \bar{c}$ is the limit point if $c_0 > c^\circ$. When $w = N$ and $\bar{c} > 1$, $c^* = 0$ is a unique GESE. In all other cases with $w > 1$, there are exactly two Bayesian equilibria, one with $c^* = 0$ and the other with $c^* > 0$. It is easily shown that $c^* = 0$ is unstable but the other equilibrium is a GESE. If $w = 1$, then there is a unique globally stable Bayesian equilibrium.[6]

There are also some asymmetric equilibria that may occur for some parameters, $\bar{c}$, w, and N. An example of such an equilibrium would be one in which a particular subset (say player numbers 1 through w) *always* contribute regardless of their cost (i.e., $c^* = \bar{c}$ for these players) and the other members of the group never contribute ($c^* = \underline{c}$). This is possible as long as $\bar{c} < 1$. We do not consider these (or other) asymmetries.

Therefore, for nearly all of our experimental parameters we will have a unique stable symmetric Bayesian equilibrium, c^*, that provides a strong prediction about individual behavior:

PREDICTION 1. Given $c^*(N,w,\bar{c})$, predict i contributes if and only if $c_i < c^*$.

---

6. Moreover, the iterated map defined by $c_{t+1} = G(c_t)$ converges globally to the GESE in all but two cases. In both these cases, $G(\cdot)$ is explosive, but there exist monotone transformations of G that will converge.

3. Explaining Deviations from the Theory

While prediction 1 is roughly supported, we will see that many individual decisions are not in accord with the rule. The model might nonetheless be correct in the aggregate. This suggests the following:

PREDICTION 2. The aggregate probability of contribution is $q* = F(c*)$.

A natural estimator of the cutpoint that players are using is to measure $\hat{q}$, the observed frequency of contribution in an experiment. Standard tests can then be used to see if this observed frequency differs significantly from $F(c*)$.

We will, in fact, find significant deviations, even in the aggregate, from the theoretical probabilities. In this section, we discuss two different approaches to "rationalizing" these deviations, one based on relaxing the rational expectations restriction of the theory, and one based on modifying the utility hypotheses of our equilibrium predictions.

The Biased Probabilities Hypothesis

In the introduction, we proposed the hypothesis that individuals consistently underestimate the probability that others free ride, but otherwise behave roughly in accordance with expected payoff maximization. What does this hypothesis, **H,** predict about these deviations? There are several alternative ways to operationalize **H** to apply it to our data. One interpretation is simply that **H** implies that individuals believe that others act according to some $c** > c*$. That is, expectations about the likelihood others will contribute exceed the equilibrium likelihood others will contribute. Using these beliefs, they then use a cutpoint, c^+, which represents the optimal decision rule, given beliefs $c**$.

To study how $c** > c*$ will affect the (observed) decision rule c^+, it suffices (for small amounts of bias) to differentiate equation 1:

$$\frac{dc^+}{dq} \gtreqless 0 \quad \text{if} \quad q \lesseqgtr \frac{w-1}{N-1}. \tag{2}$$

Let q^+ be the actual probability of contribution. (Note that $\hat{q}$ is a consistent estimator of q^+.) Relationship 2, evaluated at $q*$, immediately leads to the following predictions under **H:**

PREDICTION
3a. If $w = 1$, then $q^+ < q*$;[7]

---

7. Note that if $w = 1$, for any $F(\cdot)$, there exists a unique $q* > 0$.

3b. If $w = N$ and $0 < q^* < 1$, then $q^+ > q^*$;

3c. If $1 < w < N$ and $0 < q^*$, then $q^+ > q^*$ if $q^* < (w - 1)/(N - 1)$, and $q^+ < q^*$ if $q^* > (w - 1)/(N - 1)$.[8]

Our experimental design consists of some 1 of 3 experiments where we always expect undercontribution relative to the game-theoretic predictions, some 3 of 3 experiments where we always expect overcontribution, and some 2 of 3 and 2 of 4 where the prediction depends on the value of $\bar{c}$. We varied $\bar{c}$ to produce the appropriate contrasts.

For our design, except in the unanimity game $w = 3, N = 3$, if $c^* > 0$, c^* is unique.[9] In unanimity games, there is no $q^* > 0$ when $\bar{c} > 1$, and a unique solution $c^* = 1$ when $\bar{c} = 1$. When $\bar{c} < 1$, we have one solution with $c^* = \bar{c}^2$ and a second solution $c^* = \bar{c}$.

Combining hypothesis 1 with the auxiliary hypothesis that the bias is always with respect to the unique expectationally stable equilibrium thus leads to strong restrictions on observations. When multiple stable equilibria exist, we will assume that the bias is with respect to $c^* = 0$.

A second way to operationalize **H** is that players' expectations about the likelihood others will contribute exceeds the empirical likelihood rather than exceeding the equilibrium likelihood. In other words, the bias is with respect to actual contribution rates, not necessarily equilibrium contribution rates. Again, the measurement problem is that we only have data on contribution decisions, not on beliefs. However, for any observed rates of contribution, q^+, we can estimate a cutpoint decision rule, c^+, and infer what players beliefs would have to have been if they had been optimizing relative to those beliefs. Denoting these inferred beliefs by q^e, we then state

PREDICTION 4. $q^e \geq q^+$.

As we will discuss in the next section, this prediction, while more appealing that prediction 3 in some ways, has some drawbacks.

---

8. Note that for $w < N$, there never exists an equilibrium with $q^* = 1$.
9. Showing uniqueness is direct with $N = 3$, since $q = F(c^*)$ is linear in c^* while equation 1 is quadratic in q. In the $w = 2, N = 4$ game, uniqueness follows from noting that $\frac{dc}{dq} \gtreqless 0$ if $q \lesseqgtr 1/3$ and $\frac{d^2c}{dq^2} \gtreqless 0$ if $q \lesseqgtr 2/3$.

Alternative Models of Nonlinear Utility and Cooperation

The purpose of this section is to demonstrate that prediction 3, the prediction developed on the basis of the probability bias hypothesis, cannot be generated from plausible alternative models. We first deal with nonlinear utility and next with cooperation.

Nonlinear Utility. Since our experimental subjects were paid in dollars, it is important to rule out utility being nonlinear in money as an alternative explanation for our results. Without loss of generality, we assume that each player's utility for the outcomes is given by the function u with:

$$u(0) = 0; \tag{3}$$

$$u(c) = c + \alpha(c);$$

$$u(1) = 1;$$

$$u(1 + c) = 1 + c + \delta(c).$$

The case of risk neutrality is $\alpha = \delta = 0$. We continue to assume that all players have the same utility function[10] and that the functions α and δ are each either always weakly positive or weakly negative.[11] Again, our analysis focuses on local changes in the equilibrium. This directs our attention to $0 < c < 1$.

With equations 3, equation 1 generalizes to:

$$c^* = \text{Prob}(k = w - 1) - \alpha \cdot \text{Prob}(k < w) - \delta \cdot \text{Prob}(k \geq w). \tag{4}$$

Let us begin by considering the common form of utility in economics, global risk aversion. This requires $\alpha > 0$ and $\delta < 0$. But in unanimity games, the last term in equation 4 must be 0. That is, the outcome with payoff $1 + c$ is impossible in unanimity games. Therefore, $\alpha > 0$ implies that the utility of noncontribution is raised relative to the utility of contribution, in turn implying less contribution, contradicting prediction 3b.

Having dealt with risk aversion, we turn to models where, in spirit with

---

10. This assumption can be relaxed.

11. In the actual experiment, subjects know prior to play that, postplay, they will not only learn their payoffs but also the total number of contributors in the group. It is possible that subjects attach utility to these reports (Is being the sole noncontributor in a unanimity game worse than not contributing when no one else does?), but we choose to ignore this complexity.

prospect theory in psychology, the utility function is partly risk-averse and partly risk-acceptant. These possibilities are covered by either: (a) $\alpha > 0$ and $\delta \geq 0$, with at least one inequality strict, or (b) $\alpha \leq 0$ and $\delta \leq 0$, with at least one inequality strict.

In case a, the utility of noncontribution is raised relative to the utility of contribution. The utility function is risk-averse for lotteries between the two contribution outcomes (0 and 1), but risk-acceptant for lotteries between the noncontribution outcomes. Case a can be interpreted as the utility function for individuals who are loss-averse with respect to the natural anchor formed by their endowment. They are risk-averse for lotteries over the alternatives near the anchor point where there is a possibility of being worse off, but are risk-acceptant for lotteries that guarantee they will be no worse off than the endowment. Since the utility of noncontribution always increases, however, case a predicts that contribution always falls relative to risk neutrality. Therefore, case a is inconsistent with predictions 3b and 3c.

In case b, the situation of case a is reversed. Now the utility of contributing is always increased, and the individual is risk-acceptant for lotteries over the contribution outcomes. One can think of the individual as ascribing a nonmonetary bonus or prize effect to the successful completion of the project. Alternatively, case b captures altruism effects, including the model of Palfrey and Rosenthal (1988). But since the utility of contribution always increases relative to risk neutrality, case b is inconsistent with predictions 3a and 3c.

The remaining possibility is $\alpha < 0$ and $\delta > 0$. If $\delta \geq -\alpha c/(1 - c)$, the utility function is globally weakly risk-acceptant. We rule out this situation as a priori implausible. On the other hand, if $\delta < -\alpha c/(1 - c)$, consider 1 of N games. In these games, the outcome 0 is impossible. The inequality condition then implies that the utility of contribution has been raised relative to that of noncontributing. Therefore, contribution should increase, contradicting prediction 3a.

Cooperation. Another alternative view of behavior is provided by various models of cooperative behavior. An upper bound to what could be achieved by cooperation is the outcome that could be achieved by the players if they had full information about costs. This would have the w players with the lowest costs contribute if the sum of these lowest costs is less than N. In other words, the good is provided unless its total cost exceeds the total benefit. Another model of full information cooperation is for the w players with the lowest costs to provide the good as long as none of these costs exceeded 1.0, the value of the public good. Given that costs are private information, these highly coordinated behaviors cannot be achieved. Moreover, they lead to predicted contribution rates that are very much higher than anything we observe in the data.

A more plausible model of cooperation is for players to use (perhaps as a tacit collusion against the experimenter) a cutpoint that maximizes expected group payoff. This always implies a contribution rate greater than or equal to q^*, where q^* is an ESE. As we will see in section 5, observed contribution rates are typically much lower than the group optimal rate.

In summary, we have established that models of nonlinear utility (and models like altruism that can be interpreted in terms of nonlinear utility) cannot be used to generate predictions equivalent to those of prediction 3. To see if **H** is supported as a behavioral hypothesis, we turn to a presentation of our experimental design and results.

4. Description of the Experiments

A detailed specification of each experiment appears as table 1. The experiments at Carnegie-Mellon University used seventy-two undergraduates. The 1987 and 1988 experiments at Caltech used subjects who were undergraduates at Caltech or Pasadena Community College. The experiments in the summer of 1989 used high school students participating in a summer program at Caltech. The subjects were mainly male. None of the participants had prior experience in the tasks required in these experiments. Each experimental session used nine or twelve subjects. A given experimental session consisted of one or three experiments, an experiment constituting a different set of parameters. In the CMU setting, there were six sessions involving three matched pairs. For the paired sessions, everything was identical except the order of experiments. No important order effects were observed. Instructions are given in the appendix. These instructions varied slightly between CMU and Caltech, and within Caltech sessions. Experiments run in 1987 and 1988 used a computer program written at Caltech. Experiments run in 1989 used a computer program written at Carnegie-Mellon, with minor modifications made at Caltech. None of the factors mentioned to this point appeared to have a notable influence on results.

All experiments were designed to have twenty, twenty-five, or thirty rounds. The number of rounds was made known to the subjects before the experiment started. Three experiments were inadvertently curtailed shortly before the planned end because of computer crashes.

At the beginning of each experiment, subjects were told w, N, the value, in "francs," of the public benefit, and all other relevent information about the experimental procedures. They were also told how many cents per franc they would receive at the conclusion of the session. These values were held constant throughout an experiment. Subjects earned between \$10 and \$20 during each session. Sessions lasted between forty-five minutes and an hour and a half.

In each round, subjects were each given a single indivisible "token" (endowment). Token values in franc increments between 1 and either 90 or

TABLE 1. Description of Experiments

Date	Site	w	N	Range[a]	Cents[b]	$\bar{c}$	Subjects	Rounds[c]	Reveal[d]	Sequence[e]
4/27/89	CMU	1	3	90	0.7	2.25	12	20	No	3
5/2/89	CMU	1	3	90	0.7	2.25	12	20	No	1
7/26/89	CIT	2	4	204	0.1	2.22	12	17	No	1
7/31/89	CIT	2	4	90	0.3	2.25	12	20	No	3
8/8/89	CIT	2	4	90	0.3	2.25	12	20	Yes	3
4/27/89	CMU	2	3	90	0.7	2.25	12	20	No	1
5/2/89	CMU	2	3	90	0.7	2.25	12	20	No	3
4/27/89	CMU	3	3	90	0.7	2.25	12	20	No	2
5/2/89	CMU	3	3	90	0.7	2.25	12	20	No	2
7/13/88	CIT	1	3	90	0.5	1.50	12	30	No	—
2/15/89	CMU	1	3	90	0.3	1.50	12	20	No	2
2/16/89	CMU	1	3	90	0.3	1.50	12	20	No	2
7/31/89	CIT	1	3	90	0.3	1.50	12	20	No	2
8/8/89	CIT	1	3	90	0.3	1.50	12	18	Yes	2
11/22/87	CIT	2	3	90	1	1.50	9	20	No	—
12/3/87	CIT	2	3	90	1	1.50	9	20	No	—
12/20/87	CIT	2	3	90	1	1.50	9	20	No	—
2/15/89	CMU	2	3	90	0.3	1.50	12	20	No	1
2/16/89	CMU	2	3	90	0.3	1.50	12	20	No	3
7/31/89	CIT	2	3	90	0.3	1.50	12	20	No	1
8/8/89	CIT	2	3	90	0.3	1.50	12	20	Yes	1
7/21/88	CIT	3	3	90	0.5	1.50	12	30	No	—
2/15/89	CMU	3	3	90	0.3	1.50	12	20	No	3
2/16/89	CMU	3	3	90	0.3	1.50	12	20	No	1

204 were independently drawn with replacement from identical uniform distributions and randomly assigned to subjects, and this was carefully explained to the subjects in the instructions.[12] Then each subject was told the value of his or her token, but not told the values of the tokens of other subjects. Subjects were then asked to enter their decisions (spend or not spend the token).

---

12. These costs were generated in advance by a standard computerized pseudo–random number generator. In the three 1987 experiments, token values were assigned directly in cents. There do not seem to have been any important effects from the manner of presenting or scaling the payoffs.

TABLE 1—*Continued*

Date	Site	w	N	Range[a]	Cents[b]	c̄	Subjects	Rounds[c]	Reveal[d]	Sequence[e]
8/3/89	CIT	3	3	204	0.1	0.995	12	25	No	1
2/21/89	CMU	1	3	90	0.2	0.750	12	20	No	1
3/1/89	CMU	1	3	90	0.2	0.750	12	20	No	3
2/21/89	CMU	2	3	90	0.2	0.750	12	20	No	2
3/1/89	CMU	2	3	90	0.2	0.750	12	20	No	2
2/21/89	CMU	3	3	90	0.2	0.750	12	20	No	3
3/1/89	CMU	3	3	90	0.2	0.750	12	20	No	1
7/26/89	CIT	2	4	204	0.1	0.667	12	25	No	2
7/26/89	CIT	2	3	204	0.1	0.667	12	24	No	3

Notes: The c̄ value of 2.22 was for a treatment in the 2.25 condition in which franc values had been rescaled from 90 to 204. Setting B to the integer 91 resulted in c̄ = 2.22.

The 18 experiments at CMU form a matched set in which the same randomly drawn endowments were used with all six sets of subjects. Two sets of subjects were run for each of three different values of c̄ (2.25, 1.5, and 0.75). Within each c̄ value, the order of the $w = 1$, 2, and 3 experiments was permuted so that the first experiment and third experiments were reversed for the two sets of subjects. The endowments in the CMU 1 of 3, c̄ = 1.5 experiments were matched in the 1 of 3 experiment at CIT on 7/31/89. (The three experiments on that date and on 8/8/89 followed the same sequence but differed in endowment assignments and the reveal treatment.) Otherwise, new random draws were used in each experiment.

[a]Range gives the upper end of the uniform (in integers) distribution of endowments in francs. This number and c̄ can be used to calculate the franc value of the public benefit, $B = $ Range$/$c̄.

[b]Cents is number of cents paid per franc earned in the experiment.

[c]Rounds is the number of (nonpractice) rounds for the given (w, N, c̄) parameters. Experiments of twenty, twenty-five, or thirty rounds ran for the planned duration. Experiments of seventeen, eighteen, and twenty-four rounds were prematurely terminated by computer crashes.

[d]When the reveal parameter is "Yes," all token values were revealed after each round. Subjects could match individual token values and decisions but could not identify the individuals. Otherwise, token values were not revealed.

[e]Only one set of subjects was run on a given date. Some sets of subjects played three sets of parameters in sequence. The sequence shows the order in which the parameters were used. In the experiment on 8/3/89, subjects were used, subsequent to their play of a 3 of 3 game, for two other treatments in which groups were fixed rather than rotated. When this entry is blank, subjects were run for only one set of parameters.

If at least w of the N subjects in a group spent their token, each subject in that group received a number of francs equal to the value of the public benefit if he or she was a "contributor." If he or she was not a contributor, the payoff was this number of francs plus the token value. In table 1, c̄ shows the rescaling of the distribution of token values such that the benefit is rescaled to 1. In each round, subjects were assigned to a new group in a random rotation sequence, subject to the constraint that two subjects were never paired together in the same group in consecutive rounds. (This constraint was not imposed when $N = 4$.) The reason for doing this was to limit reputation and supergame effects that can occur with repeated play. In the ensuing analysis, we treat each decision as an independent observation.

5. Results

Testing the Bayesian-Nash Predictions

Efficiency Predictions. We begin discussion of the results by noting that the Bayesian-Nash Equilibrium is remarkably successful as a predictor of aggregate outcomes of the experiments. For each group in each round of each experiment, we computed the actual earnings of the group. Using the actual token values drawn by the subjects, we also computed the predicted earnings for the group, assuming that play conformed to the theoretical cutpoints, c^*. We then computed average earnings per subject, normalized so that the public good had a value of 1.0 in each experiment. We then compared predicted earnings to actual earnings for each experiment. These are aggregate comparisons where individual variations from round to round and group to group are averaged out. (We maintain disaggregation across replicate experiments.)

The results offer remarkably strong support for the theory. For data from all rounds, the regression equation is:

Actual earnings $= -0.054 + 1.045*$Predicted earnings,
$R^2 = 0.95, \quad N = 33.$

The estimated constant does not differ significantly from zero and the estimated intercept does not differ significantly from 1.0. The actual data points are plotted in figure 1.

Since there is substantial variation in endowments (via $\bar{c}$) across experiments (endowments and actual earnings have an R^2 of 0.40), we checked that the success of the model was not largely driven by the correlation between earnings and endowments. Therefore, we also examined the increase in per subject earnings over per subject endowments. The results, plotted in figure 2, continue to be striking:

Actual Increase $= 0.008 + 0.937*$Predicted Increase,
$R^2 = 0.93, \quad N = 33.$

Again, at conventional levels, the intercept did not differ significantly from zero and the slope did not differ significantly from unity (see fig. 2).

These impressive results occur even though the data, from other viewpoints, show systematic deviations from theoretical predictions. We discuss these deviations next with a series of tables where the rows show the value of

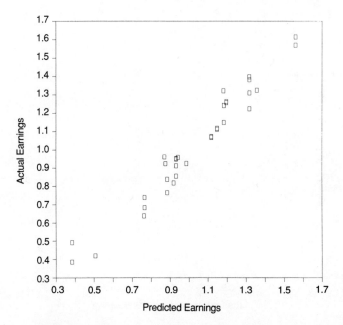

Fig. 1. Bayesian equilibrium, per subject earnings. Public good normalized to 1, all rounds.

$\bar{c}$ and the columns designate the four different w, N combinations used in the design. In each cell of the table, we present results for each experiment that matches the cell. The order of experiments within cells always matches the order given in table 1. Spaces between the rows in table 1 separate cells in the later tables.

Individual Behavior. Table 2 shows that risk-neutral game theory does not succeed at the individual level corresponding to prediction 1. There are many errors of classification using the theoretical cutpoints. (For $w < N$, the nonzero cutpoint was used where it existed. For $w = N = 3$, the zero cutpoint was used.)

On the other hand, prediction 1 is qualitatively correct. Contribution rates are decreasing in cost, as shown by probit analysis that is not reported here. For all experiments, the standard chi-square test for the 2×2 table contribute/not contribute versus endowment above or equal to cutpoint/endowment below cutpoint, is significant at $p < .01$. In the nineteen experiments with a nonzero cutpoint where subjects had endowments above or at the benefit level, after excluding such subjects, the test is significant at $p < .001$ except for $p = .0882$ in the CIT 7/26/89 2 of 4, $p = .0436$ in the CIT 7/31/89 2 of 4, and $p = .0002$ in the CIT 8/8/89 2 of 3. Thus, the prediction is

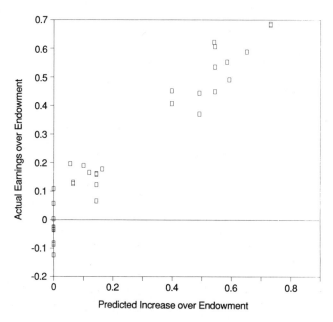

Fig. 2. Bayesian equilibrium, per subject earnings. Public good normalized to 1, all rounds.

TABLE 2. Classification Errors, Bayesian-Nash Predictions

$\bar{c}$	w/N			
	1/3	2/4	2/3	3/3
2.25	26/240	49/204	46/240	23/240
	29/240	44/240	38/240	31/240
		29/240		
1.50	64/360		43/180, 34/180	112/360
	33/240		37/180, 31/240	47/240
	34/240		39/240	60/240
	53/240		40/240	
	35/216		68/240	
0.995				132/300
0.750	61/240		46/240	126/240
	61/240		61/240	143/240
0.667		73/300	67/240	

Note: The first number for each experiment is the number of classification errors; the second number is the total number of decisions.

TABLE 3. **Endowments at Least Equal to Benefit: Contributions/Endowments**

	w/N			
c̄	1/3	2/4	2/3	3/3
2.25	0/141	6/112 *(2/36)*	6/147 *(1/34)*	2/138
	3/141	2/139	0/147	0/138
		2/139		
1.50	2/124 *(2/24)*		3/67, 2/61	19/127 *(2/17)*
	0/77		0/61, 1/89	0/87
	1/77		0/89	4/87
	1/77		0/89	
	2/69		12/89 *(2/20)*	

Note: The first number is the total number of contributions when the endowment was at least equal to the benefit. The second number is the total number of occurrences of endowments greater or equal to the endowment. The number of contributions of this type in the last five rounds of each experiment was zero, except where shown in italics. Reveal experiment results are underlined.

For the 2 × 2 comparison spend/not spend vs. endowment ≥ benefit/endowment < benefit, the standard χ^2 test was always significant at $p < .001$. The same holds true for the first ten rounds of each experiment except two experiments where the p-levels were .0003 and .062, respectively, and for the last ten rounds except for two experiments with p-levels .0006 and .0001 (last eight rounds).

qualitatively correct, even if we exclude subjects who have weakly dominant strategies of noncontributing.

When a subject has a dominant strategy, the subject almost always acts in accordance with the model, as shown in table 3. Most exceptions occur in early rounds. The classification errors of the model are thus almost entirely from the behavior of subjects without dominant strategies.[13]

Aggregate Behavior. The game-theoretic model fares somewhat better at the aggregate level of predicting the frequency of contribution, as shown in table 4. It should be noted that an important comparative static prediction of the game-theoretic model is strongly supported by the data. For w, N fixed, contribution is strongly decreasing in c̄. As contribution is cheaper on average for low c̄, contribution occurs more frequently as c̄ falls. On the other hand, for c̄ fixed, contribution is not increasing in w/N, which increases from left to right, in the table. A naive view of volunteering might claim that contribution should increase as w/N increases, since a larger fraction of the group is needed to produce the public benefit. This naive view is not supported by the data.

---

13. Finding rare violation of dominant strategies is, in fact, surprising since the same result does not occur in Prisoner's Dilemma experiments. A key difference between our experiments and the Prisoner's Dilemma is that, in our experiments, "All Contribute" does not Pareto dominate "All not Contribute."

TABLE 4. The Frequency of Contribution

$\bar{c}$	1/3		2/4		2/3		3/3	
2.25	*0.217*	(0.192)	0.309*	(0.132)	0.192	(0)	0.096	(0)
	0.213	(0.192)	0.221*	(0.104)	0.159	(0)	0.129	(0)
			0.200*	(0.104)				
1.50	0.311	(0.306)			0.394*	(0.222)	0.311	(0)
	0.221*	(0.271)			0.350*	(0.239)	0.196	(0)
	0.263	(0.271)			0.383*	(0.244)	0.250	(0)
	*0.333**	(0.271)			0.308*	(0.238)		
	0.292	(0.269)			0.308*	(0.238)		
					0.363*	(0.238)		
					0.379*	(0.238)		
0.995							0.440	(0)
0.750	0.379	(0.392)			0.521*	(0.596)	0.525	(0)
	0.404	(0.392)			0.558	(0.596)	0.596	(0)
0.667			0.500	(0.523)	0.580*	(0.674)		

Notes: The entries in parentheses in each cell are the theoretical contribution frequencies for symmetric Bayesian-Nash equilibrium under risk neutrality. The frequencies were calculated using the actual token draws in the experiment. The absence of an entry in a cell indicates that no experiments were run for the parameters corresponding to the cell. Actual frequencies that represent deviations from the theory that are not consistent with **H** are shown in italics. An asterisk (*) indicates a departure from the theoretical frequency that is statistically significant at .05 level on the basis of a *t*-test using normal approximation to the binomial.

If we examine each cell in the table, we find results that are sometimes in the "ballpark" of the theory, but we also find many statistically significant deviations, leading to rejection of prediction 2. However, these deviations are mostly consistent with **H**. Consider, first, experiments with $w < N$. Of twenty-five experiments, all but six of them have observed contribution rates that are consistent with prediction 3. Only one of the six inconsistent observations is statistically significant at the .05 level. In contrast, fifteen of the nineteen consistent observations are statistically significant. Experiments with $w = N = 3$ cannot be evaluated statistically because $q^* = 0$. (Relative to the 0 equilibrium, any positive contribution is consistent with **H**. On the other hand, there are also equilibria with 100 percent contribution rates for two of the cells. The observed contribution rates are obviously below those given theoretically and so, relative to the 100 percent contribution equilibrium are inconsistent with **H**.) Results similar to those presented in table 4 are obtained when we base the analysis only on those subjects with dominant strategies. These results are shown in table 5.

Two alternatives to **H**, nonlinear utility that leads to "altruism" and cooperative behavior, always predict contribution in excess of the Bayesian-

TABLE 5.   Frequency of Contribution, Endowment below Benefit Level

	w/N							
$\bar{c}$	1/3		2/4		2/3		3/3	
2.25	*0.525*	(0.465)	0.620*	(0.293)	0.430	(0)	0.206	(0)
	0.485	(0.465)	0.505*	(0.248)	0.409	(0)	0.304	(0)
			0.465*	(0.248)				
1.50	0.466	(0.466)			0.601*	(0.354)	0.399	(0)
	0.325	(0.399)			0.512*	(0.361)	0.366	(0)
	0.380	(0.399)			0.580*	(0.370)	0.398	(0)
	*0.485**	(0.399)			0.483*	(0.378)		
	0.415	(0.395)			0.470*	(0.378)		
					0.576*	(0.378)		
					0.523*	(0.378)		

Notes: The entries in parentheses in each cell are the theoretical contribution frequencies for symmetric Bayesian-Nash equilibrium under risk neutrality. The frequencies were calculated using the actual token draws in the experiment. The absence of an entry in a cell indicates that no experiments were run for the parameters corresponding to the cell. Actual frequencies that represent deviations from the theory that are not consistent with **H** are shown in italics. An asterisk (*) indicates a departure from the theoretical frequency that is statistically significant at .05 level on the basis of a *t*-test using normal approximation to the binomial.

Nash levels. For any parameter, one can compute a "cooperative cutpoint," which is the cutpoint that would maximize the expected payoff to the group. In all cases, it exceeds the Bayesian equilibrium cutpoint, reflecting the fact that there is a free rider problem. In table 6, we display the contribution probabilities that would result if players followed the cooperative cutpoints. (To provide readers with a sense of how parametric variation affects the probabilities, the probabilities are also shown for cells where no experiments were run.) The information in tables 4 and 6 enables us to make comparisons across the thirty-three experiments. When $w = N = 3$ and $\bar{c} = 2.25$, both the cooperative and self-interested models predict zero contribution. (In this extreme case, the expected cost of providing the good exceeds the benefits.) In the other thirty-one cases, the observed frequencies are always closer to the Bayesian predictions than to the cooperative predictions, except in the two observations where $w = N = 3$ and $\bar{c} = 3/4$. For $w = N = 3$, we always use 0 as the Bayesian equilibrium prediction. But in that case, there also exists a stable equilibrium with 100 percent contribution. On the whole, the data present strong evidence for self-interested behavior in comparison to full cooperation.

An Alternative Test of the Probability Bias Hypothesis

To this point, we have only examined the hypothesis about probability bias with reference to local properties of the predicted equilibrium probability that

TABLE 6. Theoretical Contribution Probabilities for Group Optimal Behavior

$\bar{c}$	w/N			
	1/3	2/4	2/3	3/3
2.25	0.431	0.567	0.625	0
	(0.25)	(0.134)	(0.000)	(0)
1.50	0.500	0.646	0.750	1
	(0.313)	(0.293)	(0.250)	(0)
0.995	0.567	0.712	0.834	1
	(0.381)	(0.424)	(0.500)	(0)
0.750	0.610	0.750	0.875	1
	(0.431)	(0.500)	(0.625)	(0)
0.667	0.627	0.765	0.889	1
	(0.453)	(0.529)	(0.667)	(0)

Note: The entries in parentheses in each cell are the theoretical contribution probabilities for symmetric Bayesian-Nash equilibrium under risk neutrality. The other entries are the contribution probabilities generated by the cutpoint that maximizes expected group payoff.

a randomly selected individual will contribute. That is, we began by considering a unique stable equilibrium cutpoint, then looked at the implied contribution frequencies if everyone adopts that strategy, then calculated the derivative of the reaction function (i.e., direction of change in the optimal cutpoint) if expectations departed from "rational expectations" in a neighborhood of the equilibrium. If that derivative was positive, then our prediction was an observed level of contribution greater than the equilibrium level of contribution; if the derivative was negative, then we predicted the opposite.

That method of evaluating **H** has two potential weaknesses. First, the probability bias is measured with respect to the equilibrium prediction, not with respect to the objective frequencies of what players are actually doing. Second, the sign of the derivative evaluated at the equilibrium may be different than the sign of the derivative evaluated elsewhere. That is, we are making global comparisons by extrapolating from a local calculation. To show that these are not serious problems, we next examine whether the expectations overestimated the actual frequencies of contributions. We do this in the following way.

Suppose that we observe an empirical frequency of contributions equal to $\hat{q}$. Ignoring individual differences, this implies a cutpoint rule $c(\hat{q}) = F^{-1}(\hat{q})$ that the players are following. We may then perform the following calculation. First we maintain the assumption that players are using best responses, given their beliefs, so that they are all maximizing under the *expectation* that others are contributing with probability equal to q^e (possibly not equal to $\hat{q}$). Next we ask "what value of q^e would rationalize the use of the strategy $c(\hat{q})$?"

If $q^e > \hat{q}$, then **H** is confirmed, because it means that $\hat{q}$ can only be justified as deriving from best response behavior if players beliefs, q^e, exceed $\hat{q}$. If $\hat{q} < q^e$ then **H** is contradicted.

Care is required in comparing $\hat{q}$ and q^e. First, for the 2 of 3 and 2 of 4 experiments, it is possible that $\hat{q}$ is sufficiently high that the implied cutpoint is not a best response to any cutpoint, so q^e is undefined. Thus, any such observation rejects the joint hypothesis that subjects are responding optimally to biased priors. Second, in 2 of 3 experiments where a best response can be found, there are two values of q^e that are consistent with the observed cutpoint. If both of these exceed $\hat{q}$, **H** is ambiguously supported. But the data are ambiguous if only one exceeds $\hat{q}$. Finally, for $w = N = 3$ and $\bar{c} > 1$, we are guaranteed that $q^e > \hat{q}$ unless $\hat{q} = 0$. For experiments with these parameters, **H** cannot be put to a test.

Table 7 displays $\hat{q}$ and q^e for all experiments. A dash indicates that q^e is undefined. The hypothesis is supported in all 3 of 3 experiments and all but one of the 1 of 3 experiments. In the 2 of 3 experiments, five experiments rejected the joint hypothesis since the value of $\hat{q}$ was too great to be consistent with optimizing behavior. In three other experiments, one q^e was below $\hat{q}$, the other above. In the remaining four 2 of 3 experiments, **H** was supported. It was not supported in the 2 of 4 experiments. In three of the four such experiments, there is no q^e that rationalizes $\hat{q}$; in the remaining experiment, one of the two solutions is above q^e, the other below.

Summarizing, this alternative examination of the probability bias hypothesis produces somewhat more mixed results than before. While the hypothesis seems to hold for most of the experiments, there are some parameter values for which it clearly fails.

Learning

If players have systematically inaccurate prior beliefs about the likelihood others will contribute, then, as they play the game and observe a sample of contribution rates, one would expect them to adjust their beliefs and their behavior in light of this new information. This will implicitly lead to a dynamic learning process that will be reflected in changes in the observed $\hat{q}$. If this learning process is stable and it adjusts in the direction of an equilibrium, then the difference between their beliefs and the "true" contribution rates of the other players should be smaller in later rounds. If the equilibrium is stable, then we would also expect the difference between observed contribution rates and the equilibrium contribution rates to decline over the course of the experiment.

Thus, one implication of such an adjustment process is that we will measure $\hat{q}$ closer to q^e in the later rounds than in the earlier rounds. There is some evidence in support of this. For one thing, in the first ten rounds there

TABLE 7. Estimated Prior Probabilities in the Experiments

Parameters	Date	Site	All Rounds $\hat{q}$	All Rounds q^e	Last Ten Rounds $\hat{q}$	Last Ten Rounds q^e
$w=1$, $N=3$, $\bar{c}=2.25$	4/27/89	CMU	.217	.302	.242	.263
	5/2/89	CMU	.213	.308	.225	.288
$w=2$, $N=4$, $\bar{c}=2.25$	7/26/89	CIT	.309	—	.298	—
	7/31/89	CIT	.221	—	.217	—
	8/8/89	CIT	.200	—	.192	.488
$w=2$, $N=3$, $\bar{c}=2.25$	4/27/89	CMU	.192	.315,.685	.183	.291,.719
	5/2/89	CMU	.158	.232,.768	.150	.215,.785
$w=3$, $N=3$, $\bar{c}=2.25$	4/27/89	CMU	.096	.464	.075	.411
	5/2/89	CMU	.129	.538	.108	.493
$w=1$, $N=3$, $\bar{c}=1.50$	7/13/88	CIT	.311	.317	.292	.339
	2/15/89	CMU	.221	.424	.233	.408
	2/16/89	CMU	.263	.394	.250	.387
	7/31/89	CIT	.333	.293	.342	.284
	8/8/89	CIT	.292	.338	.302	.327
$w=2$, $N=3$, $\bar{c}=1.50$	11/22/87	CIT	.394	—	.367	—
	12/3/87	CIT	.350	—	.278	.296,.704
	12/20/87	CIT	.383	—	.378	—
	2/15/89	CMU	.308	.363,.637	.317	.388,.612
	2/16/89	CMU	.308	.363,.637	.292	.323,.677
	7/31/89	CIT	.363	—	.392	—
	8/8/89	CIT	.379	—	.358	—
$w=3$, $N=3$, $\bar{c}=1.50$	7/21/88	CIT	.311	.683	.258	.622
	2/15/89	CMU	.196	.542	.142	.461
	2/16/89	CMU	.250	.613	.175	.512
$w=3$, $N=3$, $\bar{c}=0.995$	8/3/89	CIT	.440	.662	.325	.569
$w=1$, $N=3$, $\bar{c}=0.750$	2/21/89	CMU	.379	.467	.408	.446
	3/1/89	CMU	.404	.449	.408	.446
$w=2$, $N=3$, $\bar{c}=0.750$	2/21/89	CMU	.521	.266,.734	.583	.323,.677
	3/1/89	CMU	.558	.298,.702	.583	.323,.677
$w=3$, $N=3$, $\bar{c}=0.750$	2/21/89	CMU	.525	.627	.492	.607
	3/1/89	CMU	.596	.668	.575	.657
$w=2$, $N=4$, $\bar{c}=0.667$	7/26/89	CIT	.500	.156,.551	.458	.136,.582
$w=2$, $N=3$, $\bar{c}=0.667$	7/26/89	CIT	.580	.318,.682	.558	.390,.610

TABLE 8. Differences in the Frequency of Contribution (First Ten Trials Frequency minus Last Ten Trials Frequency)

$\bar{c}$	w/N			
	1/3	2/4	2/3	3/3
2.25	−.05*	+.02*a	+.02*a	+.04*a
	−.03*	+.01*a	+.02*a	+.04*a
		+.02*a		
1.50	+.10*a		+.06*a	+.09*a
	−.04*a		+.14**a	+.11**a
	+.03*		+.01*a	+.15***a
	−.02*		−.02*	
	−.02*		+.03*a	
			−.06*	
			+.04*a	
0.995				+.24***a
0.750	−.06*a		−.13**a	+.07*a
	−.01*		−.05*a	+.04*a
0.667		+.07*	+.02*	

ª Sign of difference correctly predicted by learning theory.
*$p \geq .10$.   **$p \geq .01$.   ***$p \geq .001$.

were eight experiments where the value of $\hat{q}$ was too large to rationalize with any q^e; the $\hat{q}$ for two of these experiments could be rationalized in the last ten rounds. Of the remaining twenty-five experiments, there are seventeen in which $\hat{q}$ and q^e are closer in the last ten rounds than in the first ten rounds.[14]

A second implication about learning is that the difference between $\hat{q}$ and q^* should be less in the later rounds than in the early rounds. In twenty-three of the thirty-three experiments, this is the case, when the comparison is between the first ten and the last ten rounds. Table 8 shows the differences between the contribution rates in the first ten rounds and the last ten rounds. Note ª indicates those experiments where the sign of this difference is consistent with the hypothesis that $\hat{q}$ and q^* should be closer toward the end of the experiment. As one can see, the sign is correctly predicted in all eight of the $w = 3$, $N = 3$ experiments, where contribution rates consistently exceeded the predicted equilibrium of 0 contribution. However, in the remaining experiments, the change in contribution rates is correctly predicted only about half the time (fifteen of twenty-five). Perhaps even more troublesome is that very

---

14. In those cases where there are two solutions for q^e, we use the value of q^e that is closest to $\hat{q}$ in the first ten rounds.

few of the correctly predicted changes in contribution rates (only five out of twenty-three) have differences that are statistically significant at the .01 level, so it appears that, even if there is learning, there is not very much of it going on. We find somewhat more support for a learning theory in the observation that this difference fails to be significant in all of the ten experiments where the difference goes in the opposite direction from that which a learning theory would predict.

Summarizing the evidence for the aggregate data, the direction of movement of q^e supports the hypothesis that players' priors on q are biased upward initially, but they adjust these priors in the correct direction during the course of the experiment. However, the evidence for this learning is by no means overwhelming, since roughly one-third of the experiments have the observed contribution rates moving in the opposite direction from that which this naive learning model would suggest.

We are thus left, for now at least, with a successful probability bias hypothesis, together with Bayesian-Nash equilibrium predictions, as the major sources of explanation for the variation in aggregate contribution rates. However, a more definitive statement of the results, especially regarding learning effects, would require a much more rigorous analysis of the data at the individual level. We leave this major project for another article.

APPENDIX

These are the instructions for the laboratory session run on July 31, 1989, at the California Institute of Technology. Subjects were seated in front of computer terminals that were separated by partitions. These instructions were not distributed, but were read aloud to the subjects. In addition, the payoff tables were distributed to the subjects as indicated below.

After reading the instructions for the first experiment, two practice rounds were conducted to familiarize the subjects with the procedures and the computer screens. The practice rounds were very controlled in the sense that subjects were instructed exactly what actions to take in the practice round. They were also shown how to access a "history screen" that summarized the past decisions made and outcomes in the games they had played in previous rounds. After going through these two practice rounds, all subjects were given a quiz to make sure they understood the details of the experiment and how their earnings would be computed. Any misunderstandings were clarified and the experiment commenced.

After the first experiment of the session had concluded, subjects were briefly informed of the new rules for the second experiment, and then the second experiment commenced. Because the keyboard tasks and the screen layouts were similar in all three experiments conducted in each session, practice rounds and quizzes were not always conducted before the second and third experiments. At the end of a session, subjects were paid in private in a separate room. Each subject was then dismissed from the experiment before the next subject was paid. Similar procedures were followed in the other sessions.

Instructions

This is an experiment in decision making. You will be paid in cash at the end of the experiment. The amount of money you earn will depend upon the decisions you make and on the decisions other people make. It is important that you do not talk at all or otherwise attempt to communicate with the other subjects except according to the specific rules of the experiment. If you have a question, feel free to raise your hand. One of us will come over to where you are sitting and answer your question in private. This session you are participating in is broken down into a sequence of three separate experiments. Each experiment will last twenty rounds. All money is denominated in francs. At the end of the last experiment, you will be paid $.30 for every 100 francs you have accumulated during the course of all three experiments.

Rules for Experiment 1

At the beginning of every round of every experiment, you will be randomly assigned to a group with two other subjects. Each round in the experiment you will have a single token to use in one of two ways.

> Option 1: Spend the token.
> Option 2: Keep the token.

The amount of money you earn in a round depends upon whether you keep or spend your token that round and how many others in your group spend their token. Each round, you will be told how many francs your token is worth if you do not spend it. This amount, called your token value, will change from round to round and will vary from person to person randomly. To be more specific, in each round, this amount is equally likely to be anywhere from 1 to 90 francs. There is absolutely no systematic or intentional pattern to your token values or the token values of anyone else. The determination of token values across rounds and across people is entirely random. Therefore, everyone in your group will generally have different token values. Furthermore, these token values will change from period to period in a random way. You will be informed privately what your new token value is at the beginning of each round, and you are not permitted to tell anyone what this amount is.

Specific Instructions. At the start of each round you are told your token value for that round. Remember that members of the same group will generally have different token values, and these values change randomly for everyone after each round. After being told your token value, you must wait at least ten seconds before making your decision to keep or spend. Your keyboard will be frozen for this period of time. When everyone has made a decision, you are told which members of your group spent their token and what your earnings were for that round. This will continue for twenty rounds. Following each round you are randomly given a new token value, and randomly reassigned to a new group.

Payoffs. In each round of experiment 1, if at least two out of the three members in your group decides to spend their token, every member (both spenders and nonspenders) in your group will each earn 60 francs. In addition, nonspenders in your group also earn their token value. What happens in your group has no effect on the payoffs to members of the other groups and vice versa. Therefore, in each round, you have three possible earnings. These are shown in the following table [hand out earnings table]:

Earnings Table for Experiment 1

You Spend	Number of Others Spending	Your Earnings
Yes	0	0 francs
Yes	1	60 francs
Yes	2	60 francs
No	0	Your Token Value
No	1	Your Token Value
No	2	Your Token Value + 60 francs

Specific Instructions for Experiment 2. This is exactly the same as experiment 1, except only one spender is needed for all members in that group to receive 60 francs.

Payoffs. In each round, if at least one out of the three members in your group decides to spend their token, every member (both spenders and nonspenders) in your group will each earn 60 francs. In addition, nonspenders in your group also earn their token value. What happens in your group has no effect on the payoffs to members of the other groups and vice versa. Therefore, in each round, you have three possible earnings. These are shown in the following table [hand out new table to subjects and collect old table]:

Earnings Table for Experiment 2

You Spend	Number of Others Spending	Your Earnings
Yes	0	60 francs
Yes	1	60 francs
Yes	2	60 francs
No	0	Your Token Value
No	1	Your Token Value + 60 francs
No	2	Your Token Value + 60 francs

Specific Instructions for Experiment 3. There are three differences in this experiment. First of all, each group has four members instead of three. Second, two out of the four members of a group must spend in order for all members of that group to get the extra payment. Third, the extra payment is 40 francs instead of 60 francs.

Payoffs. In each round, if at least two out of the four members in your group decides to spend their token, every member (both spenders and nonspenders) in your group will earn 40 francs. In addition, nonspenders in your group also earn their token value. What happens in your group has no effect on the payoffs to members of the other groups and vice versa. Therefore, in each round, you have three possible earnings. These are shown in the following table [hand out new table to subjects and collect old table]:

Earnings Table for Experiment 3

You Spend	Number of Others Spending	Your Earnings
Yes	0	0 francs
Yes	1	40 francs
Yes	2	40 francs
Yes	3	40 francs
No	0	Your Token Value
No	1	Your Token Value
No	2	Your Token Value + 40 francs
No	3	Your Token Value + 40 francs

REFERENCES

Bliss, C., and B. Nalebuff. 1984. "Dragon-Slaying and Ballroom Dancing: The Private Supply of a Public Good." *Journal of Public Economics* 25:1–12.
Camerer, C., and K. Weigelt. 1988. "Experimental Tests of a Sequential Equilibrium Reputation Model." *Econometrica* 56:1–36.
Cox, J., B. Roberson, and V. Smith. 1982. "Theory and Behavior of Single Object Auctions." In *Research in Experimental Economics*, ed. V. L. Smith. Greenwich: JAI Press.
Cox, J., V. Smith, and J. Walker. 1983. "Tests of a Heterogeneous Bidder's Theory of First Price Auctions." *Economics Letters* 12:207–12.
Forsythe, R., T. Palfrey, and C. Plott. 1982. "Asset Valuation in an Experimental Market." *Econometrica* 50:537–67.
Lipnowski, I., and S. Maital. 1983. "Voluntary Provision of a Pure Public Good as the Game of Chicken." *Journal of Public Economics* 20:381–86.
McKelvey, R., and T. Palfrey. 1989. "An Experimental Study of the Centipede Game." Working paper, California Institute of Technology.
Palfrey, T., and H. Rosenthal. 1984. "Participation and Provision of Discrete

Public Goods: A Strategic Analysis." *Journal of Public Economics* 24:171–93.

Palfrey, T., and H. Rosenthal. 1988. "Private Incentives and Social Dilemmas: The Effects of Incomplete Information and Altruism." *Journal of Public Economics* 28:309–32.

Palfrey, T., and H. Rosenthal. 1991. "Testing for Effects of Cheaptalk in a Public Goods Game with Private Information." *Games and Economic Behavior.* In press.

Rapoport, A. 1985. "Public Goods and the MCS Experimental Paradigm." *American Political Science Review* 79:148–55.

Van de Kragt, A., J. Orbell, and R. Dawes. 1983. "The Minimal Contributing Set as a Solution to Public Goods Problems." *American Political Science Review* 77:112–21.

Costly Communication: An Experiment in a Nested Public Goods Problem

R. Mark Isaac and James M. Walker

1. Introduction

The past decade has seen extensive experimental examination of the performance of the voluntary contributions mechanism (VCM) as a process for providing public goods in environments that, in theory, should be subject to the so-called free rider problem.[1] Several replicable facts have emerged from this literature. One is that there is a tendency for participants initially to provide the public good at levels that are substantially less than optimal but substantially more than the free-riding predictions. A second is that contributions tend to decay with repetition. A third is that prior experience in the decision environment increases the tendency for suboptimal provision of the group good. A fourth is that there are specific parameters of the economic environment (which can be captured in the experiments) that can influence the level of underprovision. Specifically, there exist certain payoff parameters that, with considerable regularity, generate experimental data that decay to levels very close to complete free riding; other parameters predictably fail to do so. A fifth replicable fact, and the one that is the basis of this article, is the power of nonbinding, face-to-face communication to ameliorate the under-

This research was supported, in part, by grants from the NSF: SES-8821067 and SES-8820897. All experimental parameters and the raw individual data on contributions to the group good are archived on PLATO permanent storage. The experiments were conducted at the facilities of the University of Arizona's Economic Science Laboratory. Our thanks go to Nat Wilcox and Alison Mehlman who provided assistance in running the experiments, and to Tom Palfrey who provided many useful editorial comments.

1. See, for example, Andreoni 1989; Bagnoli and McKee 1987; Brookshire, Coursey, and Redington 1988; Isaac, McCue, and Plott 1985; Isaac and Walker 1988b; Isaac, Walker, and Thomas 1984; Kim and Walker 1984; and Marwell and Ames 1979. There is an even larger literature on public goods provision mechanisms other than VCM and bimatrix experiments (prisoner's dilemmas, coordination games, etc.).

provision problem. The research to which we will make considerable reference is our own investigation of communication, Isaac and Walker 1988a (hereafter IW).

The success of communication as an ameliorative feature surprised us and, we suspect, many of our colleagues. An important caveat to our previous research is that participants were provided the opportunity for communication free of charge. Looked at another way, no members of the group had to incur any organization costs to initiate communication: those costs were borne by the experimenters. The purpose of the research reported here is to investigate what happens when the opportunity for communication is not free, but rather must be borne by (at least some members of) the group. This is what we call the "nested public goods" problem. Upon reflection, we saw that such nesting has an important role in the collective action problems described by Olson (1971). Being wary of making too strong a claim for communication based solely upon the IW results, we view this research as an investigation into the robustness of our previously reported results.

The paper is organized as follows. Section 2 presents a brief description of the computerized institution used in the experiments as well as a more complete description of prior research. Section 3 contains the specific experimental design for the research reported here, along with our working hypotheses. Section 4 presents the results of the initial six experiments. Section 5 offers a discussion of the current results and of some areas for further research.

2. The Voluntary Contributions Mechanism and a Discussion of Prior Research

There have been several laboratory versions of a voluntary contributions mechanism. The one used here is a PLATO computerized institution first reported by Isaac, Walker, and Thomas (1984). Each individual in a group of size n faces ten "investment" decision periods. In each period, the experimenters endow each participant, i, with Z_i tokens. Each token will be invested either in an "individual exchange" (where it will be exchanged for p_i cents with certainty) or in a "group exchange." Note that an individual is free to divide his or her tokens between the two types of exchange, but is not allowed to carry over tokens from one period to the next. Let m_i represent individual i's contribution ("investment") of tokens to the group exchange in a given period. The group exchange is the public good in that each individual receives a payment of:

$$(1|n)G(m_i + \Sigma m_j) \text{ cents,}$$

where $G(\cdot)$ is an appropriately specified function and Σm_j represents the sum of the contributions of everyone else except person i. In fact, in the experiments reported here, p_i and the $G(\cdot)$ function were chosen so the Pareto optimum (defined simply as the outcome that provides the greatest total monetary payout from the experimenters to the subjects) was for each individual to invest all tokens in the group exchange (i.e., to set $m_i = Z_i$). In addition, these parameters were chosen so that the single-period, dominant strategy (and hence the unique, backward unravelling complete information multiperiod Nash equilibrium) was for each person to invest zero tokens in the group exchange. We will refer to these zero contributions equilibria as the free-riding outcomes.

The use of communication to address the problem of suboptimal equilibria has a long experimental tradition in Prisoner's Dilemma research.[2] Our own interest grew not only out of that literature but also out of the literature of experimental industrial organization. Several laboratory studies had investigated communication as a device to enable one side of a market to obtain greater than normal profits. If one considers a successful price conspiracy as a type of a public good to its members, then these papers also touched upon the issue of communications and public goods.[3] Our research plan was to add nonbinding, face-to-face communication to the VCM. The result of this research was the IW paper mentioned in the introduction.[4] In these experiments, which can be thought of as "free communication" experiments, each group consisted of four experienced participants. The parameters, using the terminology introduced above, were:

$$Z_i = 62 \text{ tokens,}$$

$$p_i = 1 \text{ cent,}$$

$$G(\cdot) = 1.2 * \Sigma m_i \text{ cents.}$$

These parameters create a marginal per capita return (MPCR) of 0.3 for the

---

2. Some examples are Caldwell 1976; Dawes, McTavish, and Shaklee 1977; Loomis 1959; Radlow and Weidner 1966; Swenson 1967; and Wichman 1972.

3. This literature includes Daughety and Forsythe 1987; Isaac and Plott 1981; Isaac, Ramey, and Williams 1984; Isaac and Walker 1985; and DeJong et al. 1986.

4. Our communication practices follow the tradition started by Isaac and Plott (1981). The discussion is nonbinding in that sidepayments and physical threats are not allowed and private information required for enforcement is not provided. It is face to face, using (within the restrictions) all aspects of the English language and nonverbal communication. This tradition, therefore, differs from the "cheap talk" tradition (Palfrey and Rosenthal 1991) in which subjects signal (via a messenger or computer) from a much more limited message space.

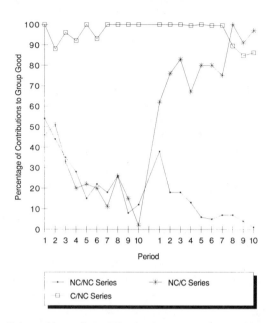

Fig. 1. Prior evidence from IW experiments, costless communication

public good.[5] Such parameters had, in previous experiments, produced the now familiar pattern of moderate contribution at the beginning followed by decay to the (Nash) free-riding predictions. (The group optimum is 100 percent contribution.) Each of the ten experiments contained twenty periods, conducted in two, ten-period blocks. There were three treatments: no communication for ten periods followed by communication (NC,C), and similarly (C,NC) and (NC,NC). The results are summarized in figure 1, which graphs, by period, the average contribution to the public good as a percentage of the optimum. These data indicate that, for this particular design, communication had a substantial ameliorative effect on the free-riding problem.

We were most surprised by the "hysteresis" effect of prior communication as exhibited in the (C,NC) experiments. These groups had no opportunities for between-period communication during the second sequence of ten

---

5. The MPCR is defined as the ratio $\dfrac{G'(\cdot)}{\dfrac{n}{p_i}}$. Thus, if an individual considers moving one token from the individual to the group exchange, the MPCR measures the ratio of the benefit in increased returns from the group exchange to the opportunity cost in foregone returns from the individual exchange.

decisions. Nevertheless, these four groups averaged greater than 95 percent contribution levels for seven periods and greater than 80 percent throughout. This "average" number masks the fact that three out of the four groups maintained essentially perfect cooperation during the no-communication rounds, while the fourth group allowed contributions to decay dramatically.

3. Experimental Design and a Working Hypothesis

The research reported here actually consisted of fourteen experiments. Because Isaac, Walker, and Thomas (1984) had found subject experience to be an important treatment, our subsequent work has all used "experienced" subjects. The six research experiments reported here each consisted of six experienced participants. The participants were experienced in the sense that each had participated in one of eight prior sessions using the voluntary contributions process (but not involving communication in any way). No group of six, however, was brought back intact from an "inexperienced" session.

Because participants' expectations about what might happen in this experiment could be important, we will discuss at more length than usual the inexperienced experiments. Each inexperienced experiment consisted of groups of six, seven, or eight persons who had never before participated in a VCM public goods experiment. The parameters were chosen with an MPCR in the range of 0.30 to 0.34.[6] Zero contribution to the public good (investment in the group exchange) was the unique multiperiod complete information Nash equilibrium.[7] The group optimum consisted of each participant contributing all tokens to the public good.[8] Table 1 summarizes the design differences between the eight inexperienced subject experiments and the six research experiments.

Figure 2 displays data from the eight inexperienced subject experiments. On this graph, we denote the average contribution of tokens to the group good as a percent of the total (and hence, with these parameters, of the optimum).

---

6. The protocol for the experiments with inexperienced subjects was designed to allow for us to use everyone who showed up for the experiments, in order to create a large pool of "experienced" subjects for the later experiments. (Often, when recruiting subjects for the first time, some will be no-shows.) Our plan was to adjust the parameters on the computer at the last minute so that, regardless of the number of subjects participating, each group would face the "low MPCR" (i.e., 0.30) condition. In one experiment, a last-minute mathematical error caused the actual MPCR to become 0.35.

7. We use this solution concept as a reference even though this is technically a game of incomplete information because the p_i's and the Z_i's are not publicly provided. Isaac and Walker (1989) present data showing that the typical pattern of these experiments is reproduced when subjects are provided these private parameters.

8. The group optimum is defined simply as the outcome that maximizes payments from the experimenters to the group.

TABLE 1. Design Parameters for the Experiments with Inexperienced Subjects and the Research Experiments with Experienced Subjects

Number of Experiments	Group Size	Group Payoff Function	MPCR	Individual Tokens per Period
		Parameters for Experiments with Inexperienced Subjects		
3	6	$\$.018\ (\Sigma m_i)$	.30	40
1	7	$\$.021\ (\Sigma m_i)$	.30	35
1	7	$\$.024\ (\Sigma m_i)$	.34	35
3	8	$\$.024\ (\Sigma m_i)$	.30	30
		Parameters for Experiments with Experienced Subjects		
6	6	$\$.018\ (\Sigma m_i)$	.30	40

These groups began period one with an average level of contributions to the group good of 43 percent, and declined by period ten to 16 percent. This pattern is very typical of the numerous inexperienced groups we have previously observed facing similar parameters. These results gave us confidence that we would be drawing experienced subjects whose behavior and, hence,

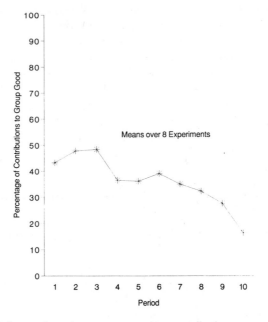

Fig. 2. Inexperienced groups, percentage contributions to group good

prior experience were consistent with experienced subjects in our prior research.

In the experienced subject experiments, the parameters were as follows:

Z_i = 40 tokens;

p_i = 1 cent;

$G(\cdot)$ = 1.8 * $\sum m_i$ cents

Again, the multiperiod Nash prediction is a free-riding outcome of zero contribution to the public good, while group optimality is obtained if all tokens are contributed. The MPCR in these experiments is 0.30.

The crux of the nested public goods problem in this design is that communication is available to the participants, but at a cost. Before the start of the experiment, additional instructions were read aloud (see the appendix). It was explained that before any decision period, the right to meet for nonbinding, face-to-face discussion could be purchased. Each participant, prior to each period, privately marked and returned to the experimenters a slip of paper stating whether they did or did not choose to contribute 10 cents to this "discussion fund." If four, five, or six persons so contributed, all six participants met for the discussion session. If fewer than four contributed, no discussion was held (but contributions were *not* refunded).

From this description, let x be the existence or nonexistence of a communication session. We will assume that each person has a private value for a communication session before period t, V_{xi}^t. Presumably, if such a value is positive, it is because the individual expects his or her earnings from the investment experiment to be higher with communication. Good x costs 40 cents to produce, and it may be produced only at levels $(0,1)$. As x is consumed equally and without excludability by the six participants, x is a discrete public good. Furthermore, x is provided through a special type of VCM. Within the category of VCM public goods mechanisms, a subset consists of those mechanisms in which there is a "provision point." In the discrete case, a provision point works as follows: contributions are collected and the good is produced if and only if the contributions sum to at least the provision point. An even more specific variant is used here: if the contributions fall short of the provision point, they are not refunded. That is, there is no money-back feature.

Provision point mechanisms with no money back typically exhibit the so-called assurance problem in which there are multiple Nash equilibria, some of which can be Pareto ranked. This type of public goods problem is very similar to what is sometimes called the "cutpoint" or "step-good" problem in bimatrix games, which has been examined theoretically by, among others, Rapoport

(1985) and Palfrey and Rosenthal (1988). The bimatrix games have received extensive experimental investigation. The results of Dawes et al. (1986) are typical. Seven participants in single-shot decisions were given a binary choice to keep a $5 promissary note or to contribute it toward a group bonus of $70, to be divided equally. In the treatment in which five of the seven were required to donate in order to achieve the group bonus, only four of ten groups succeeded. (This is in spite of the fact that, overall, 64 percent of the seventy persons contributed. There were five groups in which four of seven persons contributed.) Isaac, Schmidtz, and Walker (1989; hereafter ISW) investigated the behavior of a laboratory version of a no-money-back, provision point VCM process. Their research found that these environments usually produced the suboptimal equilibrium (specifically, zero contributions). Specifically, that paper reports on eighteen experiments whose design is, with one exception, identical to that described here. The one difference is that the return to the group exchange (public good) is given by the following:

$$1.2 \sum m_i \text{ cents} \quad \text{for} \quad \sum m_i \geq m^+, \quad \text{otherwise 0.}$$

The amount, m^+, is called the provision point of the experiment. Of the eighteen ISW experiments, six were conducted as high provision point experiments ($m^+ = 248$ out of 248 tokens), six as medium provision point experiments ($m^+ = 216$) and six as low provision point experiments ($m^+ = 108$). Each experiment lasted ten periods. Thus, across all six experiments of one type, there were sixty trials. The high provision point groups met the provision point nine of sixty times. The medium provision point groups succeeded fifteen times, the low provision point groups twenty-one times.

In the current research, the decision of the six participants about whether to contribute to organizing communication can thus be represented as one type of public goods problem. Each individual has a binary choice to contribute or not. Because the value to communicating comes from the group-individual exchange experiments, which are themselves a public goods problem, we refer to this as the *nested public goods problem*. Let us assume for a moment that $V_{xi}^t > 10$ cents for each participant. In this case, we have a public goods assurance problem. One Nash equilibrium of the game is for none of the six to contribute to the discussion fund. In addition, any permutation of the contribution pattern (10, 10, 10, 10, 0, 0) constitutes a (one-shot) Nash equilibrium (recall that we restrict contributions to either zero or 10 cents). Any one of the better equilibria Pareto-dominates the former, but among the latter set there is no Pareto ranking.

Palfrey and Rosenthal (1988) investigate the issue of mixed-strategy equilibria in assurance games. A precise derivation of any such equilibrium is problematic here because the V_{xi}^t values are unobservable. However, we can use as a benchmark the single-period difference between full cooperation and complete free riding (72 cents − 40 cents for each person). With V_{xi}^t defined as this 32 cents, and the cost of contributing 10 cents, there are two symmetric, mixed-strategy Nash equilibria. One equilibrium involves a probability of contribution of 0.50 for each player, the other a probability of 0.6947.

To this point we have argued only that our experimental technology makes it possible to structure the communications environment as a nested public goods problem. A second argument that needs to be made is why we view this as an interesting description of an economic phenomenon. In our previous work on communications in public goods situations, we noted that the experimenter organized the group discussion. The participants bore no additional organization costs of their own. There are certainly nonlaboratory examples of such situations. Legislatures are standing bodies in which organizational costs are small. Adam Smith, in *The Wealth of Nations* ([1776] 1977), worried that government rules that forced registration of craftsmen would make communication to fix prices that much easier. Likewise, a homeowners' association that holds regularly scheduled meetings to enforce deed restrictions will already be communicating if a city proposes to build a freeway through their neighborhood. But, to carry the analogy a bit further, what happens to those neighborhoods that have no homeowners' association, but are equally affected by the freeway? They might fight the freeway in a totally decentralized and uncoordinated fashion, or they might fight it as a group. If the probability of winning is greater when acting as a group than when acting individually (perhaps because of the free rider problem in the latter instance) then this neighborhood faces precisely the nested public goods problem that we have just described: first, they must see whether or not they can organize a homeowners' association where none existed before; second, they must deal with the actual public goods problem. This distinction has been made previously by Olson (1971, 10–11 and 46–48).

The results of the Dawes et al. and ISW research suggested that the VCM does not work very well in no-money-back, provision point environments. In addition, the subject groups participating in the experiments reported here had never seen the ameliorative power of communication in action. We conjectured that these groups would be unlikely to organize; that is, that they would achieve the suboptimal, zero contribution equilibrium in the first stage of the problem. As noncommunicating groups, they would then be expected to produce the familiar pattern of decay toward free riding. Thus, our working hypothesis was that these groups would generally fail to organize for communication and their investment decisions would resemble the decay toward zero contribution typical of experienced, noncommunicating groups. In fact, our original research plan was to conduct these experiments first and then a

second set, more favorable to organizing communication, in which participants were given some periods of free communication during their "trainer"
experiments. The reasons the second series was not conducted will be made
obvious in the next section.

4. Experimental Results

The results are summarized in table 2 and figure 3. The top section of table 2
displays period-by-period observations on the percentage of endowments (total tokens) contributed to the group good. (Recall that a 100 percent contribution represents the group optimum.) The bottom section of table 2 displays
period-by-period observations on the number of individuals contributing to
fund the communication mechanism. The first few periods show considerable
variance across experiments. The subjects in experiment 1 were able to fund
the mechanism with the minimum number of four contributors and agree to an
optimal level of contribution in the first period, but they met more often than
other groups and had the fewest periods of 100 percent contribution. In
contrast to this experiment, several groups struggled with attempts to fund the
communication mechanism and produced several early periods of substantially less than optimal contributions. By period 4, however, all groups had
succeeded in funding the communication mechanism. Figure 3 summarizes

TABLE 2. Contribution Results, Costly Communication Series

Experiment	1	2	3	4	5	6	7	8	9	10
	Period									

Percentage of Endowments Contributed to the Group Good

1	100.0	75.0	87.5	70.8	83.3	81.2	31.2	100	95.8	95.8
2	32.9	25.8	100.0	100.0	100.0	100.0	100.0	100	83.3	37.5
3	50.0	30.0	100.0	100.0	100.0	100.0	100.0	100	83.3	17.1
4	29.2	20.0	100.0	100.0	100.0	100.0	100.0	100	100.0	66.7
5	79.2	70.8	100.0	100.0	100.0	100.0	100.0	100	100.0	100.0
6	87.5	0.0	0.0	100.0	100.0	100.0	100.0	100	100.0	50.4

Number of Individuals Contributing to Fund the Communication Mechanism

1	4[a]	5[a]	0	0	3	2	3	4[a]	0	0
2	3	2	5[a]	0	0	0	0	0	0	0
3	3	3	5[a]	0	0	0	0	0	0	0
4	3	3	4[a]	0	0	0	0	0	0	0
5	4[a]	3	5[a]	0	0	0	0	0	0	0
6	3	1	3	4[a]	0	0	0	0	0	0

[a]Periods in which the communication mechanism was successfully funded.

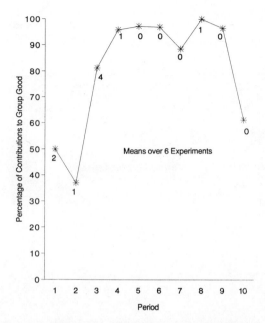

Fig. 3. Costly communication, percentage contributions to group good. Number of groups meeting included for each period.

the aggregate behavior for all six experiments. (Stars represent average contributions and the number displayed with each star represents the number of groups communicating in each period). By period 4, the average contribution was over 90 percent of optimum. Contributions stayed at these high levels until period 10, when apparent end-period effects reduced contributions to approximately 60 percent of optimum.

It seemed even more remarkable that the participants solved the larger efficiency problem by not having repeated meetings. Among thirty-six opportunities for discussion in periods 5–10 (six groups across six periods), there was only one discussion session. It is important to note that it was obvious from the conversations of the participants that this was intentional. The groups did not meet in later periods because they had agreed not to meet. Perhaps this should not have been so surprising, as these groups, once communicating, were simply recapturing the same "hysteresis" benefit of communication of the Isaac and Walker (C,NC) experiments. This level of contribution without communication suggests that there should be very little waste in expenditures on organizing costs. To examine this more closely, consider figure 4, which denotes average net efficiency for the six experiments. The term *net efficiency* indicates that it includes the costs of contribut-

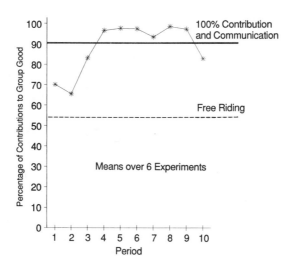

Fig. 4. Net efficiency

ing to the discussion fund. If groups fully provided the public good and never talked, they would score 100.0 percent net efficiency. If they behaved as complete free riders, they would score 55.6 percent efficiency (denoted by the solid line on fig. 4). If they fully contributed to the public good but paid 40 cents organization cost, they would score 90.7 percent efficiency (denoted by the dotted line on fig. 4). On average, the groups always earned more than full free riding and beat the active communication optimum in six periods.

These results can be compared with those obtained from parallel research by Ostrom and Walker (1989). They have been investigating the role of communication in an experimental setting designed to characterize a common pool resource. Their research examines communication using a mechanism virtually identical to that used in IW for costless communication and in this paper for costly communication. In the aggregate, the results of the two independent studies (this paper and Walker and Ostrom) are quite similar. Relative to baseline experiments with no communication, Walker and Ostrom found that efficiency increased from 30 percent to 98 percent with the introduction of costless communication. Players successfully used the opportunity to (a) calculate coordinated rent-improving strategies, (b) devise verbal agreements to implement these strategies, and (c) deal with nonconforming players. The provision problem that players faced in the costly communication experiments created a nontrivial barrier. In all three experiments, the problem of providing the institution for communication diminished the success of either (a) having the ability to develop a coordinated strategy, and/or (*b*) dealing with players who cheated on a previous agreement. On the other hand, all groups eventually succeeded in providing the communication mechanism and in dealing with the common pool resource dilemma. On average, efficiency in these groups increased from approximately 42 percent to 80 percent.

5. Discussion and Areas for Further Research

Needless to say, we consider these data to be a virtually complete refutation of our working hypothesis. There are only two minor aspects in which the costly communication experiments appear to have behaved differently from the free communication experiments. First, it took three or four periods for many of the groups to organize for communication. In these early periods, contributions to the public good followed the usual path of decay. Second, there was a larger end-period effect in the tenth period (although we have to interpret this with some caution, because none of the groups actually met immediately before period ten). For most of the interior periods (5–9), the data look indistinguishable from that of the IW free communication.

Why were our expectations so wrong? The failure of the no-money-back provision point process in ISW had convinced us that these groups would have a hard time solving the first public goods problem (organization for communication). They did not. Given that they did communicate, the highly efficient public goods provision in the second problem (the group and individual exchange) is very consistent with our prior data. We can offer the following areas for consideration.

1. In looking at the Isaac, Schmidtz, and Walker data, our pessimism over the ability of groups to solve the assurance problem is founded largely on the drastic decay across time. Early on, the groups met the provision point more often. Perhaps we should have focused more on the early period successes.

2. Perhaps participants make the decision to contribute to the discussion fund in a manner consistent with one of the Nash mixed-strategy equilibria. Unfortunately, we do not have a large amount of data on individual choices because there is an obvious regime shift once the groups have successfully met for communication the first time. For any one person, we have at most four, and sometimes only one, observation before the group meets for communication. However, taking the number of individuals (out of six possible) who contribute the 10 cents as a datum, and pooling across the six experiments and across the periods prior to communication, we have seventeen observations. Conducting a chi-square test on the distribution of the number of contributors relative to a null binomial probability of 0.50 yields a statistic that is highly insignificant, meaning that we cannot reject the null hypothesis

that the data are coming from an underlying binomial distribution with a probability of contribution equal to 0.50, one of the mixed-strategy Nash equilibria. The calculated chi-square is 5.6; the critical chi-square for $\alpha = 0.05$ is 11.07. The observed frequency of contribution is 56.86 percent. (A similar chi-square test on a null binomial probability of 0.6947, the other mixed-strategy Nash equilibrium, yields a test statistic of 13.68, which is significant for rejection at $\alpha = 0.05$.)

It appears from inspection that a regime shift occurs once groups meet for communication the first time. There are forty-three observations after communication, with an observed frequency of contribution of only 7.36 percent. We conducted the same chi-square test (relative to the 0.50 mixed-strategy equilibrium probability) with these forty-three observations. The calculated chi-square statistic, 1,890.77, is highly significant at levels of confidence much greater than .995. We conclude that, in terms of deciding whether to contribute to the "discussion fund," the participants do not use the Nash equilibrium mixed strategies after their first period of communication. Instead, for the most part, they choose the zero contribution equilibrium strategies.

3. In the Isaac, Schmidtz, and Walker experiments, each period was a new provision point problem. However, the reality of the current experiments is that the groups did not need to communicate every time in order to maintain high levels of provision of the public good. (This is consistent with Isaac and Walker 1988a). It seems that, for this environment, meeting once was enough. With this viewpoint, the question we should have asked from the Isaac, Schmidtz, and Walker data was not how many groups met the provision point in any one period, but how many groups met the provision point at least once in any of the periods. The answer to that question is as follows: one of the six high provision point groups succeeded at least once; two of six of the medium provision point experiments succeeded at least once; five of the six low provision point groups succeeded at least once. It is this last figure that seems to be in concert with the data reported here.

4. Once we consider that the participants recognized the multiperiod benefits of even a single episode of communication, a reevaluation of the costs and benefits of communication may be in order. The 10 cent (per person) cost of communication was chosen to represent a significant part of the 32 cent per period (per person) gain from full cooperation as opposed to complete free riding. On the other hand, we wanted there to remain nontrivial gains from the communication, even if it was costly. However, viewed in the light of multiperiod benefits from communication, participants' expected gains from communication in early rounds, V_{xi}^t, can reasonably be conjectured to have been much greater than 32 cents.

There are at least two reasons why recognizing this larger, multiperiod value for communication might alter behavior. First, while this does not change the nature of the pure-strategy Nash equilibria, it may change participants' willingness to try for the Pareto-superior equilibrium. Second, altering the value of contributions can affect the nature of mixed-strategy equilibria (see Palfrey and Rosenthal 1988). Calculating and testing for alternative mixed strategy equilibria using the current data is not straightforward because the V_{xi}^t values are unobservable and may differ from person to person. But the issue could be addressed indirectly in future experiments by raising the cost of communication. To address either of these conjectures, future experiments with costs of communication more like $1.00 per person might be in order.

With these considerations in mind, we are altering our plans for future research. Our original expectation was that these groups would have a difficult time with the nested public goods problems, and that we would then move on to an "easier" environment (giving participants a history of free communication). We no longer feel that this direction is the best use of our resources. Instead, we will move to new experiments in which we change the environment so that communication might be less likely to occur. Specifically, we are currently conducting experiments with much larger groups and with "naturally occurring" costs to communication. We are also considering experiments in which the subjects are asymmetric in wealth and/or in marginal per capita return from the public good. Further down the road, we would like to relax the discreteness constraint on contributions to the discussion fund so that any one person could contribute any part of their wealth toward the 40 cents required to organize the group. This takes us in the direction of an investigation of political entrepreneurship.

APPENDIX: ADDITIONAL INSTRUCTIONS

Before each decision period that follows, you will be given the opportunity to purchase the right to discuss among yourselves (as a group) your investment decisions. The rules on discussion are as follows.

You may discuss all aspects of the two markets and the experiment with the following restrictions:

1. there will be no discussion of side payments;
2. there will be no discussion of physical threats;
3. there will be no viewing or discussion of the private quantitative information on your screens;
4. there is a maximum of 4 minutes per discussion session.

How do you purchase this right to have a group discussion session?

You have been given an envelope. In the envelope there are slips of paper that say "I choose to contribute $.10" and "I do not choose to contribute

$.10." Each period you will be asked to privately mark one of the slips and return it to _____ [me, my assistant]. If four or more slips are marked "I choose to contribute $.10," the *entire* group will be allowed to meet in a discussion section. If fewer than four slips read "I choose to contribute $.10," the group will not be allowed to meet for discussion.

At the end of the experiment, all contributions made by an individual to the "discussion fund" will be deducted from that person's total experimental profits. For example, if you chose to contribute $.10 to the discussion fund in each of four periods and otherwise had profits of $10.00, then your final experimental profit would be $9.60. Note that contributions will be deducted whether or not the group contributed sufficiently to have a group discussion. So that we can keep track of this accounting, please write the participant number, written on the outside of your envelope, on your slip.

Because there are still restrictions on your discussion, if it occurs, all the discussion sessions will be held here and I will monitor your discussion to insure that you stay within the confines of the restrictions. In order to insure that no one views the private quantitative information on your screen, we will darken your screens between the time you turn in your slip and the time when the discussion, if any, has ended.

Are there any questions?

REFERENCES

Andreoni, J. 1989. "Why Free Ride?" *Journal of Public Economics* 37:291–304.
Bagnoli, M., and M. McKee. 1987. "Can the Private Provision of Public Goods be Efficient? Some Experimental Evidence." Washington University, St. Louis. Mimeo.
Brookshire, D., D. Coursey, and D. Redington. 1988. "Special Interests and the Voluntary Provision of Public Goods." Washington University, St. Louis. Mimeo.
Caldwell, M. D. 1976. "Communication and Sex Effects in a Five-Person Prisoner's Dilemma." *Journal of Personality and Social Psychology* 33:273–81.
Daugherty, A. F., and R. Forsythe. 1987. "Regulation and the Formation of Expectations." In *Public Regulation: New Perspectives on Institutions and Policies,* ed. Elizabeth E. Bailey. Cambridge, Mass.: MIT Press.
Dawes, R. M., J. McTavish, and H. Shaklee. 1977. "Behavior, Communication, and Assumptions about Other People's Behavior in a Commons Dilemma Situation." *Journal of Personality and Social Psychology* 35:1–11.
Dawes, R. M., J. M. Orbell, R. T. Simmons, and A. J. C. Van de Kragt. 1986. "Organizing Groups for Collective Action." *American Political Science Review* 80:1171–85.
DeJong, D., R. Forsythe, J. Schatzberg, and W. Uecker. 1986. "Collusion and Product Quality in Agency Relationship: A Laboratory Investigation." College of Business Administration Working Paper 86–01. University of Iowa. Mimeo.

Isaac, R. M., and C. R. Plott. 1981. "The Opportunity for Conspiracy in Restraint of Trade." *Journal of Economic Behavior and Organization* 2:1–30.

Isaac, R. M., K. McCue, and C. R. Plott. 1985. "Public Goods Provision in an Experimental Environment." *Journal of Public Economics* 26:51–74.

Isaac, R. M., V. Ramey, and A. W. Williams. 1984. "The Effects of Market Organization on Conspiracies in Restraint of Trade." *Journal of Economic Behavior and Organization* 5:191–222.

Isaac, R. M., and J. M. Walker. 1985. "Information and Conspiracy in Sealed Bid Auctions." *Journal of Economic Behavior and Organization* 6:139–59.

Isaac, R. M., and J. M. Walker. 1988a. "Communication and Free-Riding Behavior: The Voluntary Contributions Mechanism." *Economic Inquiry* 26:585–608.

Isaac, R. M., and J. M. Walker. 1988b. "Group Size Effects in Public Goods Provision: The Voluntary Contributions Mechanism." *Quarterly Journal of Economics* 103:179–99.

Isaac, R. M., and J. M. Walker. 1989. "Complete Information and the Provision of Public Goods." University of Arizona. Mimeo.

Isaac, R. M., J. M. Walker, and S. Thomas. 1984. "Divergent Evidence of Free Riding: An Experimental Examination of Some Possible Explanations." *Public Choice* 43:113–49.

Isaac, R. M., D. Schmidtz, and J. M. Walker. 1989. "The Assurance Problem in a Laboratory Market." *Public Choice* 62:217–36.

Kim, O., and M. Walker. 1984. "The Free Rider Problem: Experimental Evidence." *Public Choice* 43:3–24.

Loomis, J. 1959. "Communication: The Development of Trust and Cooperative Behavior." *Human Relations* 12:305–15.

Marwell, G., and R. E. Ames. 1979. "Experiments on the Provision of Public Goods: I. Resources, Interest, Group Size, and the Free Rider Problem." *American Journal of Sociology* 84:1335–60.

Olson, M. 1971. *The Logic of Collective Action*. Cambridge, Mass.: Harvard University Press.

Ostrom, E., and J. M. Walker. 1989. "Communication in a Commons: Cooperation without External Enforcement." Indiana University. Mimeo.

Palfrey, T. R., and H. Rosenthal. 1988. "Private Incentives in Social Dilemmas: The Effects of Incomplete Information and Altruism." *Journal of Public Economics* 35:309–32.

Palfrey, T. R., and H. Rosenthal. 1991. "Testing for the Effects of Cheap Talk in a Public Goods Game with Private Information." *Games and Economic Behavior*. In press.

Radlow, R., and M. Weidner. 1966. "Unenforced Commitments in 'Cooperative' and 'Noncooperative' Nonconstant Sum Games." *Journal of Conflict Resolution* 10:497–505.

Rapoport, A. 1985. "Provision of Public Goods and the MCS Experimental Paradigm." *American Political Science Review* 79:148–55.

Smith, A. [1776] 1977. *The Wealth of Nations*. Reprint. Harmondsworth, England: Penguin Books.

Swenson, R. 1967. "Cooperation in a Prisoner's Dilemma Game: I. The Effects of

Asymmetric Payoff Information and Explicit Communication." *Behavioral Science* 12:314–22.

Wichman, H. 1972. "Effects of Communication on Cooperation in a Two-Person Game." In *Cooperation and Competition*, ed. L. Wrightsman, J. O'Connor, and N. Baker. Belmont, Calif.: Brooks-Cole.

Communication in a Commons: Cooperation without External Enforcement

Elinor Ostrom and James M. Walker

1. Introduction

Communication in experimental social dilemmas generally increases the frequency with which players choose joint income maximizing strategies, even when individual incentives conflict with the cooperative strategies (Jerdee and Rosen 1974; Caldwell 1976; Dawes, McTavish, and Shaklee 1977; Edney and Harper 1978; Van de Kragt et al. 1986; Isaac and Walker 1988).[1] Hypotheses forwarded to explain why communication increases the selection of cooperative strategies include the following.

1. Communication promotes generalized norms that favor cooperation (Orbell, Van de Kragt, and Dawes 1988b).
2. Communication provides the opportunity for individuals to offer and extract promises of cooperation (or nonenforceable social contracts, see Braver and Wilson 1984; Orbell, Van de Kragt, and Dawes 1988b).
3. Communication alters the perceptions of subjects about the likelihood of other subjects contributing to the group good (Rapoport 1985; Braver and Wilson 1986).

An earlier version of this paper was presented at the American Political Science Meetings, Atlanta, Georgia, 1989, and at the Workshop on Rational and Boundedly Rational Principles of Strategic Behavior, Universität Bielefeld, Bielefeld, Germany, 1989. We would like to thank Roy Gardner, Mark Isaac, Rick Wilson, Edella Schlager, and Tom Palfrey for their useful comments. Financial support of the National Science Foundation (Grant No. SES-8619498) is gratefully acknowledged. Data are archived on permanent PLATO disk files.

1. The term *social dilemma* refers to a broad class of situations where strategies leading to efficient joint outcomes are strictly dominated for each individual by strategies leading to deficient equilibria (See Dawes 1975 and 1980). The Prisoner's Dilemma game is the best known example of a social dilemma.

288 Laboratory Research in Political Economy

4. Communication enables subjects to transform the problem from a social dilemma to an assurance game (Van de Kragt et al. 1983; Runge 1984).
5. Communication facilitates the boosting of subjects' prior normative orientations toward cooperation (Dawes, Orbell, and Van de Kragt 1984).
6. Communication permits subjects to develop a group identity that helps motivate cooperative behavior (Kramer and Brewer 1986; Dawes, Van de Kragt, and Orbell 1988).

Experiments designed to test these conjectures generally involve one-shot decisions where individuals face a dichotomous choice of whether to keep a promissory note or "contribute" it to a group account (Van de Kragt et al. 1983; Braver and Wilson 1984 and 1986; Orbell, Van de Kragt, and Dawes 1988b). Evidence from these one-shot, public good experiments support all but the first hypothesis. The five surviving hypotheses identify a process that communication is posited to facilitate: (1) offering and extracting promises, (2) changing the expectations of others' behavior, (3) changing payoff structure, (4) the reinforcement of prior normative orientations, and (5) the development of a group identity. Experimental examination of one-shot decisions has demonstrated the independent effect of all five of these processes, but they also appear to reinforce one another in an interactive manner.[2] Thus, prior experiments have provided important insights into the role of face-to-face discussion in one-shot public good environments.

Many problems of collective action in field settings, however, involve (1) repeated rather than one-shot decisions, (2) choices from a range of strategies rather than a choice between dichotomous strategies, and (3) common-pool resources (CPRs) rather than public goods. All three of these attributes are normally present in situations that are referred to as "the commons" (Hardin and Baden 1977). In such situations, multiple appropriators use the same resource system, such as fishing grounds, a grazing range, an irrigation system, or a jointly owned forest.[3] When all three of these attributes are

---

2. Orbell, Van de Kragt, and Dawes (1988b) summarize the findings from ten years of research on one-shot public good experiments by stressing both the independent and interdependent nature of the posited explanatory factors for why communication has such a powerful effect on rates of cooperation.

3. The major difference between a public goods environment and a common-pool resource (CPR) environment relates to the subtractability of the resource unit valued by potential users. In a public goods environment, use of a resource unit by one individual does not reduce the number of resource units available to others. In a CPR environment, the ton of fish that I harvest is not available to be harvested by any other fishermen. Both of these environments share difficulties related to exclusion and, thus, problems of free riding (see Gardner, Ostrom, and Walker 1990).

present, the decision environment is substantially different from the one-shot, dichotomous, public good environment. Instead of making a decision between clearly demarked cooperative or noncooperative strategies, individuals and groups must ascertain the consequences of a wide diversity of choice combinations. In this type of environment, individuals must determine a joint, income-maximizing strategy, should it be feasible. In addition, they must succeed in maintaining compliance to that strategy in an environment where the individual's incentive to comply is negatively correlated with the compliance of others.

The effect of communication in CPR situations, where individuals must repeatedly decide on the number of resource units to withdraw from a common pool, is open to considerable theoretical and policy debate. It is obvious that one cannot simply transfer results from a one-shot situation to a repeated situation.[4] On the one hand, the "shadow of the future" may reduce the temptation to break promises, avoiding the "unraveling" of a mutually productive verbal agreement. On the other hand, words alone—without a sword—are viewed as frail constraints when individuals choose privately between the single-period dominating strategy and the strategy negotiated verbally, even when these decisions are made repetitively.[5]

Game-theoretic models do not yield uniform answers to how individuals will (or ought to) behave in repeated, social dilemma situations. With a finite number of repetitions, the consistent prediction is that individuals will select their dominant strategy (if one exists) in each round, yielding the deficient equilibrium. With an infinite number of repetitions, some theorists argue that a rational player should play the dominant strategy (if one exists) in each round (Sobel 1985). Others rely on the capacity of players in repeated situations to use contingent strategies to "teach" one another the benefits of selecting cooperative strategies (R. Hardin 1982; Axelrod 1984). By assuming that resolute players can use strong threats of permanent retaliation instead of cooperative moves and forgiveness, other theorists develop models of repeated dilemma games—many of which are CPRs—that predict the selection of cooperative strategies without external enforcement (Friedman 1971; Aumann 1978; Levhari and Mirman 1980; Lewis and Cowens 1983; Axelrod 1984; Bendor and Mookherjee 1985). Others rely on the importance of an

---

4. One prior study had led us to expect that communication would have a positive effect on the choice of cooperative strategies in a repeated CPR experiment. Isaac and Walker (1988) found that communication dramatically enhanced efficiency in a repeated voluntary contribution/public good game.

5. This is, of course, the basis for Hobbes's observation that "covenants without the sword, are but words, and of no strength to secure a man at all." See Orbell, Van de Kragt, and Dawes 1988a.

individual's reputation to predict cooperation when repetition is not finite (Kreps et al. 1982).[6]

The literature is also inconclusive regarding the necessity of external enforcement. Some theorists presume that stable and efficient equilibria can be achieved by participants in repetitive situations without the necessity of external enforcers (Schotter 1980; Runge 1984). On the other hand, many assume that individuals in repetitive CPR situations will not reach jointly efficient outcomes unless external agents monitor and enforce agreements. Even if individuals promise to adopt strategies that generate the highest joint outcome, promises are considered worthless when individuals face a series of private decisions without individual monitoring and enforcement. Why should a person keep a general promise made to a group when the short-term payoff from breaking that promise is substantially better, especially if no one knows the identity of those who break their promise?

The most pessimistic view of the capacity for individuals to solve their own CPR problems arises when analysts make policy recommendations. Many agree with Anderson (1977, 41) when he asserts that: "It is, therefore, clear that coercive solutions are required to save the commons" (also see G. Hardin 1968; Sinn 1984). Studies of repetitive CPR situations in field settings have, however, shown that appropriators in many, but by no means all, settings adopt cooperative strategies that enhance their joint payoffs without the presence of external enforcers.[7] Many factors appear to affect the capacity for resource users to arrive at and maintain agreed upon limits to their appropriation activities.[8] The ability to communicate appears to be a necessary, but not sufficient, condition. The presence of external monitors and enforcers is neither necessary nor sufficient (Siy 1982; McKean 1986; Wade 1988; Ostrom 1990). In many natural settings, however, monitoring and enforcement activities are undertaken, often *without* external intervention.

A deeper examination of the role of communication in facilitating the selection of efficient strategies is of considerable theoretical (as well as policy) interest. The demarcation line between cooperative and noncooperative game

---

6. In a recent review of game-theoretic models of fishery resources, Kaitala (1986) describes the wide diversity of predicted strategies and equilibria.

7. See the many individual case studies reported in National Research Council 1986; McCay and Acheson 1987; Berkes 1989 and the literature cited in those volumes.

8. Among the variables that affect the capacity of individuals to devise their own rules for limiting the use of a CPR are: (1) net benefits from the restrictions; (2) discount rates of CPR users; (3) size of the appropriating group; (4) asymmetry of appropriations with regard to information, asset structure, leadership, and appropriation technologies; (5) the physical complexity of the resource; and (6) the institutional structure and incentives in place (see Libecap 1989; Ostrom 1990).

theory is based on the presumption that communication alone does not affect players' decisions unless there is external enforcement.[9]

In this article we explore the effect of communication (without the presence of external enforcement) in a repeated CPR setting. In particular, we examine the following questions.

1. To what extent does the capability to communicate improve the efficiency of joint outcomes in repeated CPR situations where individual decisions are anonymous?
2. How do subjects use communication? Do they understand the strategic structure of the CPR situation? Do they overtly search for joint, income-maximizing strategies?
3. Do subjects threaten to use trigger strategies if any cheating is detected by monitoring aggregate results?
4. How do subjects cope with cheating by unidentified players?
5. Are the initiators of proposals to adopt joint strategies primarily the most or least cooperative in decision rounds prior to communication?

The robustness of our initial results are examined in a more complex environment where subjects are presented with a second decision related to costly provision of the communication mechanism. In this environment, we examine the following questions.

6. Will individuals (with prior experience in a communication experiment) pay for the right to communicate?
7. What are the characteristics of players who contribute to a provision point game to "purchase" the right to communicate?

---

9. Harsanyi and Selten (1988) indicate that when Nash (1951) had originally distinguished between noncooperative and cooperative game theory, he used two criteria: free communication and enforceable agreements. Two criteria for distinguishing between a dichotomy is logically unsatisfactory. Contemporary game theories stress the fundamental importance of external enforcement. In discussing the Prisoner's Dilemma game, for example, Harsanyi and Selten (1988, 3) argue:

> Clearly, in playing this game, the decisive question is whether the players can make enforceable agreements, and it makes little difference whether they are allowed to talk to each other. Even if they are free to talk and to negotiate an agreement, this fact will be of no real help if the agreement has little chance of being kept. An ability to negotiate agreements is useful only if the rules of the game make such agreements binding and enforceable.

The capability to make enforceable agreements is included in noncooperative models by specifically including such an option in the extensive form of the game. A cooperative approach presumes that players are always able to make enforceable agreements, regardless of the structure of the extensive form.

8. What type of communication process is engendered when, instead of being free, it is costly to communicate?

The paper proceeds as follows. In section 2 we present a summary discussion of the experimental decision environment. Section 3 presents the experimental design, theoretical predictions, and results from our design 1 experiments, where the right to communicate was costless to the subjects. In section 4 we analyze our design 2 experiments, where provision of the communication mechanism was costly. Our summary and conclusions are presented in section 5.

2. Experimental Environment

Subjects and the Experimental Setting

The experiments reported in this article used subjects drawn from the undergraduate population at Indiana University. Students were volunteers recruited primarily from "Principles of Economics" classes. Prior to recruitment, potential volunteers were given a brief explanation in which they were told only that they would be making decisions in an "economic choice" environment and that the money they earned would be dependent upon their own investment decisions and those of the others in their experimental group. All experiments were conducted on the PLATO computer system at Indiana University. The computer facilitates the accounting procedures involved in the experiment, enhances cross-experiment control, and allows for minimal experimenter interaction.

The Choice Environment

At the beginning of each experimental session, subjects were told that they would be making a series of investment decisions, that all individual investment decisions were anonymous to the group, and that, at the end of the experiment, they would be paid privately (in cash) their individual earnings. Subjects then proceeded to go through, at their own pace, a set of instructions that described the investment decisions.[10]

Subjects were instructed that they would be endowed with a given number of tokens in each period, and that they would invest between two markets. Market 1 was described as an investment opportunity in which each token

---

10. A complete set of instructions is available from the authors upon request.

UNITS PRODUCED AND CASH RETURN FROM INVESTMENTS IN MARKET 2
commodity 2 value per unit = $ 0.01

Tokens Invested by Group	Units of Commodity 2 Produced	Total Group Return	Average Return per Token	Additional Return per Token
8	181	$ 1.81	$ 0.23	$ 0.23
16	323	$ 3.23	$ 0.20	$ 0.18
24	427	$ 4.27	$ 0.18	$ 0.13
32	493	$ 4.93	$ 0.15	$ 0.08
40	520	$ 5.20	$ 0.13	$ 0.03
48	509	$ 5.09	$ 0.11	$-0.01
56	459	$ 4.59	$ 0.08	$-0.06
64	371	$ 3.71	$ 0.06	$-0.11
72	245	$ 2.45	$ 0.03	$-0.16
80	80	$ 0.80	$ 0.01	$-0.21

The table shown above displays information on
investments in Market 2 at various levels of
group investment. Your return from Market 2
depends on what percentage of the total group
investment is made by you.

Market 1 returns you one unit of commodity 1 for
each token you invest in Market 1. Each unit of
commodity 1 pays you $ 0.05.

Press -BACK-

Fig. 1. Instructions: summary information

yielded a fixed (constant) rate of output and that each unit of output yielded a
fixed (constant) return. Market 2 (the CPR) was described as a market that
yielded a rate of output per token dependent upon the total number of tokens
invested by the entire group. The rate of output at each level of group investment was described in functional form as well as tabular form. Subjects were
informed that they would receive a level of output from market 2 that was
equivalent to the percentage of total group tokens they invested. Further,
subjects knew that each unit of output from market 2 yielded a fixed (constant)
rate of return. Figure 1 displays the actual information subjects saw as summary information in the experiment. Subjects knew with certainty the total
number of decision makers in the group, total group tokens, and that endowments were identical. They did not know the actual number of investment
decision periods. All subjects were experienced. That is, all subjects had
participated in at least one experiment using this form of decision environment.

3. Experimental Design, Theoretical Predictions, and Results—Design 1

Experimental Design

Our eight design 1 experiments fall into two categories: four baseline, non-communication experiments and four communication experiments. In the four baseline, noncommunication experiments, subjects participated in a series of decision periods (a minimum of twenty) in which no form of oral or visual communication was allowed. After each period, subjects were shown a display that recorded: (*a*) their profits in each market for the period, (*b*) total group investment in market 2, and (*c*) a tally of their cumulative profits for the experiment. During the experiment, subjects could request, through the computer, this information for all previous periods. No subject received information about the individual-level strategies of others at any point in the experiment. The parameters used in the design 1 experiments are reported in table 1.

The four "communication" experiments began with a series of ten periods conducted in a manner identical to the noncommunication experiments. After the tenth period, the subjects were brought together, and they received the following message.

> Sometimes in previous experiments, participants have found it useful, when the opportunity arose, to communicate with one another. We are going to allow you this opportunity between periods. There will be some restrictions.
> 1. You are not allowed to discuss sidepayments.
> 2. You are not allowed to make physical threats.
> 3. You are not allowed to see the private information on anyone's monitor.
> Since there are still some restrictions on communication with one another, we will monitor your discussions between periods. To make this easier, we will have all discussions at this site.
>
> Remember, after you return to your terminals there will be no further discussions for that period. We will allow a maximum of four minutes in any one discussion session between periods. If you desire, you may unanimously agree to return to your terminals earlier than that.
>
> We will be tape recording your discussions for our records.[11]

---

11. Each subject wore a tag with their player number on it so that one of the experimenters could record the player number corresponding to each statement that was made. This method enabled us to match the decision history of a subject with the statements made by that subject.

TABLE 1.   Design 1 Parameters for a Given Decision Period

Experiments	4 Noncommunication, 4 Communication
Number of subjects	8
Individual token endowment	10
Production function: market 2[a]	$15 (\Sigma x_i) - .15 (\Sigma x_i)^2$
Market 2 return per unit of output	$.01
Market 1 return per unit of output	$.05
Earnings per subject at group maximum	$.71

[a] Σx_i = the total number of tokens invested by the group in market 2. The production function shows the number of units of output produced in market 2 for each level of tokens invested in market 2.

Theoretical Predictions

We discuss three alternative predictions that will be useful in describing the results of our experiments. These predictions are illustrated in figure 2. First, consider the nature of our parameterization of the CPR environment: (*a*) entry is limited to eight players with fixed levels of inputs (tokens to invest); (*b*) the marginal opportunity cost of investing in the CPR (market 2) is constant, given that the return per token from market 1 is constant; and (*c*) the value of output units produced from investments in market 2 is constant (output from market 2 can be viewed as being sold in a perfectly competitive market). Thus, our environment most closely parallels that of a limited access CPR (see, for example, Clark 1980; Cornes and Sandler 1986). Following this

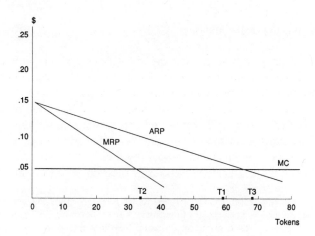

Fig. 2. Design 1 theoretical predictions

literature, Nash equilibria can be derived for this environment. Consider the specific designs for market 1 and market 2. The strategy set for each player is $x_i \in \{0,1,2, \ldots ,10\}$, where x_i denotes the number of tokens in market 2. The payoff for player i, $h_i(x)$, in cents, is:

$$h_i(x) = 50 \qquad\qquad\qquad\qquad\qquad\qquad\quad \text{if} \quad x_i = 0;$$

$$h_i(x) = 5(10 - x_i) + (x_i/\textstyle\sum x_i)[15 \sum x_i - .15(\sum x_i)^2] \quad \text{if} \quad x_i > 0,$$

where $x = (x_1, \ldots , x_8)$ is the vector of strategies of all players. This symmetric game yields multiple equilibria in pure strategies generated by having five players play $x_i = 7$, and three players play $x_i = 8$, with the $\sum(x_i) = 59$ tokens (approximately 41 percent of rents possible from market 2).[12] Note that all of these equilibria are within \$.01 of each other in individual payoff-space. The game also has a symmetric Nash equilibrium in mixed strategies, with $E(\sum x_i) = 59$ generated by each player playing $x_i = 7$ with probability 0.62 and $x_i = 8$ with probability 0.38. The Nash prediction of 59 tokens is noted as T1 in figure 2.

As benchmarks for discussion purposes, it is useful to consider two other investment predictions. As noted in figure 2, a group investment of 33 tokens yields the Pareto-optimal level of investment at which MRP = MC and thus maximum rents (denoted T2). Conversely, a group investment of 67 tokens yields a level of investment at which ARP = MC and, thus, zero rents from market 2 (denoted T3). This is the level of investment generally associated with an "open access" CPR environment.

Experimental Results, Design 1,
No Communication Experiments

We begin our interpretation of the experimental observations with a descriptive look at the data for the noncommunication baseline experiments. Our primary focus is the extent to which this environment leads to an inefficiency in resource allocations. In figure 3 we present period-by-period observations on rents accrued in market 2. Across all experiments, we observe a general pattern where rents decay toward zero and then rebound as subjects reduce the level of investment in the common-pool resource. Table 2 presents summary information on the aggregate tendencies of these four experiments. On aver-

---

12. See Walker, Gardner, and Ostrom 1991 for the complete derivation of these equilibria. Note that rents accrued as a percentage of maximum = (return from market 2 minus the opportunity costs of tokens invested in market 2)/(return from market 2 at MR = MC minus the opportunity costs of tokens invested in market 2). Opportunity costs equal the potential return that could have been earned by investing the tokens in market 1.

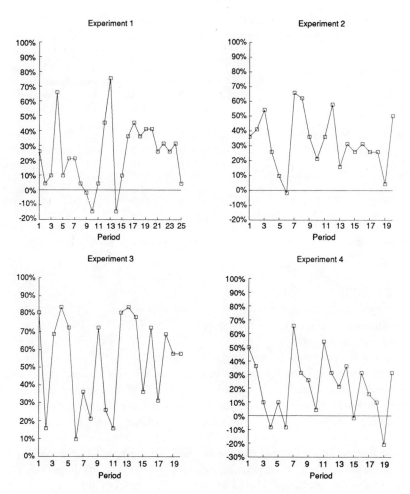

Fig. 3. Rents as a percentage of maximum in design 1, NC series

age (pooling across all experiments and the first twenty periods), we find rents equal to only 32.6 percent of optimum. Thus, even with the limited access parameterization for our environment, player strategies generate rents that fall far short of the maximum attainable. Further, from figure 3, we see that there is some tendency for rents to decrease with repetition of the decision process. At the aggregate level, it is the Nash prediction that yields the best prediction for rent dissipation.[13]

---

13. See Walker, Gardner, and Ostrom 1991 for a more complete analysis of behavior and tests of the alternative theoretical conjectures in environments without communication.

TABLE 2.   Percentage of Rents Earned in Design 1 Experiments

Experiment[a]	Periods 1–10			Periods 11–20		
	Mean	SD	Range	Mean	SD	Range
NC/NC-1	14.5	21.6	−14.5–65.7	31.9	25.5	−14.5–75.3
NC/NC-2	34.9	22.0	−1.8–65.7	30.4	15.4	4.2–57.8
NC/NC-3	48.6	29.5	9.6–83.7	58.2	23.3	15.7–83.7
NC/NC-4	21.6	24.6	−8.4–65.7	20.8	21.3	−21.1–54.2
Aggregate	29.9	27.7	−14.5–83.7	35.3	25.2	−21.1–83.7
NC/C-1	25.7	22.0	−8.4–62.0	98.1	6.1	80.7–100.0
NC/C-2	27.8	17.2	−8.4–50.0	98.6	4.4	86.1–100.0
NC/C-3	28.4	27.0	−21.1–72.3	98.6	2.9	92.8–100.0
NC/C-4	38.0	19.2	15.7–72.3	95.9	3.3	88.0–100.0
Aggregate	30.0	21.4	−21.1–72.3	97.8	4.4	80.7–100.0

[a]NC/NC designates experiments with no communication allowed in either periods 1–10 or 11–20; NC/C designates experiments with no communication allowed in periods 1–10, and communication allowed in periods 11–20.

Experimental Results, Design 1, Experiments with Communication

Figure 4 presents period-by-period observations on rents accrued in the four communication experiments. Recall that communication was allowed only in periods 11–20 of these experiments. All four experiments show a strong shift toward optimality beginning with period 11. In table 2 we see the aggregate effect of this shift in efficiency. In the first ten periods of the communication experiments, the mean level of rents is nearly identical to that observed in our baseline experiments (30.0 percent compared to 29.9 percent). In periods 11–20, rent shifts dramatically to an average of 97.8 percent. This compares to 35.3 percent in periods 11–20 of the baseline experiments. The average behavior across decision periods is summarized in figure 5. Clearly, the ability to communicate has translated into a shift in efficiency to near optimality.

Group Discussions, Design 1

In the discussion below, we examine the content of the discussion periods for each of these noncommunication/communication (NC/C) experiments.

NC/C Experiment 1. During the first ten periods of this experiment, the players achieved a mean of 26 percent of the attainable rents, with an average market 2 investment per player of 7.7 tokens. The discussion following period

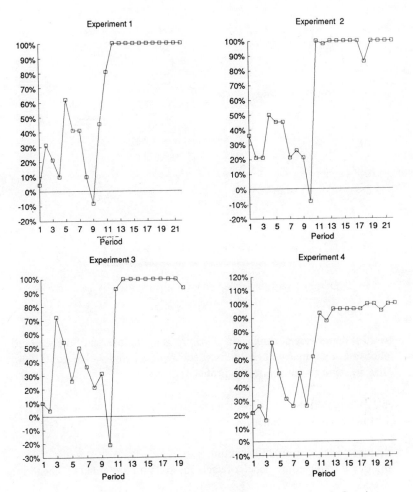

Fig. 4. Rents as a percentage of maximum in design 1, NC/C series

10 was initiated by player 2, who had invested an average of 6.5 tokens in market 2 during the first 10 periods:

> . . . I'd like to make a suggestion that will maximize our profits here. So we are going to have to come up with some quantity here for what we invest in each period. It is clear, like in game theory, you've got certain outcomes. If all the members were to decide on one outcome, and they follow through with that outcome, they would maximize the profits.

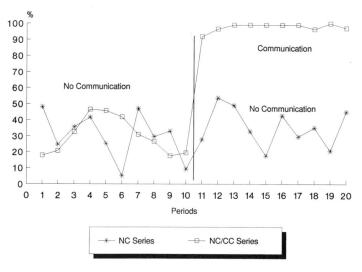

Fig. 5. Design 1 series averages, rents as a percentage of maximum

And, if there were cheating, then, you're going to lose out. So you got to choose a level that will be the best for market 2 and we've got to hold that decision to maximize the profits.[14]

Player 2 clearly understood the structure of the experiment and raised the key issues in his opening statement, namely:

the need to find a group optimum;
the threat to the continuance of such an optimum presented by cheating; and
the consequent need to "hold" all players to a decision to coordinate their strategies.

Almost the entire four-minute discussion focused on determining the group optimum. At one point, player 2 asked: "Do you all agree that it is all to our advantage to stick together on a joint investment?" No verbal response to this question was provided, simply a general nodding of heads. It took almost the entire four minutes to agree to a best strategy. As time was called, they had

---

14. The reference to game theory is somewhat surprising. Most of these subjects were recruited from lower-level economics classes. Some, however, were juniors and seniors. This particular subject was a senior.

not formulated a definite strategy. They hurriedly agreed to an inefficient strategy of 6 tokens each in market 2.

In period 11, all eight players followed the agreed upon strategy (a perfectly coordinated but incorrect joint strategy). The sole topic of conversation upon reconvening was recalculating their joint strategy. By the end of this period, they decided to change the investment to 4 tokens each in market 2. In period 12, all eight players followed the agreed upon strategy. Player 2's comment upon reconvening was: "That was 20 cents over my average—that's the easy way." In this discussion period, the players tried to come up with a strategy that would pay a little more. Player 5 suggested the possibility of a "rotation" system where a few individuals each period invested more than 4 tokens in market 2, but she did not make a specific proposal.[15] Others found player 5's general proposal confusing. They concluded this discussion with a proposal to continue their prior strategy.

All players held to their agreement in period 13. Player 2 then suggested that "we stay with 6 and 4" and was rewarded with "yeahs" all around. After two periods with perfect compliance, player 2 suggested that "we just stay with our earlier agreement." From then on until the end of the experiment, no one raised a hand to initiate a discussion between periods, and no one deviated from the agreement. The problem of cheating was mentioned twice during the first communication period and never raised again. Three persons—all of whom had invested an average of 7.0 (or below) in the first ten periods—actively participated in the discussion. The other players merely nodded when appropriate or helped in the calculation process. Thus, in this experiment, it was the "more cooperative" players who dominated the discussion period. Since they had perfect compliance with the joint strategies proposed in the communication rounds, no need arose for punishment, either by words or by heavy investments in market 2.

NC/C Experiment 2. During noncommunication periods, the investment history of this group was similar to that of the first NC/C experiment. The group had obtained an average of 35 percent of maximum rents and had invested an average of 7.6 tokens in market 2. Player 1 started the discussion with a clear formulation of the problem facing them.

What we are talking about right here is getting together to maximize profits. As far as I can see, the best we can do is if we all go in and punch

---

15. The maximal group payoff could be achieved only with an asymmetric investment pattern. When various participants noticed this asymmetry, either they rejected the idea of a joint strategy that enabled some to get more than others, or they tried to devise a "rotation" scheme whereby individuals would rotate among themselves who would get a slightly larger payoff.

in 4 into market 2 and 6 into market 1. We are all going to come up with about 70 cents apiece. If somebody decides to break the cartel, they are not going to be making more than a couple cents profit. We are all going to get real mad at them, if we find out differently. But that's not going to be a problem. Does anybody see any bigger profits than that?

Player 1 not only formulated the strategy but proposed a specific plan. After two clarifications, player 6 asked: "Do we have unanimity on that so we can return to our computer terminals?" Player 1 replied with: "The question has been called, I will second the question." Head nodding around was accepted as a sign of agreement.

In period 11, all but one player followed the agreement to invest 4 tokens in market 2. One player invested 6 tokens in market 2 but the action was not noticed.[16] Immediately upon reconvening, player 1 stated: "That worked nice. Do you just want to do that again?" Player 6 responded, "That's the best we can do," and the communication period ended with nods all around.

In period 12, two defections occurred. The first defector increased his investment in market 2 from 6 to 8 tokens, and a second player now invested 6 in market 2. This deviation from the agreement was noticed. Player 7 started this communication period by chastising the unknown (to the group) defectors:

So there were 38 [tokens]. So somebody is playing some games. They are knocking it down to 9 cents return on each token rather than 10 cents return on each token. And so, they are probably making a maximum of 4 cents off of each one. So, is it really worth busting the cartel and knocking everyone's profit down for 4 cents! . . .

So, anyway, do you want to try it again? I don't think the cartel is totally broken here. Somebody's karma is going to be really bad here. Want to try it again?

That appeal brought some success. The second defector returned to the agreed strategy (and kept to it for the rest of the experiment). The first defector reduced the "overinvestment" from 8 to 6. But a third player now invested 6 tokens in market 2, rather than 4.

Player 6 started the discussion after period 13 with the challenge, "All right, who is it?" and player 1 commented that "we have had 2 tokens of karma restored." Further appeals not to try for a few extra cents yielded a

---

16. Since the optimum investment was 33 tokens rather than the 32 tokens they had agreed upon, this small level of "cheating" did not reduce the payoffs of the other players.

period where only one player, who later "confessed" to being confused, overinvested.[17] After period 14, player 1 indicated that "we are still two tokens off, but we are back up to 70 cents, which means that some scumbucket is making an extra few tokens worth." Player 6 asserted that he didn't "care who is making a little more." Player 1 suggested that they continue without further communication as long as the group invested 34 tokens. (In other words, they should continue to follow the "agreement" to restrain their investment in market 2 to 4 tokens as long as the rate of nonconformance remained less than or equal to 2 tokens.) For the next two periods, only the confused player deviated from the agreement by investing 4 tokens in market 1 instead of market 2. Then, a second player began to deviate by overinvesting 2 tokens in market 2. No one exercised the opportunity to communicate after any of these four periods.

Period 18 produced a crisis. Players 7 and 8 both invested 10 tokens in market 2, while the confused player continued to invest 6. The 14 extra tokens in market 2 produced a noticeable drop in the average return, from 10 cents to 8 cents. Everyone wanted to talk after this period. The exchange after period 18 stressed the need for "pulling back." This discussion apparently did the trick. Periods 19, 20, and 21 produced perfect compliance. After period 21, player 7 proposed a rotation scheme where two players would invest 5 each in market 2. Player 7 simply pointed to players 1 and 3, sitting opposite from him, and suggested that they be the first ones. After some discussion as to whether it was worth adopting such a complex scheme, when they did not know how many more periods were coming, the players agreed to this "rotation" plan and implemented it for what was to be their last period.

In contrast to the first experiment, in this experiment, the major "leaders" were all individuals who had invested heavily in market 2 during the first ten periods. Player 7 was the major speaker, using such pejorative terms as *scumbucket* to refer to anyone who did not keep their "agreement." Player 7, in fact, cheated on the agreement in two of the periods where communication was allowed. (One cannot know whether player 7 was attempting to gain a few extra cents or to illustrate the danger of nonconformance so that he could obtain the willing conformance of all players. After his appeal in period 18, he did not deviate from the agreement.)

What is interesting about this experiment is that the use of terms such as *scumbucket* addressed to an unknown cheater were a sufficient "sanction" to change the behavior of the player. The players punished one another with words rather than with the behavior of investing all tokens in market 2—the predicted behavior in repeated games with trigger strategies. They did not use

---

17. On the debriefing form administered after the experiment, this player wrote: "I myself got the ratio mixed up—oops!"

behavioral punishments even when several players deviated from the agreed upon joint strategy for more than one round. Further, once the deviations from the agreement were halted, the players built on this conformance to develop a somewhat more complex rotation system that gained them a marginal improvement in joint payoffs. The players in this group conformed to their agreed upon strategies in 86 percent of their actual investment decisions—the lowest percentage in design 1.

NC/C Experiment 3. This group invested an average of 7.5 tokens in market 2 (an average rent of 35 percent of optimum) during the first ten periods. Once given the opportunity to communicate, the players rapidly agreed to coordinate their investments. They erroneously concluded, however, that their maximum payoff could be obtained if they all invested 3 tokens in market 2. After one period of perfect compliance but less than optimal payoffs, they discovered their error. They proposed and agreed to a rotation scheme whereby half of them invested 4 tokens and the other half invested 5 tokens each period. They kept this somewhat complex rotation pattern going with only one defection, in period 20. The major discussants in this experiment had been among the more cooperative players during the first ten periods. The player who proposed the rotation scheme, however, had invested the most in market 2 during the first ten periods and was the sole "defector" in period 20. This group conformed to their agreed upon strategies in 99 percent of their actual investment decisions and, thus, never faced a situation where verbal or behavioral punishment was needed.

NC/C Experiment 4. The history of the first ten no communication periods closely parallels that of the other three experiments. The average investment per player in market 2 was 7.4 tokens, resulting in the group earning 38 percent of maximum rents. The group took only four statements to reach an agreement to follow a joint strategy, but a suboptimal one—investing 5 tokens in both markets. In period 11, all players conformed to the agreement with the exception of one player who invested 7 tokens in market 2. Immediately upon convening, player 8 stated: "Someone is a traitor." After several comments concerning the agreement, the "deviant" player blurted out: "Oh, I am sorry, I did not understand."[18] Another player simply asked whether "we should do this again" and they returned to their terminals.

In period 12, the confused player followed the agreement, but another player invested 10 in market 2, rather than the agreed upon 5. This provoked a short but intense discussion. Player 8 indicated that "seeing this is a group

---

18. The player (a foreign student) seemed genuinely mortified and commented again on the debriefing form about her error.

project, let's make it that instead of trying to pimp each other over." At a later point, player 8 pointed out that the increased payoff to the defector was minimal and that "it was not worth it" to break the agreement. All players proceeded to follow the agreement in period 13.

For several more periods, the players had what they came to call "their little pep talk" about the importance of keeping their agreement to invest "5 and 5." After perfect compliance for five periods, they decided to reduce their investment in market 2 to 4 (an agreement that gained perfect compliance). In periods 20 and 22, one person deviated slightly, but in total, the players in this group conformed to their agreed upon strategies in 95 percent of their actual investment decisions.

All but two of the players participated at least once in the discussions during this experiment. The two individuals who were the most active had followed quite different strategies during the first ten periods. Player 8, the most active participant, had invested, on average, 9.7 tokens during the first ten periods, while player 2, the second most active, had invested only 5.8 tokens on average.

An Overview of the Discussion Periods

An examination of the transcripts for these four experiments reveals that the subjects clearly understood the group "dilemma." They frequently characterized the problem as that of a cartel. Given that the subjects had to determine a somewhat complex joint strategy, a considerable amount of effort was devoted to calculating and checking on whether they had found the optimum. Several groups eventually found an asymmetric strategy that produced the highest joint payoffs, while others were satisfied with symmetric payoffs that closely approached the optimum.

Given that the players received only aggregate investment information (all individual decisions were anonymous), the problem of dealing with cheating was potentially even more difficult to cope with than the problem of discovering the optimum. The subjects' method for dealing with this problem is revealing both in terms of what they did and what they did not do. They tried to arouse internal guilt in any person who deviated, and they appear to have been somewhat successful. Evocative terms, such as *scumbucket* and *pimp*, were used on the negative side. They did not threaten to use a trigger strategy. Nor did the players actually react to a deviation in outcome consistent with one or more players cheating by switching all their investments to market 2 as a punishment strategy. Several groups overtly faced the problem of small levels of nonconformance and decided to keep to their agreement as long as the level of deviation did not get too large. The potential threat of everything unraveling was clearly in view.

Finally, we do not have clear evidence concerning the behavioral characteristics of those individuals who took the greatest effort to gain agreement
and to chastise cheaters. In two of the experiments, those who participated in
the discussions were about evenly divided between those who had invested
most heavily in market 2 during the first ten periods and those who had
invested least heavily. In the other two experiments, the "big" investors dominated discussions in one and the "small" investors dominated in the other.

4. Experimental Design, Theoretical Predictions, and Results—Design 2

Experimental Design

Similar to design 1, our six design 2 experiments included a set of baseline
noncommunication experiments and a set of parallel experiments where communication was allowed. In the three baseline noncommunication experiments, subjects participated in a series of at least twenty periods in which no
form of oral or visual communication was allowed. The first ten periods of the
"communication" experiments were conducted in a manner identical to the
noncommunication experiments. Prior to period 11, however, the subjects
received the following message.

> In the decision periods that follow, you will be given the opportunity to
> purchase the right to discuss (as a group) your investment decisions. The
> rules on discussion will be exactly the same as in the discussion sessions
> in which you participated in previous experiments.
>
> 1. No sidepayments,
> 2. no physical threats,
> 3. no viewing of other individuals' monitor screens, and
> 4. a maximum of four minutes per discussion sessions.
>
> How do you purchase this right to have a group discussion session?
>
> You will be given two envelopes. In one envelope there are slips of paper
> that say "I contribute $.20." In the other envelope there are slips that say
> "I contribute $.00."
>
> Each period you will be asked to privately return one of the slips to the
> persons running the experiment. If 5 or more slips reading "I contribute
> $.20" are returned, the *entire* group will be allowed to meet in a discus-
> sion session.

TABLE 3.   Design 2 Parameters for a Given Decision Period

Experiments	3 Noncommunication, 3 Communication
Number of subjects	8
Individual token endowment	15
Production function: market 2[a]	$25\,(\Sigma x_i) - .30\,(\Sigma x_i)^2$
Market 2 return per unit of output	$.01
Market 1 return per unit of output	$.00
Earnings per subject at group maximum	$.65

[a] Σx_i = the total number of tokens invested by the group in market 2. The production function shows the number of units of output produced in market 2 for each level of tokens invested in market 2.

If fewer than 5 slips which read "I contribute $.20" are returned, the group will not be allowed to meet for discussion.

The parameters used in the design 2 experiments are reported in table 3.[19] There are several key differences relative to the design 1 experiments. In design 2, (*a*) the payoff function for market 2 was increased (shifted upward) relative to that used in design 1, (*b*) the payoff from market 1 was reduced to zero, (*c*) individual token endowments were increased to 15 tokens, and (*d*) subjects started the experiment with an initial capital endowment of $5.00. The reasons for the increased token endowments and the use of an up-front capital endowment will be made clear after we investigate the theoretical properties of this design.

The design 2 communication experiments were conducted to investigate the properties of a mechanism in which provision of the right to communicate was costly. Since our goal was to examine the "pure" effects of the costly provision structure, we wanted to control for subjects' awareness of the impact (success) of communication itself. This design feature was captured by using subjects who had participated in our previous communication experiments. Thus, these subjects had experienced the efficiency enhancing characteristics of communication. No subject group was drawn intact from a previous design 1 experiment. To utilize this design feature, however, we had to insure that subjects did not enter the decision environment with prior "implicit

---

19. It was verbally explained to the subjects that all contributions were final. If the group was not successful in funding the communication session, contributions were *not* refunded. The particular cost of $.20 per individual and the requirement that five of eight individuals must contribute to provide the mechanism were chosen to make the provision a nontrivial problem, and yet not to make the provision so costly that provision would have been virtually impossible. One would like to be able to calculate the expected cost and benefits from provision. These are not well-defined terms, however, in this context. Some groups may require only one round of communication to coordinate a strategy that stays in place for the entire experiment. Other groups may require repeated rounds of face-to-face discussion. The fact that our groups struggled with the provision problem but did eventually succeed suggests that our designs were reasonable.

bargain" agreements. That is, we needed a decision environment parallel in structure to our previous design, but with distinct cooperative equilibria. The equilibrium properties of design 2 capture this characteristic.

The provision mechanism imposed on the right to communicate placed subjects in a second-order public good dilemma situation (with a provision point). Second-order dilemma games exist whenever individuals must expend resources to provide a mechanism that may alter the strategic nature of a first-order dilemma game (Oliver 1980; Taylor 1987). The imposition of sanctions, for example, is one mechanism that can change a first-order dilemma situation into a situation where everyone's dominant strategy is to cooperate with others. But, the sanctioning mechanism itself is a public good. Once it is provided, it is simultaneously available to all participants. Since sanctioning mechanisms are costly to provide, it is in the interest of each participant that others bear the cost of solving the dilemma.[20]

The opportunity to communicate in a CPR dilemma situation can be viewed as a mechanism that enables individuals to coordinate strategies to solve the first-order CPR dilemma. In our first design, the opportunity was presented to the players at no cost. In our second design, however, we increased the realism of the experimental setting by imposing a cost for communicating. In field settings, communication is not free. Some individuals have to bear the cost of organization. If communication is going to continue, these costs must be borne repeatedly. Without continuing provision of a mechanism for communication, the communication effort may collapse and, with it, the possibility of avoiding the suboptimal outcomes of the first-order social dilemma.

Theoretical Predictions

As in design 1, design 2 allows for three useful predictions. Figure 6 illustrates group behavior that would be consistent with these alternative predictions. First, consider the specific parameterizations for market 1 and market 2. The strategy set for each player is $x_i \in \{0,1,2, \ldots ,15\}$, where x_i denotes the number of tokens in market 2. The payoff for player i, $h_i(x)$, in cents, is:

$$h_i(x) = 0 \qquad \qquad \text{if} \quad x_i = 0;$$

$$h_i(x) = 0(15 - x_i) + (x_i/\Sigma x_i)[25\Sigma x_i - .30(\Sigma x_i)^2] \quad \text{if} \quad x_i > 0,$$

where $x = (x_1, \ldots , x_8)$ is the vector of strategies of all players. This symmetric game has multiple Nash equilibria in pure strategies, with $\Sigma x_i =$

___

20. Yamagishi (1986 and 1988) examines the imposition of a sanctioning system to change the structure of a simple public good dilemma situation.

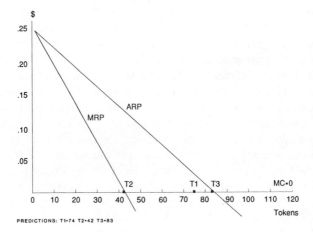

Fig. 6. Design 2 theoretical predictions

74 (approximately 40 percent of rents possible from market 2). These are generated by having six players play $x_i = 9$, and two players play $x_i = 10$. The game also has a symmetric Nash equilibrium in mixed strategies, with $E(\Sigma x_i)$ = 74 (denoted as T1 in fig. 6). This equilibrium is generated by each player playing $x_i = 9$ with probability 0.74 and $x_i = 10$ with probability 0.26.

As noted in figure 6, a group investment of 42 tokens yields a level of investment at which MRP = MC and, thus, maximum rents (denoted T2). Conversely, a group investment of 83 tokens yields a level of investment at which ARP = MC and, thus, zero rents from market 2 (denoted T3). For this design, note that this result would yield a zero total return from investments in market 2.

Given the possible payoffs for this design, one can see why we modified the design relative to design 1. We increased individual token endowments to 15 (from 10) so that full rent dissipation would not be inhibited by a binding constraint on resource endowments. Further, with this design, it is possible for subjects to actually have negative returns for a decision period. For this reason, and to increase the likelihood of subjects earning some minimal experimental earnings, we added the up-front cash endowment.

The decisions of the eight players of whether to contribute toward the opportunity to communicate can be modeled as a binary-choice decision in a public goods assurance game. Assume each player places a value on the opportunity to communicate (V_i), where $V_i > \$.20$. One Nash equilibrium to this game is for no player to contribute. In addition, any permutation of the contribution pattern (20,20,20,20,20,0,0,0) is a (one-shot) Nash equilibrium. The derivation of symmetric mixed Nash equilibria for this game depends crucially on the actual value (V_i) each player places on the opportunity to communicate.[21] One might view the limiting case as being a situation where V_i equals the difference between an individual's payoff at the group optimum and at the single-period Nash equilibrium. In this case, our parameters yield a value for V_i of approximately (\$.65 − \$.26 = \$.39). This is the limiting case in that any hypothesis where the opportunity to communicate has multiperiod, payoff-improving effects would increase the value of V_i. Our calculations for this limiting case show that there is no mixed-strategy Nash equilibrium for V_i = \$.39. Recall, however, that each subject had experienced the strong ameliorative effects of communication in prior, costless communication experiments. To the extent that subjects use this prior information, it is very plausible that subjects' subjective calculation of V_i is significantly greater than \$.39, and that a mixed-strategy equilibrium might exist for this environment.[22]

Experimental Results, Design 2, No Communication

We begin our interpretation of the results from design 2 with a descriptive look at the level of inefficiency generated in the noncommunication, baseline experiments. In figure 7 we present observations on rents accrued across experimental decision periods. As in design 1, the resource allocations between the two markets are at very low levels of efficiency. Table 4 presents summary information on the aggregate tendencies of these three experiments. On average (pooling across all experiments and the first twenty periods), we find rents equal to only 39.3 percent of optimum. Note that average rents are almost identical to the Nash prediction. Similar to previous experiments, however, these experiments demonstrated a pulsing pattern in which rents decayed toward zero and then rebounded as players reduced investments in market 2. (Table 4 presents statistics on cross-period variation in rents.)

Experimental Results, Design 2, Costly Communication

In figure 8 we present period-by-period observations on rents accrued across experimental decision periods for the three "costly communication" experi-

---

21. See Palfrey and Rosenthal (1991) for a discussion of mixed-strategy equilibria in assurance games.

22. The data on individual contributions to fund the communication mechanism is insufficient to yield meaningful tests of whether individual subjects were playing a mixed strategy. However, pooling data over all individuals in all three experiments prior to the successful provision of the opportunity to communicate, we find a contribution rate of 56 percent (27 of 48 decisions). If one assumes that 56 percent represents the probability of contributing in a mixed-strategy equilibrium, this would imply subjects placed a value on the opportunity to communicate at approximately \$.94. Once subjects successfully funded the communication mechanism, they agreed to multiperiod cooperative strategies. For this reason, we do not incorporate periods after communication into the present analysis.

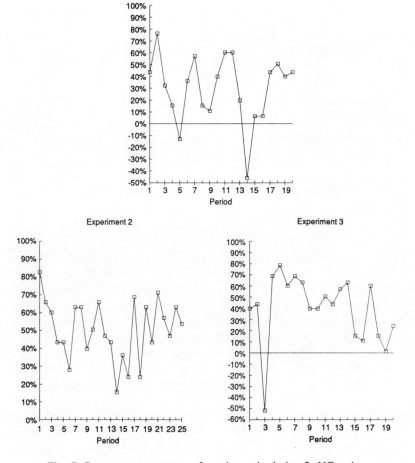

Fig. 7. Rents as a percentage of maximum in design 2, NC series

ments. Recall that the ability to fund the communication mechanism was allowed only in periods 11–20. Unlike our four experiments with "costless" communication, in two of these experiments we do not see a sudden shift in efficiency in period 11. In both of these experiments, the attempt to provide the communication mechanism failed in the initial periods, and, in both experiments, token investment remained at very low levels of efficiency (in experiment 1, efficiency dropped to its lowest level of the experiment). After period 11, all three groups found varying degrees of success in providing the communication mechanism and in coordinating strategies. From table 4 we see the aggregate effect of the communication opportunity. In the first ten

TABLE 4. Percentage of Rents Earned in Design 2 Experiments

Experiment[a]	Periods 1–10			Periods 11–20		
	Mean	SD	Range	Mean	SD	Range
NC/NC-1	31.3	25.4	−13.2–76.2	28.4	32.7	−45.9–60.1
NC/NC-2	54.0	15.9	28.0–82.7	43.1	18.6	15.4–68.7
NC/NC-3	39.5	30.5	−51.8–78.5	34.1	23.1	1.5–63.0
Aggregate	43.4	28.1	−51.8–82.7	35.2	25.4	−45.9–68.7
NC/CC-1	60.3	15.4	32.1–78.5	79.8	43.4	−23.6–100.0
NC/CC-2	38.1	29.1	−23.6–71.2	69.1	20.7	47.0–99.8
NC/CC-3	29.0	20.1	1.5–68.7	90.9	20.7	32.1–97.7
Aggregate	42.5	25.3	−23.6–78.5	79.9	30.5	−23.6–100.0

[a]NC/NC designates experiments with no communication allowed in either periods 1–10 or 11–20; NC/CC designates experiments with no communication allowed in periods 1–10, and costly communication allowed in periods 11–20.

periods of the communication experiments, the mean level of rents is nearly identical to that observed in our baseline experiments (42.5 percent compared to 43.4 percent). In periods 11–20, rents shift significantly to an average of 79.9 percent. This compares to 35.2 percent in periods 11–20 of the baseline experiments. The average behavior across decision periods is summarized in figure 9. Clearly, the ability to communicate has translated into a shift in efficiency. Unlike the four experiments in which the right to communicate was provided without cost, however, these subjects struggled to provide the communication mechanism and to coordinate strategies.

Group Discussion, Design 2

We turn now to a detailed account of the decision process in each of the three noncommunication/costly communication (NC/CC) experiments.

NC/CC Experiment 1. In the first two periods of this experiment, the players did not achieve sufficient contributions to fund the right to communicate. Three players contributed 20 cents after period 10 and again after period 11, but they failed to gain the five contributions needed to provide a communication period. After period 12, the group was successful when six players made contributions. Player 2 (who was the only player not to make a contribution in any of the prior periods) led the discussion with a suggestion that the group develop a rotation scheme for investments in market 2. (Player 2 in this experiment was player 7 in NC/C experiment 2. He was the major "verbal organizer" in both of these experiments.) Player 2 and player 7 spent a minute or so calculating the optimal strategy. Player 7 then proposed that ". . . we all

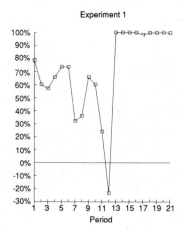

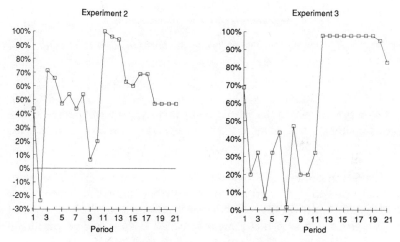

Fig. 8. Rents as a percentage of maximum in design 2, NC/CC series

put in 5, and that we rotate 2 people putting in 6. That looks pretty good, shall we do that?" It took some time to figure out how to coordinate the rotation system, but eventually a scheme was agreed upon. In this discussion, no reference was made to the problem of cheating or to the need to hold firm to the agreement to avoid paying the cost of communicating again.

After this single communication period, the players implemented the agreement perfectly for four periods. When this first "rotation" was accomplished, player 4 cast a solitary vote for a second communication period. Only minor deviations occurred during the next five periods, and no further effort was made to communicate. Overall, the players in this group conformed to their agreed upon strategies in 92 percent of their actual investment decisions.

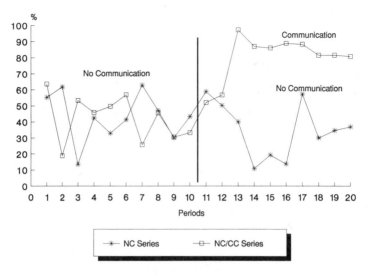

Fig. 9. Rents as a percentage of maximum in design 2, series averages

NC/CC Experiment 2. In the second costly communication experiment, five subjects contributed 20 cents at their first opportunity. Player 5 started the session with this statement:

> The reason we are here is to make a profit, so we need to lower the group investment down from 66 and 70 which we have been doing, down to say 42 or 40. And if we all agree to invest 5, then we would have 40 invested as a group. Ten in market 1 and 5 in market 2. We would get maximum profit out of this. Is that a reasonable decision?

Some further effort was made to calculate whether or not this was optimal. Relative to other groups, these subjects focused on calculations with very little discussion. Only seven statements were made during the communication period. Player 5 ended this period with the statement: "Everybody needs to do it—if you remember from last time, if everyone does not do it then someone sucks it." (Player 5 in this period was player 8 in the fourth communication experiment using design 1. The line of argument he used here was consistent with his rhetoric and experience in the previous experiment.)

Period 11 involved perfect coordination. In period 12, player 4 (who had said nothing in the discussion period) invested 15 tokens in market 2, while the others held to their agreement to invest 5. The information given to the players after period 12 clearly conveyed the fact that a major deviation from their verbal agreement had occurred. Player 4 continued to invest 15 tokens in market 2 for the remaining periods (as he had done in the first 10 periods). If the players were ever to use a behavioral punishment strategy, the extent of this defection should have triggered it. Instead, two players invested 6 tokens in market 2 and, thus, joined player 4 in the next period as defectors (but at a very low level) while the other five players held to their agreement and invested 5 tokens. In period 14, player 3 switched all tokens into market 2 and continued this strategy for the remaining periods.[23] In addition to the two players who maximally deviated, three other players deviated at a low level by investing from 1 to 4 tokens above the agreed upon level. Thus, in period 14, only three players kept to the original agreement.

If deviations from the optimal strategy to which they verbally agreed were likely to trigger punishing behavior on the part of the other players, all of the players should have switched to an investment of 15 tokens in market 2. This did not occur in any of the remaining periods. The players were obviously aware of the defections. Three players contributed 20 cents after the fourteenth period in an unsuccessful attempt to regain the right to communicate. After the fifteenth period, a solitary player contributed 20 cents toward communication, but that was the last contribution toward communication made in this experiment. During the last six periods, two players invested 15.00 tokens each in every period, two players invested, on average, in the range of 8.00 to 9.33 tokens each, and the remaining four players held their average investments in the range between 5.00 and 6.33. These behaviors do not provide empirical support for the likelihood of trigger strategies being used in a noncooperative setting.

The players in this group conformed to their agreed upon strategies in 45 percent of their actual investment decisions—the lowest percentage of any of the communication experiments. Although the players had achieved over 90 percent of the available rents in the first four periods after communication, the percentage fell steadily to 47 percent in the last three periods of the experiment.

NC/CC Experiment 3. Relative to the first two experiments in this design, this group adopted somewhat more "cooperative" strategies during the first ten noncommunication periods. The average investment in market 2 was 7.0 tokens compared to 8.5 for the first NC/CC and 9.2 for the second NC/CC experiments. Four subjects contributed toward communication after the tenth

---

23. Whether player 3 was punishing player 4 or was merely defecting from the agreement in order to obtain a higher payoff cannot be determined from behavior alone. Since player 3 had invested heavily in market 2 during the first ten periods (the second highest investor after player 4), it is reasonable to assume that the fifteen-token investment in market 2 was motivated by profit considerations more than punishment considerations.

period, falling one vote shy of the provision level. After the eleventh period, six individuals made the necessary contribution to obtain the right to communicate. Two of the players, who had been among the most active communicators in the design 1 experiments, took the lead (as well as financially contributing toward the achievement of a communication period). After some hurried calculations, the group decided to invest 6 tokens in market 2 and 9 in market 1. They obtained 97.7 percent of the available rents with this strategy. The players seemed concerned about making a quick decision and avoiding the need for further communication. As player 5 argued during the communication period: "Let's decide something so that we all know what we are doing so that we don't have to conference each time." On his debriefing form, player 5 indicated: "Instead of a complicated maximizing scheme, we chose a simple, easy-to-follow method to set relatively maximized profits."

For twelve periods, the players observed perfect compliance to their agreement with no further discussion. In period 20, player 3 invested 9 instead of 6 tokens in market 2. In period 21—the unannounced final period— player 3 continued the investment of 9 tokens while player 8 invested all 15 tokens in market 2. Player 8 had invested 15 tokens throughout the noncommunication periods, had not voted at any time to hold a communication period, did not say anything during their discussion, and had conformed to the agreement for nine periods. On his debriefing form, he "justified" his actions in the following way:

> I never purchased because I felt like the others would purchase it, consequently, I wouldn't lose $.20. I didn't feel like I was taking advantage of the group in this respect. I also felt like, since I didn't purchase the opportunity, I did not have to abide by the group's decision because I really didn't want to meet.

The players in this group conformed to their agreed upon strategies in 96 percent of their actual investment decisions.

An Overview of the Discussion Periods

The design 2 experiments demonstrate the strength as well as the fragile nature of costly communication. Since it was costly to communicate, each group funded the opportunity to communicate only once. Two of the groups had to go several periods before sufficient contributions enabled them to meet. What is rather startling, however, is that two of the groups achieved almost perfect compliance to their joint strategy after only a single opportunity to discuss the problem. The other group experienced cascading defections once it was clear that they could not mount the level of voluntary contributions needed to achieve a second or third "pep talk."

5. Summary and Conclusions

These experiments provide strong evidence for the power of face-to-face communication in a repeated CPR situation where decisions are made privately. When communication was provided as a "costless" institution, players successfully used the opportunity to (*a*) calculate coordinated rent improving strategies, (*b*) devise verbal agreements to implement these strategies, and (*c*) verbally sanction nonconforming players. On average, efficiency increased from 30 percent to 98 percent with the introduction of costless communication. Considerable time and effort were expended during the communication periods simply trying to ascertain the optimal, joint strategy, since the experiment afforded considerably more choice than a dichotomy between a "cooperative" and a "noncooperative" strategy.

In field settings, it is rare that the opportunity to communicate is costless. Someone has to invest time and effort to create and maintain arenas for face-to-face communication. The cost of providing an arena for communicating has not been overtly considered in previous experimental work. Our design 2 experiments investigated the effect of costly provision of the communication mechanism on (*a*) the ability of players to provide the mechanism, and (*b*) the impact of the second-order dilemma in solving the first-order dilemma posed by the CPR environment itself. In summary, the provision problem players faced in the costly communication experiments was not trivial and did, in fact, create a barrier. In all three experiments, the problem of providing the institution for communication diminished the success of either (*a*) having the ability to develop a coordinated strategy, and/or (*b*) dealing with players who cheated on a previous agreement. On the other hand, all groups succeeded (to some degree) in providing the communication mechanism and in dealing with the CPR dilemma. On average, efficiency in these groups increased from approximately 42 percent to 80 percent.

In our experiments, players received only aggregate information (all individual decisions were anonymous), and the problem of dealing with cheating was potentially even more difficult to cope with than the problem of discovering the optimum. How subjects dealt with this problem is revealing, both in terms of what they did and what they did not do. Verbal criticism was a common ploy used against anonymous defectors. Evocative terms, such as *scumbucket* and *pimp,* were used as negative persuasion. They did not threaten or ever adopt a trigger strategy. Several groups overtly faced the problem of small levels of nonconformance and decided to keep to their agreement as long as the level of deviation did not get too large. The potential threat of everything unraveling was clearly in view.

In general, these results are consistent with previous small-group research. Isaac and Walker (1988 and 1991) found similar results for costless and costly communication in a public good environment with symmetric payoffs. Similar to our results, they found communication to be a successful mechanism for improving market efficiency, even when the communication mechanism was provided as a second-order public good.

Of the six hypotheses forwarded to explain the impact of communication in prior studies, the evidence from our experiments clearly supports two.

1. Communication did provide an opportunity for individuals to offer and extract promises of cooperation for nonenforceable contracts.
2. Communication did facilitate the boosting of prior normative orientations.

Our experiments, however, cannot clearly differentiate between the various normative orientations that are evoked in such situations.[24] We tend to agree with Orbell, Van de Kragt, and Dawes (1988a) that keeping promises appears to be a more fundamental, shared norm than "cooperation per se." It is, of course, difficult to sort these out. When a defector is called a "scumbucket," is the reproach being used because someone is: (1) breaking a promise, (2) being uncooperative, or (3) taking advantage of others who are keeping a promise? The strength of the reproaches used probably reflects the sense of the other players that the offenders were committing all three of these offenses simultaneously.

The evidence from these experiments demonstrates that external agents are not always necessary to achieve high levels of conformance to verbal promises, even when:

1. players make repeated anonymous and private decisions and breaking the verbal agreement strongly dominates keeping the verbal agreement; and
2. players do not have an opportunity to establish a well-defined community with strong internal norms and established ways to enforce these norms.

On the other hand, the evidence from these experiments should not be interpreted as supporting arguments that communication alone is sufficient to overcome repeated dilemma problems in general. While many endogenous arrangements appear to evolve in experimental and field settings to overcome CPR dilemmas, many endogenous efforts have failed as well. The task facing all scholars interested in these questions is the development of an empirically validated theory that explains why some institutions evolve, are efficient, and are stable, and why others fail (for an effort in this direction, see Ostrom 1990).

Free communication appears to work in a setting involving a limited

---

24. This is not to say that we found evidence that contradicts the other hypotheses.

number of symmetric players who are well informed about the structure of their environment and the aggregate investment patterns. There are many field settings that approximate these conditions. The difficulties created by introducing a modest cost and the need to gain five out of eight players to contribute to a communication period illustrates that endogenous development of institutions to solve social dilemma problems do not spring forth effortlessly. In our own future research, we plan to explore a range of questions involving the development of endogenous institutions, including the effects of various types of internal and external monitoring and sanctioning mechanisms.

REFERENCES

Anderson, Jay M. 1977. "A Model of the Commons." In *Managing the Commons,* ed. Garrett Hardin and John Baden. San Francisco: W. H. Freeman.

Aumann, R. J. 1978. "Survey on Repeated Games." In *Essays in Game Theory and Mathematical Economics in Honor of Oskar Morgenstern,* ed. R. J. Aumann. Mannheim: Bibliographiches Institut.

Axelrod, Robert. 1984. *The Evolution of Cooperation.* New York: Basic Books.

Bendor, Jonathan B., and Dilip Mookherjee. 1985. "Institutional Structure and the Logic of Ongoing Collective Action." Stanford University, Graduate School of Business.

Berkes, Fikret, ed. 1989. *Common Property Resources: Ecology and Community-Based Sustainable Development.* London: Belhaven Press.

Braver, Sanford L., and L. A. Wilson. 1984. "A Laboratory Study of Social Contracts as a Solution to Public Goods Problems: Surviving on the Lifeboat." Paper presented at the Western Social Science Association, San Diego.

Braver, Sanford L., and L. A. Wilson. 1986. "Choices in Social Dilemmas: Effects of Communication within Subgroups." *Journal of Conflict Resolution* 30:51–62.

Caldwell, Michael D. 1976. "Communication and Sex Effects in a Five-Person Prisoner's Dilemma Game." *Journal of Personality and Social Psychology* 33:273–80.

Clark, Colin. 1980. "Restricted Access to Common-Property Fishery Resources: A Game-Theoretic Analysis." In *Dynamic Optimization and Mathematical Economics,* ed. P. T. Liu. New York: Plenum Press.

Cornes, Richard, and Todd Sandler. 1986. *The Theory of Externalities, Public Goods, and Club Goods.* Cambridge: Cambridge University Press.

Dawes, Robyn M. 1975. "Formal Models of Dilemmas in Social Decision Making." In *Human Judgment and Decision Processes: Formal and Mathematical Approaches,* ed. Martin F. Kaplan and Steven Schwartz. New York: Academic Press.

Dawes, Robyn M. 1980. "Social Dilemmas." *Annual Review of Psychology* 31:169–93.

Dawes, Robyn M., Jeanne McTavish, and Harriet Shaklee. 1977. "Behavior, Communication, and Assumptions about Other People's Behavior in a Commons Dilemma Situation." *Journal of Personality and Social Psychology* 35:1–11.

Dawes, Robyn M., John M. Orbell, and Alphons J. C. Van de Kragt. 1984. "Normative Constraint and Incentive Compatible Design." University of Oregon, Department of Psychology.

Dawes, Robyn M., Alphons J. C. Van de Kragt, and John M. Orbell. 1988. "Not Me or Thee but WE: The Importance of Group Identity in Eliciting Cooperation in Dilemma Situations: Experimental Manipulations." *Acta Psychologica* 68:83–97.

Edney, Julian J., and Christopher S. Harper. 1978. "The Commons Dilemma: A Review of Contributions from Psychology." *Environmental Management* 2:491–507.

Friedman, James W. 1971. "A Noncooperative Equilibrium for Supergames." *Review of Economic Studies* 28:1–12.

Gardner, Roy, Elinor Ostrom, and James Walker. 1990. "The Nature of Common-Pool Resource Problems." *Rationality and Society* 2:335–58.

Hardin, Garrett. 1968. "The Tragedy of the Commons." *Science* 162:1243–48.

Hardin, Garrett, and John Baden. 1977. *Managing the Commons.* San Francisco: W. H. Freeman.

Hardin, Russell. 1982. *Collective Action.* Baltimore: Johns Hopkins University Press.

Harsanyi, John C., and Reinhard Selten. 1988. *A General Theory of Equilibrium Selection in Games.* Cambridge, Mass.: MIT Press.

Isaac, R. Mark, and James M. Walker. 1988. "Communication and Free-Riding Behavior: The Voluntary Contribution Mechanism." *Economic Inquiry* 24:585–608.

Isaac, R. Mark, and James M. Walker. 1991. "Costly Communication: An Experiment in a Nested Public Goods Problem." In this volume.

Jerdee, Thomas H., and Benson Rosen. 1974. "Effects of Opportunity to Communicate and Visibility of Individual Decisions on Behavior in the Common Interest." *Journal of Applied Psychology* 59:712–16.

Kaitala, Veijo. 1986. "Game Theories Models of Fisheries Management—A Survey." In *Dynamic Games and Applications in Economics,* ed. T. Basar. Berlin: Springer-Verlag.

Kramer, R. M., and Marilyn M. Brewer. 1986. "Social Group Identity and the Emergence of Cooperation in Resource Conservation Dilemmas." In *Experimental Social Dilemmas,* ed. Henk A. Wilke, David M. Messick, and Christel G. Rutte. Frankfurt am Main: Verlag Peter Lang.

Kreps, David M., Paul Milgrom, John Roberts, and Robert Wilson. 1982. "Rational Cooperation in the Finitely Repeated Prisoner's Dilemma." *Journal of Economic Theory* 27:245–52.

Levhari, S., and L. H. Mirman. 1980. "The Great Fish War: An Example Using a Dynamic Cournot-Nash Solution." *Bell Journal of Economics* 11:322–34.

Lewis, Tracy R., and James Cowens. 1983. "Cooperation in the Commons: An Application of Repetitious Rivalry." University of British Columbia, Department of Economics.

Libecap, Gary D. 1989. "Distributional Issues in Contracting for Property Rights." *Journal of Institutional and Theoretical Economics* 145:6–24.

McCay, Bonnie M., and James M. Acheson. 1987. *The Question of the Commons: The*

Culture and Ecology of Communal Resources. Tucson: University of Arizona Press.

McKean, Margaret A. 1986. "Management of Traditional Common Lands (*Iriaichi*) in Japan." In *Proceedings of the Conference on Common Property Resource Management.* Washington, D.C.: National Academy Press, 1986.

Nash, John F. 1951. "Noncooperative Games." *Annals of Mathematics* 54:286–95.

National Research Council. 1986. *Proceedings of the Conference on Common Property Resource Management.* Washington, D.C.: National Academy Press.

Oliver, Pamela. 1980. "Rewards and Punishments as Selective Incentives for Collective Action: Theoretical Investigations." *American Journal of Sociology* 85: 1356–75.

Orbell, John M., Alphons J. C. Van de Kragt, and Robyn M. Dawes. 1988a. "Covenants without the Sword." Paper prepared for the conference on Normative Underpinnings of Constitutional Order, Jackson Hole, Wyoming.

Orbell, John M., Alphons J. C. Van de Kragt, and Robyn M. Dawes. 1988b. "Explaining Discussion-Induced Cooperation." *Journal of Personality and Social Psychology* 54:811–19.

Ostrom, Elinor. 1990. *Governing the Commons.* Cambridge: Cambridge University Press.

Palfrey, T. R., and H. Rosenthal. 1991. "Testing for the Effects of Cheap Talk: A Public Goods Game with Private Information." *Games and Economic Behavior.* In press.

Rapoport, Amnon. 1985. "Provision of Public Goods and the MSC Experimental Paradigm." *American Political Science Review* 79:148–55.

Runge, Carlisle Ford. 1984. "Institutions and the Free Rider: The Assurance Problem in Collective Action." *Journal of Politics* 46:154–81.

Schotter, Andrew. 1980. *The Economic Theory of Social Institutions.* New York: Cambridge University Press.

Sinn, Hans-Werner. 1984. "Common Property Resources, Storage Facilities, and Ownership Structures: A Cournot Model of the Oil Market." *Economica* 51:235–53.

Siy, Robert Y. 1982. *Community Resource Management: Lessons from the Zanjera.* Quezon City, Philippines: University of the Philippines Press.

Sobel, Jordon H. 1985. "Utility Maximizers in Iterated Prisoner's Dilemmas." In *Paradoxes of Rationality and Cooperation,* ed. Richmond Campbell and Lanning Sowden. Vancouver: University of British Columbia Press.

Taylor, Michael. 1987. *The Possibility of Cooperation.* Cambridge: Cambridge University Press.

Van de Kragt, Alphons J. C., J. M. Orbell, and R. M. Dawes. 1983. "The Minimal Contributing Set as a Solution to Public Goods Problems." *American Political Science Review* 77:112–22.

Van de Kragt, Alphons J. C., R. M. Dawes, J. M. Orbell, S. R. Braver, and L. A. Wilson. 1986. "Doing Well and Doing Good as Ways of Resolving Social Dilemmas." In *Experimental Social Dilemmas,* ed. H. Wilke, D. Messick, and C. Rutte. Frankfurt am Main: Verlag Peter Lang.

Wade, Robert. 1988. *Village Republics: Economic Conditions for Collective Action in South India.* Cambridge: Cambridge University Press.

Walker, James, Roy Gardner, and Elinor Ostrom. 1991. "Rent Dissipation and Nash Disequilibrium in Common Pool Resources: Experimental Evidence." In *Game Equilibrium Models,* ed. Reinhard Selten. Berlin: Springer-Verlag.

Yamagishi, Toshio. 1986. "The Provision of a Sanctioning System as a Public Good." *Journal of Personality and Social Psychology* 51:110–16.

Yamagishi, Toshio. 1988. "Seriousness of Social Dilemmas and the Provision of a Sanctioning System." *Social Psychology Quarterly* 51:32–42.

Contributors

Richard Boylan, Washington University

Dan S. Felsenthal, University of Haifa

Robert Forsythe, University of Iowa

Roberta Herzberg, Indiana University

R. Mark Isaac, University of Arizona

John Ledyard, California Institute of Technology

Arthur Lupia, University of California, San Diego

Zeev Maoz, University of Haifa

Richard D. McKelvey, California Institute of Technology

Forrest Nelson, University of Iowa

George Neumann, University of Iowa

Peter C. Ordeshook, California Institute of Technology

Elinor Ostrom, Indiana University

Thomas R. Palfrey, California Institute of Technology

Charles R. Plott, California Institute of Technology

Amnon Rapoport, University of Arizona

Howard Rosenthal, Carnegie-Mellon University

Kenneth C. Williams, Michigan State University

Rick Wilson, Rice University

James M. Walker, Indiana University

Jack Wright, University of Iowa